Erik H. Erikson

CHILDHOOD
AND SOCIETY

VINTAGE

Published by Vintage 1995

10

Copyright © W. W. Norton & Co Inc 1950, 1963

First published in Great Britain by
Imago Publishing Company 1951
Revised edition published by
The Hogarth Press 1965

Vintage
Random House, 20 Vauxhall Bridge Road, London SW1V 2SA

Random House Australia (Pty) Limited
20 Alfred Street, Milsons Point, Sydney,
New South Wales 2061, Australia

Random House New Zealand Limited,
18 Poland Road, Glenfield,
Auckland 10, New Zealand

Random House (Pty) Limited
Endulini, 5a Jubilee Road, Parktown 2193, South Africa

The Random House Group Limited Reg. No. 954009
www.randomhouse.co.uk

A CIP catalogue record for this book
is available from the British Library

ISBN 0 09 953291 3

Papers used by Random House are natural, recyclable
products made from wood grown in sustainable forests.
The manufacturing processes conform to the environmental
regulations of the country of origin

Printed and bound in Great Britain by
Cox & Wyman Ltd, Reading, Berkshire

To our children's children

Contents

Foreword to the Second Edition

As I re-read the Foreword to the First Edition the phrase 'conceptual itinerary' caught my eye – and I italicized it, for I was in search of a formula which would explain the fate of this book. Originally written to supplement the psychiatric education of American physicians, psychologists, and social workers, it has gone its own way, into colleges and into the graduate schools of a variety of fields in this and in a number of foreign countries. A second edition, and with it the question of a revision, has become a matter of practical urgency.

The thought that this book was being widely read by younger as well as older people who could not judge it on the basis of clinical experience, has at times embarrassed me. Before starting the revision, I took this matter up with my freshman seminar (1961–62) at Harvard, and I found that the personal unity which, for better or for worse, characterizes an itinerary may, in fact, help young students gain a first guided overview of a field which encroaches upon their self-consciousness and their vocabulary from so many divers sources. My students, incidentally, decided almost unanimously that I should not make any drastic changes – as if tampering with an itinerary written in younger years was not one of an older man's prerogatives. My thanks to their diligence and solicitude.

But the book has also been used in the training of professional workers concerned with psychoanalysis. Here, too, I have come to the conclusion that the book's shortcomings are inseparable from its character as a record of the first phase of one worker's itinerary and that like many first voyages it provides impressions which on re-visiting prove resistant to undoing or doing over. I have, therefore, revised only in order to clarify my original intentions and added only material from the same period of my work.

In what revision has taken place, then, I have first of all corrected those passages which on re-reading I did not quite understand myself. Secondly, I have amplified or corrected descriptions and explanations which have often been mis-understood or repeatedly questioned by students of whatever field. Lengthy additions are to be found primarily at the end of Part One and throughout Part Three. Finally, I have provided initialled footnotes which reflect critically on what I wrote a decade and a half ago, and refer to later writings of mine which develop the themes then initiated.

The acknowledgements in the Foreword to the First Edition do not include the name of the late David Rapaport. He had read the manuscript but I had not received his suggestions (immensely detailed, as I need not tell those who knew him) when the book went to press. In subsequent years we worked together; and he more than anybody else (and this includes me) made explicit the theoretical implications of my work and its relation to that of other psychoanalysts and psychologists. I can only gratefully refer to some of his writings which contain exhaustive bibliographies.

Longer additions to the Second Edition are based on the papers 'Sex Differences in the Play Construction of Pre-Adolescents,' *Journal of Orthopsychiatry*, XXI, 4, 1951; and 'Growth and Crises of the "Healthy Personality," ' *Symposium on the Healthy Personality* (1950), M. J. E. Senn, editor, New York, Josiah Macy, Jr, Foundation.

Centre for the Advanced Study   ERIK HOMBURGER ERIKSON.
in the Behavioral Sciences
Stanford, California
March 1963

Foreword to the First Edition

A foreword enables an author to put his afterthoughts first. Looking back on what he has written, he can try to tell the reader what lies before him.

First: this book originated in the practice of psychoanalysis. Its main chapters are based on specimen situations which called for interpretation and correction: anxiety in young children, apathy in American Indians, confusion in veterans of war, arrogance in young Nazis. In these, as in all situations, the psychoanalytic method detects conflict; for this method was first focused on mental disturbance. Through the work of Freud, neurotic conflict has become the most comprehensively studied aspect of human behaviour. However, this book avoids the easy conclusion that our relatively advanced knowledge of neurosis permits us to view mass phenomena – culture, religion, revolution – as analogies of neuroses in order to make them amenable to our concepts. We will pursue a different path.

Psychoanalysis today is implementing the study of the ego, a concept denoting man's capacity to unify his experience and his action in an adaptive manner. It is shifting its emphasis from the concentrated study of the conditions which blunt and distort the individual ego to the study of the ego's roots in social organization. This we try to understand not in order to offer a rash cure to a rashly diagnosed society, but in order first to complete the blueprint of our theory. In this sense, this is a psychoanalytic book on the relation of the ego to society.

This is a book on childhood. One may scan work after work on history, society, and mortality and find little reference to the fact that all people start as children and that all peoples begin in their nurseries. It is human to have a long childhood; it is civilized to have an ever longer childhood. Long childhood makes a technical and mental virtuoso out of man, but it also leaves a lifelong residue of emotional immaturity in him. While tribes and nations, in many intuitive ways, use child training to the end of gaining their particular form of mature human identity, their unique version of integrity, they are, and remain, beset by the irrational fears which stem from the very state of childhood which they exploited in their specific way.

What can a clinician know about this? I think that the psychoanalytic method is essentially a historical method. Even where it focuses on medical data, it interprets them as a function of past experience. To say that psychoanalysis studies the conflict between the mature and the infantile, the up-to-date and the archaic layers in the mind, means that psychoanalysis studies psychological evolution through the analysis of the individual. At the same time it throws light on the fact that the history of humanity is a gigantic metabolism of individual life cycles.

I would like to say, then, that this is a book on historical processes. Yet the psychoanalyst is an odd, maybe, a new kind of historian: in committing himself to influencing what he observes, he becomes part of the historical process which he studies. As a therapist, he must be aware of his own reaction to the observed: his 'equations' as an observer become his very instruments of observation. Therefore, neither terminological alignment with the more objective sciences nor dignified detachment from the clamouring of the day can and should keep the psychoanalytic method from being what H. S. Sullivan called 'participant', and systematically so.

In this sense, this is and must be a subjective book, a *conceptual itinerary*. There is no attempt at being representative in quotations or systematic in references. On the whole, little is gained from an effort to reinforce as yet vague meanings with seemingly conscientious quotations of vaguely similar meaning from other contexts.

This personal approach calls for a short statement of my training and of my over-all intellectual indebtedness.

I came to psychology from art, which may explain, if not justify, the fact that at times the reader will find me painting contexts and backgrounds where he would rather have me point to facts and concepts. I have had to make a virtue out of a constitutional necessity by basing what I have to say on representative description rather than on theoretical argument.

I first came face to face with children in a small American school in Vienna which was conducted by Dorothy Burlingham and Eva Rosenfeld, and directed by Peter Blos. I began my clinical career as a child analyst. In this I was guided by Anna Freud and August Aichhorn. I graduated from the Vienna Psychoanalytic Institute.

Henry A. Murray and his co-workers at the Harvard Psychological Clinic gave me my first intellectual home in this country. Over the years I had the privilege of long talks with anthropologists, primarily Gregory Bateson, Ruth Benedict, Martin Loeb, and Margaret Mead. Scudder Mekeel and Alfred Kroeber introduced me to 'the field'. My very special debt to them will be dealt with in detail in Part Two. It would be impossible to itemize my over-all indebtedness to Margaret Mead.

My comparative views on childhood developed through research to which I was first encouraged by Lawrence K. Frank. A grant from the Josiah Macy, Jr, Foundation enabled me to join in a study of incipient infantile neuroses at Yale (Department of Psychiatry, School of Medicine and Institute of Human Relations); and a grant from the General Education Board permitted me to participate for a time in Jean Walker Macfarlane's long-range study of representative California children (Institute of Child Welfare, University of California, Berkeley).

My wife, Joan Erikson, has edited this book.

In the completion of the manuscript I was counselled by Helen Meiklejohn, and also by Gregory Bateson, Wilma Lloyd, Gardner and Lois Murphy, Laurence Sears, and Don MacKinnon. I am grateful to them.

In the text a number of fictitious names appear: Sam, Ann, and Peter; the Marine, Jim the Sioux, and Fanny the shaman; Jean and her mother, Mary, and others. They were the patients and subjects who unknowingly provided me with 'specimens' of lucid behaviour which over the years stood out in my memory and gained in scope and significance. I hope that my reports convey my appreciation of their partnership in this work of clarification.

I owe certain data reported in this book to my work on the following staffs and with the following individuals: Harvard Medical School, Department of Neuropsychiatry – Frank

Fremont-Smith, M.D.; Yale School of Medicine, Department of Psychiatry – Felice Begg-Emery, M.D., Marian Putnam, M.D., and Ruth Washburn; Menninger Foundation, Southard School – Mary Leitch, M.D.; Children's Hospital of the East Bay, Child Development Centre – Wilma Lloyd; Mount Zion Hospital, Veteran's Rehabilitation Clinic – Emanuel Windholz, M.D.; Child Guidance Clinics, San Francisco Public Schools.

Parts of the book are based on previously published studies, in particular 'Configurations in Play: Clinical Observations,' *Psychoanalytic Quarterly*; 'Problems of Infancy and Early Childhood,' *Cyclopaedia of Medicine, Etc.*, Second Revised Edition, Davis and Company; *Studies in the Interpretation of Play*: *I. Clinical Observation of Play Disruption in Young Children*, Genetic Psychology Monographs; 'Observations on Sioux Education,' *Journal of Psychology*; 'Hitler's Imagery and German Youth,' *Psychiatry*; *Observations on the Yurok: Childhood and World Image*, University of California Publications in American Archaeology and Ethnology; 'Childhood and Tradition in Two American Indian Tribes,' in *The Psychoanalytic Study of the Child*, I, International Universities Press (revised and reprinted in *Personality*, edited by Clyde Kluckhohn and Henry A. Murray, Alfred A. Knopf); 'Ego Development and Historical Change,' in *The Psychoanalytic Study of the Child*, II, International Universities Press.

Orinda, California   ERIK HOMBURGER ERIKSON

Part One

Childhood and the Modalities of Social Life

1 Relevance and Relativity in the Case History

In every field there are a few simple questions which are highly embarrassing because the debate which for ever arises around them leads only to perpetual failure and seems consistently to make fools of the most expert. In psychopathology such questions have always concerned the location and the cause of a neurotic disturbance. Does it have a visible onset? Does it reside in the body or in the mind, in the individual or in his society?

For centuries this query centred around the ecclesiastical argument over the origin of lunacy: was it an indwelling devil or an acute inflammation of the brain? Such simple contraposition now seems long outdated. In recent years we have come to the conclusion that a neurosis is psycho- *and* somatic, psycho- *and* social, and *inter*personal.

More often than not, however, discussion will reveal that these new definitions too are only different ways of combining such separate concepts as psyche and soma, individual and group. We now say 'and' instead of 'either – or', but we retain at least the semantic assumption that the mind is a 'thing' separate from the body, and a society a 'thing' outside of the individual.

Psychopathology is the child of medicine which had its illustrious origin in the quest for the location and causation of disease. Our institutions of learning are committed to this quest, which gives to those who suffer, as well as to those who administer, the magic reassurance emanating from scientific tradition and prestige. It is reassuring to think of a neurosis as a disease, because it does feel like an affliction. It is, in fact, often accompanied by circumscribed somatic suffering: and we have well-defined approaches to disease, both on the individual and on the epidemiological level. These approaches have resulted in a sharp decline of many illnesses, and in a decrease of mortality in others.

Yet something strange is happening. As we try to think of neuroses as diseases, we gradually come to reconsider the whole problem of disease. Instead of arriving at a better definition of neurosis, we find that some widespread diseases, such as afflictions of the heart and stomach, seem to acquire new meaning by being considered equivalent to neurotic symptoms, or at any rate to symptoms of a central disturbance rather than of a peripheral happening in isolated afflicted parts.

Here the newest meaning of the 'clinical' approach becomes strangely similar to its oldest meaning. 'Clinical' once designated the function of a priest at the sickbed when the somatic struggle seemed to be coming to an end, and when the soul needed guidance for a lonely meeting with its Maker. There was, in fact, a time in medieval history when a doctor was obliged to call a priest if he proved unable to cure his patient within a certain number of days. The assumption was that in such cases the sickness was what we today might call spirituosomatic. The word 'clinical' has long since shed this clerical garb. But it is regaining some of its old connotation, for we learn that a neurotic person, no matter where and how and why he feels sick, is crippled at the core, no matter what you call that ordered or ordering core. He may not become exposed to the final loneliness of death, but he experiences that numbing loneliness, that isolation and disorganization of experience, which we call neurotic anxiety.

However much the psychotherapist may wish to seek prestige, solidity, and comfort in biological and physical analogies, he deals, above all, with *human anxiety*. About this he can say little that will not tell all. Therefore, before enlarging upon wider applications, he may well state explicitly where he stands in his clinical teaching.

This book consequently begins with a specimen of pathology – namely, the sudden onset of a violent somatic disturbance in a child. Our searchlight does not attempt to isolate and hold in focus any one aspect or mechanism of this case, rather it deliberately plays at random around the multiple factors involved, to see whether we can circumscribe the area of disturbance.

Early one morning, in a town in northern California, the mother of a small boy of three was awakened by strange noises emanating from his room. She hurried to his bed and saw him in a terrifying attack of some kind. To her it looked just like the heart attack from which his grandmother had died five days earlier. She called a doctor, who said that Sam's attack was epileptic. He administered sedatives and had the boy taken to a hospital in a near-by metropolis. The hospital staff were not willing to commit themselves to a diagnosis because of the patient's youth and the drugged state in which he had been brought in. Discharged after a few days, the boy seemed perfectly well, his neurological reflexes were all in order.

One month later, however, little Sam found a dead mole in the back yard and became morbidly agitated over it. His mother tried to answer his very shrewd questions as to what death was all about. He reluctantly went to sleep after having declared that his mother apparently did not know either. In the night he cried out, vomited, and began to twitch around the eyes and the mouth. This time the doctor arrived early enough to observe the symptoms, which culminated in a severe convulsion over the whole right side of his body. The hospital concurred in diagnosing the affliction as epilepsy, possibly due to a brain lesion in the left hemisphere.

When, two months later, a third attack occurred after the boy had accidentally crushed a butterfly in his hand, the hospital added an amendment to its diagnosis: 'Precipitating factor: psychic stimulus.' In other words, because of some cerebral pathology this boy had a lower threshold for convulsive explosion; but it was a psychic stimulus, the idea of death, which precipitated him over his threshold. Otherwise neither his birth history, nor the course of his infancy, nor his neurological condition between attacks showed specific pathology. His general health was excellent. He was well nourished, and his brain waves at the time only indicated that epilepsy 'could not be excluded'.

What was the 'psychic stimulus'? Obviously it had to do with death: dead mole, dead butterfly – and then we remember his mother's remark that in his first attack he had looked just like his dying grandmother.

Here are the facts surrounding the grandmother's death:

Some months before, the father's mother had arrived for her first visit to the family's new house in X. There was an undercurrent of excitement which disturbed the mother more deeply than she then knew. The visit had the connotation of an examination to her: had she done well by her husband and by her child? Also there was anxiety over the grandmother's health. The little boy, who at the time enjoyed teasing people, was warned that the grandmother's heart was not too strong. He promised to spare her, and at first everything went well. Nevertheless, the mother seldom left the two alone together, especially since the enforced restraint seemed to be hard on the vigorous little boy. He looked, the mother thought, increasingly pale and tense. When the mother slipped away for a while one day, leaving the child in her mother-in-law's care, she returned to find the old woman on the floor in a heart attack. As the grandmother later reported, the child had climbed on a chair and had fallen. There was every reason to suspect that he had teased her and had deliberately done something which she had warned him against. The grandmother was ill for months, failed to recover, and finally died a few days before the child's first attack.

The conclusion was obvious that what the doctors had called the 'psychic stimulus' in this case had to do with his grandmother's death. In fact, the mother now remembered what at the time had seemed irrelevant to her – namely, that Sam, on going to bed the night before the attack, had piled up his pillows the way his grandmother had done to avoid congestion and that he had gone to sleep in an almost sitting position – as had the grandmother.

Strangely enough, the mother insisted that the boy did not know of his grandmother's death. On the morning after it occurred she had told him that the grandmother had gone on a long trip north to Seattle. He had cried and said, 'Why didn't she say good-bye to me?' He was told that there had not been time. Then, when a mysterious, large box had been carried out of the house, the mother had told him that his grandmother's books were in it. But Sam had not seen the grandmother either bring or use such a lot of books, and he could not quite see the reason for all the tears shed over a box of books by the hastily congregated relatives. I doubted, of course, that the boy had really believed the story; and indeed, the mother had puzzled over a number of remarks made by the little teaser. Once when she had wanted him to find something which he did not want to look for, he had said mockingly, 'It has gone on a lo-ong trip, all the way to See-attle.' In the play group which he later joined as part of the treatment plan, the otherwise vigorous boy would, in dreamy concentration, build innumerable variations of oblong boxes, the openings of which he would carefully barricade. His questions at the time justified the suspicion that he was experimenting with the idea of how it was to be locked up in an oblong box. But he refused to listen to his mother's belated explanation, now offered almost pleadingly, that the grandmother had, in fact, died. 'You're lying,' he said. 'She's in Seattle. I'm going to see her again.'

From the little that has been said about the boy so far, it must be clear that he was a rather self-willed, vigorous, and precociously intelligent little fellow, not easily fooled. His ambitious parents had big plans for their only son: with his brains he might go east to college and medical school, or maybe to law school. They fostered in him a vigorous expression of his intellectual precocity and curiosity. He had always been wilful and from his first day unable to accept a 'no' or a 'maybe' for an answer. As soon as he could reach, he hit – a tendency which was not considered unsound in the neighbourhood in which he had been born and raised: a neighbourhood mixed in population, a neighbourhood in which he must have received at an early age the impression that it was good to learn to hit first, just in case. But now they lived, the only Jewish family, in a small but prosperous town. They had to tell their little boy not to hit the children, not to ask the ladies too many questions, and – for heaven's sake and also for the sake of business – to treat the Gentiles gently. In his earlier *milieu*, the ideal image held out for a little boy had been that of a tough guy (on the street) and a smart boy (at home). The problem now was to become quickly what the Gentiles of the middle class would call 'a nice little boy, in spite of his being Jewish'. Sam had done a remarkably intelligent job in adjusting his aggressiveness and becoming a witty little teaser.

Here the 'psychic stimulus' gains in dimensions. In the first place, this had always been an irritable and an aggressive child.

Attempts on the part of others to restrain him made him angry; his own attempts at restraining himself resulted in unbearable tension. We might call this his *constitutional intolerance,* 'constitutional' meaning merely that we cannot trace it to anything earlier, he just always had been that way. I must add, however, that his anger never lasted long and that he was not only a very affectionate, but also an outstandingly expressive and exuberant child, traits which helped him adopt the role of one who commits good-natured mischief. About the time of his grandmother's arrival, however, something, it now appeared, had robbed him of his humour. He had hit a child, hard. A little blood had trickled, ostracism had threatened. He, the vigorous extravert, had been forced to stay at home with his grandmother, whom he was not allowed to tease.

Was his aggressiveness part of an epileptic constitution? I do not know. There was nothing feverish or hectic about his vigour. It is true that his first three major attacks were all connected with ideas of death and two later ones with the departures of his first and second therapists, respectively. It is also true that his much more frequent minor attacks – which consisted of staring, gagging, and swooning from which he would recover with the worried words, 'What happened?' – often occurred immediately after sudden aggressive acts or words on his part. He might throw a stone at a stranger, or he might say, 'God is a skunk,' or, 'The whole world is full of skunks,' or (to his mother), 'You are a stepmother.' Were these outbursts of primitive aggression for which he was then forced to atone in an attack? Or were they desperate attempts at discharging with violent action a foreboding of an impending attack?

These were the impressions I had gathered from the doctor's case history and the mother's reports when I took over the boy's treatment about two years after the onset of his illness. And soon I was to witness one of his minor spells. We had played dominoes, and in order to test his threshold I had made him lose consistently, which was by no means easy. He grew very pale and all his sparkle dimmed out. Suddenly he stood up, took a rubber doll, and hit me in the face, hard. Then his glance turned into an aimless stare, he gagged as if about to vomit, and swooned slightly. Coming to, he said in a hoarse and urgent voice, 'Let's go on,' and gathered together his dominoes, which had tumbled over. Children are apt to express in spatial configuration what they cannot or dare not say. As he rearranged them hurriedly, he built an oblong, rectangular configuration: a miniature edition of the big boxes he had liked to build previously in the nursery school. The dominoes all faced inward. Now fully conscious, he noticed what he had done and smiled very faintly.

I felt that he was ready to be told what I thought I understood. I said, 'If you wanted to see the dots on your blocks, you would have to be inside that little box, like a dead person in a coffin.'

'Yes,' he whispered.

'This must mean that you are afraid you may have to die because you hit me.'

Breathlessly, 'Must I?'

'Of course not. But when they carried your grandmother away in the coffin you probably thought that you made her die and therefore had to die yourself. That's why you built those big boxes in your school, just as you built this little one today. In fact, you must have thought you were going to die every time you had one of those attacks.'

'Yes,' he said, somewhat sheepishly, because he had actually never admitted to me that he had seen his grandmother's coffin, and that he knew she was dead.

Here one might think we have the story. In the meantime, however, I had worked with the mother also and had learned of her part in it – an essential portion of the whole account. For we may be sure that whatever deep 'psychic stimulus' may be present in the life of a young child, it is identical with his mother's most neurotic conflict. Indeed, the mother now succeeded in remembering, only against severe emotional resistance, an incident when, in the middle of her busiest preparations for the mother-in-law's arrival, Sam had thrown a doll into her face. Whether he had done this 'deliberately' or not, he had aimed only too well; he had loosened one of her front teeth. A front tooth is a precious possession in many ways. His mother had hit him right back, harder and with more anger than she had ever done before. She had not exacted a tooth for a tooth, but she had shown a rage which neither she nor he had known was in her.

Or had he known it before she did? This is a crucial point. For I believe that this boy's low tolerance for aggression was further lowered by the over-all connotation of violence in his family. Above and beyond individual conflict, the whole milieu of these children of erstwhile fugitives from ghettoes and pogroms is pervaded by the problem of the Jew's special fate in the face of anger and violence. It had all started so significantly with a God who was mighty, wrathful, and vindictive, but also sadly agitated, attitudes which he had bequeathed to the successive patriarchs all the way from Moses down to this boy's grand-parents. And it all had ended with the chosen but dispersed Jewish people's unarmed helplessness against the surrounding world of always potentially violent Gentiles. This family had dared the Jewish fate, by isolating itself in a Gentile town; but they were carrying their fate with them as an inner reality, in the midst of these Gentiles who did not actively deny them their new, if somewhat shaky, security.

Here it is important to add that our patient had been caught in this, his parents' conflict with their ancestors and with their neighbours, at the worst possible time for him. For he was going through a maturational stage characterized by a developmental intolerance of restraint. I refer to the rapid increase in locomotor vigour, in mental curiosity, and in a sadistic kind of infantile maleness which usually appears at the age of three or four, manifesting itself according to differences in custom and individual temperament. There is no doubt that our patient had been precocious in this as in other respects. At that stage any child is apt to show increased intolerance of being restrained from moving wilfully and from asking persistently. A vigorous increase in initiative both in deed and in fantasy makes the growing child of this stage especially vulnerable to the talion principle – and he had come uncomfortably close to the tooth-for-a-tooth penalty. At this stage a little boy likes to pretend that he is a giant because he is afraid of giants, for he knows all too well that his feet are much too small for the boots he wears in his fantasies. In addition, precocity always implies relative isolation and disquieting imbalance. His tolerance, then, for his parents' anxieties was specifically low at the time when the grandmother's arrival added latent ancestral conflicts to the social and economic problems of the day.

This, then, is our first 'specimen' of a human crisis. But before further dissecting the specimen, let me say a word about the therapeutic procedure. An attempt was made to synchronize the paediatric with the psychoanalytic work. Dosages of sedatives were gradually decreased as psychoanalytical observation began to discern, and insight to steady, the weak spots in the child's emotional threshold. The stimuli specific for these weak areas were discussed not only with the child but also with his father and mother so that they too, could review their roles in the disturbance and could gain some insight before their precocious child could overtake them in his understanding of himself and of them.

One afternoon soon after the episode in which I was struck in the face, our little patient came upon his mother, who lay resting on a couch. He put his hand on her chest and said, 'Only a very bad boy would like to jump on his mommy and step on her; only a very bad boy would want to do that. Isn't that so, Mommy?' The mother laughed and said, 'I bet you would like to do it now. I think quite a good little boy might think that he wanted to do such a thing, but he would know that he did not really want to do it' – or something like that: such things are hard to say, and wording is not too important. What counts is their spirit, and the implication that there are two different ways of wanting a thing, which can be separated by self-observation and communicated to others. 'Yes,' he said, 'but I won't do it.' Then he added, 'Mr E. always asks me why I throw things. He spoils everything.' He added quickly, 'There won't be any scene tonight, Mommy.'

Thus the boy learned to share his self-observation with the very mother against whom his rages were apt to be directed, and to make her an ally of his insight. To establish this was of utmost importance, for it made it possible for the boy to warn his mother and himself whenever he felt the approach of that peculiar cosmic wrath or when he perceived the (often very slight) somatic indications of an attack. She would immediately get in touch with the paediatrician, who was fully informed and most cooperative. He would then prescribe some preventative measure. In this way minor seizures were reduced to rare and fleeting occurrences which the boy gradually learned to handle with a minimum of commotion. Major attacks did not recur.

The reader, at this point, may rightfully protest that such attacks in a small child might have stopped anyway, without any such complicated procedures. This is possible. No claim is advanced here of a cure of epilepsy by psychoanalysis. We claim less – and, in a way, aspire to more.

We have investigated the 'psychic stimulus' which at a particular period in the patient's life cycle helped to make manifest a latent potentiality for epileptic attacks. Our form of investigation gains in knowledge as it gives insight to the patient, and it corrects him as it becomes a part of his life. Whatever his age, we apply ourselves to his capacity to examine himself, to understand, and to plan. In doing so, we may effect a cure or accelerate a spontaneous cure – no mean contribution when one considers the damage done by the mere habitualness and repetitiveness of such severe neurological storms. But in claiming less than the cure of the epilepsy, we would in principle like to believe that with therapeutic investigations into a segment of one child's history we help a whole family to accept a crisis in their midst as a crisis in the family history. For a psychosomatic crisis is an emotional crisis to the extent to which the sick individual is responding specifically to the latent crises in the significant people around him.

This, to be sure, has nothing to do with giving or accepting *blame* for the disturbance. In fact, the mother's very self-blame, that she may have caused damage to the child's brain with that one hard slap, constituted much of the 'psychic stimulus' we were looking for: for it increased and reinforced that general fear of violence which characterized the family's history. Most of all, the mother's fear that she may have harmed him was a counterpart and thus an emotional reinforcement of what we finally concluded was the really dominant pathogenic 'psychic stimulus' which Sam's doctors wanted us to find – namely, the boy's fear *that his mother, too, might die* because of his attack on her tooth and because of his more general sadistic deeds and wishes.

No, blame does not help. As long as there is a sense of blame, there are also irrational attempts at restitution for the damage done – and such guilty restitution often results only in more damage. What we would hope that the patient and his family might derive from our study of their history is deeper humility before the processes which govern us, and the ability to live through them with greater simplicity and honesty. What are they?

The nature of our case suggests that we begin with the processes *inherent in the organism*. We shall in these pages refer to the organism as a process rather than as a thing, for we are concerned with the homeostatic quality of the living organism rather than with pathological items which might be demonstrable by section or dissection. Our patient suffered a somatic disturbance of a kind and an intensity which suggests the possibility of a somatic brain irritation of anatomic, toxic, or other origin. Such damage was not demonstrated, but we must ask what burden its presence would place on the life of this child. Even if the damage were demonstrable, it would, of course, constitute only a potential, albeit necessary, condition to convulsion. It could not be considered the cause of the convulsion, for we must assume that quite a number of individuals live with similar cerebral pathology without ever having a convulsion. The brain damage, then, would merely facilitate the discharge of tension, from whatever source, in convulsive storms. At the same time, it would be an ever present reminder of an inner danger point, of a low tolerance for tension. Such an inner danger can be said to decrease the child's threshold for outer dangers, especially as perceived in the irritabilities and anxieties of his parents, whose protection is needed so sorely, precisely because of the inner danger. Whether the brain lesion thus would cause the boy's temperament to be more impatient and more irritable, or whether his irritability (which he shared with other relatives and to which he was exposed in other relatives) would make his brain lesion more significant than it would in a boy of a different kind among different people – this is one of the many good questions for which there is no answer.

All we can say, then, is that at the time of the crisis Sam's 'constitution' as well as his temperament and his stage of development had specific trends in common; they all converged on the intolerance of restrictions in locomotor freedom and aggressive expression.

But then, Sam's needs for muscular and mental activity were not solely of a physiological nature. They constituted an important part of his personality development and thus belonged to his defensive equipment. In dangerous situations Sam used what we call the 'counterphobic' defence mechanism: when he was scared, he attacked, and when faced with knowledge which others might choose to avoid as upsetting, he asked questions with anxious persistence. These defences, in turn, were well suited to the sanctions of his early milieu, which thought him cutest when he was toughest and smartest. With a shift in focus, then, many of the items originally listed as parts of his physiological and mental make-up prove to belong to a second process of organization, which we shall call *the organization of experience in the individual ego*. As will be discussed in detail, this central process guards the coherence and the individuality of experience by gearing the individual for shocks threatening from sudden discontinuities in the organism as well as in the milieu; by enabling it to anticipate inner as well as outer dangers; and by integrating endowment and social opportunities. It thus assures to the individual a sense of coherent individuation and identity: of being one's self, of being all right, and of being on the way to becoming what other people, at their kindest, take one to be. It is clear that our little boy tried to become an intelligent teaser and questioner, a role which he had first found to be successful in the face of danger and which he now found provoked it. We have described how this role (which prepared him well for the adult role of a Jewish intellectual) became temporarily devaluated by developments in neighbourhood and home. Such devaluation puts the defensive system out of commission: where the 'counterphobic' cannot attack, he feels open to attack and expects and even provokes it. In Sam's case, the 'attack' came from a somatic source.

'Roles', however, grow out of the third principle of organization, the *social*. The human being, at all times, from the first kick *in utero* to the last breath, is organized into groupings of geographic and historical coherence: family, class, community, nation. A human being, thus, is at all times an organism, an ego, and a member of a society and is involved in all three processes of organization. His body is exposed to pain and tension; his ego, to anxiety; and as a member of a society, he is susceptible to the panic emanating from his group.

Here we come to our first clinical postulates. That there is no anxiety without somatic tension seems immediately obvious; but we must also learn that there is no individual anxiety which does not reflect a latent concern common to the immediate and extended group. An individual feels isolated and barred from the sources of collective strength when he (even though only secretly) takes on a role considered especially evil, be it that of a drunkard or a killer, a sissy or a sucker, or whatever colloquial designation of inferiority may be used in his group. In Sam's case, the grandmother's death had only confirmed what the Gentile children (or rather, their parents) had indicated, namely that he was an overwhelmingly bad boy. Behind all of this, of course, there was the fact that he was different, that he was a Jew, a matter by no means solely or even primarily brought to his attention by the neighbours: for his own parents had persistently indicated that a little Jew had to be especially good in order not to be especially bad. Here our investigation, in order to do justice to all the relevant facts, would have to lead back into history at large, it could do nothing less than trace the fate of this family back from Main Street to a ghetto in a far eastern province of Russia and to all the brutal events of the Diaspora.

We are speaking of three processes, the somatic process, the ego process, and the societal process. In the history of science these three processes have belonged to three different scientific disciplines – biology, psychology, and the social sciences – each of which studied what it could isolate, count, and dissect: single organisms, individual minds, and social aggregates. The knowledge thus derived is knowledge of facts and figures, of location and causation; and it has resulted in argument over an item's allocation to one process or another. Our thinking is dominated by this trichotomy because only through the inventive methodologies of these disciplines do we have knowledge at all. Unfortunately, however, this knowledge is tied to the conditions under which it was secured: the organism undergoing dissection or examination; the mind surrendered to experiment or interrogation; social aggregates spread out on statistical tables. In all of these cases, then, a scientific discipline prejudiced the matter under observation by actively dissolving its total living situation in order to be able to make an isolated section of it amenable to a set of instruments or concepts.

Our clinical problem, and our bias, are different. We study individual human crises by becoming therapeutically involved in them. In doing so, we find that the three processes mentioned are three aspects of one process – i.e., human life, both words being equally emphasized. Somatic tension, individual anxiety, and group panic, then, are only different ways in which human anxiety presents itself to different methods of investigation. Clinical training should include all three methods, an ideal to which the studies in this books are gropingly dedicated. As we review each relevant item in a given case, we cannot escape the conviction that the meaning of an item which may be 'located' in one of the three processes is co-determined by its meaning in the other two. An item in one process gains relevance by giving significance to and receiving significance from items in the others. Gradually, I hope, we may find better words for such *relativity in human existence*.

Of the catastrophe described in our first specimen, then, we know no 'cause'. Instead we find a convergence in all three processes of specific intolerances which make the catastrophe retrospectively intelligible, retrospectively probable. The plausibility thus gained does not permit us to go back and undo causes. It only permits us to understand a continuum, on which the catastrophe marked a decisive event, an event which now throws its shadow back over the very items which seem to have caused it. The catastrophe has occurred, and we must now introduce ourselves, as a curing agent, into the post-catastrophic situation. We will never know what this life was like before we became involved in it. These are the conditions under which we do therapeutic research.

For comparison and confirmation we now turn to another crisis, this time in an adult. The presenting symptom is, again, somatic; it consists of a severe chronic headache, which owes its onset to one of the exigencies of adult social life, combat in war.

A COMBAT CRISIS IN A MARINE

A young teacher in his early thirties was discharged from the armed forces as a 'psychoneurotic casualty'. His symptoms, primarily an incapacitating headache, followed him into his first peacetime job. In a veterans' clinic he was asked how it had all started. He reported:

A group of marines, just ashore, lay in the pitch darkness of a Pacific beachhead within close range of enemy fire. They once had been, and they still acted like, a group of tough and boisterous men who are sure that they can 'take anything'. They had always felt that they could count on the 'brass' to relieve them after the initial assault and to let mere infantry do the holding of the positions taken. Somehow it had always contradicted the essential spirit of their corps to have 'to take it lying down'. Yet it had happened in this war. And when it happened, it had exposed them not only to damnable sniping from nowhere, but also to a strange mixture of disgust, rage, and fear – down in their stomachs.

Here they were again. The 'supporting' fire from the Navy had not been much of a support. Something seemed to be wrong again. What if it were true that the 'brass' considered them expendable?

Among these men lay our patient. The last thought which at that time would have occurred to him was that he could ever become a patient himself. He was, in fact, a medical soldier. Unarmed, according to convention, he seemed unsusceptible to the slowly rising wave of rage and panic among the men. It was as if it could not get at him. Somehow, he felt in the right place as a medical corps man. The griping of the men only made him feel that they were like children. He had always liked working with children, and he had always been considered to be especially good with tough kids. But he was not a tough kid himself. In fact, at the beginning of the war he had chosen the medical corps because he could not bring himself to carry a gun. He had no hate whatsoever for anyone. (As he now reiterated this exalted sentiment, it became apparent that he must have been too good to be true, at any rate for the Marine Corps, for he never drank or smoked – and he never swore!) It was good now to show that he could take it and, more, that he could help these boys to take it too, and could be of help when their aggressive mission ended. He kept close to his medical officer, a man like himself, a man whom he could look up to and admire.

Our medical man never quite remembered what happened during the remainder of the night. There were only isolated memories, more dreamlike than real. He claims that the medical corps men were ordered to unload ammunition instead of setting up a hospital; that the medical officer, somehow, became very angry and abusive; and that some time during the night somebody pressed a sub-machine gun into his hands. Here his memory becomes a blank.

The following morning the patient (for he was now a patient) found himself in the finally improvised hospital. Overnight he had developed severe intestinal fever. He spent the day in the twilight of sedatives. At nightfall the enemy attacked from the air. All the able-bodied men found shelter or helped the sick to find one. He was immobilized, unable to move, and, much worse, unable to help. Here for the first time he felt fear, as so many courageous men did at the moment when they found themselves on their backs, inactivated.

The next day he was evacuated. When not under fire he felt calmer – or so he thought, until the first meal was served on board. The metallic noise of the mess utensils went through his head like a salvo of shots. It was if he had no defence whatsoever against these noises, which were so unbearable that he crawled under a cover while the others ate.

From then on his life was made miserable by raging headaches. When temporarily free of headaches, he was jumpy, apprehensive of possible metallic noises, and furious when they occurred. His fever (or whatever had caused it) was cured; but his headaches and his jumpiness made it necessary for him to be returned to the States and to be discharged.

Where was the seat of his neurosis? For a 'war neurosis' it was, if we accept his doctors' diagnosis. From the physiological viewpoint the fever and the toxic state had justified his first headache, but only the first one.

Here we must ask something seemingly far removed from headaches: why was this man such a good man? For even now, though practically surrounded with annoying postwar circumstances, he seemed unable to verbalize and give vent to anger. In fact, he thought that his medical officer's swearing anger that night had, by disillusioning him, exposed him to anxiety. Why was he so good and so shocked by anger?

I asked him to try to overcome his aversion to anger and to list for me the things that had irritated him, however slightly, during the days preceding the interview. He mentioned the vibration of buses; high-pitched voices, such as the children's at work; the squeaking of tyres; the memory of foxholes full of ants and lizards; the bad food in the Navy; the last bomb which had exploded pretty close; distrustful people; thieving people; high-hat, conceited people of 'whatever race, colour, or religion';

the memory of his mother. The patient's associations had led from metallic noises and other war memories proper to thievery and distrust – and to his mother.

He had not seen his mother, it appeared, since he was fourteen years old. His family had then been on an economic and moral decline. He had left home abruptly when his mother, in a drunken rage, had pointed a gun at him. He had grabbed the gun, broken it, and thrown it out of the window. Then he had left for good. He had secured the secret help of a fatherly man – in fact, his principal. In exchange for protection and guidance, he had promised never to drink, to swear, or to indulge himself sexually – and then, never to touch a gun. He had become a good student and a teacher and an exceptionally even-tempered man, at least on the surface, until that night on the Pacific beachhead, when amidst the growing anger and panic of the men, his fatherly officer had exploded with a few violent oaths, and when immediately afterwards somebody had pressed a sub-machine gun into his hands.

There have been many war neuroses of this kind. Their victims were in a constant state of potential panic. They felt attacked or endangered by sudden or loud noises as well as by symptoms that flashed through their bodies: palpitations, waves of fever heat, headaches. They were just as helpless, however, in the face of their emotions: childlike anger and anxiety without reason were provoked by anything too sudden or too intense, a perception or a feeling, a thought, or a memory. What was sick in these men, then, was their screening system, that ability *not* to pay attention to a thousand stimuli which we perceive at any given moment but which we are able to ignore for the sake of whatever we are concentrating on. Worse, these men were unable to sleep deeply and to dream well. Through long nights they would hang between the Scylla of annoying noises and the Charybdis of the anxiety dreams which would startle them out of finally achieved moments of deep sleep. In the daytime they would find themselves unable to remember certain things; in their own neighbourhoods they would lose their way or suddenly detect, in conversation, that they had unwittingly misrepresented things. They could not rely on the characteristic processes of the functioning ego by which time and space are organized and truth is tested.

35

What had happened? Were these the symptoms of physically shaken, somatically damaged nerves? In some cases, undoubtedly the condition started with such damage, or at least with momentary traumatization. More often, however, several factors combined to cause a real crisis and to make it a lasting one. The case presented included all of these factors: the lowering of group morale and the gradual growth of imperceptible group panic because of doubt in the leadership; immobilization under enemy fire that could not be located and returned; the inducement to 'giving up' in a hospital bed; and finally, immediate evacuation and a lasting conflict between two inner voices, one of which said, 'Let them take you home, don't be a sucker,' and the other, 'Don't let the others down; if they can take it, you can.'

What impressed me most was the loss in these men of a sense of identity. They knew who they were; they had a personal identity. But it was as if, subjectively, their lives no longer hung together – and never would again. There was a central disturbance of what I then started to call ego identity. At this point it is enough to say that this sense of identity provides the ability to experience one's self as something that has continuity and sameness, and to act accordingly. In many cases there was at the decisive time in the history of the breakdown a seemingly innocent item such as the gun in our medical soldier's unwilling hands: a symbol of evil, which endangered the principles by which the individual had attempted to safeguard personal integrity and social status in his life at home. Likewise, the anxiety often broke out with the sudden thought, I should now be at home, painting the roof, or paying that bill, or seeing this boss or calling on that girl; and the despairing feeling that all of this which should have been would never be. This, in turn, seemed to be intrinsically interwoven with an aspect of American life which will be fully discussed later – namely, the fact that many of our young men keep their life plans and their identities tentative on the principle suggested by the early course of American history – that a man must have and must preserve and defend the freedom of the step and the right to make a choice and grasp opportunities. To be sure, Americans too settle down and, in fact, can be sedentary with a vengeance. But sitting with conviction presupposes also the assurance that they could move if they chose to, move geographically or socially or both. It is the free choice that counts and the conviction that nobody can either 'fence you in' or 'push you around'. Thus contrasting symbols become all-important, symbols of possession, of status, and of sameness, and symbols of choice, change, and challenge. Depending on the immediate situation, these symbols can become good or evil. In our marine, the gun had become the symbol of his family's downfall and represented all the angry and ugly things which he had chosen *not* to do.

Thus again, three contemporaneous processes, instead of supporting one another, seem to have mutually aggravated their respective dangers: (1) The group. These men wanted to have the situation well in hand as a group, with a defined identity among the armed forces of this country. Mistrust in leadership, instead, caused grumbling panic. Our man countered this panic, of which he could not possibly be oblivious, by the defensive position so often taken in his life, that he was the well-composed, tolerant leader of children. (2) The patient's organism struggled to maintain homeostasis under the impact of both the (subliminal) panic and symptoms of an acute infection, but was sabotaged by the severe fever. Against this the man held out to the breaking-point because of that other 'conviction' that he could 'take anything'. (3) The patient's ego. Already overtaxed by the group panic and the increasing fever, to neither of which he was at first willing to give in, the patient's balance was further upset by the loss of an outer support for an inner ideal: the very superiors on whom he had relied ordered him (or so he thought) to break a symbolic vow on which his self-esteem was so precariously based. No doubt, then, this occurrence opened the floodgate of infantile urges which he had so rigidly held in abeyance. For in all of his rigidity only part of his personality had genuinely matured, while another part had been supported by the very props which now collapsed. Under such conditions he was unable to endure inactivity under air bombardment and something in him gave in only too easily to the offer of evacuation. Here the situation changed, introducing new complications. For once evacuated, many men felt, as it were, unconsciously obligated to continue to suffer and to suffer somatically, in order to justify the evacuation, not to speak of the later discharge, which some men could never have forgiven themselves on the grounds of a 'mere neurosis'. After the First World War, much emphasis was put on a compensation neurosis – neuroses unconsciously prolonged so as to secure continued financial help. The Second World War experience has indicated insight into what might be called an *over* compensation neurosis – i.e., the unconscious wish to continue to suffer in order to over-compensate psychologically for the weakness of having let others down; for many of these escapists were more loyal than they knew. Our conscientious man, too, repeatedly felt 'shot through the head' by excruciating pain whenever he seemed definitely better, or rather whenever he became aware of having felt well for some time without taking note of it.

We could say with reasonable assurance that this man would not have broken down in this particular way had it not been for the conditions of war and combat – just as most doctors would be reasonably certain that young Sam could not have had convulsions of such severity without some 'somatic compliance'. In either case, however, the psychological and therapeutic problem is to understand how the combined circumstances weakened a central defence and what specific meaning the consequent breakdown represents.

The combined circumstances which we recognize are an aggregate of simultaneous changes in the organism (exhaustion and fever), in the ego (breakdown of ego identity), and in the milieu (group panic). These changes aggravate one another if traumatic suddenness in one set of changes makes impossible demands on the balancing power of the other two, or if a con-vergence of main themes gives all changes a high mutual specificity. We saw such a convergence in Sam's case, where a hostility problem came to a critical focus all at once in his milieu, in his maturational stage, in his somatic condition, and in his ego defences. Sam's and the marine's cases both showed another dangerous trend – namely, ubiquity of change, a condition existing when too many props are endangered in all three spheres at once and the same time.

We have presented two human crises in order to illustrate an over-all clinical viewpoint. The laws and mechanisms involved will be discussed in the bulk of this book. The cases presented are not typical: in the daily run of the clinical mill, few cases demonstrate such dramatic and clear-cut 'beginnings'. Nor did these beginnings really mark the onset of the disturbance which eventually overcame these patients. They only marked moments of concentrated and representative happening. But we did not stray too far from clinical, and indeed, historical habit when, for purposes of demonstration, we chose cases which highlight in an unusually dramatic way the principles governing the usual.

These principles can be expressed in a didactic formula. The relevance of a given item in a case history is derived from the relevance of other items to which it contributes relevance and from which by the very fact of this contribution, it derives additional meaning. To understand a given case of psychopathology you proceed to study whatever set of observable changes seem most accessible either because they dominate the symptom presented or because you have learned a methodological approach to this particular set of items, be they the somatic changes, the personality transformations, or the social upheavals involved. Wherever you begin, you will have to begin again twice over. If you begin with the organism, it will be necessary to see what meanings these changes have in the other processes and how aggravating these meanings, in turn, are for the organism's attempt at restoration. To really understand this it will be necessary, without fear of undue duplication, to take a fresh look at the data and begin, say, with variations in the ego process, relating each item to the developmental stage and the state of the organism, as well as to the history of the patient's social associations. This, in turn, necessitates a third form of reconstruction – namely, that of the patient's family history and of those changes in his social life which receive meaning from and give meaning to his bodily changes as well as to his ego development. In other words, being unable to arrive at any simple sequence and causal chain with a clear location and a circumscribed beginning, only triple bookkeeping (or, if you wish, a systematic going around in circles) can gradually clarify the relevances and the relativities of all the known data. The fact that this may not lead to a clear beginning and may not end with either a clear pathogenic reconstruction nor a well-founded prognostic formulation is unfortunate for the appearance of our files, but it may be just as well for our therapeutic endeavour; for we must be prepared not only to understand but also to influence all three processes at the same time. This means that in our best clinical work, or in the best moments of our clinical work, we do not strenuously think of all the relativities involved, explicit as we may have been able to make them in staff meetings and summaries; we must act upon them as we add ourselves to them.

To demonstrate the therapeutic aspect of our work is not the purpose of this book. Only in the conclusion shall we return to the problem of psychotherapy as a specific relationship. Our formula for clinical thinking has been presented here mainly as a rationale for the organization of this book.

In the remainder of Part I, I will discuss the *biological* basis of psychoanalytic theory, Freud's timetable of *libido development*, and relate it to what we now know about the ego and are beginning to learn about society. Part II deals with a *societal* dilemma – namely, the education of American Indian children today and in the tribal past, and its significance for cultural adaptation.

Part III will concern itself with the laws of the *ego* as revealed in ego pathology and in normal childhood play. We will present a chart of psychosocial gains which are the result of the ego's successful mediation between physical stages and social institutions.

In the light of such insight, we will review in Part IV selected aspects of the end of childhood and of entrance into adulthood under the changing conditions of industrialization in this country, in Germany, and in Russia. This will provide a historical rationale for our study, for in our time man must decide whether he can afford to continue the exploitation of childhood as an arsenal of irrational fears, or whether the relationship of adult and child, like other inequalities, can be raised to a position of partnership in a more reasonable order of things.

2 The Theory of Infantile Sexuality

As an introduction to a review of Freud's theories concerning the infantile organism as a powerhouse of sexual and aggressive energies, let me now present observations on two children who seemed strangely deadlocked in combat with their own bowels. As we try to understand the social implications of the eliminative and other body apertures, it will be necessary to reserve judgement regarding the children studied and the symptoms observed. The symptoms seem odd; the children are not. For good physiological reasons the bowels are farthest away from the zone which is our prime interpersonal mediator, namely the face. Well-trained adults dismiss the bowels, if they function well, as the non-social backside of things. Yet for this very reason bowel dysfunction lends itself to confused reflection and to secret response. In adults this problem is hidden behind somatic complaints; in children it appears in what seem to be merely wilful habits.

Ann, a girl of four, enters the office, half gently pulled, half firmly pushed by her worried mother. While she does not resist or object, her face is pale and sullen, her eyes have a blank and inward look, and she sucks vigorously on her thumb.

I have been informed of Ann's trouble. She seems to be losing her usual resilience; in one way she is much too babyish, in another much too serious, too unchildlike. When she does express exuberance, it is of an explosive kind which soon turns to silliness. But her most annoying habit is that of holding on to her bowel movements when requested to relinquish them, and then of stubbornly depositing them in her bed during the night, or rather in the early morning just before her sleepy mother can catch her. Reprimands are borne silently, and in reverie behind which lurks obvious despair. This despair seems recently to have increased following an accident in which she was knocked down by an automobile. The damage to her body is only superficial, but she has withdrawn even further from the reach of parental communication and control.

Once inside the office the child lets go of the mother's hand and walks into my room with the automatic obedience of a prisoner who no longer has a will of his own. In my playroom she stands in a corner, sucking tensely on her thumb and paying only a very reserved kind of attention to me.

In Chapter 6 I shall go into the dynamics of such an encounter between child and psychotherapist and indicate in detail what I think is going on in the child's mind and what I know is going on in mine during these first moments of mutual sizing up. I shall then discuss the role of play observation in our work. Here I am merely interested in recording a clinical 'specimen' as a springboard for theoretical discussion.

The child indicates clearly that I will not get anything out of her. To her growing surprise and relief, however, I do not ask her any questions; I do not even tell her that I am her friend and that she should trust me. Instead I start to build a simple block house on the floor. There is a living-room; a kitchen; a bedroom with a little girl in a bed and a woman standing close by her; a bathroom with the door open; and a garage with a man standing next to a car. This arrangement suggests, of course, the regular morning hour when the mother tries to pick the little girl up 'on time', while the father gets ready to leave the house.

Our patient, increasingly fascinated with this wordless statement of a problem, suddenly goes into action. She relinquishes her thumb to make space for a broad and toothy grin. Her face flushes and she runs over to the toy scene. With a mighty kick she disposes of the woman doll; she bangs the bathroom door shut, and she hurries to the toy shelf to get three shiny cars, which she puts into the garage beside the man. She has answered my 'question': she, indeed, does not wish the toy girl to give to her mother what is her mother's, and she is eager to give to her father more than he could ask for.

I am still pondering over the power of her aggressive exuberance when she, in turn, seems suddenly overpowered by an entirely different set of emotions. She burst into tears and into a desperate whimper, 'Where is my mummy?' In panicky haste she takes a handful of pencils from my desk and runs out into the waiting-room. Pressing the pencils into her mother's hand, she sits down close to her. The thumb goes back into the mouth, the child's face becomes uncommunicative, and I can see the game is over. The mother wants to give the pencils back to me, but I indicate that I do not need them today. Mother and child leave.

Half an hour later the telephone rings. They have hardly reached home when the little girl asks her mother whether she may see me again that same day. Tomorrow is not early enough. She insists with signs of despair that the mother call me immediately for an appointment the same day so that she may return the pencils. I must assure the child over the phone that I appreciate her intentions but that she is quite welcome to keep the pencils until the next day.

The next day, at the appointed time, Ann sits beside her mother in the waiting-room. In the one hand she holds the pencils, unable to give them to me. In the other she clutches a small object. She shows no inclination to come with me. It suddenly becomes quite noticeable that she has soiled herself. As she is picked up to be taken to the bathroom, the pencils fall to the floor and with them the object from the other hand. It is a tiny toy dog, one of whose legs has been broken off.

I must add here the information that at this time a neighbour's dog plays a significant role in the child's life. This dog soils too; but he is beaten for it, and the child is not. And the dog, too, has recently been knocked down by a car; but he has lost a leg. Her friend in the animal world, then, is much like herself, only more so; and he is much worse off. Does she expect (or maybe even wish) to be punished likewise?

I have now described the circumstances of a play episode and of an infantile symptom. I shall not go further here into the relativities and relevances which led up to the described situation; nor shall I relate how the deadlock was finally resolved in work with parents and child. I appreciate and share the regret of many a reader that we are not able here to pursue the therapeutic process and, in fact, the passing of this infantile crisis. Instead I must ask the reader to accept this story as a 'specimen' and to analyse it with me.

The little girl had not come of her own free will. She had merely let herself be brought by the very mother against whom, as everything indicated, her sullenness was directed. Once in my room, my quiet play apparently had made her forget for a moment that her mother was outside. What she would not have been able to say in words in many hours she could express in a few minutes of non-verbal communication: she 'hated' her mother and she 'loved' her father. Having expressed this, however, she must have experienced what Adam did when he heard God's voice: 'Adam, where art thou?' She was compelled to atone for her deed, for she loved her mother too and needed her. In her very panic, however, she did compulsively what ambivalent people always do: in turning to make amends to one person they 'inadvertently' do harm to another. So she took my pencils to appease the mother, and then wanted to force the mother to help her make restitution.

The next day her eagerness to conciliate me is paralysed. I think I had become the tempter who makes children confess in unguarded moments what nobody should know or say. Children often have such a reaction after an initial admission of secret thoughts. What if I told her mother? What if her mother refused to bring her back to me so she could modify and qualify her unguarded acts? So she refused to act altogether, and let her symptom speak.

Soiling represents a sphincter conflict, an anal and urethral problem. This aspect of the matter we shall call the zonal aspect, because it concerns a *body zone*. On closer review, however, it becomes clear that this child's behaviour, even where it is not anal in a zonal sense, has the quality of a sphincter problem. One may almost say that the whole little girl acts like a multiple sphincter. In her facial expression, as well as in her emotional communication, she closes up most of the time, to open up rarely and spasmodically. As we offer her a toy situation so that she may reveal and commit herself in its 'unreality', she performs two acts: she closes, in vigorous defiance, the bathroom door of the toy house, and she gives in manic glee three shiny cars to the father doll. More and more deeply involved in the opposition of the simple modalities of taking and giving, she gives to the mother what she took from me and then wants desperately to return to me what she has given to her mother. Back again, her tense little hands hold pencils and toy tight, yet drop them abruptly, as equally suddenly the sphincters proper release their contents.

Obviously then this little girl, unable to master the problem of how to give without taking (maybe how to love her father without robbing her mother), falls back on an automatic alternation of retentive and eliminative acts. This alternation of holding on and letting go, of withholding and giving, of opening up and closing up, we shall call the *mode* aspect of the matter. The anal–urethral sphincters, then, are the anatomic models for the *retentive* and *eliminative* modes, which, in turn, can characterize a great variety of behaviours, all of which, according to a now widespread clinical habit (and I mean bad habit) would be referred to as 'anal'.

A similar relationship between a zone and a mode can be seen in this child's moments of most pronounced babyishness. She becomes all mouth and thumb, as if a milk of consolation were flowing through this contact of her very own body parts. She is now 'oral'. But upon uncoiling from this withdrawal into herself, the young lady can become quite animated indeed, kicking the doll and grasping the cars with a flushed face and a throaty laugh. From the retentive-eliminative position then, an avenue of regression seems to lead further inward (isolation) and backward (regression), while a progressive and aggressive avenue leads outward and forward, towards an initiative which, however, immediately causes guilt. This, then, circumscribes the kind of aggravated crisis in which a child and a family may need help.

The pathways of such regression and progression are the subject-matter of this chapter. In order to demonstrate further the systematic relationship between zones and modes, I shall describe a second episode, concerning a little boy.

I had been told that Peter was retaining his bowel movements, first for a few days at a time, but more recently up to a week. I was urged to hurry when, in addition to a week's supply of faecal matter, Peter had incorporated and retained a large enema in his small, four-year-old body. He looked miserable, and when he thought nobody watched him he leaned his bloated abdomen against a wall for support.

His paediatrician had come to the conclusion that this feat could not have been accomplished without energetic support from the emotional side, although he suspected what was later revealed by X-ray, namely that the boy indeed had by then an enlarged colon. While a tendency towards colonic expansion may initially have contributed to the creation of the symptom, the child was now undoubtedly paralysed by a conflict which he was unable to verbalize. The local physiological condition was to be taken care of later by diet and exercise. First it seemed necessary to understand the conflict and to establish communication with the boy as quickly as possible so that his cooperation might be obtained.

It has been my custom before deciding to take on a family problem to have a meal with the family in their home. I was introduced to my prospective little patient as an acquaintance of the parents who wanted to come and meet the whole family. The little boy was one of those children who make me question the wisdom of any effort at disguise. 'Aren't dreams wonderful?' he said to me in a decidedly artificial tone as we sat down to lunch. While his older brothers ate heartily and quickly and then took to the woods behind the house, he improvised almost feverishly a series of playful statements which, as will be clear presently, revealed his dominant and disturbing fantasy. It is characteristic of the ambivalent aspect of sphincter problems that the patients surrender almost obsessively the very secret which is so strenuously retained in their bowels. I shall list here some of Peter's dreamy statements and my silent reflections upon them.

'I wish I had a little elephant right here in my house. But then it would grow and grow and burst the house.' The boy is eating at the moment. His intestinal bulk is growing to the bursting point.

'Look at that bee – it wants to get at the sugar in my stomach.' 'Sugar' sounds euphemistic, but it does transmit the thought that he has something valuable in his stomach and that somebody wants to get at it.

'I had a bad dream. Some monkeys climbed up and down the house and tried to get in to me.' The bees wanted to get at the sugar in his stomach; now the monkeys want to get at him in his house. Increasing food in his stomach – growing baby elephant in the house – bees after sugar in his stomach – monkeys after him in the house.

After lunch coffee was served in the garden. Peter sat down underneath a garden table, pulled the chairs in towards himself as if barricading himself, and said, 'Now I am in my tent and the bees can't get at me.' Again he is inside an enclosure, endangered by intrusive animals.

He then climbed out and showed me to his room. I admired his books and said, 'Show me the picture you like best in the book you like best.' Without hesitation he produced an illustration showing a gingerbread man floating in water towards the open mouth of a swimming wolf. Excitedly he said, 'The wolf is going to eat the gingerbread man, but it won't hurt the gingerbread man because (loudly) *he's not alive*, and food can't feel it when you eat it!' I thoroughly agreed with him, reflecting in the meantime that the boy's playful sayings converged on the idea that whatever he had accumulated in his stomach was alive and in danger of either 'bursting' him or of being hurt. I asked him to show me the picture he liked next best in any of the other books. He immediately went after a book called *The Little Engine That Could* and looked for a page which showed a smoke-puffing train going into a tunnel, while on the next page it comes out of it – its funnel *not smoking*. 'You see,' he said, 'the train went into the tunnel and in the dark tunnel it *went dead*!' Something alive went into a dark passage and came out dead. I no longer doubted that this little boy had a fantasy that he was filled with something precious and alive; that if he kept it, it would burst him and that if he released it, it might come out hurt or dead. In other words, he was pregnant.

The patient needed immediate help, by interpretation. I want to make it clear that I do not approve of imposing sexual enlightenment on unsuspecting children before a reliable relationship has been established. Here, however, I felt 'surgical' action was called for. I came back to his love for little elephants and suggested that we draw elephants. After we had reached a certain proficiency in drawing all the outer appointments and appendages of an elephant lady and of a couple of elephant babies, I asked whether he knew where the elephant babies came from. Tensely he said he did not, although I had the impression that

47

he merely wanted to lead me on. So I drew as well as I could a cross section of the elephant lady and of her inner compartments, making it quite clear that there were two exits, one for the bowels and one for the babies. 'This,' I said, 'some children do not know. They think that the bowel movements and the babies come out of the same opening in animals and in women.' Before I could expand on the dangers which one could infer from such misunderstood conditions, he very excitedly told me that when his mother had carried him she had had to wear a belt which kept him from falling out of her when she sat on the toilet; and that he had proved too big for her opening so she had to have a cut made in her stomach to let him out. I had not known that he had been born by Caesarean section, but I drew him a diagram of a woman, setting him straight on what he remembered of his mother's explanations. I added that it seemed to me that he thought he, too, could have babies; that while this was impossible in reality it was important to understand the reason for his fantasy; that, as he might have heard, I made it my business to understand children's thoughts; and that, if he wished, I would come back the next day to continue our conversation. He did wish; and he had a superhuman bowel movement after I left.

There was no doubt, then, that once having bloated his abdomen with retained faecal matter this boy thought he might be pregnant and was afraid to let go lest he hurt himself or 'the baby'. But what had made him retain in the first place? What had caused in him an emotional conflict at this time which found its expression in bowel retention and a pregnancy fantasy?

The boy's father gave me a key to one immediate 'cause' of the deadlock. 'You know,' he said, 'that boy begins to look just like Myrtle.' 'Who is Myrtle?' 'She was his nurse for two years; she left three months ago.' 'Shortly before his symptoms became so much worse?' 'Yes.'

Peter, then, has lost an important person in his life: his nurse. A soft-spoken Oriental girl with a gentle touch, she had been his main comfort for years because his parents were out often, both pursuing professional careers. In recent months he had taken to attacking the nurse in a roughhousing way, and the girl had seemed to accept and quietly enjoy his decidedly 'male' approach. In the nurse's homeland such behaviour is not only not unusual, it is the rule. But there it makes sense, as part of the whole culture. Peter's mother, so she admitted, could not quite suppress a feeling that there was something essentially wrong about the boy's sudden maleness and about the way it was permitted to manifest itself; and, indeed, it did not quite fit *her* culture. She became alerted to the problem of having her boy brought up by a foreigner, and she decided to take over herself.

Thus it was during a period of budding, provoked, and disapproved masculinity that the nurse left. Whether she left or was sent away hardly mattered to the child. What mattered was that he lived in a social class which provides paid mother substitutes from a different race or class. Seen from the children's point of view this poses a number of problems. If you like your ersatz mother, your mother will leave you more often and with a better conscience. If you mildly dislike her, your mother will leave you with mild regret. If you dislike her very much and can provoke convincing incidents, your mother will send her away – only to hire somebody like her or worse. And if you happen to like her very much in your own way or in her own way, your mother will surely send her away sooner or later.

In Peter's case, insult was added to injury by a letter from the nurse, who had heard of his condition and who was now trying her best to explain to him why she had left. She had originally told him that she was leaving in order to marry and was going to have a baby of her own. This had been bad enough in view of the boy's feelings for her. Now she informed him that she had taken another job instead. 'You see,' she explained, 'I always move on to another family when the child in my care becomes too big. I like best to tend babies.' It was then that something happened to the boy. He had tried to be a big boy. His father had been of little help because he was frequently absent, preoccupied with a business which was too complicated to explain to his son. His mother had indicated that male behaviour in the form provoked or condoned by the nurse was unacceptable behaviour. The nurse liked babies better.

So he 'regressed'. He became babyish and dependent, and in desperation, lest he lose more, *he held on*. This he had done before. Long ago, as a baby, he had demonstrated his first stubbornness by holding food in his mouth. Later, put on the toilet and told not to get up until he had finished, he did not finish and he did not get up until his mother gave up. Now he held on to his bowels – and to much more, for he also became tight-lipped, expressionless, and rigid. All of this, of course, was one symptom with a variety of related meanings. The simplest meaning was: I am holding on to what I have got and I am not going to move, either forward or backward. But as we saw from his play, the object of his holding on could be interpreted in a variety of ways. Apparently at first, still believing the nurse to be pregnant, he tried to hold on to her by becoming the nurse and by pretending that he was pregnant too. His general regression, at the same time, demonstrated that he too, was a baby and thus as small as any child the nurse might have turned to. Freud called this the *overdetermination* of the meaning of a symptom. The over-determining items, however, are always systematically related: the boy identifies with *both partners of a lost relationship*; he is the nurse who is now with child and he is the baby whom she likes to tend. Identifications which result from losses are like that. In mourning, we become the lost person *and* we become again the person we were when the relationship was at its prime. This makes for much seemingly contradictory sympto-matology.

Yet, we can see that here *retention* is the mode and the elimina-tive trace the model zone used to dramatize holding back, holding on, and holding in. But once it looked and felt as if he did indeed have the equivalent of a baby in him, he remembered what his mother had said about birth and about the danger of birth to mother and child. He could not let go.

The interpretation of this fear to him resulted in a dramatic improvement which released the immediate discomfort and danger and brought out the boy's inhibited autonomy and boyish initiative. But only a combination of dietetic and gymnastic work as well as interviews with mother and child could finally overcome a number of milder setbacks.

LIBIDO AND AGGRESSION

We are now acquainted with two pathological episodes, one in the life of a girl and one in that of a boy. These incidents were chosen because of their clear and observable structures. But what kinds of laws can account for such happenings?

Freud and the early psychoanalysts first pointed to the psychologically uncharted regions of the body's orifices as zones of vital importance for emotional health and illness. To be sure, their theories were based on the observation of adult patients, and it may be worth while to indicate briefly in what way an adult patient observed in psychoanalysis may offer an analogy to what we have seen in our child patients.

An adult's neurotic 'anality' may, for example, express itself in a ritualistic overconcern with his bowel functions, under the guise of meticulous hygiene, or a general need for absolute order, cleanliness, and punctuality. In other words, he would seem to be anti-anal rather than anal; he would be averse to either prolonged retention or careless elimination. But his very anti-anal avoidances would make him at the end spend more thought and energy on anal matters than, say, an ordinary person with a mild tendency towards the enjoyment or repudiation of bowel satisfactions. Such a patient's conflict over the modes of retention and elimination might express itself in a general over-restraint, now firmly entrenched in his character. He would not be able to let go: he would allot his time, his money, and his affection (in whatever order) only under carefully ritualized conditions and at appointed times. Psychoanalysis, however, would reveal that, more or less consciously, he entertains peculiarly messy fantasies and violently hostile wishes of total elimination against selected individuals, especially those close to him who by necessity are forced to make demands on his inner treasures. In other words he would reveal himself as highly ambivalent in his loves, and often as quite unaware of the fact that the many arbitrary rights and wrongs which guard his personal restraints constitute at the same time autocratic attempts at controlling others. While his deeds of passive and retentive hostility often remain unrecognizable to him and to his intended victims, he would be constantly compelled to undo, to make amends, to atone for something done in fact or fantasy. But like our little girl after she had tried to balance her withholdings and givings, he would only find himself in ever deeper conflicts. And like her, the adult compulsive would, deep down, have a stubborn wish for punishment because to his conscience – and he has a peculiarly severe conscience – it seems easier to be punished than to harbour secret hate and go free. It seems easier because his egocentric hate has made him mistrust the redeeming features of mutuality. Thus, what in the child is still free for manifold expression and amelioration in the adult has become fixed character.

In the reconstructed early history of such cases Freud regularly found crises of the kind demonstrated *in statu nascendi* by our child patients. We owe to him the first consistent theory which took systematic account of the tragedies and comedies which centre in the apertures of the body. He created this theory by cutting through the hypocrisy and artificial forgetfulness of his time which kept all of man's 'lower' functions in the realms of shame, of questionable wit, and of morbid imagination. He was forced to conclude that the nature of these tragedies and comedies was sexual, and as such he determined to describe them. For he found that neurotics and perverts are not only infantile in their attitudes towards their fellow men, but also regularly impaired in their genital sexuality and given to overt or covert gratifications and comforts from other than genital body zones. Moreover, their sexual impairment and their social infantility are all systematically related to their early childhood and particularly to clashes between the impulses of their infantile bodies and the inexorable training methods of their parents. He concluded that during successive stages of childhood zones providing special gratification were endowed with *libido*, a pleasure-seeking energy which before Freud had received official and scientific recognition as *sexual* only when it became *genital* at the conclusion of childhood. Mature genital sexuality, he concluded, is the end product of an infantile sexual development, which he consequently called *pre-genitality*. Thus, the kind of compulsive neurotic whom we have just described was to Freud an individual who although overtly anti-anal, was unconsciously *fixated* on or partially *regressed* to a stage of infantile sexuality called the *anal-sadistic* stage.[1]

Similarly, other emotional afflictions prove to be fixations or regressions to other infantile zones and stages.

Addicts, for example, depend, as the baby once did, on the incorporation by mouth or skin of substances which make them feel both physically satiated and emotionally restored. But they

[1] Sigmund Freud, 'Three Contributions to the Theory of Sex', in *The Basic Writings of Sigmund Freud*, The Modern Library, New York, 1938.

are not aware that they yearn to be babies again. Only as they whine and boast and challenge are their disappointed and babyish souls revealed.

Manic-depressive patients, on the other hand, feel hopelessly empty, without substance; or full of something bad and hostile that needs to be destroyed; or again, so permeated with sudden goodness that their sense of power and exuberance knows no bounds and accepts no limitations. Yet they do not know either the source or the nature of all these inner goodnesses and bad-nesses.

Hysterics, if they are women, act as if strangely victimized, attacked and revolted by things and yet fascinated by them: while genitally frigid, they are preoccupied with events which, on analysis, dramatize the woman's inceptive role. They are uncon-sciously obsessed with their sexual role, although (or because) it became unacceptable far back in childhood.

All these tormented people, then, whether addicted, depressed, or inhibited, have somehow failed to integrate one or another of the infantile stages, and they defend themselves against these infantile patterns – stubbornly, wastefully, unsuccessfully.

On the other hand, for each omission by repression there is a corresponding commission by perversion. There are those adults who, far from disguising the original infantile pattern, receive the most complete sexual gratification they are capable of from stimulation received or given by the mouth. There are those who prefer the anus to other orifices which lend themselves to inter-course. And there are perverts who above all want to gaze at genitals or display their own; and those who want to use them, impulsively and promiscuously, for the mere sadistic 'making' of other human beings.

Having at last understood the systematic relationship between sexual acts unconsciously desired by neurotics and acts overtly committed by perverts, Freud proceeded to erect the edifice of his libido theory. *Libido*, then, is that sexual energy with which zones other than the genital are endowed in childhood and which enhances with specific pleasures such vital functions as the intake of food, the regulation of the bowels, and the motion of the limbs. Only after a certain schedule of such pregenital uses of libido is successfully resolved does the child's sexuality graduate to a short-lived infantile genitality, which must immediately become

53

more or less 'latent', transformed, and deflected. For the genital machinery is still immature; and the first objects of immature sexual desire are forever barred by universal incest taboos.

As to the remnants of pregenital desires, all cultures permit to a degree some kinds of non-genital sexual play which should be called perversion only if they tend to replace and crowd out the dominance of genuine genitality. A significant amount of the pregenital libido, however, is *sublimated* – i.e., is diverted from sexual to non-sexual aims. Thus a measure of infantile curiosity concerning the 'doings' in the mother's body may reinforce man's eagerness to understand the workings of machines and of test tubes; or he may eagerly absorb the 'milk of wisdom' where he once desired more tangible fluids from more sensuous containers; or he may collect all kinds of things in all kinds of boxes instead of overloading his colon. In pregenital trends which are *repressed*, instead of outgrown, sublimated, or admitted to sex play, Freud saw the most important source of neurotic tension.

Most successful sublimations are, of course, part and parcel of cultural trends and become unrecognizable as sexual derivatives. Only where the preoccupation appears to be too strenuous, too bizarre, too monomanic, can its 'sexual' origin be recognized in adults; but at that point the sublimation is on the verge of breaking up – and it was probably faulty at the beginning. It is here that Freud, the physician, became a critic of his Victorian age. Society, so he concluded, is too blindly autocratic in demanding impossible feats of sublimation from her children. True, some sexual energy can and must be sublimated; society depends on it. Therefore, by all means, render unto society that which is society's; but first render unto the child that libidinal vitality which makes worth-while sublimations possible.

Only those who specialize in the extreme intricacies of mental disturbances and of ordinary mental quirks can fully appreciate what clear and unifying light was thrown into these dark recesses by the theory of a libido, of a mobile sexual energy which contributes to the 'highest' as well as to the 'lowest' forms of human endeavour – and often to both at the same time.

However, far-reaching theoretical and terminological problems remain to be solved. In determining to focus on truly relevant matters in psychology Freud found that the re-discovery

54

of sexuality was the most important job to be done. Here a historical hiatus had to be bridged with a terminology which strangely mingled ancient wisdom and modern thinking. Take the term 'hysteria'. The Greeks had assumed (or at any rate had expressed their assumptions in a form which seemed to say) that hysteria in women was caused by a tearing loose of the uterus from its mooring: it wandered about the body, pinching here and blocking there. To Freud, of course, it was a genital idea, not a genital organ, which had become dissociated from its goal, causing blocking in the libidinal supply to the genitals (frigidity). The libidinal supply could be converted and displaced along the pathway of some symbolic association with infantile zones and modes. A retching throat, then, may express defensive ejection above, warding off repressed genital hunger below. To express the fact that libidinization withdrawn from the genitals thus manifests itself elsewhere, Freud used the thermodynamic language of his day, the language of the preservation and transformation of energy. The result was that much that was meant to be a working hypothesis appeared to be making concrete claims which neither observation nor experiment could even attempt to substantiate.

Great innovators always speak in the analogies and parables of their day. Freud, too, had to have the courage to accept and to work with what he himself called his 'mythology'. True insight survives its first formulation.

It seems to me that Freud has done with the libido something analogous to George Stewart's handling of a storm. In his book *Storm* Stewart makes a major cataclysm of nature the central character of his story.[2] He delineates the life cycle and the individuality of a natural event. It is as if the world and its people existed for the glory of that storm – which proves to be a powerful way of enriching our perspective on the oversize happenings around and within. Early psychoanalysis similarly describes human motivation as if libido were the prime substance, individual egos being mere defensive buffers and vulnerable layers between this substance and a vague surrounding 'outer world' of arbitrary and hostile social conventions.

But the doctor here goes beyond the author. The doctor learns

[2] George R. Stewart, *Storm*, Random House, New York, 1941.

to investigate and to master clinically the storms which he has first identified and circumscribed. By delineating the life of the libido, Freud expanded our theoretical acumen as well as our therapeutic effectiveness over all those impairments of individual and group life which stem from the meaningless mismanagement of sensuality. It was clear to him, and it becomes clearer to us – who deal with new areas of the mind (ego), with different kinds of patients (children, psychotics), with new applications of psychoanalysis (society) – that we must search for the proper place of the libido theory in the totality of human life. While we must continue to study the life cycles of individuals by delineating the possible vicissitudes of their libido, we must become sensitive to the danger of forcing living persons into the role of marionettes of a mythical Eros – to the gain of neither therapy nor theory.

Freud the investigator, in turn, went beyond Freud the doctor. He did more than explain and cure pathology. Being by training a developmental physiologist, Freud showed that sexuality develops in stages, a growth which he firmly linked with all epigenetic development.

For when Freud first studied the matter of sex he found that sexology, popular as well as scientific, seemed to assume sex to be a new entity which at puberty springs into being as the result of newly initiated physiological changes. Sexology then stood where embryology stood in medieval times, when the concept of the homunculus, a minute, but complete, preformed man waiting in the man's semen to be delivered into a woman's uterus, there to expand and from there to jump into life, was generally accepted. Embryology now understands *epigenetic* development, the step-by-step growth of the foetal organs. I think that the Freudian laws of psychosexual growth in infancy can best be understood through an analogy with physiological development *in utero*.

In this sequence of development each organ has its time of origin. This time factor is as important as the place of origin. If the eye, for example, does not arise at the appointed time, 'it will never be able to express itself fully, since the moment for the rapid outgrowth of some other part will have arrived, and this will tend to dominate the less active region and suppress the belated tendency for eye expression'.[3]

[3] C. H. Stockard, *The Physical Basis of Personality*, W. W. Norton & Co. Inc., New York, 1931.

After the organ has begun to arise at the right time, still another time factor determines the most critical stage of its development:

A given organ must be interrupted during the early stage of its development in order to be completely suppressed or grossly modified . . . After an organ has arisen successfully from the 'Anlage', it may be lamed or runted, but its nature and actual existence can no longer be destroyed by interrupting the growth.[4]

The organ which misses its time of ascendancy is not only doomed as an entity; it endangers at the same time the whole hierarchy of organs.

Not only does the arrest of a rapidly budding part, therefore, tend to suppress its development temporarily, but the premature loss of supremacy to some other organ renders it impossible for the suppressed part to come again into dominance so that it is permanently modified . . .[5]

The result of normal development is proper relationship of size and function among the body organs: the liver adjusted in size to the stomach and intestine, the heart and lungs properly balanced, and the capacity of the vascular system accurately proportioned to the body as a whole. Through developmental arrest one or more organs may become disproportionally small: this upsets functional harmony and produces a defective person.

If 'proper rate' and 'normal sequence' are disturbed, the outcome may be a 'monstrum in excessu' or a 'monstrum in defectu':

The fact that the normal individual stands between these two arbitrary classes of abnormalities has no significance other than that the abnormal deviations are simple modifications of the normal condition resulting from unusual reductions in the rate of development during certain critical stages.[6]

The most critical time in terms of possible organic monstrosities are the months before birth. Once born, the body has 'successfully arisen from its "Anlage"', or can soon be diagnosed as being too defective for integrated maturation. Still a

[4] ibid.   [5] ibid.   [6] ibid.

'precerebrate' bundle fit only for a slow increase of limited kinds and intensities of stimulation, the infant has now left the chemical exchange of the womb for maternal care within the training system of his society. How the maturing organism continues to unfold by developing not new organs, but a prescribed sequence of locomotor, sensory, and social capacities is described in the literature of child development. Psychoanalysis has added to this an understanding of the more idiosyncratic experiences and conflicts by which an individual becomes a distinct person. Whether they are the child's official habits for which tests have been found because they are obvious steps to certain skills, or his unofficial ways which become the open delight or secret concern of mothers, it is first of all important to realize that in the sequence of significant experiences the healthy child, if halfway properly guided, merely obeys and on the whole can be trusted to obey inner laws of development, namely those laws which in his prenatal period had formed one organ after another and which now create a succession of potentialities for significant interaction with those around him. While such interaction varies widely from culture to culture, in ways to be indicated presently, proper rate and proper sequence remain critical factors guiding and limiting all variability.

From the point of view of the individual child's 'libido economy', then, we would say that in our two patients the rate and the sequence of budding impulses had been disturbed: they were stuck on the theme of anal retention and elimination like a phonograph record with a faulty groove. They repeatedly regressed to babyish themes and repeatedly failed in their attempts to advance to the next theme, the management of their love for significant people of the opposite sex. Ann's love for her father was suggested by the great release of manic joy when she gave three shiny cars to the toy father; while in Peter's case his phallic behaviour towards the nurse had immediately preceded the pathogenic events. The libido theory would suggest that the rectal expulsion in the one case and the colonic accumulation in the other had at one time given these children sexual pleasure which they were now trying to regain – only that their by now faulty brake system made them regress further and faster than anticipated. Yet, no longer being innocent infants enjoying as yet untrained bowels, these children apparently indulged in fantasies of expelling hated persons (remember how Ann kicked the mother doll) and retaining loved ones; while the effect of what they did, in all its terrifying consequences, constituted a sadistic triumph over the parent who wished to control them. There is no doubt that there was triumph as well as fear in the eyes of that little girl when she sat in her mess in the early morning and watched her mother come in; and there was a quiet satisfaction in the boy's remote face even when he was manifestly bloated and uncomfortable. But the poor mothers knew from short and intensely painful experiment that to react to the child's tyranny with angry methods would only make things worse. For say what you wish, these children loved and wanted to be loved and they very much preferred the joy of accomplishment to the triumph of hateful failure. Do not mistake a child for his symptom.

Here some would say that children when undergoing such experiences are at the mercy of that second primeval power the assumption of which followed the concept of the libido in the psychoanalytic system – namely, an instinct of destruction, of death. I shall not be able to discuss this problem here, because it is essentially a philosophical one, based on Freud's original commitment to a mythology of primeval instincts. His nomenclature and the discussion which ensued have blurred the clinical study of a force which will be seen to pervade much of our material without finding essential clarification; I refer to the *rage* which is aroused whenever action vital to the individual's sense of mastery is prevented or inhibited. What becomes of such rage when it, in turn, must be suppressed, and what its contributions are to man's irrational enmity and eagerness to destroy, is obviously one of the most fateful questions facing psychology.

In order to determine more concretely what kinds of forces are operative in a given clinical situation, it may be more profitable to ask what it is that we are called upon to accomplish. Maybe by clarifying our function in the situation we can come to grips with the forces which we are trying to understand. I would say it is our task to re-establish a mutuality of functioning between the child patient and his parents so that instead of a number of fruitless, painful, and destructive attempts at controlling one another, a mutual regulation is established which restores self-control in both child and parent.

The prescription betrays the diagnosis. In growing up together, families are apt to lose a certain mutual regulation as a group. As a consequence each family member has somehow lost the self-control appropriate to his age and status in the family. Instead of controlling himself and of serving the mutual regulation of the group, each member has searched for and found substitute controls, areas of autonomy which exclude the others: the parents in hectic work and social life, the children in the only area of seemingly absolute autonomy that is theirs, their bodies. Auto-erotism is an important weapon in this guerrilla warfare in that it gives the child seeming independence from the lost mutuality with others. Such self-absorbed autonomy, however, dissembles the true condition. For in seemingly enjoying the pleasures of his body zones, the child is using organ modes in hostile fantasies of controlling others by total usurpation, whether with a sadistic or a masochistic emphasis. Only this twist, this being turned against the self or against others, causes the organ to become a vehicle of aggression in the more usual, the more hostile sense. Before this happens, organ modes are naïve – i.e., pre-hostile – patterns of going at things, modes of approach, modes of seeking relationships: this is what ad-gression means before it becomes aggression.

Parents who are faced with the development of a number of children must constantly live up to a challenge. They must develop with them. We distort the situation if we abstract it in such a way that we consider the parent as 'having' such and such a personality when the child is born and then, remaining static, impinging upon a poor little thing. For this weak and changing little being moves the whole family along. Babies control and bring up their families as much as they are controlled by them; in fact, we may say that the family brings up a baby by being brought up by him. Whatever reaction patterns are given biologically and whatever schedule is predetermined developmentally must be considered to be a series of *potentialities for changing patterns of mutual regulation*.

It will seem to some that I am abandoning this point of view as I now proceed to review the whole field of what Freud called pregenital stages and erotogenic zones in childhood and attempt to build a bridge from clinical experience to observations on societies. For I will again speak of biologically given potentialities which develop with the child's organism. I do not think that psychoanalysis can remain a workable system of inquiry without its basic biological formulations, much as they may need periodic reconsideration.

For semantic and conceptual reasons, then, the next section will be the most difficult one – for the reader and for myself. I have indicated where we stand on this side of the shore, the clinical one; now a bridge must be begun, the contemplated end of which on the other shore cannot be visible to the reader as yet.

To make the job easier for myself I shall, as I go along, reconstruct the final version of a chart of pregenitality which I first presented over a decade ago. Perhaps this will make it easier for the reader, too. Charts, to paraphrase Lincoln, are the kind of thing which help the kind of people who are helped by that kind of thing. To give the reader the fullest opportunity to be his own kind, I shall try to write this chapter in such a way that what is understandable at all can be understood with or without the chart. By 'understood' I mean that the reader will be able to check his knowledge and vocabulary against my way of phrasing the problem. It is in the very nature of the problem that its description and evaluation should differ from observer to observer and from period to period. From our own observation, we will attempt to chart an order and a sequence of relevant events.

What kind of events do we wish to chart? How 'normative' (in the statistical sense) are these events, how indicative and predictive are our charts?

Let us consider a little boy's normative behaviour before a mirror as studied by Gesell.[7] The examiner, intent on studying the child's 'perceptual, prehensory, and adaptive behaviour' at age 56 weeks, raises ('with a moderately decisive manoeuvre') a curtain from a full-length mirror before which the child has been placed. It is noted that the naked little boy alternately regards his own image and that of the examiner, as he leans

[7] Arnold Gesell, *An Atlas of Infant Behavior*, Vol. 1, Yale University Press, New Haven, 1934.

forward, slaps the mirror, assumes a kneeling posture, moves to and from the mirror, 'contacts mirror with mouth', withdraws, etc. Arnold Gesell once showed me the original series of photographs and it was clear that on pictures not included in the Atlas the little boy's penis was erect. But this bit of sexual behaviour, while by no means abnormal, has nothing to do with the sequence to be photographed as normative. Such behaviour was not invited to the test; it has, as it were, crashed a good, clean party. It seems out of place for cultural reasons because up to the time when zoologists entered the field of human sexuality we did not experiment with sexuality. It seems out of place for systematic reasons because such sexual behaviour happens, but not on schedule. In a given situation it may happen; it may not: it is not 'normative'. However, if it does happen and this at an inopportune moment – i.e., when somebody in the vicinity (mother, attendant) thinks it should not happen – then it may, or may not, elicit from that somebody a drastic reaction which might consist merely in a rare and bewildering change of voice or a general diffused attitude. This may or may not happen in relation to a person or at a time of the life cycle that would give the event decisive importance for the child's relation to himself, to sex, to the world. If it does, it may take a psychoanalyst many months of reconstruction in which no normative charts will be of help. For this item of behaviour concerns an area of the body richly endowed with nerve endings and elaborately supplied with connotations by the reactions of the environment.

What we must try to chart, then, is the approximate sequence of stages when according to clinical and common knowledge the nervous excitability as well as the coordination of the 'erogenous' organs and the selective reactivity of significant people in the environment are apt to produce decisive encounters.

ZONES, MODES, AND MODALITIES

Mouth and Senses

The first such encounter occurs when the newborn, now deprived of his symbiosis with the mother's body, is put to the breast. His inborn and more or less coordinated ability to take in by mouth meets the breast's and the mother's and the society's more or less coordinated ability and intention to feed him and to welcome him. At this point he lives through and loves with his mouth; and the mother lives through and loves with her breasts. For her this is highly dependent on the love she can be sure of from others, on the self-esteem that accompanies the act of nursing – and on the response of the newborn. To him the oral zone, however, is only the focus of a first and general mode of approach, namely *incorporation*. He is now dependent on the delivery of 'materia' of all kinds directly to the receptive doors of his organism. For a few weeks at least, he can only react if and when material is brought into his field. As he is willing and able to suck on appropriate objects and to swallow whatever appropriate fluids they emit, he is soon also willing and able to 'take in' with his eyes what enters his visual field. (As if nearly ready also to hold on to things, he opens and closes his fist when properly stimulated.) His tactile senses too seem to take in what feels good. But all of these readinesses are most vulnerable. In order to assure that his first experience may not only keep him alive but also help coordinate his sensitive breathing and metabolic and circulatory rhythms, deliveries to his senses must have the proper intensity and occur at the right time; otherwise his openness changes abruptly into diffuse defence. While it is quite clear, then, what *must* happen to keep the baby alive (the minimum supply necessary) and what *must not* happen, lest he die or be severely stunted (the maximum frustration tolerable) there is increasing leeway in regard to what *may* happen; and different cultures make extensive use of their prerogative to decide what they consider workable and insist on calling necessary. Some people think that a baby, lest he scratch his own eyes out, must necessarily be swaddled completely for the better part of the day throughout the greater part of the first year; but also that he should be rocked or fed whenever he whimpers. Others think that he should feel the freedom of his kicking limbs as early as possible, but should 'of course' be forced to wait for his meals until he, literally, gets blue in the face. All of this depends on the culture's general aim and system. As will be pointed out in the next chapter, there seems to be an intrinsic wisdom, or at any rate an unconscious planfulness, in the seemingly arbitrary varieties of cultural conditioning: in fact, homogeneous cultures provide certain balances in later life for the very desires, fears, and rages which they provoked in childhood.

What then, is 'good for the child', what *may* happen to him, depends on what he is supposed to become, and where.

But while the mode of incorporation dominates this stage, it is well to get acquainted with the fact that the functioning of any orificial body zone requires the presence of all modes as auxiliary modes. Thus, there is in the first incorporative stage a clamping down with jaws and gums (second incorporative mode); there is spitting up and out (eliminative mode); and there is a closing up of the lips (retentive mode). In vigorous babies even a general intrusive tendency of the whole head and neck can be noticed, a tendency to fasten itself upon the nipple and, as it were, into the breast (oral–intrusive). Any one of the auxiliary modes may be especially pronounced in some children and hardly noticeable in others; and then again such modes may grow into near dominance by a lack or loss of inner control and a lack or loss of mutual regulation with the sources of food and oral pleasure.

The interplay of one zone with all modes is represented diagrammatically in the first line of the chart (Figure 1).[8] Each big circle represents the whole organism. Within it we differentiate three zones: (a) 'oral–sensory', which includes the facial apertures and the upper nutritional organs; (b) 'anal', the excretory organs; (c) the genitalia. (The emphasis here is on neurological coherence rather than on anatomic vicinity: the urethral tract, for example, is part of the anal and part of the genital zone, depending on the innervations mobilized.)

Each small circle represents an organ mode:

    1 = incorporative 1   4 = eliminative
    2 = incorporative 2   5 = intrusive
    3 = retentive

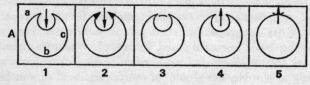

FIGURE 1

In the first oral stage (A), the first incorporative mode dominates the oral zone. However, we prefer to call this stage the *oral–respiratory–sensory stage* because the first incorporative mode at the time dominates the behaviour of all these zones, including the whole skin surface;

[8] References to the charts appear in smaller print so that the reader so inclined may first read the chapter and then study the charts.

the sense organs and the skin too are receptive and increasingly hungry for proper stimulation. This generalization of the *incorporative mode* from its focus in the oral zone to all the sensitive zones of the body surface is represented by the outlining of the large circle in AI.

The other circles (2, 3, 4, 5) represent the auxiliary modes: second oral–incorporative (= biting), oral–retentive, oral–eliminative, and oral–intrusive. These modes become variably important according to individual temperament. But they remain subordinated to the first incorporative mode unless the mutual regulation of the zone with the providing mother is disturbed either by a loss of inner control in the baby or by unfunctional behaviour on the part of the mother.

An example of a lack of inner control would be pyloric spasm which thrusts food out again shortly after intake. In such cases the oral–eliminative mode takes its place beside the supposedly dominant incorporative mode: they are regularly experienced together, a fact which in severe cases and under improper management may determine an individual's basic orientation once and for all. The consequence may be an early overdevelopment of the retentive mode, an oral closing up which becomes a generalized mistrust of whatever comes in because it is apt not to stay.

The loss of mutual regulation with the maternal source of supply is exemplified by a mother's habitual withdrawal of the nipple because she has been nipped or because she fears she will be. In such cases the oral machinery, instead of relaxedly indulging in sucking, may prematurely develop a biting reflex. Our clinical material often suggests that such a situation is the model for one of the most radical disturbances of interpersonal relations. One hopes to get, the source is withdrawn, whereupon one tries reflexively to hold on and to take; but the more one holds on, the more determinedly does the source remove itself. But let us now turn from the clinical to the normative.

As the child's radius of awareness, coordination, and responsiveness expands, he meets the educative patterns of his culture, and thus learns the basic modalities of human existence, each in personally and culturally significant ways. These basic modalities are admirably expressed in 'basic' English, which is so precise when it comes to the definition of interpersonal patterns. To our great relief, therefore, we can at this point take recourse to some of the simplest English words instead of inventing new Latin combinations.

To get (when it does not mean 'to fetch') means to receive and to accept what is given. This is the first social modality learned in life; and it sounds simpler than it is. For the groping and unstable newborn organism learns this modality only as it learns to regulate its organ systems in accordance with the way in which the maternal environment integrates its methods of child care.

It is clear, then, that the optimum total situation implied in the baby's readiness to get what is given is his mutual regulation with a mother who will permit him to develop and coordinate his means of getting as she develops and coordinates her means of giving. There is a high premium of libidinal pleasure on this coordination – a libidinal pleasure which one feels is only insufficiently formulated by the term 'oral'. The mouth and the nipple seem to be the mere centres of a general aura of warmth and mutuality which are enjoyed and responded to with relaxation not only by these focal organs, but by both total organisms. The mutuality of relaxation thus developed is of prime importance for the first experience of friendly otherness. One may say (somewhat mystically, to be sure) that in thus *getting what is given*, and in learning to *get somebody to do* for him what he wishes to have done, the baby also develops the necessary ego groundwork to *get to be* a giver. Where this fails, the situation falls apart into a variety of attempts at controlling by duress or fantasy rather than by reciprocity. The baby will try to get by random activity what he cannot get by central suction; he will exhaust himself or he will find his thumb and damn the world. The mother too may try to force matters by urging the nipple into the baby's mouth, by nervously changing hours and formulas, or by being unable to relax during the initially painful procedure of suckling.

There are, of course, methods of alleviating such a situation, of maintaining reciprocity by giving to the baby what he can get through good artificial nipples and of making up for what is missed orally through the satiation of other than oral receptors: his pleasure in being held, warmed, smiled at, talked to, rocked, etc. We cannot afford to relax our remedial inventiveness. However, it seems (here as elsewhere) that if we expend a fraction of our curative energy on thoughtful prevention, we may abet the cure and make it simpler.

Now to the second stage, during which the ability to make a more active and directed approach, and the pleasure derived from it, grow and ripen. The teeth develop, and with them the pleasure in biting *on* hard things, in biting *through* things, and in biting pieces *off* things. With a little configurational play we can see that the biting mode serves to subsume a variety of other activities (as did the first incorporative mode). The eyes, first part of a relatively passive system of accepting impressions as they come along, have now learned to focus, to isolate, to 'grasp' objects from the vaguer background, and to follow them. The organs of hearing have similarly learned to discern significant sounds, to localize them, and to guide an appropriate change in position (lifting and turning the head, lifting and turning the upper body). The arms have learned to reach out and the hands to grasp more purposefully.

With all of this a number of interpersonal patterns are established which centre in the social modality of *taking* and *holding on to* things – things which are more or less freely offered and given, and things which have more or less of a tendency to slip away. As the baby learned to change positions, to roll over, and very gradually to sit up, he must perfect the mechanisms of grasping, investigating, and appropriating all that is within his reach.

We now add stage B to our chart (Figure 2)[9]

In stage B, mode 2 (incorporation by biting) dominates the oral zone. Thus, progress from stage A to stage B (and later to further stages) is represented as a diagonal progression upward and to the right. Progress here means that the child's libido moves on in order now to endow with power a second organ mode which in turn will lead to the integration of a new social modality: *taking*. A new stage does not mean the initiation of a new zone or mode, but the readiness to experience both more exclusively, to master them more coordinately, and to learn their social meaning with a certain finality.

But what if this progress is impeded, accelerated, or arrested? Then a deviation must be charted either horizontally or vertically. The horizontal deviation (A1 to A2) corresponds to a precocious

[9] In the First Edition the chart was so arranged as to read down as print does. Since then I have accepted the repeated recommendation that a chart of growth should ascend, like family trees and pictorializations of evolutionary descent.

E.H.E.

progression to the mode of the following stage: the baby's 'mouth, instead of sucking relaxedly, clamps down. The vertical deviation (AI to BI) represents a clinging to a mode which has proved satisfactory. The horizontal deviation leads to a *zone* fixation, i.e., the individual holds on to *oral* pleasures of various mode characteristics. The vertical fixation is a *mode* fixation – i.e., the individual is apt to overdevelop mode A in a variety of zones: he always wants to *get* whether by mouth and senses, or by other apertures, receptors, or behaviours. This kind of fixation will later be carried over to other zones.

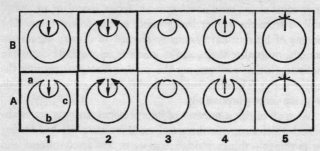

FIGURE 2

At this stage, however, not even the kindest environment can save the baby from a traumatic change – one of the severest because the baby is so young and the difficulties encountered are so diffuse. I refer to the general development of impulses and mechanisms of active prehension, the eruption of the teeth and the proximity of this process to that of weaning and to the increasing separation from the mother, who may go back to work, or be pregnant again, or both.

For it is here that 'good' and 'evil' enter the baby's world, unless his basic trust in himself and others has already been shaken in the first stage by unduly provoked or prolonged paroxysms of rage and exhaustion. It is, of course, impossible to know what the infant feels, as his teeth 'bore from within' – in the very oral cavity which until then was the main seat of pleasure, and a seat mainly of pleasure; and what kind of masochistic dilemma results from the fact that the tension and pain caused by the teeth, these inner saboteurs, can be alleviated only by biting harder. This, in turn, adds a social dilemma to a physical one. For where breast feeding lasts into the biting stage (and, all in all, this has been the rule on earth) it is now necessary to learn how to continue sucking without biting, so that the mother may not withdraw the nipple in pain or anger. Our clinical work indicates that this point in the individual's early history can be the origin of an evil dividedness, where anger against the gnawing teeth, and anger against the withdrawing mother, and anger with one's impotent anger all lead to a forceful experience of sadistic and masochistic confusion leaving the general impression that once upon a time one destroyed one's unity with a maternal matrix. This earliest catastrophe in the individual's relation to himself and to the world is probably the ontogenetic contribution to the biblical saga of Paradise, where the first people on earth forfeited forever the right to pluck without effort what had been put at their disposal; they bit into the forbidden apple, and made God angry. We must understand that the profundity as well as the universality of this subject makes it seem the more important that the early unity should be a deep and satisfactory one and that a baby should be exposed to the unavoidable 'evil' in human nature gently and reassuringly, and without avoidable aggravation.

In regard to the first oral stage, we spoke of a mutual regulation of the baby's pattern of accepting things and the mother's (the culture's) way of giving them. There are stages, however, which are marked by such unavoidable development of rage and anger that mutual regulation by complementary behaviour cannot be the pattern for meeting them. The rages of teething, the tantrums of muscular and anal impotence, the failures of falling, etc. – all are situations in which the intensity of the impulse leads to its own defeat. Parents and cultures use and exploit just these infantile encounters with inner gremlins for the reinforcement of their outer demands. But parents and cultures must also meet these stages by seeing to it that as little as possible of the original mutuality is lost in the process of moving from phase to phase. Weaning, therefore, should not mean sudden loss of the breast and loss of the mother's reassuring presence too, unless, of course, the cultural situation is a homogeneous one and other women can be depended on to sound and feel pretty much like the mother. A drastic loss of accustomed mother-love without proper substitution at this time can lead (under otherwise aggravating conditions) to acute infantile depression or to a mild but chronic stage of mourning which may give a depressive under-tone to the whole remainder of life.[10] But even under the most favourable circumstances, this stage leaves a residue of a primary sense of evil and doom and of a universal nostalgia for a lost paradise.

The oral stages then, form in the infant the springs of the *basic sense of trust* and the *basic sense of mistrust* which remain the autogenic source of both primal hope and of doom throughout life. These will be discussed later as the first nuclear conflict in the developing personality.

Eliminative Organs and Musculature

When discussing self-preservation Freud suggests that at the beginning of life the libido associates itself with the need for keeping alive by sucking drinkables and biting edibles. Not that the mere intake of food would take care of the libidinal need. Levy, in his famous experiments with puppies and chicks, has shown that in these groups of young there is an independent quantity of need for sucking and pecking beyond the mere intake of food. In humans, who live more by training and less by instinct, one suspects greater cultural variability as to the inborn and provoked quantities of a need. What we are discussing here are *potential* patterns which cannot be ignored or reduced below a certain minimum without risking deficiencies and which, on the other hand, must be provoked in specific ways by environ-mental procedures in order to be promoted to full development. Yet it is clear that oral erotism and the development of the social modalities of 'getting' and 'taking' are based on the need to breathe, to drink, to eat, and to grow by absorption.

What would be the self-preservative function of anal erotism? First of all, the whole procedure of evacuating the bowels and the bladder as completely as possible is made pleasurable by a feeling of well-being which says, 'Well done'. This feeling, at the beginning of life, must make up for quite frequent discom-fort and tensions suffered as the bowels learn to do their daily work. Two developments gradually give these anal experiences the necessary volume: the arrival of better-formed stool and the

[10] Rene Spitz has called this 'anaclitic depression'. See his contributions to *The Psychoanalytic Study of the Child*, Vols. I–IV, International Universities Press, New York, 1945–49.

general development of the muscle system which adds the dimension of voluntary release, of dropping and throwing away, to that of grasping appropriation. These two developments together suggest a greater ability to alternate withholding and expelling at will. As far as anality proper is concerned, at this point very much depends on whether the cultural environment wants to make something of it. There are cultures (as we shall see) where the parents ignore anal behaviour and leave it to older children to lead the toddler out to the bushes, so that his wish to comply in this matter gradually coincides with his wish to imitate the bigger ones. Our Western civilization, however, has chosen to take the matter more seriously, the degree of pressure being dependent upon the spread of middle-class *mores* and of the ideal image of a mechanized body. For it is assumed that early and rigorous training not only keeps the home atmosphere nicer but is absolutely necessary for the development of orderliness and punctuality. Whether this is so or not we shall discuss later. There is no doubt, however, that the neurotics of our time include the compulsive type, who has more mechanical orderliness, punctuality, and thrift, and this in matters of affection as well as faeces, than is good for him and, in the long run, for his society. Bowel and bladder training has become the most obviously disturbing item of child training in wide circles of our society.

What then, makes the anal problem potentially so difficult?

The anal zone lends itself more than any other to the display of stubborn adherence to contradictory impulses because, for one thing, it is the modal zone for two conflicting modes of approach, which must become alternating, namely *retention* and *elimination*. Furthermore, the sphincters are only part of the muscle system with its general duality of rigidity and relaxation, of flexion and extension. The development of the muscle system gives the child a much greater power over the environment in the ability to reach out and hold on, to throw and to push away, to appropriate things and to keep them at a distance. This whole stage, then, which the Germans called the stage of stubbornness, becomes a battle for autonomy. For as he gets ready to stand more firmly on his feet the infant delineates his world as 'I' and 'you', 'me' and 'mine'. Every mother knows how astonishingly pliable a child may be at this stage, if and when he has made the decision that he *wants* to do what he is supposed to do. It is hard, however, to find the proper formula for making him want to do just that. Every mother knows how lovingly a child at this stage will snuggle up and how ruthlessly he will suddenly try to push the adult away. At the same time the child is apt both to hoard things and to discard them, to cling to possessions and to throw them out of the window. All of these seemingly contradictory tendencies, then, we include under the formula of the retentive–eliminative modes.

As to new social modalities developed at this time, the emphasis is on the simple antithesis of *letting go* and *holding on*, the ratio and sequence of which is of decisive importance both for the development of the individual personality and for that of collective attitudes.

The matter of mutual regulation now faces its severest test. If outer control by too rigid or too early training insists on robbing the child of his attempt gradually to control his bowels and other ambivalent functions by his free choice and will, he will again be faced with a double rebellion and a double defeat. Powerless in his own body (and often fearing his faeces as if they were hostile monsters inhabiting his insides) and powerless outside, he will again be forced to seek satisfaction and control either by regression or by false progression. In other words, he will return to an earlier, oral control – i.e., by sucking his thumb and becoming whiny and demanding; or he will become hostile and intrusive, using his faeces as ammunition and pretending an autonomy, an ability to do without anybody to lean on, which he has by no means really gained. (In our two 'specimens' we have seen regressions to this position.)

Adding the anal–urethral–muscular stage to our chart, we arrive at the formulation shown in Figure 3.

The diagonal has extended to the establishment of the retentive (3) and eliminative (4) modes in the anal–urethral zone (bottoms of circles) in the new stage C. The outlining of the circle itself again indicates a generalization of these modes over the whole of the developing muscular system, which, before serving more intricate and varied ends, must have gained some form of self-control in the matter of dual expression, such as letting go and holding on. Where such control is disturbed by maldevelopments in the anal–urethral sphere, lasting emphases on retention and/or elimination are established which may lead to a variety of disturbances in the zone itself (spastic rectum or colon), in the muscle system (general flabbiness or rigidity), in obsessional fantasy (paranoid fear of inimical substances within one's body), and in the social spheres (attempts at controlling the environment by compulsive systematization).

At this point it is possible to illustrate the clinical use of the as yet unfinished chart. We indicated that our anal–retentive boy patient, in early infancy, went through a period of retaining food in his mouth and of closing up in general. Such a 'deviant' development, which could, of course, pass without the serious turn which it took temporarily

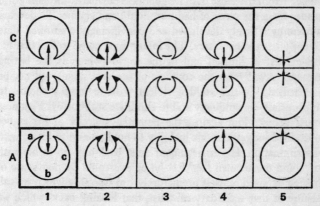

FIGURE 3

in this case, can be entered in the chart by outlining B3. This boy then, while giving up the attempt at holding on to his mother (B2), attempted to control the situation by retention, a mode fixation which pre-destined him for a difficult period in stage C, when he was supposed to learn to 'let go'. The real crisis, however, occurred when he was about to abandon this stage: he regressed and held on for dear life.

Other escape routes at the disposal of children are indicated in the chart. Modes C2 and C1 (anal–urethral–incorporative) are concretely known to paediatricians who have to free children from objects which they have stuck up the anus. In the urethral counterpart to this habit straws and little sticks are introduced into the urethra. Such concrete mode expressions exist, but are rare. More common are fantasies of a kind which may prepare for future perversions. Any anal fixation on one of these modes is especially apt to prepare for a homosexual attitude with the implied idea of gaining love and control forever through anal incorporation. With girls matters are entirely different, owing to the fact that a girl's 'graspiness' does not need to remain fixated in the mouth or perverted in the anus: it can normally shift to the vagina and dominate genital behaviour. We shall come back to this point when discussing genitality.

The other possible 'sideward' escape is an undue emphasis on mode C5 – i.e., the use of faeces as ammunition to be shot at people. This may take the form of aggressive evacuation or deposition of faecal matter. The temptation to do so survives in adults as the tendency to hurl profanities referring to faecal matter – a magic way of attacking your enemy, and easy if you can get away with it.

What enduring qualities are rooted in this muscular and anal stage? From the sense of inner goodness emanates autonomy and pride; from the sense of badness, doubt and shame. To develop autonomy a firmly developed and convincingly continued state of early trust is necessary. The infant must come to feel that his basic trust in himself and in the world (which is the lasting treasure saved from the conflicts of the oral stage) will not be jeopardized by this sudden violent wish to have a choice, to appropriate demandingly and to eliminate stubbornly. Firmness must protect him against the potential anarchy of his as yet untrained judgement, his inability to hold on and to let go with discrimination. His environment must back him up in his wish to 'stand on his own feet' lest he be overcome by that sense of having exposed himself prematurely and foolishly which we call shame or that secondary mistrust, that looking back, which we call doubt.

Autonomy versus *shame* and *doubt*, therefore, is the second nuclear conflict, the resolving of which is one of the ego's basic tasks.

Locomotion and the Genitals

I have mentioned no ages so far. We are now approaching the end of the third year, when walking is getting to be a thing of ease, of vigour. The books tell us that a child 'can walk' much before this; but to us he is not really on his feet as long as he is only able to accomplish this, more or less well, with more or fewer props, for short spans of time. The ego has incorporated walking and running into the sphere of mastery when gravity is felt to be within, when the child can forget that he is *doing* the walking and instead can find out what he can *do with* it. Only then have his legs become an integral part of him instead of being an ambulatory appendage.

To look back: the first way–station was prone relaxation. The trust based on the experience that the basic mechanisms of breathing, digesting, sleeping, etc., have a consistent and familiar relation to the foods and comforts offered gives zest to the developing ability to raise oneself to a sitting and then standing position. The second way–station (accomplished only towards the end of the second year) is that of being able to sit not only securely but, as it were, untiringly, a feat which permits the muscle system gradually to be used for finer discrimination and for more autonomous ways of selecting and discarding, of piling things up – and of throwing them away with a bang.

The third way–station finds the child able to move independently and vigorously. He not only is ready to manifest his sex role, but also begins either to comprehend his role in economy or, at any rate, to understand what roles are worth imitating. More immediately, he can now associate with his age mates and, under the guidance of older children or special women guardians, gradually enter into the infantile politics of nursery school, street corner, and barnyard. His learning now is intrusive; it leads away from him into ever new facts and activities; and he becomes acutely aware of differences between the sexes. This, then, sets the stage for infantile genitality and for the first elaboration of the intrusive and inclusive modes.

Infantile genitality, of course, is destined to remain rudimentary, a mere promise of things to come. If not specifically provoked into precocious manifestation by special frustrations or special customs (such as sex play in groups), it is apt to lead to no more than a series of fascinating experiences which are frightening and pointless enough to be repressed during the stage which Freud called the 'latency' period – i.e., the long delay of physical sexual maturation.

The sexual orientation of the boy at this stage is phallic. While erections undoubtedly occur earlier (either reflexively or in clear sexual response to things and people that make the child feel intensively) there now develops a focused interest in the genitalia of both sexes, together with a vague urge to perform sex acts. Observations of primitive societies show acts of intercourse between children of three or four – acts which, to judge from the attendant laughter, are primarily playful imitation. Such open and playful acts probably help to ease a development that is potentially dangerous: namely, the exclusive direction of early sexual impulses towards the parents, especially where there is a complete taboo on the communication of such desire. For the increased locomotor mastery and the pride of being big now and *almost* as good as Father and Mother receives its severest setback in the clear fact that in the genital sphere one is vastly inferior; and furthermore that not even in the distant future is one ever going to be the father in sexual relationship to the mother or the mother in sexual relationship to the father. The very deep consequences of this insight make up what Freud has called the oedipus complex.

This term, of course, has complicated matters in that it compares what is to be inferred in childhood with what is to be inferred from the story of King Oedipus. The name thus establishes an analogy between two indefinables. The idea is that Oedipus, who inadvertently killed his father and married his mother, became a mythical hero and on the stage is viewed with intense pity and terror because to possess one's mother and to replace one's father is a universal wish, universally tabooed.

Psychoanalysis verifies in daily work the simple conclusion that boys attach their first genital affection to the maternal adults who have otherwise given comfort to their bodies and that they develop their first sexual rivalry against the persons who are the genital owners of those maternal persons. To conclude, as Diderot did, that if the little boy had the power of a man he would rape his mother and murder his father is intuitive and yet meaningless. For if he had such power he would not be a child and would not need to stay with his parents – in which case he might simply prefer other sex objects. As it is, infantile genitality attaches itself to the protectors and ideals of childhood and suffers intense complications therefrom.

The *intrusive mode* dominating much of the behaviour of this stage characterizes a variety of configurationally 'similar' activities and fantasies. These include the intrusion into other bodies by physical attack: the intrusion into other people's ears and minds by aggressive talking; the intrusion into space by vigorous locomotion; the intrusion into the unknown by consuming curiosity. In general it seems clear that to children of this age adult sex acts seem to be dangerous acts of mutual aggression. Even where there is group sex-play, the child seems to interpret the sex acts of his elders as intrusive on the part of the male and incorporative in a spidery way on the part of the female; and this especially where darkness surrounds adult sex life, where sounds accompanying it are interpreted as expressions of pain, where menstrual blood is observed surreptitiously, and where a hostile aftermath is perceived in insufficiently satisfied parents.

Girls have a fateful experience at this stage in that they must comprehend the finality of the fact that although their locomotor, mental, and social intrusiveness is equally increased and as adequate as that of the boys, they lack one item: the penis. While the boy has this visible, erectable, and comprehensible organ to attach dreams of adult bigness to, the girl's clitoris cannot sustain dreams of sexual equality. And she does not yet have breasts as analogously tangible tokens of her future; her maternal instincts are relegated to play fantasy or baby tending. Where the necessities of economic life and the wisdom of its social plan make the female role and its specific powers and rewards comprehensible, all this is, of course, more easily integrated and female solidarity established. Otherwise the girl is apt to develop, together with the basic modes of feminine *inception* and maternal *inclusion*, either a teasing, demanding, grasping attitude, or a clinging and overly dependent childishness.

The chart can now nearly be completed (Figures 4 and 5).

In both Figure 4 (male) and Figure 5 (female) we add line D, the locomotor and infantile genital stage, during which the mode of intrusion (5) is suggested in ambulatory exuberance, in aggressive mentality, and in sexual fantasies and activities. Both sexes partake of the general development of ambulatory and intrusive patterns, although in the girl patterns of demanding and mothering inception (1, 2) develop in a ratio determined by previous experience, temperament, and cultural emphasis.

Figure 5 shows the girl's psychosexual progress at stage D as a partial reversion to incorporative modes, originally developed on oral and sensory lines. This, I think is not an accidental result of our method of charting. For the girl at this stage matches the boy's potentially more vigorous muscular life with the potentiality of richer sensory discrimination and with the perceptive and acceptant traits of future motherhood. She also is apt to become again more dependent and more demanding and, in fact, is permitted to do so, except where the culture chooses to cultivate the auxiliary mode of intrusive and strongly locomotor behaviour (D5). We shall return later to the general exploitability which has been women's fate due to this closeness of her genital modes (inception, inclusion) to those of orality (incorporation).

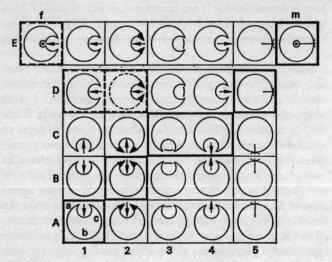

FIGURE 4

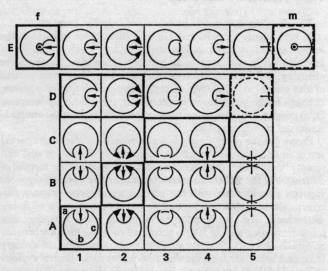

FIGURE 5

The ambulatory and infantile genital stage adds to the inventory of basic social modalities in both sexes that of 'making' in the sense of 'being on the make'. There is no simpler, stronger word to match the social modalities previously enumerated. The word suggests head-on attack, enjoyment of competition, insistence on goal, pleasure of conquest. In the boy, the emphasis remains on 'making' by phallic–intrusive modes: in the girl it sooner or later changes to making by teasing and provoking or by milder forms of 'snaring' – i.e., by making herself attractive and endearing. The child thus develops the prerequisites for *initiative*, i.e., for the selection of goals and perseverance in approaching them.

At once, however, this general readiness for initiative meets its arch-enemy in the necessity of delaying and displacing its sexual core: for this sexual core is both biologically incomplete and culturally opposed by incest taboos. The 'oedipal' wishes (so simply and so trustingly expressed in the boy's assurance that he will marry his mother and make her proud of him and in the girl's that she will marry her father and take much better care of him) lead to vague fantasies bordering on murder and rape. The consequence is a deep sense of guilt – a strange sense, for it forever seems to imply that the individual has committed a crime which, after all, was not only not committed, but would have been biologically quite impossible. This secret guilt, however, also helps to drive the whole weight of initiative and the power of curiosity towards desirable ideals and immediate practical goals, towards the knowledgeable world of facts and to methods of making things, not of 'making' people.

This, however, presupposes that a lasting solution is being found for the third nuclear conflict, to be discussed in the chapter on the ego – namely, the conflict between *initiative* and *guilt*.

This concludes our restatement of the theory of infantile sexuality, which is really a theory of pregenital stages leading to a rudimentary genitality. But we must add both to text and chart a further development, namely, a rudimentary generative mode, representing the dim anticipation of the fact that genitality has a procreative function. In the fourth and final section of this chapter we will present some evidence pointing to what a clinician knows and works by even if he does not always know how to conceptualize it, namely, that boys and girls are differentiated not only by differences in organs, capacities, and roles, but by a

79

unique quality of experience. This is the result of the ego's organization of all that one has, feels, and anticipates. It is never enough, then, to characterize the sexes by the way they differ from each other, although such difference is counterpointed by cultural roles. Rather, each sex is characterized by a uniqueness which includes (but is not summed up by) its difference from the other sex; a uniqueness which is founded on the preformed functions of the future inseminator and the future child-bearer, in whatever system of distribution of labour and cultural style. Here the modes of intrusion and inclusion are polarized in the service of production and procreation.

In line E (Figure 4 and Figure 5) the rudimentary 'genital stage' is anticipated. The additional little circle in both the male and the female interior designates two new modes, female generative (Ef) and male generative (Em), and conveys the fact that female inclusion as well as male intrusion are increasingly oriented towards a dimly divined inner potentiality – namely, the coming together of ovum and sperm in an act of procreation.

But while our method of developing the chart was *additive*, as if at each stage something entirely new was emerging, the whole chart should now be reconsidered as one that represents a *successive differentiation* of parts all of which exist in some form from beginning to end, and always within an organic whole, the maturing organism. In this sense, the modes added last (male and female generative) can be assumed to have been a central, if rudimentary, factor throughout earlier development.[11]

[11] The chart is now completed. To many (including myself) it will at times seem to be a forbiddingly stereotyped way of accounting for phenomena of growth. Such stereotypy is to some extent the result of the origin of the schema in clinical observation. But then, that is where this book originates; and we should not discard too lightly what once proved useful in giving order to observed data. If, for example, the chart depicts *inceptive* and *inclusive* modes as a renewal of *incorporative* ones, it may be well to ponder the social as well as the clinical implications. For it suggests a tendency towards a corresponding recapitulation of the theme of infantile *dependence*, and this both in the sense of a (regressive) need for being dependent and a (progressive) turn towards a generative concern for dependants. In certain cultural schemes this tendency, in turn, may form the basis for a specific exploitability of the female as one who is expected to remain dependent and to be primarily concerned with dependants; while in the male a corresponding fear of regressive dependence may lead to an over-compensation in excessively intrusive pursuits. What becomes of this in unconscious differentiation and mutual identification may have to be understood before a liberation both from exploitability and from the need to exploit is truly possible. That the concept of mode-emphasis is thus applicable to non-clinical data will become clear in the conclusion of this chapter, while its applicability to cultural phenomena is suggested in Part II.

Pregenitality and Genitality

A system must have its Utopia. For psychoanalysis the Utopia is 'genitality'. This was first conceived of as the integration of the pregenital stages to a point of perfection which, later on (after puberty), would ensure three difficult reconciliations: (1) the reconciliation of genital orgasm and extragenital sexual needs; (2) the reconciliation of love and sexuality; (3) the reconciliation of sexual, procreative, and work-productive patterns.

It is a fact that all neurotics, on close study, prove to be handicapped in their sexual cycles: their intimacy is disturbed as they approach potential partners, as they initiate or execute or finish the sexual act, or as they turn away from the respective 'parts' and from the partner. In this the traces of pregenitality are most obvious although rarely conscious. Neurotic people, deep down, would rather incorporate or retain, eliminate or intrude, than enjoy the mutuality of genital patterns. Many others would rather be or make dependent, destroy or be destroyed, than love maturely, and this often without being overtly neurotic in any classifiable, diagnosable, and curable sense. Undoubtedly rich sex-play serves best to take care of pregenital leftovers. But the relationship of sex and play, of play and work, and of work and sex, calls for a later, more comprehensive discussion.

At this point, then, the chart can be used to classify the ways in which pregenital deviation disturbs genitality. In Figure 4 the mode of feminine procreation (Ef) and modes E1 and E2 are not to be taken too literally. The rudiments of a wish to give birth are utilized in identification with and support of the female; or they are absorbed in creativity. As for receptive tendencies, the male organ has no morphological similarity to the mouth, although there are rudiments of a feminine organ around and behind the base of the penis which is erotized in passive–receptive individuals. Otherwise, mouth and anus must take over the sexual remnants of the man's incorporative wishes. Mode E1, if dominant or as dominant as E5, would signify an emphasis on genital receptivity, a wish to get rather than to give. A dominance of E2 would represent the male 'bitch' – for example, the homosexual who seeks intercourse with men in order (more or less consciously) to snare their power. Mode E3 would mean a retentive quality, E4 an eliminative quality in the man's genital behaviour; forms of inhibited and incomplete ejaculation and of premature and 'flowing' ejaculation belong here. E5 has been described as the phallic–aggressive attitude. These deviations, then, can be traced backward along the vertical paths of mode fixation to other zones from which they originated and to which they are apt to regress. In mature male sexuality, of course, all of these modes must be integrated and will accept the dominance of the male procreative mode (Em).

The last line of Figure 5 has a double application: to sex life and to childbearing (and child care). Ef has been formulated as the dominant final position. E1 and E2 have been dealt with as the most common deviation: relative frigidity in conjunction either with receptive passivity or with sexual avarice – at its worst an inability to give genitally and thus to acknowledge the male's performance, which is nevertheless demanded, teased, and provoked. E3 is the inability to relax enough to let the male enter, to make him feel at home, or to let him go. E4, eliminative genitality, is expressed in frequent orgastic spasms which do not add up to one adequate experience. E5 is the unreconstructed phallic position as expressed in exclusively clitoral erotism, and in all forms of intrusive coercion Em, in a woman, is that ability to partake in and to identify with the male's procreative role, which makes woman an understanding companion and a firm guide of sons. Furthermore, creativity in both sexes calls for a certain ratio of Em and Ef.

For both the male and female charts the rule holds that all deviations if subordinated to the dominant mode, are as normal as they are frequent. Where they replace the normal dominant mode, they lead to, imbalances in the total libidinal household which cannot exist for long without decisively distorting the individual's social modalities. This, in turn, cannot happen too frequently without distorting the social life of a group unless the group, for a while, can manage the matter by establishing organized subgroups of deviants.

But does pregenitality exist only for genitality? It seems not. In fact, the very essence of pregenitality seems to be the absorption of libidinal interests in the early encounter of the maturing organism with a particular style of child care and in the transformation of its inborn forms of approach (aggression) into the social modalities of the culture.

To begin once more with what may appear to be a biological beginning: when we say that animals have 'instincts', we mean that at least the lower forms have relatively inborn, relatively early, ready-to-use ways of interacting with a segment of nature as part of which they have survived. These patterns vary widely from species to species, but within one species they are highly inflexible; animals can learn little. Here we think of the story of the swallows from England who were imported to New Zealand by homesick ex-Englishmen. When winter came they all flew south and never returned, for their instincts pointed southward, not warmward. Let us remember that our domesticated animals and our pets, whom we so easily think of as the measure of the animal world, are highly selected and bred creatures who learn to serve our practical and emotional needs as they are taken care of by us. What they learn from us does not improve their chances of surviving in any segment of nature or in any cooperation with their own kind. In this context we do not ask what an individual animal can learn, but what a species can teach its young from generation to generation.

In the higher forms of animals we observe a *division of instinct* (a term here used in analogy to 'division of labour'). Here it is the mutual regulation of instinctive contact-seeking in the young and of instinctive contact-giving in the parent which completes adaptive functioning in the young. It has been observed, for example, that certain mammals can learn to defecate only by having the rectum licked by the mother animal.

We could assume that human childhood and human child training are merely the highest form of such instinctive reciprocity. However, the drives man is born with are not instincts; nor are his mother's complementary drives entirely instinctive in nature. Neither carry in themselves the patterns of completion, of self-preservation, of interaction with any segment of nature; tradition and conscience must organize them.

As an animal, man is nothing. It is meaningless to speak of a human child as if it were an animal in the process of domestication; or of his instincts as set patterns encroached upon or moulded by the autocratic environment. Man's 'inborn instincts' are drive fragments to be assembled, given meaning, and organized during a prolonged childhood by methods of child training and schooling which vary from culture to culture and are determined by tradition. In this lies his chance as an organism, as a member of a society, as an individual. In this also lies his limitation. For while the animal survives where his segment of nature remains predictable enough to fit his inborn patterns of instinctive response or where these responses contain the elements for necessary mutation, man survives only where traditional child training provides him with a conscience which will guide him without crushing him and which is firm and flexible enough to fit the vicissitudes of his historical era. To accomplish this, child training utilizes the vague *instinctual* (sexual and aggressive) forces which energize instinctive patterns and which, in man, just because of his minimal *instinctive* equipment, are highly mobile and extraordinarily plastic.[12]

Here we merely wish to gain an initial understanding of the timetable and the systematic relationship of the organ modes of pregenitality which establish the basic orientation that an organism or its parts can have to another organism and its parts and to the world of things. A being with organs can take things or another being into itself; it can retain them or let them out; or it can enter them. Beings with organs can also perform such modal acts with another being's parts. The human child during its long childhood learns these modes of physical approach and with them the modalities of social life. He learns to exist in space and time as he learns to be an organism in the space–time of his culture. Every part-function thus learned is based on some integration of all the organ modes with one another and with the world image of their culture.

If we take intellectual functioning as an example of a part function, we find that it is either integrated with or will be distorted by organ modes. We perceive an item of information; as we incorporate it, we apprehend that part of it which seems worth appropriating; by digesting it we try to comprehend it in our own way, assimilating it to other items of information; we retain parts of it and eliminate others; and we transmit it to another person in whom the appropriate digestion or insemination repeats itself. And just as the modes of adult genitality may bear the more or less distorting imprint of early organ-mode experiences, so a man's intellectuality may be – for better or worse – characterized by the under- or overdevelopment of one or the other of the basic modes. Some grasp at knowledge as avidly as the cartoonist's goat who was asked by another whether she had eaten a good book lately; others take their knowledge into a corner and chew on it as on a bone; again, others transform themselves into storehouses of information with no hope of ever digesting it all; some prefer to exude and spread information which is neither digested nor digestible; and intellectual rapists

[12] For revisions and clarifications of the psychoanalytic theory of instincts see the work of H. Hartman, E. Kris, and R. Loewenstein (*The Psychoanalytic Study of the Child*, Vols. I–IV, International Universities Press, New York, 1945–49).

insist on making their points by piercing the defences of unrecep-
tive listeners.

But these are caricatures, illustrating merely that not only
genital intercourse but also every other kind of intercourse
develops on a proper (or improper) ratio of the organ modes of
pregenitality, and that every form of intercourse can be characterized by a relative mutuality of modes of approach or by one-
sided forms of aggression. To establish a particular ratio, the
societal process requisitions early sexual energy as well as early
modes of approach. It completes by traditional child-training
the fragmentary drives with which the human child is born. In
other words, where instinct fragments in the young non-human
mammal are assembled (relatively) more completely in a (relatively) shorter time by the instinctive care afforded by the parent
animals, the human child's much more fragmentary patterns
depend on the process of tradition which guides and gives meaning to parental responses. The outcome of this more variable
completion of drive patterns by tradition – glorious as it is in its
cooperative achievements and in its inventive specializations and
refinements – forever ties the individual to the traditions and to
the institutions of his childhood *milieu*, and exposes it to the –
not always logical and just – autocracy of his inner governor, his
conscience.

GENITAL MODES AND SPATIAL MODALITIES

This chapter began with two clinical episodes in which zones
and modes were shown to dominate the play as well as the
symptoms and the behaviour of two small patients. I will conclude
it with observations made on a large number of children who
were not patients, but the subjects of a developmental study
made at the University of California.[13] Neither were they children of play age. Ten, eleven, and twelve years old, they had
already been interviewed and observed regularly for a decade,
and all discernible aspects of the growth and development of
their bodies, their minds, and their personalities had been carefully recorded. When I joined the staff of the study to review

[13] J. W. Macfarlen, 'Studies in Child Guidance. I. Methodology of Data
Collection and Organization'. Society for Research in Child Development
Monographs, Vol. III, No. 6, 1938.

their records, we thought it might be interesting to test on this large sample the clinical proposition which guides such observation as that of Ann's and Peter's play, namely, that play observation can add significant pointers to available data from other sources. Would an appropriate procedure provide me with specimens of play which could serve as live clues to the data accumulated in the files of the study? Here, maybe, what I had learned from case histories could be applied to ongoing life histories.

I set up a play table and a random selection of toys and invited the boys and girls of the study, one at a time, to come in and to imagine that the table was a movie studio, and the toys actors and sets. I then asked them to 'construct on the table an exciting scene out of an imaginary moving picture'. This instruction was given to spare these children, the majority of whom were eleven years old, the indignity of having to play at 'kids' stuff'; at the same time it was thought to be a sufficiently impersonal 'stimulus' for an unselfconscious use of the imagination. But here was the first surprise: although, for over a year and a half, about 150 children constructed about 450 scenes, not more than a half dozen of these were movie scenes, and only a few dolls were named after a particular actor. Instead, after a moment of thoughtfulness, the children arranged their scenes as if guided by an inner design, told me a brief story with more or less exciting content, and left me with the task of finding out what (if anything) these constructions 'meant'. I remembered, however, that years before, when I had tried out an analogous method on a smaller group of Harvard and Radcliffe students, all English majors, who were asked to construct a 'dramatic' scene, not one scene was reminiscent of a Shakespearian or any other drama. It appears, then, that such vague instructions do accomplish what the encouragement to 'associate freely' (i.e., to let thoughts wander and words flow without self-censorship) effects in a psychoanalytic interview, as does, indeed, the suggestion to play in interviews with children: seemingly arbitrary themes tend to appear which on closer study prove to be intimately related to the dynamics of the person's life history. In the present study, what I came to call 'unique elements' often provided the key to such significance. For example, one of the few coloured boys in the study, and the smallest of these, is the only child to build his scene *under* the table. He thus offers stark and chilling evidence of the meaning of his smiling meekness: he 'knows his place'. Or consider the only scene in which the piano chair is pushed under the piano so that it is quite clear that nobody is playing. Since the girl who constructed the scene is the only subject whose mother is a musician, it becomes probable that the dynamic meaning of musical noise in her childhood (if suggested in other data as well) deserves our attention. Finally, to mention one of the main instances where a child reveals in her play an awareness of something she was not supposed to know: a girl, since deceased, who suffered from a malignant blood disease was said to be ignorant of the fact that she was kept alive only by a new medical invention then in its experimental stages. She constructed the only ruin built by a girl and put in the centre of her scene 'a girl who miraculously returned to life after having been sacrificed to the gods'. These examples do not touch on the difficult problem of interpreting unconscious content, but they indicate that the scenes often enough proved to be close to life. However, this is not what is to be discussed at this point. Here, I intend only to consider the manifestations of the power of organ modes in spatial modalities.

In order to convey a measure of my surprise at finding organ modes among what (in contrast to *unique* elements) I came to call the *common* elements in these children's constructions, it is necessary to claim what is probably hard to believe, namely, that I tried not to expect anything in particular, and was, in fact, determined to enjoy the freshness of the experience of working with so many children, and healthy ones. To be ready to be surprised belongs to the discipline of a clinician; for without it clinical 'findings' would soon lose the instructive quality of new (or truly confirming) finds.

As one child after another concentrated with a craftsman's conscientiousness on configurations which had to be 'just right' before he would announce that his task was done, I gradually became aware of the fact that I was learning to expect different configurations from boys than from girls. To give an example which brings us immediately to the mode of female inclusion (DI), girls much more often than boys would arrange a room in the form of a circle of furniture, without walls. Sometimes a circular configuration of furniture was presented as being intruded upon by something threatening, even if funny, such as a pig (see Figure 6) or 'father coming home riding on a lion'. One day, a boy arranged such a 'feminine' scene, with wild animals as intruders, and I felt that uneasiness which I assume often betrays to an experimenter what his innermost expectations are. And, indeed, on departure and already at the door, the boy exclaimed, 'There is something wrong here', came back, and with an air of relief arranged the animals along a tangent to the circle of

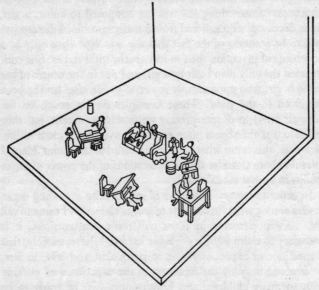

FIGURE 6

furniture. Only one boy built and left such a configuration, and this twice. He was of obese and effeminate build. As thyroid treatment began to take effect, he built, in his third construction (a year and a half after the first) the highest and most slender of all towers – as was to be expected of a boy.

That this boy's tower, now that he himself had at last become slimmer, was the slenderest, was one of those 'unique' elements which suggested that some sense of one's physical self influenced the spatial modalities of these constructions. From here it was only one step to the assumption that the modalities *common* to either sex may express something of the sense of being male or female. It was then that I felt grateful for the kind of investigation which we had embarked on. For building blocks provide a wordless medium quite easily counted, measured, and compared in regard to spatial arrangement. At the same time, they seem so impersonally geometric as to be least compromised by cultural connotations and individual meanings. A block is *almost* nothing but a block. It seemed striking, then (unless one considered it a mere function of the difference in themes), that boys and girls differed in the *number* of blocks used as well as in the *configurations* constructed.[14]

So I set out to define these configurations in the simplest terms, such as towers, buildings, streets, lanes, elaborate enclosures; simple enclosures, interiors with walls, and interiors without walls. I then gave photographs of the play scenes to two objective observers;[15] to see whether they could agree on the presence or the absence of such configurations (and of combinations of them). They did agree 'significantly', whereupon it could be determined how often these configurations were said by these observers (who did not know of my expectations) to have occurred in the constructions of boys and of girls. I will abstract their conclusions here in general terms. The reader may assume that each item mentioned occurs more (and often considerably more) than two thirds of the time in the constructions of the sex specified and that in the remaining one third special conditions prevail which often can be shown to 'prove the rule'.

The most significant sex difference was the tendency of boys to erect structures, buildings, towers, or streets (see Figure 7); the girls tended to use the play table as the interior of a house, with simple, little, or no use of blocks (see Figure 6).

High structures, then, were prevalent in the configurations of the boys. But the opposite of elevation, i.e. *downfall*, was equally typical for them: ruins or fallen-down structures were exclusively found among boys. (I quoted the one exception.) In connection with the very highest towers, something in the nature of a downward trend appears regularly, but in such diverse forms that only 'unique' elements can illustrate it: one boy, after much

[14] M. P. Honzik, 'Sex Differences in the Occurrence of Materials in the Play Constructions of Preadolescents', *Child Development*, XXII, 15–35.
[15] Frances Orr and Alex Sherriffs.

indecision, took his extraordinarily high and well-built tower down in order to build a final configuration of a simple and low structure without any 'exciting' content; another balanced his tower very precariously and pointed out that the immediate danger of collapse was the 'exciting' element in his story: in fact, *was* his story. One boy who built an especially high tower laid a boy doll at the foot of it and explained that this boy had fallen

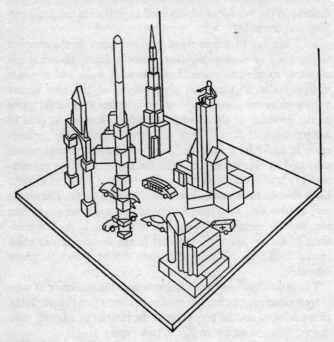

FIGURE 7

from the top of the tower; another boy left the boy doll sitting high on one of several elaborate towers but said that the boy had had a mental breakdown (Figure 7). The very highest tower was built by the very smallest boy; and, as pointed out, a coloured boy built his *under* the table. All these variations make it apparent that *the variable high–low* is a *masculine variable*. Having studied a number of the histories of these children I would add the clinical judgement that extreme height (in its combination with an element of breakdown or fall) reflects a need to overcompensate a doubt in, or a fear for, one's masculinity.

The boys' structures enclosed fewer people and animals inside a house. Rather, they channelled the traffic of motorcars, animals, and Indians. And they blocked traffic: the single policeman was the doll used most often by boys! (Figure 8).

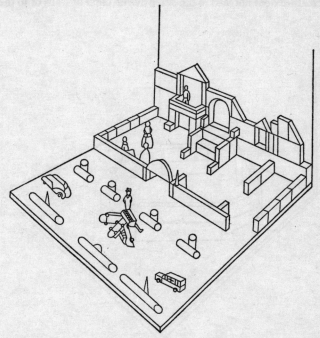

FIGURE 8

Girls rarely built towers. When they did, they made them lean against, or stay close to, the background. The highest tower built by any girl was not on the table at all but on a shelf in a niche behind the table.

If 'high' and 'low' are masculine variables, 'open' and 'closed' are feminine modalities. Interiors of houses without walls were built by a majority of girls. In many cases the interiors were expressly peaceful. Where it was a home rather than a school, a little girl often played the piano: a remarkably tame 'exciting movie scene' for girls of that age. In a number of cases, however, a disturbance occurred. An intruding pig throws the family in an uproar and forces the girl to hide behind the piano; a teacher has jumped on a desk because a tiger has entered the room. While the persons thus frightened are mostly women, the intruding element is always a man, a boy, or an animal. If it is a dog, it is expressly a boy's dog. Strangely enough, however, this idea of an intruding creature does not lead to the defensive erection of walls or to the

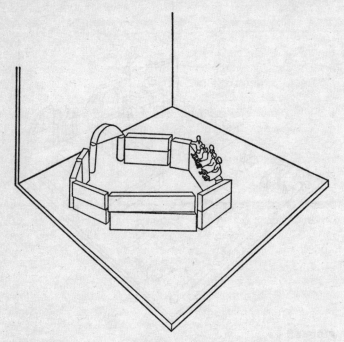

FIGURE 9

closing of doors. Rather, the majority of these intrusions have an element of humour and of pleasurable excitement.

Simple enclosures with low walls and without ornaments were the largest item among the configurations built by girls. However, these enclosures often had an elaborate gate (Figure 9): the only configuration which girls cared to construct and to ornament richly. A blocking of the entrance or a thickening of the walls could on further study be shown to reflect acute anxiety over the feminine role.

The most significant sex differences in the use of the play space, then, added up to the following modalities: in the boys, the outstanding variables were height and downfall and strong motion (Indians, animals, motor cars) and its channelization or arrest (policemen); in girls, static interiors, which are open, simply enclosed, and peaceful or intruded upon. Boys adorned high structures; girls, gates.

It is clear by now that the spatial tendencies governing these constructions are reminiscent of the *genital modes* discussed in this chapter, and that they, in fact, closely parallel the morphology of the sex organs: in the male, *external* organs, *erectable* and *intrusive* in character, *conducting* highly *mobile* sperm cells; *internal* organs in the female, with a vestibular *access* leading to *statically expectant* ova. Does this reflect an acute and temporary emphasis on the modalities of the sexual organs owing to the experience of oncoming sexual maturation? My clinical judgement (and the brief study of the 'dramatic productions' of college students) incline me to think that the dominance of genital modes over the modalities of spatial organization reflects a profound difference in the sense of space in the two sexes, even as sexual differentiation obviously provides the most decisive difference in the ground plan of the human body which, in turn, co-determines biological experience and social roles.

Play construction can also be seen as spatial expression of a variety of social connotations. A boy's tendency to picture outward and upward movement may, then, be only another expression of a general sense of obligation to prove himself strong and aggressive, mobile and independent in the world, and to achieve 'high standing'. The girls' representation of house interiors (which has a clear antecedent in their infantile play with dolls) would then mean that they are concentrating on the anticipated task of taking care of a home and of rearing children.

But this commonsense interpretation poses more questions than it answers. If the boys, in building these scenes, think primarily of their present or anticipated roles, why are not boy dolls the figures most frequently used by them? The policeman is their favourite; yet it is safe to say that few anticipate being policemen or believe that we expect them to be. Why do the boys not arrange any sports fields in their play constructions? With the inventiveness born of strong motivation, this could have been accomplished, as could be seen in the construction of one football field, with grandstand and all. But this was arranged by a girl who at the time was obese and tomboyish and wore 'affectedly short-trimmed hair' – all of which suggests a unique determination in her case.

As mentioned before, World War II approached and broke out during the early stages of the study; to be an aviator became one of the most intense hopes of many boys. Yet the pilot received preferred treatment only over the monk, and over the baby; while the policeman occurs twice as often as the cowboy, who certainly is the more immediate role-ideal of these Western boys and the one most in keeping with the clothes they wear and the attitudes they affect.

If the girls' prime motivation is the love of their present homes and the anticipation of their future ones to the exclusion of all aspirations which they might be sharing with boys, it still would not immediately explain why the girls build fewer and lower walls around their houses. Love for home life might conceivably result in an increase in high walls and closed doors as guarantors of intimacy and security. The majority of the girl dolls in these peaceful family scenes are playing the piano or peacefully sitting with their families in the living-room: could this really be considered representative of what they want to do or think they should pretend they want to do when asked to build an exciting movie scene?

If a piano-playing little girl seems as specific for the representation of a peaceful interior in the girls' constructions as traffic halted by the policeman is for the boys' street scenes, the first can be understood to express *goodness indoors*; the second, *caution outdoors*. Such emphasis on goodness and caution, in response to the explicit instruction to construct an 'exciting movie scene', suggests that in these responses dynamic dimensions and acute conflicts are expressed which are not explained by a theory of mere compliance with cultural and conscious ideals.

We may accept, then, the evidence of organ-modes in these constructions as a reminder of the fact that experience is anchored in the ground plan of the body. Beyond the organ-modes and their anatomical models, we see a suggestion of a male and a female experience of space. Its outlines become clearer if, instead of mere configurations, we note the specific functions emphasized in the various ways of using (or not using) blocks. Some constructions (lanes, tunnels, crossings) serve the *channelization* of traffic. Other structures are an expression of an *erecting*, *constructing*, and *elaborating* tendency. Simple walls, on the other hand, *include* and *enclose*, while open interiors *hold safely* without the necessity of an exclusion of the outside.

Together, then, the space structured and the themes depicted suggest that interpenetration of the biological, cultural, and psychological which is the subject of this book. If psychoanalysis as yet differentiates the psychosexual from the psychosocial, I have endeavoured in this chapter to build a bridge between the two.

Cultures, we will now try to demonstrate, elaborate upon the biologically given and strive for a division of function between the sexes, which is, simultaneously, workable within the body's scheme, meaningful to the particular society, and manageable for the individual ego.[16]

[16] For other accounts of this study see 'Sex Differences in the Play Configurations of Pre-Adolescents', *American Journal of Orthopsychiatry*, XXI, No. 4 (1951); revised in *Childhood in Contemporary Cultures*, Margaret Mead and Martha Wolfenstein, editors, University of Chicago Press, 1955; and in *Discussions of Child Development*, Vol. III; Tavistock Publications, London, 1958, and International Universities Press, New York, 1958. Quite recently I have been able to observe the first stages of an investigation of the play constructions of pre-adolescents in India. First impressions indicate that the general characteristics of the play universe differ markedly and in accordance with differences in the social universe, while sex differences are expressed by the spatial modalities described in this chapter. A final word on this, however, must await further investigations by Kamalini Sarabhai and her co-workers in the B.M. Institute in Ahmdabad.

E.H.E.

Part Two

Childhood in Two American Indian Tribes

Introduction to Part Two

In now turning from children and patients to Indians, we follow a traditional course of modern inquiry which seeks, in fields peripheral to our complicated adult world, some simplified demonstration of the laws man lives by. The study of the stereotypy of mental dysfunction is one such field: crystals, Freud said, disclose their invisible structure when and where they are broken. In the field of childhood we seek to find regularities through the study of the step-by-step development of something out of nothing, or at least of something more differentiated out of something more simple. Finally we turn to cultural primitiveness at the apparent infancy of humanity where people seem, to us, to be at one moment as naïve as children, at another as possessed as lunatics. Comparative research in these three fields has demonstrated many arresting analogies. But the consequent attempt at exploiting a seeming parallelism between the total human conditions of being a savage and those of being a child or a symptom-ridden adult has proved to be misleading. We know now that primitives have their own adult normality, that they have their own brands of neurosis and psychosis and, most important, that they too have their own varieties of childhood.

Up to recent decades child training has been an anthropological no-man's-land. Even anthropologists living for years among aboriginal tribes failed to see that these tribes trained their children in some systematic way. Rather, the experts tacitly assumed with the general public that savages had no child training at all and that primitives grew up 'like little animals' – an idea which in the overtrained members of our culture arouses either angry contempt or romantic elation.

The discovery of primitive child-training systems makes it clear that primitive societies are neither infantile stages of mankind nor arrested deviations from the proud progressive norms

99

which we represent: they are a complete form of mature human living, often of a homogeneity and simple integrity which we at times might well envy. Let us rediscover the characteristics of some of these forms of living by studying specimens taken from American Indian life.

The people collectively called American Indians constitute today a very diverse American minority. As stable societies they are extinct. True, remnants of their timeless cultures can be found: in ancient relics, high up on mesas only a few miles off our busy highways, and in a few immensely dignified but culturally mummified individuals. Even where isolated ancient Indian ways are tolerantly encouraged by government agencies, or exploited by commerce for the sake of the tourist trade, these ways are no longer a part of a self-supporting societal existence.

One may ask, then, why I prefer to use American Indian tribes as an illustration for what I have to say: why not use material collected by another worker in areas which are still truly primitive? My answer is: Because this book deals not only with facts but also with the clinical experience of searching out these facts; and I owe two of my most instructive experiences to anthropologists who suggested that I come with them and see their favourite tribes among the American Indians. It was H. Scudder Mekeel who introduced me to the field by taking me to a Sioux Indian reservation in South Dakota; and it was Alfred Kroeber who subsequently helped me to make the image of the Sioux (all too easily considered 'the' Indian) soundly comparative. He took me to his Yurok, a fishing and acorn-gathering tribe on the Pacific coast.

This exposure to anthropology became rewarding for the following reasons. My guides had put personal notes and other material at my disposal before we left for our trips. The tribes in question having been their first and their lasting loves in field work, the two men could by way of personal communication articulate spontaneously more than had been ready for publication at the time of their original studies.[1] They had their trusted and trusting informants among the oldest members of the tribe,

[1] A. L. Kroeber, 'The Yurok', in *Handbook of the Indians of California*, Bureau of American Ethnology, Bulletin 78, 1925; H. S. Mekeel, *A Modern American Community in the Light of Its Past*, Dissertation for the degree of Doctor of Philosophy, Yale University, 1932.

who alone would remember the folkways of ancient child-training. Above all, both men had had some psychoanalytic training which they were eager to integrate with their anthropological work. If I, in a measure, served as an integrator, it was because as a psychoanalyst of children I was close to formulating what has been outlined in the preceding chapter. Feeling that together we might be able to salvage some neglected facts in the recent history of the American aboriginals, each of these men took me to his favourite and best-trained informants in the field and urged them to talk to me as they would have talked to him, had he known earlier what to ask regarding a number of items significant for childhood and society.

3   Hunters Across the Prairie

At the time of our trip to South Dakota, Scudder Mekeel was field representative of the Commissioner of Indian Affairs. Our investigation had the immediate and most urgent purpose of trying to find out whence came the tragic apathy with which Sioux Indian children quietly accepted and then quietly discarded many of the values taught them in the immensely thoughtful and costly experiment of federal Indian education. What was wrong with these children was obvious enough: there were two rights for them, one white and one Indian. But only by investigating this discrepancy did we find the remnants of what was once right for children on the prairie.

To be true to the clinical nature of our investigations, I must introduce the material on ancient child-training to be presented here with a great deal of circumstantial description. In order to arrive at a clearing where we may see the matter of infancy and society in better light, I must take the reader through the thorny underbrush of contemporary race relations.

The Pine Ridge Indian Reservation lies along the Nebraska state line in the south-west corner of South Dakota. It shares the fate of the rolling high plains:

> The slow hot wind of summer and its withering
> or again the crimp of the driving white blizzard
> and neither of them to be stopped
> neither saying anything else than:
>   'I'm not arguing. I'm telling you.'[1]

Here 8,000 members of the Oglala subtribe of the Sioux, or Dakota, live on land allotted to them by the government. When the Indians settled on this reservation, they turned their political

[1] Carl Sandburg, *The People, Yes*, Harcourt, Brace, New York, 1936.

and economic independence over to the United States government on condition that the government keep all whites from hunting and settling in their territory.

Only the most stubborn of romantics will expect to find on a reservation of today anything resembling the image of the old Dakotas who were once the embodiment of the 'real Indian' – a warring and hunting man, endowed with fortitude, cunning, and cruelty. His image until recently adorned the American nickel, a strange tribute to a strange relationship, for this defeated predecessor thus occupies a place reserved for monarchs and presidents. But this historical reality stems from the far past.

Life was good on the high plains of the Dakotas before the white man came . . . Buffalo moved in dark masses on the grasslands; the Black Hills and Rockies were populous with deer, beaver, bear and other game . . . Starvation was usually far from their tepees.[2]

Organized in a flexible system of 'bands', the Dakota once followed the buffalo over the vast plains in long queues on horses and with travois. Periodically they gathered in well-organized camps of light tepees. Whatever they did together – camping, big buffalo hunting, and dancing – was strictly regulated. But constantly small groups, colourful and noisy, followed the impulse to radiate from the main body, to hunt small game, to steal horses, and to surprise enemies. The cruelty of the Sioux was proverbial among the early settlers. It extended unsparingly to themselves when in solitary self-torture they sought a guiding vision from the Great Spirit.

But this once proud people had been beset by an apocalyptic sequence of catastrophes, as if nature and history had united for a total war on their too manly offspring. It must be remembered that it had been only a few centuries before the whites settled among them that the Sioux had come to the high plains from the upper Missouri and Mississippi and had organized their lives around the hunt of the buffalo. The relative youth of this adjustment may well be the explanation of the fact that, as Wissler put it:

When the buffalo died, the Sioux died, ethnically and spiritually. The buffalo's body had provided not only food and material for

[2] P. I. Wellman, *Death of the Prairie*, Macmillan, New York, 1934.

clothing, covering and shelter, but such utilities as bags and boats, strings for bows and for sewing, cups and spoons. Medicine and ornaments were made of buffalo parts; his droppings, sun-dried, served as fuel in winter. Societies and seasons, ceremonies and dances, mythology and children's play extolled his name and image.'[3]

First, then, the buffalo was vanishing. The whites, eager for trade routes to the greener pastures of the West, upset the hunting-grounds and playfully, stupidly, slaughtered buffalo by the hundred thousands. In search for gold they stampeded into the Black Hills, the Sioux' holy mountains, game reservoir, and winter refuge. The Sioux tried to discuss this violation of their early treaties with United States generals, warrior to warrior, but found that the frontier knew neither federal nor Indian law.

The ensuing wild and sporadic warfare did not come to a definite end until 1890, when the Seventh Cavalry revenged the death – many years earlier – of their highly exhibitionistic comrade, General Custer. In the massacre at Wounded Knee, hundreds of Sioux, outnumbered four to one, were killed by well-armed soldiers, although the majority had already surrendered. 'The bodies of some of the women and children were found two or three miles away where they had been pursued and killed.'[4] In 1937, photographs picturing these bodies were still tacked to the walls of Pine Ridge's only drugstore and soda fountain.

During this historical period of a search for a new economy, the Sioux encountered in successive waves many kinds of new Americans who typified the white man's restless search for space, power, and new ethnic identity. The roaming trappers and fur traders seemed acceptable enough to the nomadic Sioux. They shared the Indian's determination to keep the game intact; they brought knives and guns, beads and kettles; and they married Indian women and became devoted to them. Some American generals too, were entirely acceptable, and in fact were almost defied for the very reason that they had fought well. Even the Negro cavalry fitted into Sioux values. Because of their impressive charges on horseback, they were given the precious name of 'Black Buffaloes'. Neither did the consecrated belief in

[3] C. Wissler, 'Depression and Revolt', *Natural History*, 1938, Vol. 41, No. 2.
[4] Wellman, op. cit.

man demonstrated by the Quakers and early missionaries fail to impress the dignified and religious leaders of the Sioux. But as they looked for fitting images to connect the past with the future, the Sioux found least acceptable the class of white man who was destined to teach them the blessings of civilization – namely, the government employee.

The young and seething American democracy lost the peace with the Indian when it failed to arrive at a clear design of either conquering or colonizing, converting or liberating, and instead left the making of history to an arbitrary succession of representatives who had one or another of these objectives in mind – thus demonstrating an inconsistency which the Indians interpreted as insecurity and bad conscience. Red tape is no substitute for policy; and nowhere is the discrepancy between democratic ideology and practice more obvious than in the hierarchy of a centralized bureaucracy. For this the older Indian who had been reared in the spirit of a hunter democracy, levelling every potential dictator and every potential capitalist, had a good, not to say malicious, eye. It is hard to imagine the exposed and yet responsible role in which the agents of the government found themselves in the early days. Yet some managed well by sheer humanity.

But then followed the guerrilla war over the children which makes the beginning of federal education, as remembered by the older Sioux, anything but appealing. In some places

'. . . children were virtually kidnapped to force them into government schools, their hair was cut and their Indian clothes thrown away. They were forbidden to speak in their own language. Life in the school was under military discipline and rules were enforced by corporal punishment. Those who persisted in clinging to their own ways and those who ran away and were recaptured were thrown into gaol. Parents who objected were also gaoled. Where possible, children were kept in school year after year to avoid the influence of their families.'[5]

This general attitude was not completely abandoned until 1920.

During all this time, only one white type stirred the Indian's imagination to the point of influencing his dress, his bearing, his customs, and his children's play: the cowboy. From 1900 to 1917, the Sioux made a determined attempt to develop and to

[5] G. MacGregor, *Warriors without Weapons*, University of Chicago Press, 1946.

enjoy a cattle economy. But Washington, aware of the higher power both of the erosion of the soil and of Midwestern cattle interests, was forced to decree that the Sioux could not be cowboys on the land allotted to them. The loss of their herds, which had rapidly increased, and the later land boom which made petty capitalist spendthrifts out of the unprepared Sioux, were modern catastrophes which, psychologically, equalled the loss of the buffalo. No wonder, then, that some missionaries convinced the aquiline-nosed Sioux that they were the lost tribe of Israel – and under God's lasting curse.

There followed the most recent period, when the Sioux were supposed to turn into farmers on allotted land which was already eroded and just about to become subject to the great drought. Even today only a fraction of this land is suitable for wheat, corn, and grain crops.

It is understandable, then, that the Sioux have consistently and fruitlessly blamed the United States government for the breaches of promise and for the administrative mistakes of former regimes. As for the whites, instances of error and faithlessness have never been denied even by those who unwittingly or helplessly perpetrated them. There are accounts of American generals reporting to the government and of Indian commissioners reporting to Congress which speak of the deep shame felt by these men as they listened to the dignified reproaches of the old Indians. In fact, the conscience of the American people was at times so readily awakened that sentimentalists and politicians could exploit it for purposes entirely detrimental to a realistic approach to Indian problems.

The government has withdrawn the soldier and has created an imposing and humane organization for the American Indian. The administrator has been superseded by the teacher, the physician, and the social anthropologist. But the years of disappointment and dependence have left the Plains Indians unable to trust where they can hardly afford to distrust. Where once the Indian was a man wronged, he is now comparable to what in psychiatry is called a 'compensation neurotic'; he receives all his sense of security and identity out of the status of one to whom something is owed. Yet it must be suspected that even if the millions of buffaloes and the gold taken from the Black Hills could be returned, the Sioux would not be able to forget the habits of dependence or manage to create a community adapted to the present-day world, which, after all, dictates to the conquerors as well as to the conquered.

No wonder, then, that the visitor on the reservation after a short while feels as if he were a part of a slow-motion picture, as if a historical burden arrested the life around him. True, the town of Pine Ridge looks much like a rural country seat anywhere in a poorer section of the Middle West. The government buildings and schools are clean, roomy, and well appointed. The teachers and employees, Indian and white, are well shaven and friendly. But the longer one stays on the reservation, the wider one roams and the closer one looks, the more it becomes apparent that the Indians themselves own little and maintain it badly. Seemingly calm, usually friendly, but generally slow and apathetic, the Indians show surprising signs of undernourishment and disease. Only at an occasional ritual dance and at the drunken brawls in bootleg cafés off the reservation can some of the immense energy be seen which is smouldering beneath the idle surface. At the time of our visit to Pine Ridge, the Indian problem seemed to be caught somewhere between the majestic turn of the wet and dry cycles, the divine wastefulness of the democratic process and the cheerful ruthlessness of the free-enterprise system: and we know that for those who are caught unprepared in these wheels the mills of proletarization grind fast and fine. Here the Indian problem loses its ancient patina and joins the problems of coloured minorities, rural and urban, which are waiting for busy democratic processes to find time for them.

JIM

One day at the trader's, Mekeel and I had met Jim, a lean and sincere young Sioux, obviously one of the more assimilated high-school graduates and therefore, as we had learned to expect, troubled in mind. Jim had left the reservation years before to marry a girl belonging to another closely related Plains Indian tribe and to live among her people. After a conversation during which it was explained to him what my vocation was, he said that he was not satisfied with the way things were going with the education of his children, and that he wished we had come to his

107

reservation instead of to Pine Ridge so that his wife and he could talk things over with me. We promised to make an early excursion to his town.

When we neared the simple, clean homestead, the little sons were playing the small Indian boy's favourite game, roping a tree stump, while a little girl was lazily sitting on her father's knees, playing with his patient hands. Jim's wife was working in the house. We had brought some additional supplies, knowing that with Indians nothing can be settled in a few hours; our conversation would have to proceed in the slow, thoughtful, shy manner of the hosts. Jim's wife had asked some women relatives to attend our session. From time to time she went to the door to look out over the prairie which rolled away on every side, merging in the distance with the white processions of slow-moving clouds. As we sat and said little, I had time to consider what Jim's place among the living generations of his people might be.

The few long-haired old men among the present inhabitants of these reservations remember the days when their fathers were the masters of the prairie who met the representatives of the United States government as equals. Once the actual fighting had ceased, these Indians had learned to know the older generation of Americans whose God was a not-too-distant relative of the Indian's Great Spirit and whose ideas of an aggressive but dignified and charitable human life were not so very different from the brave and generous characteristics of the Indian's 'good man'.

The second generation of Indians knew hunting and fur trading only from hearsay. They had begun to consider a parasitic life based on government rations their inalienable right by treaty, and thus a 'natural' way of life.

Jim obviously belonged to the third generation, who have had the full benefit of government boarding-school education and who believe that they, with their superior education, are better equipped for dealing with the white man. They cannot point to any basic accomplishment, however, beyond a certain superficial adaptation, for the majority of them have as little concept of the future as they are beginning to have of the past. This youngest generation, then, finds itself between the impressive dignity of its grandparents, who honestly refuse to believe that the white man is here to stay, and the white man himself, who feels that the Indian persists in being a rather impractical relic of a dead past.

After a period of pensive waiting, Jim's wife announced that her women relatives were coming. It was some minutes before we also were able to see the two figures approaching in the distance.

When they finally arrived, there was a round of bashful, yet amused, greetings, and we sat down in a circle under the shade of pine boughs. By chance I was sitting on the highest fruit crate (chairs are scarce on the prairie). Saying jokingly that it was uncomfortable to be elevated like a preacher, I turned the box so that it would be lower. But it was weaker in this position and I had to turn it back again. Jim then silently turned his seat so that he was sitting as high as I was. I remember this as but one incident typical of a quiet tact which Indians are apt to show.

While Jim looked plainly worried, his wife had the expression of one who is preparing for a very serious conversation about which she has already made up her mind.

Mekeel and I had decided that in our conversation we would not aim directly at Jim's domestic difficulties, whatever they might be, but would ask the group for comments on what we had heard at Pine Ridge about the various phases of child life on the Plains. So we talked about the customs concerning childbirth and child rearing, securing fragmentary accounts of what was once done and of present changes. The women showed a humorous frankness throughout, though their bashful smiles indicated that they would not have dared to bring up certain subjects in the presence of men had Mekeel not been able to throw details into the conversation which surprised them and set their memories and critical powers to work. They had obviously never thought that such details could be of any interest to white people or had anything to do with the world reflected in the English language.

Jim did not add much to this conversation, which lasted for several hours. When the middle of the first decade of life was being considered, the contrast between his grim silence and the women's amused acceptance of the various ways in which children anticipate the activities of adulthood became more marked.

Finally it was time for lunch, and the women went into the house to prepare it. It was now Jim's turn, and he went right to his problem. His children used sexual words in their play, and he could not tolerate it. His wife laughed about them and at him, claiming that all children use these words and that it did not make any difference. He was sensitive to the white men's insinuations that Indians were obscene and had undesirable sexual habits. We agreed that white men did secretly accuse Indians of being sexually indulgent, but then all peoples do accuse their neighbours of the perversions which they themselves are most ashamed of; in fact, they like to give foreign names to their own perversions. But Jim did not wish to make this matter relative. He held that in reality the Sioux were 'strong' men who mastered their sexual urges and did not allow their children to use obscene language; and that there was no reason why his children should do what Sioux children were not allowed to do. He thus demonstrated that he had always held with the belief that the Sioux were essentially 'stronger' than his wife's very closely related tribe and that, in fact, he held against his wife's tribe the identical prejudices which the whites held against his tribe, the Sioux. Such reflection of the prejudices of the dominant group in the mutual discrimination of subgroups is, of course, universal. Thus it happens that Sioux with considerable admixture of white blood call their full-blooded fellows 'niggers' and are, in turn, called 'white trash'.

As patients do in therapeutic interviews, Jim then contradicted himself so openly that it amounted to a confession. He related that on his last visit to his childhood home in Pine Ridge, he had been disturbed by the language which his relatives' children were using. Such a state of affairs could not have existed when he was a child, he said. We asked him who would have been the person to suppress it. 'My father,' he answered.

Further questioning revealed that Jim's father had spent most of his childhood in foreign countries. As Jim enlarged on this it became more and more obvious that foreign conditioning had induced his father, after returning to his own people, to hold up standards for his children which were different from those of the other Sioux children. In so doing he had built a wall between his children and those of his tribesmen: the wall which now isolated Jim from his children – and from himself. Unhappy as he had become in consequence of this inner blocking, Jim found himself helplessly creating conflicts in his own family by insisting that his warm-hearted wife interfere, by the use of outright parental prohibition, with habits which the Sioux as well as her own tribe let pass as a matter to be taken care of eventually by shaming or, if necessary, by the grandparents' calm admonishment.

We tried to explain to Jim the power of ambivalence conflicts. He must have secretly rebelled against his father's wish to estrange him from his playmates. He had suppressed open rebellion only at the price of doing to his children now what his father had done to him. But because he had never really made his father's foreign cause his own, his actions only caused anger in his wife, vexation in his children, and paralysing doubt in himself.

He thought about this for a few minutes and then said, 'I guess you have told me something' – high and wordy praise from an Indian. Lunch was prepared. The rebellious wife and her woman auxiliaries waited ceremoniously outside the door until the master of the house and his guests had finished.

Such, then, were the intimate conversations with heavy-hearted Indians in their homes on the high prairie. These conversations were one of the main sources of our material concerning Sioux childhood as it once was. It is obvious that in this field there are no facts free of the most far-reaching connotation. Jim's desperate attempt at regaining a sense of rightness by means inimical to himself and those close to him may give us a first glimpse into a strange mechanism – namely, the compulsive identification of the man whose tribal integrity has been destroyed, with the very destroyer himself. People's feelings have, it seems, always been aware of what we have learned to conceptualize only recently – that small differences in child training are of lasting and sometimes fatal significance in differentiating a people's image of the world, their sense of decency, and their sense of identity.

Our second major source of data was a small seminar in which Mekeel and I were joined by educators and social workers of both white and Indian origin, and in which we discussed the various opinions voiced by the teachers in the Indian Service. Here it was necessary to realize first the fact that the same childhood data which in neurotic conflicts are subject to repression and falsification, in biracial dispute underlie a nearly impenetrable mutual defensiveness. Every group, of whatever nature, seems to demand sacrifices of its children which they later can bear only in the firm belief or in the determined pretence that they were based on unquestionable absolutes of conduct: to question one of these implicit absolutes means to endanger all. Thus it comes about that peaceful neighbours, in the defence of some little item of child training, will rear up on their hind legs like angry bears who have come to believe that their cubs are in mortal danger.

On the surface, the complaints brought to our seminar had a professional and reasonable ring. Truancy was the most outstanding complaint: when in doubt Indian children simply ran home. The second complaint was stealing, or at any rate gross disregard of property rights as we understand them. This was followed by apathy, which included everything from lack of ambition and interest to a kind of bland passive resistance in the face of a question or of a request. Finally, there was too much sexual activity, a term used for a variety of suggestive situations ranging from excursions into the dark after dances to the mere huddling together of homesick girls in boarding-school beds.

The least frequent complaint was impertinence, and yet one felt that the very absence of overt resistance was feared by the teachers as if it were the Indians' secret weapon. The discussion was pervaded by the mystified complaint that no matter what you do to these children they do not talk back. They are stoical and non-committal. They make you feel that maybe they understand, until they suddenly prove to have acted otherwise. You 'cannot get at them'.

The deep and often unconscious fury which this fact had gradually aroused in the most well-meaning and best-disciplined educators really came to expression only in 'personal' opinions which teachers here and there added to their official opinions. One time-bitten old educator's ire was aroused by the quiet reference made by some teachers of Indian origin to the Indians' love of children. He exclaimed that Indians did not know what it meant to love a child. Challenged, he based his opinion on the observation of the simple fact that Indian parents who had not seen their children for as long as three years neither kissed them nor cried when they finally came to call for them. He was unable to accept the suggestion, corroborated by the oldest observers, that such reserve governed, from the earliest times, the meeting between Indian relatives, especially in the presence of non-relatives. For him such book knowledge was contradicted by two decades of personal and indignant observation. Indian parents, he insisted, felt less for their children than animals do for their young.

Granted that cultural disintegration and inability to care for children economically or spiritually may bring with it apathy in personal relations, it was, of course, appalling to be confronted with such a radical misunderstanding which could by no means be considered a relic of a less understanding period. Colonel Wheeler, who knew the Sioux as conqueror, not as educator, did 'not believe that any race of people exists on earth who are more fond of their families than are the American Indians'. Who was right? Had the conquering general turned too sentimental or the worn-out educator too cynical?

A number of the strongest opinions were volunteered only privately. 'Enuresis is really the worst difficulty,' a male teacher, part Indian, said, adding, 'but we Indians could not discuss enuresis in a group including women.' He felt that the lack of proper toilet training was the cause of most of the trouble in Indian education. A white employee volunteered to point to another problem as being 'really the worst'. Quoting confidential remarks of medical authorities in the Indian Service, he said, 'Indian parents not only let their children masturbate, they teach them to masturbate.' He thought this was the cause of all trouble, but was unwilling to discuss the subject in the presence of Indians. As far as facts could be determined, neither enuresis nor masturbation was more frequent in Indian schools than in boarding-schools or foster homes anywhere. Masturbation was, actually, a mere assumption, nobody having remembered seeing any but small children touch themselves. It was interesting, then, to note that the 'real', the most indignant, and the most unofficial complaints concerned areas of early conditioning which have aroused the attention of psychoanalysts in Western culture (and which were discussed in the section on pregenitality).

The whites, activists in educational matters, proved to consider every omission in child training, such as the complete lack of attention paid by Indian parents to anal, urethral, and genital matters in small children, a most flagrant omission with most definite malicious intent. The Indians, on the other hand, being permissive towards smaller children and only verbally cruel towards older ones, considered the white man's active approach to matters of child care a destructive and most deliberate attempt to discourage children. Whites, they thought, want to estrange their children from this world so as to make them pass through to the next world with the utmost dispatch. 'They teach their children to cry!' was the indignant remark of an Indian woman when confronted with the sanitary separation of mother and child in the government hospital, and especially with the edict of government nurses and doctors that it was good for babies to cry until blue in the face. Older Indian women expecting the birth of a grandchild would quietly wail like the Jews before their sacred Wall, becrying the destruction of their nation. But even educated Indians could not suppress the feelings that all the expensive care given their children was essentially a diabolic system of national castration. Beyond that there was on the Indian side the strange assumption that the whites wanted to destroy their own children too. Since the earliest contacts between the two races the Indians have considered most repugnant the white habit of slapping or beating children into compliance. Indians would only scare the child by saying the owl might come and get him – or the white man. What conflicts they were thus causing and perpetuating in their children, the Indians, in turn, could not see.

The unofficial complaints, then, assume (with our most advanced theoretical assumptions) that even seemingly arbitrary items of child training have a definite function, although in secret complaints this insight is used for the most part as a vehicle of mutual prejudice and as a cover-up for individual motivations and unconscious intentions. Here is truly a field for 'group therapy' of a kind which would not aim at psychiatric improvement for the individual participant but at an improvement of the cultural relations of those assembled.

Of items significant in cultural prejudice, I shall briefly illustrate three: respect for property, cleanliness, efficiency.

One day a schoolteacher brought with him a list of his pupils. There was nothing very remarkable about any of these children except, perhaps, the poetic flavour of their names (equivalents: Star-Comes-Out, Chase-in-the-Morning, Afraid-of-Horses). They were all well-behaved, yielding to the white teacher that which is the teacher's and to the Indian home that which belongs to the home. 'They have two sets of truths,' the teacher explained, putting it more politely than did some of his colleagues, who are convinced that Indians are 'born liars'. He was satisfied, on the whole, with their scholastic achievements. The only problem he wished to discuss was one presented by a certain little boy who lived a relatively isolated existence among the other children as if he were, somehow, an outcast.

We inquired into the status of the boy's family among the Indians and the whites. Both groups characterized the father of the boy with the same three fateful words, 'He has money.' The father's regular visits to the bank in the nearest town gave him, it appeared, that 'foreign smell' which an ant acquires when crossing over the territory of another 'tribe', so that it is killed on return. Here the traitor apparently becomes dead socially, after he and his family, once and for all, have acquired the evil identity of He-Who-Keeps-His-Money-to-Himself. This offends one of the oldest principles of Sioux economy – generosity.

The idea of storage over a prolonged period of time is foreign. If a man has enough to keep starvation at least around the corner, has sufficient time for meditation, and something to give away now and then, he is relatively content . . . When a man's food is low, or all gone, he may hitch up his team and take his family for a visit. Food is shared equally until none is left. The most despised man is he who is rich but does not give out his riches to those about him. He it is who is really 'poor'.[6]

[6] H. S. Mekeel, *The Economy of a Modern Teton-Dakota Community*, Yale Publications in Anthropology, Nos. 1–7, Yale University Press, New Haven, 1936.

In the Sioux system, the crowning expression of the principle of levelling wealth was the 'give-away', the offering of all the host's possessions to his guests at a feast in honour of a friend or relative. To perceive by contrast the ideal antithesis to the evil image of the miser, one must see, even today, an Indian child on some ceremonial occasion give away what meagre pennies or possessions his parents have saved for just such an occasion. He radiates what we shall later formulate as a sense of ideal identity: 'The way you see me now is the way I really am, and it is the way of my forefathers.'

The economic principle of the give-away and the high prestige of generosity was, of course, once allied with necessity. Nomads need a safe minimum of household property which they can carry with them. People who live by hunting depend on the generosity of the luckiest and most able hunters. But necessities change more rapidly than true virtues, and it is one of the most paradoxical problems of human evolution that virtues which were originally designed to safeguard an individual's or a group's self-preservation become rigid under the pressure of anachronistic fears of extinction and thus can render a people unable to adapt to changed necessities. In fact, such relics of old virtues become stubborn and yet elusive obstacles to re-education. For, once deprived of their over-all economic meaning and universal observance, they fall apart. They combine with other character traits, of which some individuals have more, others less, and fuse with surrounding group traits, such as poor-white prodigality and carelessness. In the end the administrator and teacher cannot possibly know when they are dealing with an old virtue, when with a new vice. Take the relief checks and the supplies of food and machinery due to individual families on the basis of old treaties and officially distributed according to need and desert: one could always know when a man had received such 'gifts', for all over the prairie little wagons would bring his temporarily less lucky relatives towards their rightful participation in a feast of primitive communism. Thus, after all the decades of educational efforts towards Indian participation in our monetary civilization, the ancient attitudes prevail.

The first insight which emerged from the discussion of these items was that nothing is more fruitless in the relationships between individuals or groups than to attempt to question the ideals of the adversary by demonstrating that, according to the logic of one's own conscience, he is inconsistent in his preaching. For every conscience, whether in an individual or a group, has not only specific contents but also its own particular logic which safeguards its coherence.

'They are without initiative,' the exasperated white teachers would say; and indeed the wish of an Indian boy to excel and to compete, while fully developed under certain circumstances, may disappear completely under others. The members of a running team, for example, may hesitate at the start of a race. 'Why should we run?' they say. 'It is already certain who is going to win.' In the backs of their minds there may be the reflection that he who wins will not have too good a time afterwards. For the story of the little Boy-Whose-Father-Has-Money has its parallels in the fate of all those Indian boys and girls who show signs of actually accepting the demands of their educators and of finding delight and satisfaction in excelling in school activities. They are drawn back to the average level by the intangible ridicule of the other children.

Mekeel illustrated the Indian girl's special problems by pointing to a particularly tragic detail. The first impression the little Indian girl must get on entering a white school is that she is 'dirty'. Some teachers confess that they cannot possibly hide their disgust at the Indian child's home smell. The movable tepee, of course, was freer of accumulated smell than the frame houses are now. During school time the child is taught cleanliness, personal hygiene, and the standardized vanity of cosmetics. While having by no means fully assimilated other aspects of white female freedom of motion and of ambition which are presented to her with historically disastrous abruptness, the adolescent girl returns home prettily dressed and clean. But the day soon comes when she is called a 'dirty girl' by mothers and grandmothers. For a clean girl in the Indian sense is one who has learned to practise certain avoidances during menstruation; for example, she is not supposed to handle certain foods, which are said to spoil under her touch. Most girls are unable to accept again the status of a leper while menstruating. Yet they are by no means comfortably emancipated. They are almost never given the opportunity, nor are they indeed prepared or willing, to live

117

the life of an American woman; but they are only rarely able to be happy again in the spatial restrictions, the unhygienic intimacies, and the poverty of their surroundings.

Ingrained world-images cannot be weakened by the evidence of discrepancies nor reconciled by arguments. In spite of the ideological chasm demonstrated in these examples, many Indian parents were reported to make honest and successful attempts to induce obedience to the white teacher in their children. However, the children seemed to accept this pressure as a form of compliance not backed up by a sense of deeper obligation. They often responded to it with unbelievable stoicism. This, it seemed to us, was the most astonishing single fact to be investigated: that Indian children could live for years without open rebellion or any signs of inner conflict between two standards which were incomparably further apart than are those of any two generations or two classes in our culture. We found among the Sioux little evidence of individual conflicts, inner tensions, or of what we call neuroses – anything which would have permitted us to apply our knowledge of mental hygiene, such as it was, to a solution of the Indian problem. What we found was cultural pathology, sometimes in the form of alcoholic delinquency or of mild thievery, but for the most part in the form of a general apathy and an intangible passive resistance against any further and more final impact of white standards on the Indian conscience. Only in a few 'white man's Indians', usually successfully employed by the government, did we find neurotic tension, expressed in compulsions, overconscientiousness, and general rigidity. The average Indian child, however, did not seem to have what we call a 'bad conscience' when, in passive defiance of the white teacher, he retreated into himself; nor was he met by unsympathetic relatives when he chose to become truant. On the whole, then, no true inner conflict reflected the conflict of the two worlds in both of which the individual child existed.

But the tonus and tempo of life seemed to recover some of its old vitality only in those rare but vivid moments when his elders extolled the old life; when the larger family or the remnant of the old band packed their horse carts and converged somewhere on the prairie for a ceremony or a festival to exchange gifts and memories, to gossip and to calumniate, to joke and – now on rarer occasions – to dance the old dances. For it was then that his parents and especially his grandparents came closest to a sense of identity which again connected them with the boundless past wherein there had been no one but the Indian, the game, and the enemy. The space in which the Indian could feel at home was still without borders and allowed for voluntary gatherings and, at the same time, for sudden expansion and dispersion. He had been glad to accept centrifugal items of white culture such as the horse and the gun and, later, motorcars and the dream of trailers. Otherwise there could be only passive resistance to the senseless present and dreams of restoration: when the future would lead back into the past, time would again become ahistoric, space unlimited, activity boundlessly centrifugal, and the buffalo supply inexhaustible. The Sioux tribe as a whole is still waiting for the Supreme Court to give the Black Hills back to them and to restore the lost buffalo.

Their federal educators, on the other hand, continued to preach a life plan with centripetal and localized goals; homestead, fireplace, bank account – all of which receive their meaning from a space–time in which the past is overcome and in which the full measure of fulfilment in the present is sacrificed to an ever higher standard of living in the ever distant future. The road to this future is not outer restoration but inner reform and economic 'betterment'.

Thus we learned that geographic–historic perspectives and economic goals and means contain all that a group has learned from its history, and therefore characterize concepts of reality and ideals of conduct which cannot be questioned or partially exchanged without a threat to existence itself. Items of child training, as we shall now demonstrate, are part and parcel of such concepts of reality. They persist when possible in their original form, but if necessary in distorted facsimiles as stubborn indications that the new way of life imposed by the conquerors has not yet been able to awaken images of a new cultural identity.

SIOUX CHILD–TRAINING

Birth

The Dakota women who gave us information on the old methods of child training were at first reticent. To begin with, they were

Indians. Then also, Mekeel, whom they had known as anthropologist and friend, was now a government man. And then, it was not quite decent to talk to men about things concerning the human body. Especially the subject of the unavoidable beginning, namely pregnancy, always caused some giggling. Although vomiting and other physiological disorders of pregnancy are said to be a rare occurrence among them, Indian women seem conscious of a radical change of character during this time which in retrospect appears embarrassing. It is said that only when pregnant do the usually gentle Indian women abuse their husbands and even, upon occasion, strike their children. Thus different cultural systems have different outlets for the expression of the deep ambivalence which pervades the woman who, much as she may have welcomed the first signs of pregnancy and much as she may be looking forward to the completed baby, finds herself inhabited for nine long months by a small and unknown, but utterly dictatorial, being.

Customs in regard to delivery have, of course, changed completely. White women usually speak with scorn about the 'unhygienic' custom of the older Indian woman, who made herself a bed of sand in or near her home on which she lay or knelt to have her baby, pressing her feet against two pegs driven into the ground and grasping two other pegs with her hands. However, this bed, called 'a pile of dirt' by the whites, seems to have been an important feature of the specific Plains hygiene system, according to which every bodily waste is given over to sand, wind, and sun. The manifestations of this system must have puzzled white people: menstrual pads and even placentas were hung in trees; the bodies of the dead were placed on high scaffolds; and defecation took place in specified dry places. On the other hand, it is hard for the Indians to see the hygienic superiority of the outhouse, which, though admittedly more modest, prevents sun and wind, but not flies from reaching the bodily waste.

White and Indian women regularly remark that 'no moaning or groaning' was heard from Indian women of the older generation during childbirth. There are stories which tell of Indian women who followed their people a few hours after being left behind to give birth to a baby. It seems that the old wandering life, which necessitated adapting to the change of seasons and to the sudden movement of buffalo and enemy, often left little or no time for aftercare and recuperation. Older women see in the changes which modern hygiene and hospitals are bringing about in the younger generation's custom of childbearing not only a danger to the tradition of fortitude, but also an injustice to the baby, who thus learns to cry 'like a white baby'.

Getting and Taking

As we now present a list of data significant in the Sioux system of child-rearing, the single datum owes its significance largely to the women's wish to convey a point dear to their traditional ethos, and yet sometimes also to our wish to check a point dear to our theoretical anticipations. Such a list, then, can neither be exhaustive nor entirely conclusive. Yet we thought we detected a surprising convergence between the rationale given by the Indians for their ancient methods, and the psychoanalytic reasoning by which we would come to consider the same data relevant.

The colostrom (the first watery secretion from the milk glands) was normally considered to be poison for the baby; thus the breast was not offered to him until there seemed to be a good stream of perfect milk. The Indian women maintained that it was not right to let a baby do all the initial work only to be rewarded with a thin, watery substance. The implication was clear: how could he trust a world which greeted him thus? Instead, as a welcome from the whole community, the baby's first meal was prepared by relatives and friends. They gathered the best berries and herbs the prairie affords and put their juice into a buffalo bladder, which was fashioned to serve as a breast-like nursing bottle. A woman who was considered by all to be a 'good woman' stimulated the baby's mouth with her finger and then fed him the juice. In the meantime, the watery milk was sucked out of the breast and the breast stimulated to do efficient work by certain older women who had been commanded in their dreams to perform this office.

Once the Indian baby began to enjoy the mother's breast he was nursed whenever he whimpered, day or night, and he also was allowed to play freely with the breast. A small child was not supposed to cry in helpless frustration, although later to cry in rage could 'make him strong'. It is generally assumed that

Indian mothers return to their old 'spoiling' customs as soon as they can be sure they will not be bothered by the health authorities.

In the old order the baby's nursing was so important that, in principle at least, not even the father's sexual privileges were allowed to interfere with the mother's libidinal concentration on the nursing. A baby's diarrhoea was said to be the result of a watery condition of the mother's milk brought about by intercourse with the father. The husband was urged to keep away from the wife for the nursing period, which, it is said, lasted from three to five years.

It is said that the oldest boy was nursed longest and that the average nursing period was three years. Today it is much shorter, although instances of prolonged nursing persist, to the dismay of those whose job it is to foster health and morals. One teacher told us that an Indian mother quite recently had come to school during recess to nurse her eight-year-old boy, who had a bad cold. She nursed him with the same worried devotion with which we ply our sniffling children with vitamins.

Among the old Sioux there was no systematic weaning at all. Some mothers, of course, had to stop nursing for reasons beyond their control. Otherwise the children weaned the mother by gradually getting interested in other foods. Before finally abandoning the breast altogether, however, the infant may have fed himself for many months on other food, allowing time for his mother to give birth to the next child and to restore her milk supply.

In this connection I remember an amusing scene. An Indian child of about three was sitting on his mother's lap eating dry crackers. He frequently became thirsty. With a dictatorial gesture and an experienced motion he reached into his mother's blouse (which, as of old, had openings on the sides from the armpits down), in an attempt to reach a breast. Because of our presence she prevented him bashfully, but by no means indignantly, with the cautious movement of a big animal pushing aside a little one. But he clearly indicated that he was in the habit of getting a sip now and then while eating. The attitude of the two was more telling than statistical data in indicating when such little fellows, once they can pursue other adventures, definitely stop reaching into their mother's blouse – or, for that matter, into the blouse of any woman who happens to have milk. For such milk, where it exceeds the immediate needs of her suckling baby, is communal property.

This paradise of the practically unlimited privilege of the mother's breast also had a forbidden fruit. To be permitted to suckle, the infant had to learn not to bite the breast. Sioux grandmothers recount what trouble they had with their indulged babies when they began to use nipples for the first vigorous biting. They tell with amusement how they would 'thump' the baby's head and how he would fly into a wild rage. It is at this point that Sioux mothers used to say what our mothers say so much earlier in their babies' lives: let him cry, it will make him strong. Good future hunters, especially, could be recognized by the strength of their infantile fury.

The Sioux baby, when thus filled with rage, was strapped up to his neck in the cradleboard. He could not express his rage by the usual violent motion of the limbs. I do not mean to imply that the cradleboard or tight swaddling-clothes are cruel restrictions. On the contrary, at first they are undoubtedly comfortably firm and womblike things to be wrapped and rocked in and a handy bundle for the mother to carry around while working. But I do wish to suggest that the particular construction of the board, its customary placement in the household, and the duration of its use, are variable elements used by different cultures as amplifiers of the basic experiences and the principal traits which they develop in their young.

What convergence can we see between the Sioux child's orality and the tribe's ethical ideals? We have mentioned generosity as an outstanding virtue required in Sioux life. A first impression suggests that the cultural demand for generosity received its early foundation from the privilege of enjoying the nourishment and the reassurance emanating from unlimited breast feeding. The companion virtue of generosity was fortitude, in Indians a quality both more ferocious and more stoical than mere bravery. It included an easily aroused quantity of quickly available hunting and fighting spirit, the inclination to do sadistic harm to the enemy, and the ability to stand extreme hardship and pain under torture and self-torture. Did the necessity of suppressing early biting-wishes contribute to the tribe's always ready ferocity? If so, it cannot be without significance that the generous mothers themselves aroused a 'hunter's ferocity' in their teething infants, encouraging an eventual transfer of the infant's provoked rage to ideal images of hunting, encircling, catching, killing, and stealing.

We are not saying here that their treatment in babyhood *causes* a group of adults to have certain traits – as if you turned a few knobs in your child-training system and you fabricated this or that kind of tribal or national character. In fact, we are not discussing traits in the sense of irreversible aspects of character. We are speaking of goals and values and of the energy put at their disposal by child-training systems. Such values persist because the cultural ethos continues to consider them 'natural' and does not admit of alternatives. They persist because they have become an essential part of an individual's sense of identity, which he must preserve as a core of sanity and efficiency. But values do not persist unless they work, economically, psychologically, and spiritually; and I argue that to this end they must continue to be anchored, generation after generation, in early child-training; while child training, to remain consistent, must be embedded in a system of continued economic and cultural synthesis. For it is the synthesis operating within a culture which increasingly tends to bring into close-knit thematic relationship and mutual amplification such matters as climate and anatomy, economy and psychology, society and child-training.

How can we show this? Our proof must lie in the coherent meaning which we may be able to give to seemingly irrational data within one culture and to analogous problems in comparable cultures. We shall, therefore, indicate in what way various items of our material on Sioux culture seem to derive meaning from our assumptions, and then proceed from this hunter tribe to a comparison with a tribe of fishermen.

As we watched Sioux children sitting in the dark corners of their tents, walking along the trails, or gathered in great numbers around the Fourth of July dance, we noticed that they often had their fingers in their mouths. They (and some adults, usually women) were not sucking their fingers, but playing with their teeth, clicking or hitting something against them, snapping chewing-gum or indulging in some play which involves teeth and finger-nails on one or both hands. The lips, even if the hand

was as far inside the mouth as is at all possible, did not participate. Questioning brought the astonishing answer: yes, of
course, they had always done this, didn't everybody? As
clinicians we could not avoid the deduction that this habit was
the heir of the biting-wishes which were so ruthlessly interrupted
in early childhood – just as we assume in our culture that
thumb-sucking and other sucking-habits of our children (and
adults) compensate for sucking-pleasures which have been
frustrated or made uncertain by inconsistent handling.

This led to an interesting further question: why were women
more apt to display this habit than the equally frustrated men?
We found a twofold answer to this: women, in the olden days,
used and abused their teeth to chew leather and flatten the
porcupine quills which they needed for their embroidery. They
thus could apply the teething-urges to a toothy activity of high
practicality. And indeed, I saw a very aged woman sitting in her
tent, dreamily pulling a strip of moving picture film between her
few remaining teeth, just as she may have flattened the porcupine
quills long ago. It seems then, that tooth habits persisted in
women because for them they were considered 'normal', even
when no longer specifically useful.

Generosity in the Sioux child's later life was sustained not by
prohibition, but by the example set by his elders in the attitude
which they took towards property in general and to his property
in particular. Sioux parents were ready at any time to let go of
utensils and treasures, if a visitor so much as admired them,
although there were, of course, conventions curbing a visitor's
expression of enthusiasm. It was very bad form to point out
objects obviously constituting a minimum of equipment. The
expectation, however, that an adult should and would dispose
of his surplus caused much consternation in the early days, when
the 'Indian giver' offered to a white friend not what the friend
needed, but what the Indian could spare, only to walk off with
what he decided the white man could spare. But all of this concerned only the parent's property. A parent with a claim to
good character and integrity would not touch a child's possessions, because the value of possessions lay in the owner's right
to let go of them when *he* was moved to do so – i.e., when it
added prestige to himself and to the person in whose name he

might decide to give it away. Thus a child's property was sacrosanct until the child had enough of a will of his own to decide on its disposition.

Holding and Letting Go

Generosity, we are interested to note, was not inculcated by calling stinginess bad and 'money' dirty but by calling the give-away good. Property as such, with the exception of the afore-mentioned minimum equipment for hunting, sewing, and cooking, had no inherent goodness. The traders never tire of repeating stories of the Indian parents who come to town to buy long-needed supplies with long-expected money, only to smilingly grant their children their every whim, including their wish to take new gadgets apart, and then to return home without supplies.

In the chapter on pregenitality we enlarged upon the clinical impression that there is an intrinsic relationship between the holding on to and letting go of property and the infantile dis-position of excrement as the body's property.

And, indeed, it seems that the Sioux child was allowed to reach by himself a gradual compliance with whatever rules of modesty or cleanliness existed. Although the trader complained that even five-year-olds would in no way control their excretory needs while at the store with their shopping parents, teachers say that as soon as the very young Indian child knows what is expected of him – and, most important, sees the older children comply – accidents of soiling or wetting at day school are extremely rare. The complaint that they, like children of other cultures, wet their beds in boarding-schools is another matter. For some reason enuresis seems to be the 'normal' symptom of the homesick, the billeted child. Therefore, one may say that these children, far from not having learned any control, seem able to adapt to two standards without compulsive tendencies to retention or elimination. The bowels become regulated because of the example set by other children, rather than by measures reflecting the vagaries of the parent–child relationship. Thus the small child, as soon as he can walk, is taken by the hand by older children and is led to places designated by convention for purposes of defecation. It is probably in this connection that the small child first learns to be guided by that coercion to imitate and by that avoidance of 'shaming' which characterizes so much of primitive morality. For these 'unprincipled savages' often prove to be timidly concerned about gossip which indicates that they have not done the proper thing or have done a thing improperly. The Sioux child undoubtedly becomes aware of the changing wavelengths of didactic gossip before he quite understands its detailed contents, until gradually, inexorably, this gossip includes him, encouraging his autonomous pride in being somebody who is looked upon with approval; making him mortally afraid of standing exposed and isolated; and diverting whatever rebellion may have been thus aroused in him by permitting him to participate in gossip against others.

It can be said that the Sioux attitude towards anal training in childhood does not contradict that concerning property. In regard to both, the emphasis is on free release rather than on rigid retention, and in both, the final regulation is postponed to a stage of ego development when the child can come to an autonomous decision which will give him immediate tangible status in the community of his peers.

'Making' and Making

In Sioux childhood, the first strict taboos expressed verbally and made inescapable by a tight net of ridiculing gossip did not concern the body and its modes, but rather patterns of social intimacy. When a certain stage, soon after the fifth year, was reached, brother and sister had to learn neither to look at nor to address one another directly. The girl would be urged to confine herself to female play and to stay near the mother and tepee, while the boy was encouraged to join the older boys, first in games and then in the practice of hunting.

A word about play. I had been most curious to see the Indian children's toys and to observe their games. When for the first time I approached the Indian camp near the agency, proceeding carefully and as if uninterested, so that at least a few of the children might not be disturbed in their play, the little girls ran into the tents to sit beside their mothers with their knees covered and their eyes lowered. It took me some time to realize that they were not really afraid but just acting 'proper'. (The test: they were immediately ready to play peek-a-boo from behind their mother's backs.) One of them, however, who was about six years old, sat behind a large tree and obviously was too intent on solitary play to notice me or to comply with the rules of feminine shyness. As I eagerly stalked this child of the prairie, I found her bent over a toy typewriter. And her lips as well as her fingernails were painted red.

Even the youngest of the girls are thus influenced in their play by the radical change taking place in their older sisters, the pupils of the boarding-school. This became obvious when the women of the camp made small tepees, wagons, and dolls for me in order to demonstrate what they had played with as children. These toys were clearly intended to lead little girls along the path to Indian motherhood. One little girl, playing with one of these old-fashioned toy wagons, however, unhesitatingly put two doll women in the front seat, threw the babies in the rear compartment, and had the ladies 'drive to the movies in Chadron'. However, all of this is still feminine play: a girl would be ridiculed mercilessly should she indulge in a 'boyish' game, or dare to become a tomboy.

The aspirations developed in the boys' play and games have changed less than those of the girls, although cowboy activities have largely displaced those of the buffalo hunter. Thus while I was observing the little dolls 'going off to town', a tree stump near which I was sitting was roped by the girl's little brother with gleeful satisfaction. Psychologically, such a game is obviously still considered serious training by the older children and adults, although it is 'useless' in reality. Upon one occasion I laughed, as I thought, with and not at a little boy who told his mother and me that he could catch a wild rabbit on foot and with his bare hands. I was made to feel that I had made a social blunder. Such daydreams are not 'play'. They are the preparations for skills which, in turn, assure the development of the hunter or cowboy identity.

In this respect one very old custom is of special interest, namely, the play with 'bone horses', small bones three or four inches long which the boys gather at places where cattle (formerly buffalo) have been killed. According to their shape, they are called horses, cows, or bulls, and are either fingered continuously in the boys' pockets or are used by them when playing together at games of horse racing and buffalo hunting. These bones are for the Sioux boys what small toy cars are in the lives of our boys. The phallic shape of these bones suggests that they may be the medium which allows little boys in the phallic and locomotor stage, while fingering 'horses', 'buffaloes', 'cows', and 'bulls', to cultivate competitive and aggressive daydreams common to all males of the tribe. It fell to the older brothers, at this stage, to introduce the small boy to the ethos of the hunter and to make loyalty between brothers the cement of Dakota society. Because of their exclusive association with the boasting older boys, the smaller ones must have become aware early enough of the fact that direct phallic aggressiveness remained equated with the ferocity of the hunter. It was considered proper for a youth to rape any maiden whom he caught outside the areas defined for decent girls: a girl who did not know 'her place' was his legitimate prey, and he could boast of the deed.

Every educational device was used to develop in the boy a maximum of self-confidence, first by maternal generosity and assurance, then by fraternal training. He was to become a hunter after game, woman, and spirit. The emancipation of the boy from his mother, and the diffusion of any regressive fixation on her, was accomplished by an extreme emphasis on his right to autonomy and on his duty of initiative. Given boundless trust, and gradually learning (through the impact of shaming rather than through that of inner inhibition) to treat his mother with reticence and extreme respect, the boy apparently directed all sense of frustration and rage into the chase after game, enemy, and loose women – and against himself, in his search for spiritual power. Of such deeds he was permitted to boast openly, loudly, and publicly, obliging his father to display pride in his superior offspring. It is only too obvious that such a sweeping initial invitation to be male and master would necessitate the establishment of balancing safeguards in the girls. While the arrangement of these safeguards is ingenious, one cannot help feeling that the woman was exploited for the sake of the hunter's unbroken 'spirit'; and, indeed, it is said that suicides were not uncommon among Sioux women, although unknown among men.

The Sioux girl was educated to be a hunter's helper and a future hunter's mother. She was taught to sew, to cook and conserve food, and to put up tents. At the same time she was subjected to a rigorous training towards bashfulness and outright fear of men. She was trained to walk with measured steps, never to cross certain boundaries set around the camp, and – with approaching maturity – to sleep at night with her thighs tied together to prevent rape.

She knew that if a man could claim to have touched a woman's vulva, he was considered to have triumphed over her virginity. This victory by mere touch was analogous to his right to 'count coup' – i.e., to claim a new feather in his bonnet when he had succeeded in touching a dangerous enemy in battle. How similar these two victories are could still be seen in the gossip column of an Indian Reservation school paper put out by the children: it specified the number of times certain boys had 'counted coup' against certain girls – i.e., had kissed them. In the old days, however, any public bragging on the part of the boys was insulting to the girl concerned. The girl learned that she might be called on during the Virgin Feast to defend her claim to virginity against any accusation. The ceremony of this feast consisted of symbolic acts apparently compelling the admission of the truth. Any man who, under these ceremonial conditions, would and could claim that he had so much as touched a girl's genitals could have that girl removed from the élite group.

It would be wrong to assume, however, that such ritual warfare precluded affectionate love between the sexes. In reality the seemingly paradoxical result of such education was doubly deep affection in individuals who were ready to sacrifice prestige points for love; in the boy, whose tenderness tamed his pride to the extent that he would court a girl by calling her with the love flute and by enveloping her and himself in the courting blanket in order to ask her to marry him – and in the girl, who responded without suspecting him of other than honourable intentions and without making use of the hunting knife which she carried with her always, just in case.

The girl, then, was educated to serve the hunter and to be on her guard against him – but also to become a mother who would surely not destroy in her boys the characteristics necessary to a hunter. By means of ridiculing gossip – 'people who did such and such an unheard-of thing' – she would, as she had seen her mother do, gradually teach her children the hierarchy of major and minor avoidances and duties in the relations between man and man, between woman and woman, and especially between man and woman. Brother and sister, or parent-in-law and child-in-law of the opposite sex, were not permitted to sit with one another or to have face-to-face conversations. A brother-in-law and sister-in-law, and a girl and her maternal uncle, were allowed to speak only in a joking tone to one another.

These prohibitions and regulations, however, were made part of highly significant relationships. The little girl old enough to avoid her brother knew that she would ultimately use her skill in sewing and embroidery, on which she was to concentrate henceforth, for the fabrication and ornamentation of beautiful things for his future wife – and for his children, cradles and layettes. 'He has a good sister' would be high praise for the warrior and hunter. The brother knew that he would give her the best of all he would win by hunting or stealing. The fattest prey would be offered his sister for butchering, and the corpses of his worst enemies left to her for mutilation. Thus she too would, via her brother's fortitude and generosity, find an opportunity to participate actively and aggressively in at least some aspects of the high moments of hunt and war. Above all, in the Sun Dance, she would, if proven virtuous, bathe the brother's self-inflicted wounds, thus sharing the spiritual triumph of his most sublime masochism. The first and basic avoidance – that between brother and sister – thus became a model of all respect-relationships and of helpfulness and generosity among all the 'brothers' and 'sisters' of the extended kinship; while the loyalty between brothers became the model of all comradeship.

I think it would be too simple to say that such avoidances served to forestall 'natural' incestuous tension. The extreme to which some of these avoidances go, and the outright suggestions that the joking between brothers-in-law and sisters-in-law *should* be sexual, rather point to an ingenious provocation as well as diversion of potential incestuous tension. Such tension was utilized within the universal task of creating a social atmosphere of respect in the ingroup (to each according to his family status); and of diverting safely to the prey, to the enemy, and to the outcast all the need for manipulative control and general aggressiveness provoked and frustrated at the biting stage. There was, then, a highly standardized system of 'proper' relationships which assured kindness, friendliness, and considerateness within the extended family. All sense of belonging depended on the ability to acquire a reputation as somebody who deserves praise for being proper. But he who, after the gradual increase of the pressure of shaming, should persist in improper behaviour, would become the victim of ruthlessly biting gossip and deadly calumniation: as if, by refusing to help in the diversion of the concerted aggressiveness, he himself had become an enemy.

Today the Sioux boy will catch a glimpse of the life for which his play rituals still prepare him only by observing and (if he can) joining in the dances of his elders. These dances have often been described as 'wild' by whites who obviously felt in them a two-fold danger growing out of the gradually rising group spirit and the 'animalistic' rhythm. However, when we observed older Sioux dancers in one of the isolated dance-houses, they seemed, as the hours of the night passed, to express with their glowing faces a deepening concentration on a rhythm which possessed their bodies with increasing exactness. Lawfulness kept step with wildness. In comparison, it was almost embarrassing to observe the late arrival of a group of young men, who obviously had learned to dance jazz also. Their dance was completely 'out of joint', and their gaze wandered around in a conceited way, which by comparison made the spiritual concentration of their elders only the more impressive. Old Indians tried to hide pitying smiles behind their hands at this display.

Thus on occasion the dances and ceremonies still proclaim the existence of the man with the 'strong heart' who has learned to use the tools of his material culture to expand his hunting powers beyond his body's limitations. Mastering the horse, he has gained a swiftness of which his legs were incapable in order to approach animal and enemy with paralysing suddenness. With bow and arrow and tomahawk he has extended the skill and strength of his arm. The breath of the sacred pipe has won him the good will of men; the voice of the love flute, the woman's favour. Charms have brought him all kinds of luck with a power stronger than naked breath, word, or wish. But the Great Spirit, he has learned, must be approached only with the searching concentration of the man who, naked, alone, and unarmed, goes into the wilderness to fast and to pray.

The Sun Dance

The paradise of orality and its loss during the rages of the biting stage, as we suggested in the preceding chapter, may be the ontogenetic origin of that deep sense of badness which religion transforms into a conviction of primal sin on a Universal scale. Prayer and atonement, therefore, must renounce the all too avaricious desire for 'the world' and must demonstrate, in reduced posture and in the inflection of urgent appeal, a return to bodily smallness, to technical helplessness, and to voluntary suffering.

The religious ceremony of higher significance in the life of the Dakota was the Sun Dance, which took place during two four-day periods in summer, 'when the buffalo were fat, the wild berries ripe, the grass tall and green'. It started with ritual feasting, the expression of gratitude to the Buffalo Spirit, and the demonstrations of fellowship among fellow men. Fertility rites followed, and acts of sexual licence such as characterize similar rites in many parts of the world. Then there were war and hunting games which glorified competition among men. Men boisterously recounted their feats in war; women and maidens stepped forward to proclaim their chastity. Finally, the mutual dependence of all the people would be glorified in give-aways and in acts of fraternization.

The climax of the festival was reached with the summation of self-tortures in fulfilment of vows made at critical times during the year. On the last day the 'candidates of the fourth dance' engaged in the highest form of self-torture by putting through the muscles of their chest and back skewers which were attached to the sun pole by long thongs. Gazing directly into the sun and slowly dancing backwards, the men could tear themselves loose by ripping the flesh of their chests open. Thus they became the year's spiritual élite, who through their suffering assured the continued benevolence of the sun and the Buffalo Spirit, the providers of fecundity and fertility. This particular feat of having one's chest ripped open *ad majorem gloriam* constitutes, of course, only one variation of the countless ways in which, all over the world, a sense of evil is atoned for and the continued generosity of the universe assured, and this often after an appropriately riotous farewell to all flesh (*carnevale*).

The meaning of an institutionalized form of atonement must be approached both ontogenetically, as a fitting part of the majority's typical sequence of experiences, and phylogenetically, as part of a religious style. In the particular tribal variation here under discussion I find it suggestive that there should be a relationship between the earliest infantile trauma suffered (the ontogenetic yet culturewide loss of paradise) and the crowning feature of religious atonement. The ceremony would then be the climax to the vicissitudes of that deliberately cultivated (yet, of course, long forgotten) rage at the mother's breast during a biting stage which interferes with the long sucking licence. Here the faithful would turn the consequently awakened sadistic wishes which the mothers assigned to the future hunter's ferocity, back against themselves by making their own chests the particular focus of their self-torture. The ceremony, then, would fulfil the old principle of 'an eye for an eye' – only that the baby, of course, would have been incapable of perpetrating the destruction for which the man now voluntarily atones. It is hard for our rational minds to comprehend – unless we are schooled in the ways of irrationality – that frustrated wishes, and especially early, preverbal, and quite vague wishes, can leave a residue of sin which goes deeper than any guilt over deeds actually committed and remembered. In our world only the magic sayings of Jesus convey a conviction of these dark matters. We take His word for it, that a wish secretly harboured is as good – or rather, as bad – as a deed committed; and that whatever organ offends us with its persistent desires should be radically extirpated. It is, of course, not necessary that a whole tribe or congregation should follow such a precept to the letter. Rather, the culture must provide for a convention of magic belief and a consistent system of ritual which will permit a few exceptional individuals who feel their culture's particular brand of inner damnation especially deeply (and, maybe, are histrionic enough to want to make a grand spectacle of it) to dramatize, for all to see, the fact that there is a salvation. (In our times, logical doubters and disbelievers often have to take refuge in disease, seemingly accidental mutilation or unavoidable misfortune in order to express the unconscious idea that they had wanted too much in this world – and had got away with it.)

Vision Quest

We begin slowly to comprehend that homogeneous cultures have a systematic way of giving rewards in the currency of higher inspiration and exalted prestige for the very sacrifices and frustrations which the child must endure in the process of becoming good and strong in the traditional sense. But how about those who feel that they are 'different', and that the prestige-possibilities offered do not answer their personal needs? How about those men who do not care to be heroes and those women who do not easily agree to be heroes' mates and helpers?

In our own culture Freud has taught us to study the dreams of neurotic individuals in order to determine what undone deed they could not afford to leave undone, what thought unthought, what memory unremembered in the course of their all too rigid adaptation. We use such knowledge to teach the suffering individual to find a place in his cultural milieu or to criticize an educational system for endangering too many individuals by demanding excessive compliance – and thus endangering itself.

The Sioux, like other primitives, used the dream for the guidance of the strong as well as for the prevention of anarchic deviation. But they did not wait for adult dreams to take care of faulty developments; the adolescent Sioux would go out and seek dreams, or rather visions, while there was still time to decide on a life plan. Unarmed, and naked, except for loincloth and moccasins, he would go out into the prairie, exposing himself to sun, danger, and hunger, and tell the deity of his essential humility and need of guidance. This would come, on the fourth day, in the form of a vision which, as afterwards interpreted by a special committee of dream experts, would encourage him to do especially well the ordinary things such as hunting, warring, or stealing horses; or to bring slight innovations into the institutions of his tribe, inventing a song, a dance, or a prayer; or to become something special such as a doctor or a priest; or finally, to turn to one of those few roles available to confirmed deviants.

For example: a person who was convinced he saw the Thunderbird reported this to his advisers, and from then on at all public occasions was a '*heyoka*'. He was obliged to behave as absurdly and clownishly as possible until his advisers thought he had cured himself of the curse. Wissler reports the following instructive *heyoka* experience of an adolescent:

One time when I was about thirteen years old, in the spring of the year, the sun was low and it threatened rain and thunder, while my people were in a camp of four tepees. I had a dream that my father and our family were sitting together in a tepee when lightning struck into their midst. All were stunned. I was the first to become conscious. A neighbor was shouting out around the camp. I was doubled up when first becoming conscious. It was time to take out the horses, so I took them.

As I was coming to my full senses I began to realize what had occurred and that I should go through the *heyoka* ceremony when fully recovered. I heard a herald shouting this about, but am not sure it was real. I knew I was destined to go through the *heyoka*. I cried some to myself. I told my father I had seen the Thunder-Bird: 'Well, son,' he said, 'you must go through with it.' I was told that I must be a *heyoka*. If I did not go through with the ceremony, I would be killed by lightning. After this I realized that I must formally tell in the ceremony exactly what I experienced.[7]

As can be seen, it was important that the dreamer should succeed in conveying to his listeners the feeling of an experience which complied with a recognized form of manifest dream and in which he was the overwhelmed recipient, in which case the higher powers were assumed to have given him a convincing sign that they wished him to plan or change his life's course in a certain way.

The expiation could consist of anti-natural behaviour during a given period, or for life, depending on the interpretation of the advisers. The absurd activities demanded of the unlucky dreamer were either simply silly and absurd or terrifying. Sometimes he was even condemned to kill somebody. His friends would urge compliance, for defence against evil spirits was more important than the preservation of individual life.

One conversant with the ego's tricky methods of overcoming feelings of anxiety and guilt will not fail to recognize in the *heyoka*'s antics the activities of children playing the clown or

[7] C. Wissler, *Societies and Ceremonial Associations in the Oglala Division of the Teton-Dakota*, Anthropological Papers of the American Museum of Natural History, Vol. XI, Part 1, New York, 1912.

debasing and otherwise harming themselves when they are frightened or pursued by a bad conscience. One method of avoiding offence to the gods is to humiliate oneself or put oneself in the wrong light before the public. As everybody is induced to permit himself to be fooled and to laugh, the spirits forget and forgive and may even applaud. The clown with his proverbial secret melancholy and the radio comedian who makes capital of his own inferiorities seem to be professional elaborations in our culture of this defence mechanism. Among the Sioux, too, the much-despised *heyoka* could prove to be so artful in his antics that he could finally become a headman.

Others might dream of the moon, a hermaphrodite buffalo, or the double-woman and thus learn that they were not to follow the life plan designed for their sex. Thus a girl may encounter the double-woman who leads her to a lone tepee.

As the woman comes up to the door and looks in she beholds the two deer-women sitting at the rear. By them she is directed to choose which side she shall enter. Along the wall of one side is a row of skin-dressing tools, on the other, a row of parfleche headdress bags. If the former is chosen, they will say, 'You have chosen wrong, but you will become very rich.' If she chooses the other side, they will say, 'You are on the right track, all you shall have shall be an empty bag.'[8]

Such a girl would have to leave the traditional road of Sioux femininity and be active in her quest after men. She would be called *witko* (crazy) and be considered a whore. Yet she too could gain fame in recognition of her artfulness, and achieve the status of a *hetaira*.

A boy may see:

. . . the moon having two hands, one holds a bow and arrows, the other the burden strap of a woman. The moon bids the dreamer take his choice; when the man reaches to take the bow, the hands suddenly cross and try to force the strap upon the man who struggles to waken before he takes it, and he also tries to succeed in capturing the bow. In either event he escapes the penalty of the dream. Should he fail and become possessed of the strap he is doomed to be like a woman.[9]

If such a boy does not prefer to commit suicide he must give up the career of warrior and hunter and become a *berdache*, a man-

[8] ibid.
[9] T. S. Lincoln, *The Dream in Primitive Cultures*, Cresset Press, London, 1935.

woman who dresses like a woman and does woman's work. The *berdaches* were not necessarily homosexuals, though some are said to have been married to other men, some to have been visited by warriors before war parties. Most *berdaches*, however, were like eunuchs simply considered not dangerous to women, and therefore good companions and even teachers for them, because they often excelled in the arts of cooking and embroidery.

A homogeneous culture such as that of the Sioux, then, deals with its deviants by giving them a secondary role, as clown, prostitute, or artist, without, however, freeing them entirely from the ridicule and horror which the vast majority must maintain in order to suppress in themselves what the deviant represents. However, the horror remains directed against the power of the spirits which have intruded themselves upon the deviant individual's dreams. It does not turn against the stricken individual himself. In this way, primitive cultures accept the power of the unconscious. If the deviant can only claim to have dreamed convincingly, his deviation is considered to be based on supernatural visitation rather than on individual motivation. As psychopathologists, we must admire the way in which these 'primitive' systems undertook to maintain elastic mastery in a matter where more sophisticated systems often fail.

SUMMARY

The Sioux, under traumatic conditions, has lost the reality for which the last historical form of his communal integrity was fitted. Before the white man came, he was a fighting nomad and a buffalo hunter. The buffalo disappeared, slaughtered by invaders. The Sioux then became a warrior on the defence, and was defeated. He almost cheerfully learned to round up cattle instead of encircling buffalo: his cattle were taken from him. He could become a sedentary farmer, only at the price of being a sick man, on bad land.

Thus, step for step, the Sioux has been denied the bases for a collective identity formation and with it that reservoir of collective integrity from which the individual must derive his stature as a social being.

Fear of famine has led the Sioux to surrender communal functions to the feeding conqueror. Far from remaining a transitional matter of treaty obligation, federal help has continued to be necessary, and this more and more in the form of relief. At the same time, the government has not succeeded in reconciling old and new images, nor indeed in laying the nucleus for a conscience new in both form and content. Child training, so we claim, remains the sensitive instrument of one cultural synthesis until a new one proves convincing and inescapable.

The problem of Indian education is, in reality, one of culture contact between a group of employees representative of the middle-class values of a free-enterprise system on the one hand, and on the other, the remnants of a tribe which, wherever it leaves the shadow of government sustenance, must find itself among the underprivileged of that system.

In fact, the ancient principles of child training still operating in the remnants of the tribe undermine the establishment of a white conscience. The developmental principle in this system holds that a child should be permitted to be an individualist while young. The parents do not show any hostility towards the body as such nor do they, especially in boys, decry self-will. There is no condemnation of infantile habits while the child is developing that system of communication between self and body and self and kin on which the infantile ego is based. Only when strong in body and sure in self is he asked to bow to a tradition of unrelenting shaming by public opinion which focuses on his actual social behaviour rather than on his bodily functions or his fantasies. He is incorporated into an elastic tradition which in a strictly institutionalized way takes care of his social needs, diverting dangerous instinctual tendencies towards outer enemies, and always allowing him to project the source of possible guilt into the supernatural. We have seen how stubborn this conscience has remained even in the face of the glaring reality of historical change.

In contrast, the dominating classes in Western civilization, represented here in their bureaucracy, have been guided by the conviction that a systematic regulation of functions and impulses in earliest childhood is the surest safeguard for later effective functioning in society. They implant the never-silent metronome of routine into the impressionable baby and young child to regulate his first experiences with his body and with his immediate physical surroundings. Only after such mechanical socialization is he encouraged to proceed to develop into a rugged individualist. He pursues ambitious strivings, but compulsively remains within standardized careers which, as the economy becomes more and more complicated, tend to replace more general responsibilities. The specialization thus developed has led this Western civilization to the mastery of machinery, but also to an under-current of boundless discontent and of individual disorientation.

Naturally the rewards of one educational system mean little to members of another system, while the costs are only too obvious to them. The undisturbed Sioux cannot understand how anything except *restoration* is worth striving for, his racial as well as his individual history having provided him with the memory of abundance. The white man's conscience, on the other hand, asks for continuous *reform* of himself in the pursuit of careers leading to ever higher standards. This reform demands an increasingly internalized conscience, one that will act against temptation automatically and unconsciously, without the presence of critical observers. The Indian conscience, more preoccupied with the necessity of avoiding embarrassing situations within a system of clearly defined honours and shames, is without orientation in conflicting situations which depend for their solution on an 'inner voice'.

The system underlying Sioux education is a primitive one – i.e., it is based on the adaptation of a highly ethnocentric, relatively small group of people, who consider only themselves to be relevant mankind, to one segment of nature. The primitive cultural system limits itself:

In specializing the individual child for one main career, here the buffalo hunter;

In perfecting a narrow range of the tool world which extends the reach of the human body over the prey;

In the use of magic as the only means of coercing nature.

Such self-restriction makes for homogeneity. There is a strong synthesis of geographic, economic, and anatomic patterns which in Sioux life find their common denominator in *centri-fugality*, as expressed in a number of items discussed, such as:

The social organization in bands, which makes for easy dispersion and migration;

The dispersion of tension in the extended family system;

Nomadic technology and the ready use of horse and gun;

The distribution of property by the give-away;

The division of aggression towards prey and outgroup.

Sioux child training forms a firm basis for this system of centrifugality by establishing a lasting centre of trust, namely the nursing mother, and then by handling the matter of teething, of infantile rage, and of muscular aggression in such a way that the greatest possible degree of ferocity is provoked, channelized socially, and finally released against prey and enemy. We believe that we are dealing here, not with simple causality, but with a mutual assimilation of somatic, mental and social patterns which amplify one another and make the cultural design for living economical and effective. Only such integration provides a sense of being at home in this world. Transplanted into our system, however, the very expression of what was once considered to be efficient and aristocratic behaviour – such as the disregard for property and the refusal to compete – only leads to an alignment with the lowest strata of our society.

A SUBSEQUENT STUDY

In 1942, five years after my field trip with Mekeel, a companion of our 1937 reservation days, Gordon MacGregor, directed an intensive and extensive study of 200 Pine Ridge children. This was part of a larger Indian Education Research Project which undertook to gather detailed material on childhood and tribal personality in five American Indian tribes. The study was jointly sponsored and staffed by the University of Chicago and by the Indian Service. MacGregor and his group had the opportunity, as we had not, of having Indian children observed in school and home throughout a year, and this by a team of observers who had had experience with other Indian tribes as well as with white children, and who mastered a variety of specially adapted tests. His study, therefore, can serve as an example of the verification of clinical impressions – and as a progress report.

I shall first abstract here a few of the items of old child-training which – according to MacGregor's account[10] – seem to have persisted in one form or another, especially among the full-blood or less mixed-blood Indians of the reservation population.

Babies, so MacGregor reports, are pinned into a tight bundle. While held, they are lightly rocked without interruption. Some children are weaned as early as nine months, some as late as thirty-six months; most of them somewhere between eleven and eighteen months. There is little thumb-sucking. Pacifiers were observed in three cases: one was of rubber, one was of pork, and one was a wiener. The habit of 'snapping the thumbnail against the front teeth' is a common Dakota habit. Tooth-clicking occurs predominantly among women and girls.

The early development of the child is watched by adults with amusement and patience. There is no hurrying along the path of walking or talking. On the other hand, there is no baby talk. The language usually taught first is the old Indian one: English is still a problem to many children when they enter school.

Toilet training is accomplished primarily by example. When no white people are around, the infant perambulates without diapers or underpants. However, there is a tendency to hasten bowel control and to specify localities for excretion.

Modern Dakota children are carefully trained to be generous. They still receive valuable gifts such as horses. Children of five, six, and seven give freely – and pleasantly. 'At one funeral where there was much giving, a small boy of the bereaved family spent his only dime to buy artificial orange powder in order to give a bucket of orangeade ceremonially to the visiting youngsters.' Property is sometimes removed but otherwise not protected against children, a fact watched by white people 'in bewilderment and utter frustration'.

The main means of education are warning and shaming. The children are allowed to scream in rage; it 'will make them strong'. Spanking, while more frequent, is still rare. Shaming is intensified, especially if the child continues to misbehave, and adults at

[10] G. MacGregor, *Warriors without Weapons*, University of Chicago Press, 1946.

142

home single out as misbehaviour primarily selfishness and competitiveness, the seeking after gains based on the disadvantage of others. Tense home situations are evaded by visiting homes at some distance.

Little boys (instead of playing with bow and arrow, and buffalo-foot bones) are given ropes and slingshots and, for the glory of the hunter's spirit, are encouraged to chase roosters and other small animals. Girls play with dolls and at keeping house.

By the time he is five or six, the Dakota child has acquired a feeling of security and affection in the family. Some separation of sexes is initiated, but the institution of avoidance has been abandoned: this, in fact, is noted by all observers as the most outstanding change. It is only in paired dances that brothers and sisters will avoid one another.

In school those of more mixed blood are learning to enjoy competition, and school in general is enjoyed as a get-together when family ties are outgrown. Yet many withdraw from competitive activities, and some refuse to respond at all. 'To be asked to compete in class goes against the grain with the Dakota child, and he criticizes the competitive ones among his fellows.' This difficulty, paired with the inability to speak English and fear of the white teacher, leads to frequent instances of embarrassed withdrawal or running away. The child is not punished when he runs home: his parents themselves are used to quitting work or community when embarrassed or angered.

Younger boys hit girls more than is usual in white schools. In older boys, competitive games such as baseball may on occasion lead to embarrassment because of the necessary display of competitiveness. However, there is an increased tendency among boys to fight in anger both at home and in school.

The older girls still act afraid of boys and men, always travel with other girls, refuse to ride horseback, and keep completely apart from boys.

The boarding-school, which (compared to the homes) is a place of physical luxury and of rich opportunities for varied interests, affords the pleasantest years in the child's life – and yet the great majority of students who enter high school do not graduate; they sooner or later play truant and finally quit for good. Causes are, again and again, embarrassment over situations in which the problem of shame and competition, of full blood and mixed blood, and of male and female, have become insoluble because of the changes in *mores*. Moreover, long training does not seem to promise a better-defined identity – or a more secure income.

Except in boom years, grown boys and girls tend to stay in the reservation or to return to it. Because of their early training, their home seems to be the most secure place, although the school years have made both home and youngster less acceptable to one another. Having learned that poverty can be avoided, the youngsters mind seeing their fathers idle, or shiftless; now more ambitious, they deplore the persistent trend towards dependence upon the government; now more accustomed to white ways, they find the continuous pressure of critical gossip destructive, especially where it undermines what little they themselves have assimilated of white ways. As for themselves, what they have learned in school has prepared them for a homogeneous development of tribal rehabilitation which is kept from jelling by the inducements of the armed services, of migratory labour, and of industrial work. The latter trends expose them to the problems of the poorest white rural and coloured urban populations. Only to be a soldier gives new lustre to an ancient role – when there happens to be a war on.

Those who follow their teachers' example and go to college, or prepare for civil-service positions, as a rule seek employment on other reservations to escape the double standard, which recognizes them as better trained, yet expects them to be silent when their more experienced elders speak. Thus potential leaders are lost to the community. Young men and women of integrity and stamina still emerge; but they are the exceptions. Reliable new models for Dakota children have not yet crystallized.

We have outlined what, according to MacGregor's study, has remained constant in Indian child-rearing. Let us now see what is changing.

The greatest change in Dakota life has probably been in the status of the family as a whole: instead of being a reinforcement of self-sufficiency it has become the refuge of those who feel isolated and inefficient. The strongest remaining tie seems to be that between brothers: a healthy tie, easily transferable and usable for the establishment of new communal pursuits. The weakest relationship, however, seems to be that between the children and their fathers, who cannot teach them anything and who, in fact, have become models to be avoided. Instead, boys seek praise from their age mates. Among girls, almost all of the old avoidances have been abandoned or weakened to the point where they are little more than empty acts of compliance. A strange mixture of sadness, anger, and, again and again, shame and embarrassment seems to have stepped into the breach of these old respect-relationships. Getting an education and getting a job are new and strong ambitions, which, however, are apparently soon exhausted because they cannot attach themselves to any particular roles and functions. The children feel what their elders know – namely, that (and these are my words) 'Washington', the climate, and the market make all prediction impossible.

MacGregor's study employed an extensive 'battery' of interviews and tests in order to arrive at a formulation of the 'Dakota personality', a composite picture which, he says, represents neither the 'personality of any one child nor the personalities of a majority of the children: it could not be said to exist in all its elements in any one child, let alone in a majority'. I shall not question or discuss the methodology used in the study, but shall merely abstract some of the data which throw light on these children's inner life.

To settle one question which, I am sure, many a reader has been wanting to ask: the intelligence of the Dakota children is slightly above that of white children. Their health, however, corresponds to that of the underprivileged rural whites. Chronic hunger, no doubt, causes apathy, and much of the slowness, the lack of ambition, and also the grinding bitterness of reservation life is simply due to hunger. Yet MacGregor's group, after exhaustive study, feels that the general apathy is as much the cause as it is the result of the hunger; for it has hindered initiative and industry in situations which offered chances of improvement.

Tests of thematic imagination among the Dakota children and spontaneous stories told by them reflect their image of the world. In the following, it must be kept in mind that such tests do not ask: how do you see the world and how do you look at things? – since few adults, fewer children, and no Indian children would know what to say. The testers therefore present a picture, or a story, or pages with vague inkblots on them, and say: what do you see in *this*? – a procedure which makes the child forget his reality, and yet unconsciously give away his disappointments, his wishes, and, above all, his basic attitude towards human existence.

Dakota children, so their testers saw after careful quantitative analysis of the themes produced and the apperceptions revealed, describe the world as dangerous and hostile. Affectionate relationships in early home-life are remembered with nostalgia. Otherwise the world for them seems to have little definiteness and little purpose. In their stories the characters are not named, there is no clear-cut action and no definite outcome. Correspondingly, caution and negativism become the major characteristics of the utterances of the group as a whole. Their guilt and their anger are expressed in stories of petty and trivial criticism, of aimless slapping or of impulsive stealing, just for vengeance. Like all children, they like stories in which to escape from the present, but the Dakota child's imaginativeness returns to the time before the coming of the white man. Fantasies of the old life 'are not recounted as past glories but as satisfactions that may return to make up for the hardships and fears of the present'. In the children's stories, action is mostly initiated by others, and it is mostly inconsiderate, untrustworthy, and hostile action, leading to fights and to the destruction of toys and property, and causing in the narrator sadness, fear, and anger. The narrator's action leads almost always to fighting, damaging of property, breaking of rules, and stealing. Animals, too, are represented as frightening, and this not only in the traditional cases of rattlesnakes, roaming dogs, and vicious bulls, but also in that of horses, which these children, in actuality, learn to handle early and with pleasure. In the frequency of themes, worry about the death of other people, their sickness, or their departure, is second only to descriptions of hostility emanating from people or from animals. On the positive side there is the universal wish to go to movies, fairs, and rodeos, where (as the testers interpret it) children can be with many without being with anybody in particular.

The study concludes that the children in the earliest age-group tested (6 to 8) promise better-organized personalities than they will later have; that the group from 9 to 12 seem relatively the freest, the most at ease with themselves, although already behind white children in exuberance and vivacity; and that with the advent of puberty, the children begin to retire more completely within themselves and to lose interest in the world around them. They resign themselves and become apathetic and passive. The boys, however, show more expression and ambition, though in a somewhat unbalanced way; while the girls, as they enter pubescence, are prone to display agitation, followed by a kind of paralysis of action. In adolescence, stealing triples and the fear of the ill will of society seems to include elders and institutions, white and Indian.

In view of all of these observations it is hard to see how Mac-Gregor's group can have come to their main conclusion, namely, that the 'crippled and negative' state of Dakota child personality, and its rejection of life, emotion, and spontaneity, are due to 'repressive forces set in action early in the child's life'. My conclusion would be, as before, that early childhood among the Dakota, within the limits of poverty and general listlessness, is a relatively rich and spontaneous existence which permits the school child to emerge from the family with a relative integration – i.e., with much trust, a little autonomy, and some initiative. This initiative between the ages of nine and twelve is still naïvely and not too successfully applied to play and work; while it becomes inescapably clear only in puberty that what initiative has been salvaged will not find an identity. Emotional withdrawal and general absenteeism are the results.

MacGregor's material makes it particularly clear and significant that the breakdown of the respect-relationships, together with the absence of goals for initiative, leaves unused and undiverted the infantile rage which is still provoked in early child-training. The result is apathy and depression. Similarly, without the balance of attainable rewards, shaming becomes a mere sadistic habit, done for vengeance rather than for guidance.

The view of the adult world as hostile, understandable as it is on grounds of social reality, seems to have received a powerful reinforcement from the projection of the child's inner rage – which is why the environment is pictured not only as forbidding but also as destructive, while loved ones are in danger of departing or dying. Here I feel strongly that the Dakota child now *projects* where in his old system he *diverted*. A striking example would be the horse, once a friendly animal, which here becomes the object of projection. But at the same time it seems to me to be the now hopelessly misplaced and distorted original image of an inimical beast of prey. In the buffalo days, as we saw, there was an animal on whom all the early provoked affective imagery of hunting and killing could be concentrated. There is now no goal for such initiative. Thus the individual becomes afraid of his own unused power of aggression, and such fear expresses itself in his seeing, outside of himself, dangers which do not exist, or which are exaggerated in fantasy. In social reality impulsive and vengeful stealing finally becomes the lone expression of that 'grasping and biting' ferocity which once was the well-guided force behind hunting and warring. The fear of the relatives' death or departure is probably a sign of the fact that the home, with all its poverty, represents the remnant of a once integrated culture; even as a mere dream of restoration it has more reality – than reality. It is, then, not this system of training as such and its 'repressive forces' which stunt the child, but the fact that for the last hundred years the integrative mechanisms of child-training have not been encouraged to sustain a new promising system of significant social roles, as they had done once before when the Dakota became buffalo hunters.

The cattle economy, we are happy to hear from MacGregor, is making consistent progress, together with the rehabilitation of the soil and the return of the high grass. However, the establishment of a healthy cattle economy again called for government rations, which, with the forgetful advance of history, are losing their original character of a right acquired by treaty and are becoming common dole. Industrial opportunities still call the Indian away from a consistent concentration on his communal rehabilitation, while they offer the shiftless Indian only the lower identities in the American success-system. But at least they pay well, and they pay for work rendered, not for battles lost in the last century. In the end, with all respect and understanding for the Indian's special situation and nature, and with fervent wishes for the success of his rehabilitation, the conclusion remains inevitable that he can in the long run benefit only from a cultural and political advance of the rural poor and of the non-white population of the whole nation. Child-training systems change to advantage only where the universal trend towards larger cultural entities is sustained.

4 Fishermen Along a Salmon River

THE WORLD OF THE YUROK

For comparison and counterpoint, let us turn from the melancholy 'warriors without weapons' to a tribe of fishermen and acorn gatherers on the Pacific coast: the Yurok.[1]

The Sioux and the Yurok seem to have been diametrically opposite in the basic configurations of existence. The Sioux roamed the plains and cultivated spatial concepts of centrifugal mobility; their horizons were the roaming herds of buffalo and the shifting enemy bands. The Yurok lived in a narrow, mountainous, densely forested river valley and along the coast of its outlet into the Pacific. Moreover, they limited themselves within the arbitrary borders of a circumscribed universe.[2] They considered a disc of about 150 miles in diameter, cut in half by the course of their Klamath River, to include all there was to this world. They ignored the rest and ostracized as 'crazy' or 'of ignoble birth' anyone who showed a marked tendency to venture into territories beyond. They prayed to their horizons, which they thought contained the supernatural 'homes' from which generous spirits sent the stuff of life to them: the (actually non-existent) lake upriver whence the Klamath flows; the land across the ocean which is the salmon's home; the region of the sky which sends the deer; and the place up the coast where the shell money comes from. There was no centrifugal east and west, south and north. There was an 'upstream' and a 'downstream', a 'towards the river', and an 'away from the river', and then, at the borders of the world (i.e., where the next tribes live), an elliptical 'in back and around': as centripetal a world as could be designed.

[1] A. L. Kroeber, 'The Yurok', in *Handbook of the Indians of California*, Bureau of American Ethnology, Bulletin 78, 1925.
[2] T. T. Waterman, *Yurok Geography*, University of California Press, 1920.

Within this restricted radius of existence, extreme localization took place. An old Yurok asked me to drive him to his ancestors' home. When we arrived, he proudly pointed to a hardly noticeable pit in the ground and said: 'This is where I come from.' Such pits retain the family name for ever. In fact, Yurok localities exist by name only in so far as human history or mythology has dignified them. These myths do not mention mountain peaks or the gigantic redwoods which impress white travellers so much; yet the Yurok will point to certain insignificant-looking rocks and trees as being the 'origin' of the most far-reaching events. The acquisition and retention of possessions is and was what the Yurok thinks about, talks about, and prays for. Every person, every relationship, and every act can be exactly valued and becomes the object of pride or ceaseless bickering. The Yurok had money before they ever saw a white man. They used a currency of shells of different sizes which they carried in oblong purses. These shells were traded from inland tribes; the Yurok, of course, never 'strayed' near the places on the northern coast where they could have found these shells in inflationary numbers.

This little, well-defined Yurok world, cut in two by the Klamath, has, as it were, its 'mouth open' towards the ocean and the yearly mysterious appearance of tremendous numbers of powerful salmon which enter the estuary of the Klamath, climb its turbulent rapids, and disappear upriver, where they spawn and die. Some months later their diminutive progeny descend the river and disappear out in the ocean, in order that two years later, as mature salmon, they may return to their birthplace to fulfil their life cycles.

The Yurok speak of 'clean' living, not of 'strong' living as do the Sioux. Purity consists of continuous avoidance of impure contacts and contaminations, and of constant purification from possible contaminations. Having had intercourse with a woman, or having slept in the same house with women, the fisherman must pass the 'test' of the sweat house. He enters through the normal-sized door: normal meaning an oval hole through which even a fat person could enter. However, the man can leave the sweat house only through a very small opening which will permit only a man moderate in his eating habits and supple with the perspiration caused by the sacred fire to slip through. He is required to conclude the purification by swimming in the river. The conscientious fisherman passes this test every morning.

This is only one example of a series of performances which express a world image in which the various channels of nature and anatomy must be kept apart. For that which flows in one channel of life is said to abhor contaminating contact with the objects of other channels. Salmon and the river dislike it if anything is eaten on a boat. Urine must not enter the river. Deer will stay away from the snare if deer meat has been brought in contact with water. Salmon demands that women on their trip up or down river keep special observances, for they may be menstruating.

Only once a year, during the salmon run, are these avoidances set aside. At that time, following complicated ceremonies, a strong dam is built which obstructs the ascent of the salmon and permits the Yurok to catch a rich winter supply. The dam building is 'the largest mechanical enterprise undertaken by the Yurok, or, for that matter, by any California Indians, and the most communal attempt' (Kroeber). After ten days of collective fishing, orgies of ridicule and of sexual freedom take place along the sides of the river, reminiscent of the ancient pagan spring ceremonials in Europe, and of Sioux licence before the Sun Dance.

The supreme ceremony of the fish dam is thus the counterpart of the Sioux's Sun Dance; it begins with a grandiose mass dramatization of the creation of the world, and it contains pageants which repeat the progress of Yurok ethos from centrifugal licence to the circumscribed centripetality which finally became its law and its reassurance of continued supply from the Supernatural Providers.

To these ceremonials we shall return when we can relate them to Yurok babyhood. What has been said will be sufficient to indicate that in size and structure the Yurok world was very different from – if not in almost systematic opposition to – that of the Sioux.

And what different people they are, even today! After having seen the apathetic erstwhile masters of the prairie, it was almost a relief, albeit a relief paired with shock, on arrival at a then nearly inaccessible all-Yurok village, to be treated as a member of an unwelcome white minority and to be told to go and room with the pigs – 'they are the white man's dog'.

There are several all-Yurok villages along the lower Klamath, the largest representing a late integration, in the Gold Rush days, of a number of very old villages. Situated on a sunny clearing, it is accessible only by motorboat from the coast, or over foggy, hazardous roads. When I undertook to spend a few weeks there in order to collect and check my data concerning Yurok childhood, I met immediately with the 'resistive and suspicious temperament' which the Yurok as a group are supposed to have. Luckily I had met and had worked with some Yurok individuals living near the estuary of the Klamath; and Kroeber had prepared me for folkways of stinginess, suspicion, and anger. I could therefore refrain from holding their behaviour against them – or, indeed, from being discouraged by it. So I settled down in an abandoned camp by the river and waited to find out what might in this case be specifically the matter. It appeared that, at the coast, I had visited and had eaten meals with deadly enemies of an influential upriver family. The feud dated back to the eighties of the last century. Furthermore, it seemed that this isolated community was unable to accept my declaration of scientific intention. Instead, they suspected me of being an agent come to investigate such matters as the property feuds brought about by the discussion of the Howard-Wheeler Act. According to ancient maps, existing only in people's minds, Yurok territory is a jigsaw puzzle of community land, land with common ownership, and individual family property. Opposition to the Howard-Wheeler Act, which forbids the Indians to sell their land except to one another, had taken the form of disputing what the single Yurok could claim and sell if and when the act should be repealed, and one of my suspected secret missions apparently was that of trying under false pretences to delineate property rights which the officials had been unable to establish. In addition, the fatal illness of a young Shaker and the visit of high Shaker clergy from the north had precipitated religious issues. Noisy praying and dancing filled the night air. Shakerism was opposed at the time not only by the government doctor, which whom I had been seen downriver, and by the few survivors of the ancient craft of Yurok medicine, but also by a

153

newly arrived missionary. He was a Seventh-Day Adventist, the only other white man in the community, who by greeting me kindly, although with undisguised disapproval of the cigarette in my hand, compromised me further in the eyes of the natives. It took days of solitary waiting before I could discuss their suspicions with some of the Indians, and before I found informants who further clarified the outlines of traditional Yurok childhood. Once he knows you are a friend, however, the individual Yurok loses his prescribed suspicion and becomes a dignified informant.

The unsubdued and overtly cynical attitude of most Yurok towards the white man must, I think, be attributed to the fact that the inner distance between Yurok and whites is not as great as that between whites and Sioux. There was much in the centripetal ABC of Yurok life that did not have to be relearned when the whites came. The Yurok lived in solid frame-houses which were half sunk in the ground. The present frame-houses are next to pits in the ground which once contained the subterranean dwellings of ancestors. Unlike the Sioux, who suddenly lost the focus of his economic and spiritual life with the disappearance of the buffalo, the Yurok still sees and catches, eats and talks salmon. When the Yurok man today steers a raft of logs, or the Yurok woman grows vegetables, their occupations are not far removed from the original manufacture of dugouts (a one-time export industry), the gathering of acorns, and the planting of tobacco. Above all, the Yurok has been concerned all his life with property. He knows how to discuss a matter in dollars and cents, and he does so with deep ritual conviction. The Yurok need not abandon this 'primitive' tendency in the money-minded white world. His grievances against the United States thus find other than the inarticulate, smouldering expression of the prairie man's passive resistance.

On the Fourth of July, when 'the mourners of the year' were paid off in an all-night dance ritual, I had the opportunity to see many children assembled to watch a dance, the climax of which was not scheduled until dawn. They were vigorous and yet graceful, even-tempered, and well-behaved throughout the long night.

Fanny, one of Alfred Kroeber's oldest informants, called herself, and was called by others, a 'doctor'. So far as she treated somatic disorders or used the Yurok brand of physiological treatment, I could not claim to be her professional equal. However, she also did psychotherapy with children, and in this field it was possible to exchange notes. She laughed heartily about psychoanalysis, the main therapeutic principles of which, as will be shown presently, can easily be expressed in her terms. There was a radiant friendliness and warmth in this very old woman. When melancholy made her glance and her smile withdraw behind the stone-carved pattern of her wrinkles, it was a dramatic melancholy, a positive withdrawal, not the immovable sadness sometimes seen in the faces of other Indian women.

As a matter of fact, Fanny was in an acute state of gloom when we arrived. Some days before, on stepping out into her vegetable garden and glancing over the scene, a hundred feet below, where the Klamath enters the Pacific, she had seen a small whale enter the river, play about a little and disappear again. This shocked her deeply. Had not the creator decreed that only salmon, sturgeon, and similar fish should cross the fresh-water barrier? This breakdown of a barrier could only mean that the world disc was slowly losing its horizontal position, that salt water was entering the river, and that a flood was approaching comparable to the one which once before had destroyed mankind. However, she told only a few intimates about it, indicating that perhaps the event could still become untrue if not talked about too much.

It was easy to converse with this old Indian woman because usually she was merry and quite direct, except when questions came up bordering on taboo subjects. During our first interviews Kroeber had sat behind us, listening and now and again interrupting. On the second day, I suddenly noticed that he was absent from the room for some time, and I asked where he had gone. The old woman laughed merrily, and said, 'He give you chance to ask alone. You big man now.'

What are the causes of child neuroses (bad temper, lack of appetite, nightmares, delinquency, etc.) in Yurok culture? If a child, after dark, sees one of the 'wise people', a race of small beings which preceded the human race on earth, he develops a neurosis, and if he is not cured he eventually dies.

The 'wise people' are described as not taller than a small child. They are always 'in spirit', because they do not know sexual intercourse. They are adult at six months of age, and they are immortal. They procreate orally, the female eating the male's lice. The orifice of birth is unclear; however, it is certain that the 'wise' female has not a 'woman's inside' – that is, vagina and uterus, with the existence of which, as will be shown later, sin and social disorder entered the world.

We observe that the 'wise people' are akin to infants. They are small, oral, and magic, and they do not know genitality, guilt, and death. They are visible and dangerous only for children because children are still fixated on earlier stages and may regress when the stimulation of the daylight is waning – then, becoming dreamy, they may be attracted by the 'wise people's' childishness and by their intuitive and yet anarchic ways. For the 'wise people' are without social organization. They are creative, but they know no genitality and, consequently, what it means to be 'clean'. Thus the 'wise' men could well serve the projection of the pregenital state of childhood into phylogeny and prehistory.

If a child shows disturbances or complains of pain indicating that he may have seen 'wise people', his grandmother goes out in the garden or to the creek, or wherever she has been informed that the child has played after dark, cries aloud, and speaks to the spirits: 'This is our child; do not harm it.' If this is of no avail, the grandmother next door is asked to 'sing her song' to the child. Every grandmother has her own song. American Indian cultures seem to have an amazing understanding of ambivalence, which dictates that in certain crises near relatives are of no educational or therapeutic use. If the neighbour grandmother does not avail, Fanny is finally appealed to and a price is set for the cure.

Fanny says she often feels that a patient is coming:

Sometimes I can't sleep; somebody is after me to go and doctor. I not drink water, and sure somebody come. 'Fanny, I come after you, I give you ten dollars.' I say, 'I go for fifteen dollars.' 'All right.'

The child is brought by his whole family and put on the floor of Fanny's living-room. She smokes her pipe to 'get into her power'. Then, if necessary, the child is held down by mother and father while Fanny sucks the first 'pain' from above the child's navel. These 'pains', the somatic 'causes' of illness (although they, in turn, can be caused by bad wishes), are visualized as a kind of slimy, bloody materialization. To prepare herself for this task Fanny must abstain from water for a given period. 'As she sucks, it is as if her chin were going through to your spine, but it doesn't hurt,' one informant reports. However, every 'pain' has a 'mate'; a thread of slime leads Fanny to the place of the 'mate', which is sucked out also.

We see that to the Yurok disease is bisexual. One sex is represented as being near the centre of the body, which is most susceptible to sorcery, while the other has wandered to the afflicted part, like the floating uterus in the Greek theory of hysteria or the displaced organ cathexis in the psychoanalytic system.

Having swallowed two or three 'pains', Fanny goes to a corner and sits down with her face to the wall. She puts four fingers, omitting the thumb, into her throat and vomits slime into a basket. Then, when she feels that the 'pains' she has swallowed are coming up, she holds her hands in front of her mouth, 'like two shells', and with spitting noises spits the child's 'pain' into her hands. Then she dances, making the 'pains' disappear. This she repeats until she feels that all the 'pains' have been taken out of the child.

Then comes the Yurok version of an interpretation. She smokes again, dances again, and goes into a trance. She sees a fire, a cloud, a mist, then sits down, fills her pipe anew, takes a big mouthful of smoke, and then has a more substantial vision, which makes her say to the assembled family something like this: 'I see an old woman sitting in the Bald Hills and wishing something bad to another woman. That is why this child is sick.' She has hardly spoken when the grandmother of the child rises and confesses that it was she who on a certain day sat in the Bald Hills and tried to practise sorcery upon another woman. Or Fanny says, 'I see a man and a woman doing business [having intercourse], although the man has prayed for good luck and should not touch a woman.' At this, the father or the uncle gets up and confesses to his guilt. Sometimes Fanny has to accuse a dead person of sorcery or perversion, in which event the son or the daughter of the deceased tearfully confesses to his misdeeds.

It seems that Fanny has a certain inventory of sins (comparable to the 'typical events' of our psychotherapeutic schools), which she attaches, under ritualistic circumstances, to a certain disturbance. She thus makes people confess as facts tendencies which, in view of the structure of the culture, can be predicted, and the confession of which is profitable for anybody's inner peace. Having an exalted position in a primitive community, Fanny is, of course, in possession of enough gossip to know her patients' weaknesses even before she sees them and is experienced enough to read her patients' faces while she goes about her magic business. If she, then, connects a feeling of guilt derived from secret aggression or perversion with the child's symptoms, she is on good psychopathological grounds, and we are not surprised to hear that neurotic symptoms usually disappear after Fanny has put her finger on the main source of ambivalence in the family and has provoked a confession in public.

YUROK CHILD-TRAINING

Here are the data on childhood in the Yurok world.

The birth of a baby is safeguarded with *oral* prohibitions in addition to the genital ones observed by the Sioux. During the birth, the mother must shut her mouth. Father and mother eat neither deer meat nor salmon until the child's navel is healed. Disregard of this taboo, so the Yurok believed, is the cause of convulsions in the child.

The newborn is not breast-fed for ten days, but is given a nut soup from a tiny shell. The breast feeding begins with Indian generosity and frequency. However, unlike the Sioux, the Yurok have a definite weaning time around the sixth month – that is, around the teething period: a minimal breast-feeding period for American Indians. Weaning is called 'forgetting the mother' and, if necessary, is enforced towards the end of the first year by the mother's going away for a few days. The first solid food is salmon or deer meat well salted with seaweed. Salty foods are the Yurok's 'sweets'. The attempt at accelerating autonomy by early weaning seems to be part of a general tendency to encourage the baby to leave the mother and her support as soon as this is possible and bearable. It begins *in utero*. The pregnant woman eats little, carries much wood, and preferably does work which forces her to bend over forward, so that the foetus 'will not rest against her spine' – i.e., relax and recline. She rubs her abdomen often, especially when daylight is waning, in order to keep the foetus awake, and to forestall an early tendency to regress to the state of prehistory which, as we saw, is the origin of all neuroses. Later, not only does early weaning further require him to release his mother; the baby's legs are left uncovered in the Yurok version of the cradleboard, and from the twentieth day on they are massaged by the grandmother to encourage early creeping. The parents' cooperation in this matter is assured by the rule that they may resume intercourse when the baby makes vigorous strides in creeping. The baby is kept from sleeping in the late afternoon and early evening, lest dusk close his eyes for ever. The first postnatal crisis, therefore, has a different quality for the Yurok child from the one experienced by the little Sioux. It is characterized by the close proximity in time of teething, enforced weaning, encouraged creeping, and the mother's early return to old sex ways and new childbirths.

We have referred to the affinity between the Sioux baby's oral training and the desirable traits of a hunter of the plains; and we would expect the Yurok newborn to find a systematically different reception. And, indeed, the Yurok child is exposed to early and, if necessary, abrupt weaning before or right after the development of the biting stage, and this after being discouraged by a number of devices from feeling too comfortable in, with, and around his mother. He is to be trained to be a fisherman: one who has his nets ready for a prey which (if he only behaves nicely and says 'please' appropriately) will come to him. The Yurok attitude towards supernatural providers is a lifelong fervent 'please' which seems to be reinforced by a residue of infantile nostalgia for the mother from whom he has been disengaged so forcefully. The good Yurok is characterized by an ability to cry while he prays in order to gain influence over the food-sending powers beyond the visible world. Tearful words, such as 'I see a salmon', said with the conviction of self-induced hallucination, will, so he believes, draw a salmon towards him.

But he must pretend that he is not too eager, lest the supply elude him, and he must convince himself that he means no real harm. According to the Yurok, the salmon says: 'I shall travel as far as the river extends. I shall leave my scales on nets and they will turn into salmon, but I, myself, shall go by and not be killed.'

This concentration on the sources of food is not accomplished without a second phase of oral training at the age when the child 'has sense' – i.e., when he can repeat what he has been told. It is claimed that once upon a time, a Yurok meal was a veritable ceremony of self-restraint. The child was admonished never to grab food in haste, never to take it without asking for it, always to eat slowly, and never to ask for a second helping – an oral puritanism hardly equalled among other primitives. During meals, a strict order of placement was maintained and the child was taught to eat in prescribed ways; for example, to put only a little food on the spoon, to take the spoon up to his mouth slowly, to put the spoon down while chewing the food – and above all, to think of becoming rich during the whole process. There was supposed to be silence during meals so that everybody could keep his thoughts concentrated on money and salmon. This ceremonial behaviour may well have served to lift to the level of a kind of hallucination that nostalgic need for intake which may have been evoked by the early weaning from the breast and from contact with the mother, at the stage of strong biting wishes. All 'wishful thinking' was put in the service of economic pursuits. A Yurok could make himself see money hanging from trees and salmon swimming in the river during the off-season, and he believed that this self-induced hallucinatory thought would bring action from the Providers. Later, the energy of genital day-dreams is also harnessed to the same economic endeavour. In the 'sweat house' the older boy will learn the dual feat of thinking of money and *not* thinking of women.

The fables told to children underline in an interesting way the ugliness of lack of restraint. They isolate one outstanding item in the physiognomy of animals and use it as an argument for 'clean behaviour':

The buzzard's baldness is the result of his having impatiently put his whole head into a dish of hot soup.

The greedy eel gambled his bones away.

The hood of the ever-scolding blue jay is her clitoris, which she tore off and put on her head once when she was enviously angry with her husband.

The bear was always hungry. He was married to the blue jay. One day they made a fire and the bear sent the blue jay to get some food. She brought back only one acorn. 'Is that all?' the bear said. The blue jay got angry and threw the acorn in the fire. It popped all over the place, and there was acorn all over the ground. The bear swallowed it all down and got awfully sick. Some birds tried to sing for him, but it did not help. Nothing helped. Finally the hummingbird said, 'Lie down and open your mouth,' and then the hummingbird zipped right through him. This relieved him. That's why the bear has such a big anus and can't hold his faeces.

This, then, leads us to the anal phase. In Yurok childhood, there seems to be no specific emphasis on faeces or on the anal zone, but there is a general avoidance of all contaminations caused by the contact of antagonistic fluids and contents. The infant learns early that he may not urinate into the river or into any subsidiary brook because the salmon that swims in the river would not like to float in the body's fluids. The idea, then, is not so much that urine is 'dirty', but that fluids of different tube systems are antagonistic and mutually destructive. Such lifelong and systematic avoidance calls for special safeguards built into personality and identity; and, indeed, the official behaviour of the Yurok shows all the traits which psychoanalysis, following Freud and Abraham, has found to be of typical significance in patients with 'anal fixations': compulsive ritualization; pedantic bickering; suspicious miserliness; retentive hoarding, etc. Compulsiveness in our society is often the expression of just such a general avoidance of contaminations, focused by phobic mothers on the anal zone; but in our culture it is reinforced by excessive demands for a punctuality and orderliness which are absent from Yurok life.

The groundwork for the Yurok's genital attitudes is laid in the child's earlier conditioning, which teaches him to subordinate all instinctual drives to economic considerations. The girl knows that virtue, or shall we say an unblemished name, will gain her a husband who can pay well, and that her subsequent status, and consequently her children's and her children's children's status, will depend on the amount her husband will offer to her father when asking for her. The boy, on the other hand, wishes to accumulate enough wealth to buy a worth-while wife and to pay in full. If he were to make a worthy girl prematurely pregnant – i.e., before he could pay her price in full – he would have to go into debt. And among the Yurok, all deviant behaviour and character disorders in adults are explained as a result of the delinquent's mother or grandmother or great-grandmother not having been 'paid for in full'. This, it seems, means that the man in question was so eager to marry that he borrowed his wife on a down payment without being able to pay the instalments. He thus proved that in our terms his ego was too weak to integrate sexual needs and economic virtues. Where sex does not interfere with wealth, however, it is viewed with leniency and humour. The fact that sex contact necessitates purification seems to be considered a duty or a nuisance, but does not reflect on sex as such or on individual women. There is no shame concerning the surface of the human body. If the young girl between menarche and marriage avoids bathing in the nude before others, it is to avoid offending by giving evidence of menstruation. Otherwise, everybody is free to bathe as he pleases in whatever company.

As we have seen, Sioux children learned to associate the locomotor and genital modes with hunting. The Sioux, in his official sexuality, was more phallic–sadistic in that he pursued whatever roamed: game, enemy, woman. The Yurok in all of this is more phobic and suspicious. He avoids being snared. For it even happened to God: the creator of the Yurok world was an extraordinarily lusty fellow who roamed around and endangered the world with his lawless behaviour. His sons prevailed upon him to leave this world. He promised to be a good god, but as he ventured down the coast farther than any sensible and well-bred person would do, he found the skate woman lying on the beach, invitingly spreading her legs. (The skatefish, the Yurok say, look like 'a woman's inside'.) He could not resist her. But as soon as he had entered her, she held on to him with her vagina, wrapped her legs around him, and abducted him. This story serves to demonstrate where centrifugal wandering, and lawless lust will lead. In the lawfully restricted Yurok world which was established by the delinquent creator's overconscientious sons, a sensible man avoids being 'snared' by the wrong woman or at the wrong time or place – 'wrong' meaning any circumstances that would compromise his assets as an economic being. To learn to avoid this means to become a 'clean' individual, an individual with 'sense'.

COMPARATIVE SUMMARY

The worlds of the Sioux and the Yurok are primitive worlds according to the criteria employed earlier. They are highly ethnocentric, only concerned with tribal self-regulation in relation to a specific segment of nature, and with the development of sufficient tools and appropriate magic. We have found the Yurok world to be oriented along cautiously centripetal lines, whereas we found the Sioux to be vigorously centrifugal.

As a society the Yurok had almost no hierarchic organization. All emphasis was on mutual vigilance in the daily observance of minute differences of value. There was little 'national' feeling, and, as I have neglected to point out, no taste for war whatsoever. Just as the Yurok could believe that seeing salmon meant making salmon come, he obviously also took it for granted that he could keep war away by simply not seeing potential enemies. Upriver Yurok are known to have ignored hostile tribes who traversed their territory in order to fight downriver Yurok. War was a matter of those concerned directly, not one of national or tribal loyalty.

Thus they felt secure in a system of avoidances: avoidance of being drawn into a fight, into a contamination, into a bad business deal. Their individual lives began with an early banishment from the mother's breast, and with subsequent instruction (for boys) to avoid her, to keep out of her living quarters, and to beware of snaring women in general. Their mythology banishes the creator from this world by having him snared and abducted by a woman. While the fear of being caught thus dominated their avoidances, they lived every moment for the purpose of snatching an advantage from another human being.

In the Yurok world, the Klamath River may be likened to a nutritional canal, and its estuary to a mouth and throat for ever opened towards the horizon whence the salmon come; their world-image thus starkly suggests the oral mode of incorporation. All through the year the prayers of the Yurok world go out in that direction, protesting humility and denying the wish to hurt. Once a year, however, the Yurok tearfully lure their god back into this world just long enough to assure his good will – and to snare his salmon. As the Sioux world finds its highest expression in the performances surrounding the Sun Dance, the Yurok world dramatizes all it stands for during those exalted days when, with utmost communal effort and organization, it builds the fish dam: gradually closing, as if they were gigantic jaws, the two parts extended from the opposite shores of the river. The jaws close and the prey is trapped. The creator once more rejuvenates the world by grudgingly bequeathing it parts of himself, only to be banished for another year. Again, as in the case of the Sioux, this ceremonial climax follows a cycle of rituals which deals with the dependence of the people on supernatural providers. At the same time, the ceremonial represents a grandiose collective play with the themes of earliest danger in the individual life cycle: the ontogenic loss of the mother's breast at the biting stage corresponds to the phylogenetic danger of possible loss of the salmon supply from across the ocean. Here the conclusion is inevitable that the great themes of fertility and fecundity find their symbolic expression in an equation of the sacred salmon with the paternal phallus and the maternal nipple: the organ which generates life and that which nurtures it.

During the rejuvenation festivals – that is when their prayer was reinforced by technological teeth – the Yurok were not permitted to cry, for anyone who cried would not be alive in a year. Instead, 'the end of the dam building is a period of freedom. Jokes, ridicule, and abuse run riot; sentiment forbids offence; and as night comes, lovers' passions are inflamed' (Kroeber). This one time, then, the Yurok behaved as licentiously as his phallic creator, proud that by an ingenious mixture of engineering and atonement he had again accomplished the feat of his world: to catch his salmon – and have it next year, too.

To be properly avoidant and yet properly avid, the individual Yurok must be *clean*; i.e., he must pray with humility, cry with faith, and hallucinate with conviction, as far as the Supernatural Providers are concerned; he must learn to make good nets, to locate them well, and to collaborate in the fish dam, as his technology requires; he must trade and haggle with stamina and persistence when engaged in business with his fellow men; and he must learn to master his body's entrances, exits, and interior tubeways in such a manner that nature's fluid-ways and supply routes (which are not accessible to scientific understanding and technical influence) will find themselves magically coerced. In the Yurok world, then, homogeneity rests on an integration of economic ethics and magic morality with geographic and physiological configurations. We have outlined in what way this integration is prepared in the training of the young organism.[3]

In trying to gain access to the meaning, or even the mere configurations, of Yurok behaviour we have not been able to avoid analogies with what is considered deviant or extreme behaviour in our culture. Within his everyday behaviour the Yurok cries to his gods 'like a baby'; he hallucinates in his meditation 'like a psychotic'; he acts 'like a phobic' when confronted with contamination; and he tries to act avoidant, suspicious, and stingy 'like a compulsive neurotic'. Am I trying to say that the Yurok *is* all of this or that he behaves '*as if*'?

The anthropologist who has lived long enough among a people can tell us what his informants care to enlarge upon, and whether what the people are said to be doing actually corresponds to what can be observed in daily and yearly life. Observations which would indicate whether or not traditional traits, such as nostalgia or avarice or retentiveness, are also dominant personal traits in typical individuals are still rare. Take the Yurok's ability to pantomime a crying helpless being or a deeply grieved mourner. True, in characterizing the Yurok's institutionalized claiming of recompense, Kroeber, during a few minutes of one seminar evening, used the expressions 'whining around', 'fussing', 'bickering', 'crying out', 'self-pity', 'excuses a child might give', 'claimants who make nuisances of themselves', etc. Does this mean that the Yurok anywhere within his technology is more helpless, more paralysed by sadness, than are members of a tribe which does not develop these 'traits'? Certainly not; his institutionalized helplessness *eo ipso* is neither a trait nor a neurotic symptom. It does not interfere with the individual's

[3] For a more detailed analysis of the Yurok world see E. H. Erikson, *Observations on the Yurok: Childhood and World Image*, University of California Publications in American Archaeology and Ethnology, Vol. 35, No. 10, University of California Press, 1943.

efficiency in meeting technological demands which were adequate for the segment of nature within which the Yurok lives. His crying is based on the learned and conditioned ability to dramatize an infantile attitude which the culture chooses to preserve and to put at the disposal of the individual, to be used by him and his fellow men within the limited area of magic. Such an institutionalized attitude neither spreads beyond its defined area nor makes impossible the development to full potency of its opposite. It is probable that the really successful Yurok was the one who could cry most heartbreakingly or haggle most effectively in some situations and be full of fortitude in others – that is, the Yurok whose ego was strong enough to synthesize orality and 'sense'. In comparison, oral and anal 'types' whom we may be able to observe today in our culture are bewildered people who find themselves victims of over-developed organ modes without the corresponding homogeneous cultural reality.

The configuration of Yurok retentiveness seems to be as alimentary as it is anal: it includes the demanding mouth and the storing stomach as well as the stingy sphincters. It thus is prototypal also for the anal tendency to accumulate creatively for the sake of making the most of the collected values which belong to the whole social system, where they in turn give communal pleasure, prestige, and permanence.

Where the anal character in our culture approaches the neurotic, it often appears to be a result of the impact on a retentive child of a certain type of maternal behaviour in Western civilization, namely, a narcissistic and phobic over-concern with matters of elimination. This attitude helps to over-develop retentive and eliminative potentialities and to fixate them in the anal zone. It creates strong social ambivalence in the child, and it remains an isolating factor in his social and sexual development.

The Yurok's 'pleasure of final evacuation and exhibition of stored-up material' is most conspicuous at dances, when, to-wards morning, the Yurok with a glowing face produces his fabulous treasures of obsidian or of headwear ornamented with woodpecker scalps. Here, the institutionalized obstinacy which made it possible for him to accumulate these treasures seems counteracted by the highly social experience of seeing his treasures enhance the prestige of the whole tribe. What I am arguing here is that neurosis is an individual state in which irrational trends are irreconcilably split off from a relatively advanced rationality; while primitivity is a state of human organization in which pre-rational thinking is integrated with whatever rationality is made possible by the technology.

Because both irrational and pre-rational 'logic' makes use of magical images and impulses, Freud could shed light on the second as he deciphered the first; but the study of the ego – and that is, to me, the study of the interdependence of inner and social organization – must as yet determine the function of magic thinking in different human states.

Furthermore, if we know the official behaviour required for successful participation in the traditional spectacle of a certain culture, we stand only at the beginning of the inquiry into the 'character' of individuals: for to know how generous or how thrifty a people or an individual 'is', we must know not only what the verbalized and the implied values of his culture are, but also what provisions are made for an individual's 'getting away' with transgressions. Each system, in its own way, tends to make similar people out of all its members, but each in a specific way also permits exemptions and deductions from the demands with which it thus taxes the individuality of the individual ego. It stands to reason that these exemptions are less logical and much less obvious, even to the people themselves, than are the official rules.

Let it be stated, then, that in describing conceptual and behavioural configurations in the Yurok and in the Sioux world, we have not attempted to establish their respective 'basic character structures'. Rather, we have concentrated on the configurations with which these two tribes try to synthesize their concepts and their ideals in a coherent design for living. This design inculcates efficiency in their primitive ways of technology and magic and protects them from individual anxiety which might lead to panic: the anxiety among the Plains hunters over emasculation and immobilization, among the Pacific fishermen over being left without provisions. To accomplish this a primitive culture seems to use childhood in a number of ways: it gives specific meanings to early bodily and interpersonal experience in order to create the right combination of organ modes and the proper emphasis on social modalities; it carefully and systematically channelizes throughout the intricate pattern of its daily life the energies thus provoked and deflected; and it gives consistent supernatural meaning to the infantile anxieties which it has exploited by such provocation.

In doing all this, a society cannot afford to be arbitrary and anarchic. Even 'primitive' societies must avoid doing just what our analogistic thinking would have them do. They cannot afford to create a community of wild eccentrics, of infantile characters, or of neurotics. In order to create people who will function effectively as the bulk of the people, as energetic leaders, or as useful deviants, even the most 'savage' culture must strive for what we vaguely call a 'strong ego' in its majority or at least in its dominant minority – i.e., an individual core firm and flexible enough to reconcile the necessary contradictions in any human organization, to integrate individual differences, and above all to emerge from a long and unavoidably fearful infancy with a sense of identity and an idea of integrity. Undoubtedly each culture also creates character types marked by its own mixture of defect and excess; and each culture develops rigidities and illusions which protect it against the insight that no ideal, safe, permanent state can emerge from the blueprint it has gropingly evolved. Nevertheless, we may do well to try to understand the nature of these 'instinctive' blueprints, as mankind works towards a different kind of adaptation, at once more rational, more conscious and more universal.

In Part Three we will approach the whole matter of childhood and society from another angle entirely. We must temporarily take the individual ego as the apparent measure of all things, somatic and social, and this from its formless beginning to the formulated consciousness of its self.

Freud has said that the study of dreams is the royal road to the adult's unconscious. In analogy to this, the best clue to the understanding of the infantile ego is the study of the child's play – 'fantasies woven around real objects' (Waelder). Therefore let us now turn from the fateful make-believe of primitive magic to the play of the children among us.

Part Three

The Growth of the Ego

Introduction to Part Three

When, at moments of slight and vague inner disequilibrium, we stop and ask ourselves what we have daydreamed about while pursuing our rational occupations during the preceding hours, we are in for a number of surprises. Assuming that our capacity for self-perception outweighs that of self-deception, we will find that our thoughts and feelings have described a constant (more or less intense, more or less eccentric) seesaw towards and away from a state of relative equilibrium. In one direction our thoughts pursue a series of fantasies concerning things which we wish we could do or wish we had done. Often, stepping out of the confines and possibilities of our circumscribed existence, we imagine how it would have been or how it would be if and when we might come to realize certain fantasies of omnipotent control or of sovereign choice or of sexual licence. The innocence of such fancy comes to an end when in the pursuit of our daydreams we calmly ignore or blithely manipulate, accidentally damage, or consider as nonexistent, some of the people dearest to us.

The shift of the seesaw is a reduction which often follows with irrational suddenness. Without becoming aware of a change in mood, we find ourselves involved in thoughts of 'oughtness': what we ought to have done instead of what we did do; what we ought to be doing now in order to undo what we have done; and what we ought to do in the future instead of what we would wish we could do. Here again, our irrational worry over 'spilled milk', our fear of having aroused actually quite disinterested, and antagonized quite well-meaning, people, our fantasied atonements and childish repetitions, may well surprise us.

The third position, the resting-place between the extremes, is harder to remember, although it is least offensive, for in this third state we are least impulsive, neither wishing that we could, nor feeling that we ought to, do anything different from what we should and would and could do. Here, where we are least self-conscious, we are most ourselves. Only for many of us it is hard to daydream for any length of time without, sooner or later, meeting our limits or transgressing somebody else's – and then we are off again, usurping, atoning.

Thus we may be able to observe dimly what is fully revealed only in the disguise of dreams arising from deepest sleep. It is easy to say that we do not 'really mean' what is thus shown on the private screen of our inner stage. Unfortunately for our self-esteem (but in the end, we hope, for the good fortune of mankind), Freud's psychoanalytic method has shown that we are able to become conscious of, to account for, and to neutralize by fantasy, play, and dream, only a fraction of these ups and downs: the rest is both unconscious and eminently powerful. Remaining unconscious, it finds its way into irrational personal action or into collective cycles of usurpation and atonement.

The practice of psychoanalytic observation fosters the habit of searching out the points of greatest inner resistance and focusing on them. The clinical observer asks an adult patient to verbalize freely; whereupon he watches the threshold of verbalization not only for themes which cross easily in the form of straight effect, clear memory, determined statement, but also for themes which remain elusive. Such themes may alternately appear half-remembered, dreamily disguised, bitterly repudiated, brazenly projected on others, half-heartedly joked about and clumsily avoided, or followed by silent pauses. In other words, the psychoanalyst looks for disguises and omissions, and for changing quantities and qualities of awareness as expressed in seemingly willing verbalization.

In looking at *cultures*, the psychoanalytic observer weighs themes which appear on a dynamic scale of collective behaviour: in one variation as historical memory and in another as mythological theology; in one disguise re-enacted in a heavy ritual, in another as a light game, in a third entirely represented by strict avoidance. Whole complexes of such themes may be recognizable in culture-pattern dreams or in individual dreams, in humorous or hateful projections on the neighbour, on the prehuman race, or on the animal world; they may be represented in deviating behaviour open only to the select or to the damned or to both.

It is in this general way that we have arrived, in the case of the Sioux and the Yurok, at a bridge between infantile themes and themes of great communal and religious fervour. We have pointed to the fact that a Sioux Indian – at the height of his religious endeavours – drives little sticks through his breast, ties the sticks to a thong, the thong to a pole, and then, in a peculiar trance, dances backwards until the thong tightens and the sticks split his breast so that the gushing blood runs freely down his body; and we have endeavoured to find a meaning in his extreme behaviour. This ritual, we said, may be a symbolic restitution necessitated by a critical experience which once upon a time caused an intense conflict between his rage against the frustrating mother – and that part of him which forever feels dependent and in need of faith, as assured by the love of the parents in this world and the parental powers in the supernatural.

The Yurok, once a year, having organized themselves for the great engineering feat of bridging the river with a fish dam that yields a winter's food supply, indulge in promiscuous licence and throw atonement and purification to the winds – whereupon they reach a sobering stage of satiation and reinstate self-restraint which secures for one more year the divine right to pursue and snare the sacred salmon.

In both cases we suspect that the cycle of usurpation and atonement represents a collective magic means of coercing nature.

In psychoanalysis we think we have learned to understand something about this cycle, because we observe it again and again in individual histories. We have a name for the pressure of excessive wishes (the 'id') and for the oppressive force of conscience (the 'superego'), and we have appropriate theories for the two extreme stages, when people or peoples are dominated by one or the other of these forces. But if we try to define the state of relative equilibrium between the well-known extremes, if we ask what characterizes an Indian when he does no more than just calmly be an Indian, bent on the daily chores of the year's cycle, our description of this positive state is expressed only in negations. We look for small tokens of the fact that he continues to betray in minute emotional and ideational changes that same conflict which, as Freud puts it, is manifested in a change of mood from a vague anxious depression through a certain in-between stage to heightened well-being – and back. Because psychoanalysis developed as psychopathology, it had at first little to say about this 'in-between stage', except that neither a manic nor a depressive trend is, at the time, clearly noticeable; that the superego is temporarily non-belligerent, that the id has agreed to an armistice, and that a momentary lull exists on the battlefield of the ego.

Let us pause at this point to re-trace the term 'ego' to its beginnings in psychoanalysis. The id Freud considered to be the oldest province of the mind, both in individual terms – for he held the young baby to be 'all id' – and in phylogenetic terms, for the id is the deposition in us of the whole of evolutionary history. The id is everything that is left in our organization of the responses of the amoeba and of the impulses of the ape, of the blind spasms of our intra-uterine existence, and of the needs of our postnatal days – everything which would make us 'mere creatures'. The name 'id', of course, designates the assumption that the 'ego' finds itself attached to this impersonal, this bestial layer like the centaur to his equestrian underpinnings: only that the ego considers such a combination a danger and an imposition, whereas the centaur makes the most of it. The id, then, has some of the pessimistic qualities of Schopenhauer's 'will', the sum of all desire which must be overcome before we can be quite human.

The other inner institution recognized and designated by Freud is the 'super-ego', a kind of automatic governor which limits the expression of the id by opposing to it the demands of conscience. Here, too, the emphasis was at first on the foreign burden imposed on the ego by its super-ego. For this super-imposed, this superior ego was 'the (internalized) sum of all the restrictions to which the ego must bow'. But conscience, too, contains traces of the cruel forces of suppression in human history – i.e., the threat of mutilation or isolation. In moments of self-reproach and depression, the super-ego uses against the ego methods so archaic and so barbaric that they become analogous to those of the blindly impulsive id. So, too, in the cruelties of religious or political inquisition, it is hard to see where mere sadistic perversion ends and an all too hearty form of piety begins.

Between the id and the super-ego, then, the ego dwells. Consistently balancing and warding off the extreme ways of the other two, the ego keeps tuned to the reality of the historical day, testing perceptions, selecting memories, governing action, and otherwise integrating the individual's capacities of orientation and planning. To safeguard itself, the ego employs 'defence mechanisms'. These, contrary to the more colloquial way of speaking of an overtly 'defensive' attitude, are unconscious arrangements which permit the individual to postpone satisfaction, to find substitutions, and otherwise to arrive at compromises between id impulses and super-ego compulsions. Such compromises we found in Sam's 'counterphobic' defence, his proclivity to attack when he was frightened. We recognized in the Marine's all-around abstinence the defence mechanism of 'self-restriction'; and we interpreted his exaggerated goodness as 'overcompensation' for all the rage that had accumulated in his much-deprived childhood. Other defence mechanisms will be described as further cases are referred to. However, in studying this area we wish to extend our reach beyond the mere defensive aspects of the ego which have been so conclusively formulated in Anna Freud's *The Ego and the Mechanisms of Defence*:

Then ego is victorious when its defensive measures . . . enable it to restrict the development of anxiety and so to transform the instincts that, even in difficult circumstances, some measure of gratification is secured, thereby establishing the most harmonious relations possible between the id, the super-ego, and the forces of the outside world.[1]

The ego, then, is an 'inner institution' evolved to safeguard that order within individuals on which all outer order depends. It is not 'the individual', nor his individuality, although it is indispensable to it. In order to grasp the nature of this indispensability we will describe a tragic failure, a specimen of psychopathology, a description of difficult circumstances within the individual. We shall see a very young ego struggle for coherence, and fail. Turning to the play-acting of normal childhood, we shall then observe children as they temporarily fail and then lastingly succeed in overcoming the worst of their infantile anxiety.

[1] Anna Freud, *The Ego and the Mechanisms of Defence*, The Hogarth Press and the Institute of Psycho-Analysis, London, 1937.

5 Early Ego-Failure: Jean

To come face to face with a 'schizophrenic' child is one of the most awe-inspiring experiences a psychotherapist can have. It is not the bizarreness of the child's behaviour which makes the encounter so immediately challenging, but rather the very contrast of that behaviour with the appeal of some of these children. Their facial features are often regular and pleasing, their eyes are 'soulful' and seem to express deep and desperate experience, paired with a resignation which children should not have. The total impression first goes to the heart and immediately convinces the clinical observer, even against the better knowledge of previous experience, that the right person and the right therapeutic regime could bring the child back on the road to coherent progress. This conviction has the more or less explicit corollary that the child has been in the wrong hands and, in fact, has every reason to mistrust his 'rejecting' parents. (We saw how far Indians and whites would go in accusing one another of doing deliberate harm to their children; our occupational prejudice is 'the rejecting mother'.)

I first saw Jean when she was almost six years old. I did not see her at her best. She had just made a train trip, and my house was strange to her. What glimpses I could catch of her (for she was frantically on the move through garden and house) showed her to be of graceful build, but tense and abrupt in her movements. She had beautiful dark eyes which seemed like peaceful islands within the anxious grimace of her face. She ran through all the rooms of the house, uncovering all the beds she could find, as if she were looking for something. The objects of this search proved to be pillows, which she hugged and talked to in a hoarse whisper and with a hollow laugh.

Yes, Jean was 'schizophrenic'. Her human relationships were centrifugal, away from people. I had observed this strange phenomenon of a 'centrifugal approach', often interpreted as mere lack of contact, years before in the behaviour of another little girl who was said to 'notice nobody'. When that little girl came down a flight of stairs towards me, her glance drifted in an absent way over a series of objects, describing concentric circles around my face. She focused on me negatively, as it were. This flight is the common denominator for a variety of other symptoms, such as the preoccupation with things far away and imagined; the inability to concentrate on any task at hand; violent objection to all close contact with others unless they fit into some imaginary scheme; and immediate diffused flight from verbal communication, when it happens to become nearly established. Meaning is quickly replaced by parrotlike repetition of stereotyped phrases, accompanied by guttural sounds of despair.

The observation that Jean, on her mad rush through my house, again and again paused long enough to concentrate her attention and to lavish her affection on bed pillows seemed significant for the following reason. Her mother had told me that Jean's extreme disorientation had begun after the mother had become bedridden with tuberculosis. She was permitted to stay at home in her own room, but the child could speak to her only through the doorway of her bedroom, from the arms of a good-natured but 'tough' nurse. During this period the mother had the impression that there were things which the child urgently wanted to tell her. The mother regretted at the time that, shortly before her illness, she had let Jean's original nurse, a gentle Mexican girl, leave them. Hedwig, so the mother anxiously noticed from her bed, was always in a hurry, moved the baby about with great energy, and was very emphatic in her disapprovals and warnings. Her favourite remark was, 'Ah, baby, you stink!' and her holy war was her effort to keep the creeping infant off the floor so that she would not be contaminated by dirt. If the child were slightly soiled, she scrubbed her 'as if she were scrubbing a deck'.

When after four months of separation Jean (now thirteen months old) was permitted to re-enter the mother's room, she spoke only in a whisper:

She shrank back from the pattern of the chintz on the armchair and cried. She tried to crawl off the flowered rug and cried all the time, looking very fearful. She was terrified by a large, soft ball rolling on the floor and terrified of paper crackling.

These fears spread. First, she did not dare to touch ashtrays and other dirty objects, then she avoided touching or being touched by her elder brother and gradually by most people around her. Although she learned to feed herself and to walk at the normal time, she gradually became sad and silent.

Maybe the child's frantic affection for pillows had to do with that period when she was prevented from approaching her mother's bed. Maybe, for some reason, she had not been able to take the separation, had 'adjusted' to it by a permanent pattern of fleeing from all human contact, and was now expressing her affection for the bedridden mother in her love for pillows.

The mother confirmed that the child had a fetish, a small pillow or sheet which she would press over her face when going to sleep. For her part, the mother seemed desirous of making restitution to the child for what she felt she had denied her, not only during those months of illness, but by what now seemed like a general kind of neglect by default. This mother by no means lacked affection for the child, but she felt that she had not given Jean the relaxed affection she needed most *when* she needed it most.

Some such maternal estrangement may be found in every history of infantile schizophrenia. What remains debatable is whether the maternal behaviour such as the mother's relative absence and the nurse's total presence could possibly be a 'cause' for such a radical disturbance in a child's functioning; or whether such children, for some intrinsic and perhaps constitutional reasons, have idiosyncratic needs which no mother would understand without professional help – and professional people, until very recently, could not even spot these children when they were young enough to be (supposedly) saved with special dosages of well-planned mother love.

On the children's part, early oral traumata are often suggested in the history. Take Jean's feeding history. The mother tried to nurse her for one week but had to give up because of a breast infection. The baby vomited, cried excessively, seemed always hungry. When Jean was ten days old, she began to suffer from thrush, which remained acute for three weeks and persisted as a low-grade infection for the remainder of her first year. Drinking was often painful. At one time during the first half of the first year, an infected layer of skin was removed from the underside of her tongue. Early moving pictures of the little girl show a heavy lower lip and a protruding, hyperactive tongue. No doubt the oral trauma had been severe. It should be noted here that Jean's main fetish consisted of a sheet which she made into a ball and pressed against her mouth with one piece between her teeth. Besides these pillows, Jean loved only instruments and machines: egg-beaters, vacuum cleaners, and radiators. She smiled at them, whispered to them, and hugged them, and was impelled by their very presence to a kind of excited dancing – all this, while she remained completely uninterested in people unless they invaded her preoccupations, or unless she wished to invade theirs.

In the mother's early notes there was another item which seemed of great relevance to me. She showed me the statement of a psychologist who, when testing the child at the age of four, noted his impression that 'the child had turned against speech'. For it seems important to understand that these children repudiate their own sense organs and vital functions as hostile and 'outside'. They have a defective screening system between the inner and the outer world; their sensory contacts fail to master the overpowering impressions as well as the disturbing impulses which intrude themselves upon consciousness. They therefore experience their own organs of contact and communication as enemies, as potential intruders into a self which has withdrawn 'under the skin'. It is for this reason that these children close their eyes and hold their hands over their ears, or hide their whole heads in blankets, in reaction to unsuccessful contacts. Thus, only a carefully dosed and extraordinarily consistent application of maternal encouragement could enable the child's ego to reconquer, as it were, its own organs, and with them to perceive the social environment and to make contact with it more trustingly.

When I saw Jean she had not lived with her parents for many months, but had been taken care of by a devoted professional woman. Most of the time she appeared not to care. Yet, on the previous Christmas, after attending a party at her parents' house, the child had thrown all the presents which she had received from her parents on the street outside her foster home, stamped on them, and cried wildly. Maybe she did care. I proposed that the family move together and that, for some extended time, the mother should take over Jean's care under my guidance to be given on regular trips to their home in a college town. This family-treatment plan, I felt, should precede any direct therapy with the child.

When she found herself back within her family, with her mother in untiring attendance, Jean expressed appreciation by a determined attempt to restore intimate contact. But these attempts were often too determined and too specific in their goal. She became fascinated with *parts* of people. Her shocked brothers (older and younger) found their penises grabbed – and politely withdrew their sincere wish to cooperate in the treatment plan. Her father found her an enthusiastic attendant at his showers, where she waited for opportunities to grab his genitals. He could not hide, first, his amused consternation, and then his somewhat nervous annoyance. When he was dressed she concentrated on a bump on his hand which she called a 'lumpy', and his cigarettes, which she would tear from his lips and throw out of the window. She knew where people are vulnerable; these children, so vulnerable themselves, are masters at such diagnosis.

Luckily, Jean's greatest 'partialistic' interest was in her mother's breasts; luckily, because the mother could indulge this interest for a period. The child would love to sit on the mother's lap and take sly pokes at breasts and nipples. Climbing on the mother, she would say 'gloimb you, gloimb you', which apparently meant 'climb on you'. The mother let her sit on her for hours. The 'gloimb you' gradually expanded into sing-songs such as this (I quote from the mother's diary):

Gloimb you, gloimb you, not hurt a chest – not touch a didge – not touch a ban – not touch a dage – not touch a bandage – throw away a chest – hurt a chest.

This apparently meant that the child was preoccupied with the idea that touching her mother's chest-bandage (brassière) might hurt her. The desperate intensity and repetitiveness of these phrases even made us surmise that she communicated the idea that she had hurt the mother when she developed 'chest trouble' and that she had been banished from her mother's room for this reason. For her talk seemed to indicate that the 'throwing away' she referred to really meant that she had been thrown away: here again, we see that most basic imagery of expulsion and atonement. It must be understood that the most difficult verbal (and maybe conceptual) feat for these children, even where they have acquired extensive vocabularies, is to differentiate between active and passive, and between 'I' and 'you': the basic grammar of two-ness. As the game with the mother progressed, Jean could be heard whispering to herself 'spank you' or 'not pick you finger off'. She apparently associated her attacks on penises with those on the mother's breasts, for she would continue, 'Brother has a penis. Be gentle. Don't hurt. Don't cut off your nailfingers. Bola. Jean has a bola (vulva).' Gradually she became outspokenly self-punitive and asked to be 'thrown away'. In solitary games she would go back to her old fears of dirt, and would act as if she were brushing away a cobweb or throwing away something disgusting.

Let us pause here to note that Jean was already describing here the basic cycle of an infantile schizophrenic conflict. There seems to be little doubt that the child, given a chance to communicate with the mother in her own way, referred back to the time, five years earlier, when the mother was ill. These children have an excellent memory – in spots, in vulnerable spots – but their memory does not seem to sustain the rudiments of a sense of identity. Their sayings, like dream images, indicate what they want to talk about, but do not indicate what causal connection is to be communicated. In talking about her mother's illness, then, so we must infer, Jean alluded to the possibility that she had hurt the mother's chest, that as token of her hurt condition the mother had worn a 'bandage', and that for that reason the child had been thrown away (not permitted to come and hug her mother). The confusion as to what was hurt, the child's finger or the mother's chest, we may ascribe to semantic difficulties as well as to the faulty boundary between self and other. Adults are of little help in these matters when they say, 'Don't touch it, you will hurt it,' and then switch to 'Don't touch it, or else you will hurt your fingers.' Yet one might say that the confusion of adult dicta here fits only too well that early ego stage when all pain is experienced as 'outside', all pleasure as 'inside', no matter where its actual source is. Jean may never have outgrown that stage; and yet, there was also the early experience of being abandoned by the mother to a nurse who was a 'don't touch' zealot. In re-testing the reality of that prohibition, of course, she only had to do what she did to the men in the family. With her mother she was more fortunate. But here an important item enters – namely, the immense self-punitive tendency in these driven children. Their law is 'all or none'; they take the dictum, 'If thine eye offend thee, pluck it out', literally and quite seriously. Thus it may happen that a little boy in a schizophrenic episode requests his horrified parents in all sincerity to cut off his penis because it is no good.

The mother continued to explain patiently to Jean that her illness had not been the child's fault. She let Jean sleep with her, let her sit on her lap, and, in general, gave her the attention and consideration usually awarded only to an infant. Jean seemed to begin to believe her. After several months she showed marked improvement. She became more graceful in her movements; her vocabulary increased, or, as one should say in such cases, became apparent, for it is usually there before its presence is suspected. And she began to play! She put a little black toy dog to bed and said, 'Go to sleep, dog, stay under covers; shut your eyes, have to spank you, dog.' Also she began to build long block trains which were 'going east'. During one of these games she looked her mother in the eyes with one of her rare, completely direct glances and said, 'Not go on long ride on the train some-time.' 'No,' said the mother, 'we are going to stay together.'

Such improvements seemed most rewarding. They were usually interrupted by crises which led to emergency calls. I would visit the family and talk with all the members of the household until I had ascertained what was going on in all their lives. A whole series of difficulties arose in this one-patient sanitarium. One can live with schizophrenic thought only if one can make a profession out of understanding it. The mother had accepted this task, which demands a particular gift of empathy and at the same time the ability to keep oneself intact. Other-wise one must refute such thinking in order to be protected against it. Each member of the household, then, in being forced to take a glance into Jean's mind, characterized as it was by the alternation of naked impulsiveness and desperate self-negation, was endangered in his own equilibrium and self-esteem. This had to be pointed out repeatedly, because Jean would constantly change the direction of her provocation. And she would withdraw repeatedly for no apparent reason.

The following incident will serve to illustrate the impact of the mother's first attempts to make Jean sleep by herself. Suddenly a pathological attachment to spoons developed, and it assumed such proportions that it led to the first crisis of despair both in Jean and in her parents. Jean would insistently repeat such sentences as 'not sleep in the light in Jean's room', 'light in the spoon', 'incinerator in the spoon', 'blankets in the spoon', etc. During dinnertime she would often sit and merely look at the 'light in the spoon'. Unable to make herself understood, she began to withdraw and to stay in bed for hours and days. Yet she refused to go to sleep at night. The parents put in an emergency call and asked me to try to clear up the matter. When I asked Jean to show me the light in the spoon, she showed me a plug behind a bookcase. Some weeks ago she had broken off one piece of this plug and had caused a short circuit. As I went with her to her room to investigate the electrical appliances there I found that she had a dim bulb in her room with a small spoonlike shade attached to it which was intended to keep the light from shining on her bed. Was that the original 'light in the spoon'? Jean indicated it was. Now it became clear. On returning home, Jean had first slept in the mother's bed. Then the mother had slept with her in her bed. Then the mother had slept in her own bed and Jean in hers, the door ajar and the hall light on. Finally the hall light had been turned off and only the light from a small bulb ('the light in the spoon') left in Jean's room. Apparently at night, then, Jean would look at this light as her last consolation – the last 'part' of her mother – and endow it with the same partialistic affection and fear which she had demonstrated in relation to her mother's breast, her father's and her brothers' penises, and all the fetishes before. It was at that time that she touched the plug in the living-room with those problem fingers of hers, causing a short circuit and making everything dark, including the 'light in the spoon'. Again she had brought on catastrophe: by touching something she had caused a crisis which threatened to leave her alone in the dark.

The circumstances having been explained all around, the spoon fetish was abandoned, and the course of restoration resumed. However, one could not fail to be impressed with the persistence of the pathogenic pattern and the violence of its eruption, for Jean was now a whole year older (nearly seven). Yet she seemed to begin to feel that her fingers could do no irreparable harm and that she could not only keep them but also use them for learning and for making beautiful things.

First, she became enchanted by the finger play which says that 'this little pig does this' and 'that little pig does that'. She made the little pigs do what she had been doing during the day, namely, 'go to market', 'go to ten-cent store', 'go to escalator', or 'cry all the way home'. Thus, in referring to the coherent series of her fingers she learned to integrate time and to establish a continuity of the various selves which had done different things at different times. But she could not say, '*I* did this' and '*I* did that'. Not that I consider this a problem of mere mental capacity. The ego of schizoid (as well as schizophrenic) people is dominated by the necessity of repeating the testing and integrating experience just because it provides an inadequate sense of the trustworthiness of events at the time when they happen. Jean, then, accomplished such reintegration, together with its communication, by the use of her fingers, which, now permitted, could be readmitted to the body ego. She learned the letters of the alphabet by drawing them with her fingers, after studying them with the help of the Montessori touch method. And she learned to play melodies by scratching a xylophone with her nails. The mother reported:

Since the time when Jean began to show such a disturbing, because apparently senseless, interest in the xylophone, I have noticed that she is actually playing it with her fingernails. She does it so quietly one cannot distinguish what she is doing. Tonight, however, I discovered that she could play 'Water, Water Wild Flower' all the way through. This song requires every note in the scale. I asked for it to be repeated and watched her hand travel up and down the scale. I was amazed and made a big fuss over her, saying it was wonderful. I said, 'Let's go downstairs to the others and play it for them.' She came down willingly, even self-consciously, and very pleased. She now played it aloud for them, and they were astounded. She then played several other things: 'Rain is Falling Down', 'ABCDEFG', etc. We all praised her and she ate it up. She did not want to go upstairs but seemed to want to stay and play on for the audience, a new delightful feeling.

Thus Jean 'sublimated' and gained friends; but as she regained parts of herself she also made new enemies, in new ways. For she also used her fingers for poking people and came so near to hurting a visitor's eyes that she had to be energetically stopped. She especially liked to poke her father, obviously as a sequence to her penis- and cigarette-grabbing activities. When, at this point, the father had to go on a trip, she regressed to whining, resumed her sheet fetish (saying 'blanket is mended'), spoke only in a soft voice, and ate little, even refusing ice cream. She had again made somebody go away by touching him! She seemed particularly desperate because she had, in fact, begun to respond to her father's devoted efforts to help her.

At the height of this new crisis, Jean lay down beside her mother in bed and with desperate crying repeated over and over, 'No vulva on Jean, no eggplant, take it off, take it off, no egg in the plant, not plant the seed, cut off your finger, get some scissors, cut it off.' This obviously represented the old deep self-punitive reaction.

Jean's mother gave her appropriate explanations concerning her father's 'disappearance'. She also told Jean that it was not because she had touched herself that her 'eggplant' had disappeared; in fact, she still had one of her own way inside. Jean resumed her play with her fingers. She had to work her way again through previous stages of existence by chanting: 'This little girl sleeps in the refrigerator, this little girl sleeps in the vacuum cleaner,' etc. Gradually her interest in animals and now also in other children reappeared, and the fingers would represent 'this little boy is jumping, this little boy is running . . . is walking . . . is racing', etc. Her interest in finger skill then was applied to various forms of locomotion both of children and of animals. She learned to read and to list the names of various domestic animals and, again using her fingers, to recite the days of the week, and adding her toes, count up to twenty. At the same time her play on the xylophone began to include more difficult French folk-songs, all of which she played with great ease and abandon, knowing always exactly where to find the first note. The pleasure of having the use of her fingers restored can be seen from the mother's report:

Last Sunday Jean made a painting of a little girl in a yellow dress. At night she went up to the picture on the wall silently and felt the paint. She paused long over the hands, each of which was bigger than the whole girl, and very carefully done with five fingers each. Then she said, 'The hands are nice.' I agreed, repeating the words. Then in a minute she said, 'The hands are pretty.' Again I agreed appreciatively. She retreated to the bed without taking her eyes off the picture as she sat down on the bed, still studying it. Then she burst out loudly, 'The hands are *lovely*.'

During all this time, Jean had, off and on, played the xylophone and sung songs. Now the parents were fortunate enough to find a piano teacher who was willing to base her methods on Jean's auditory gift and ingenuity in imitating. At my next visit, after being taken to my room, I heard somebody practising some phrases of Beethoven's first sonata, and innocently remarked on the strong and sensitive touch. I thought a gifted adult was playing. To find Jean at the piano was one of the surprises which are so gripping in work with these cases – and which often prove so misleading, because again and again they make one believe in the child's total progress where one is justified in believing only in isolated and too rapid advances of special faculties. This I say with feeling and conviction, for Jean's piano playing, whether it was Beethoven, Haydn, or boogie-woogie, was truly astounding – until she turned against this gift, just as she had 'turned against speech', in the words of the first psychologist who had seen her.

This completes one episode in Jean's improvement: her relation to her hands. It also completes the specimen to be reported here as an illustration of the essential ego-weakness which causes these children to be swayed at one time by a 'drivenness' focused on a part of another person; and at another by cruel self-punitiveness and paralysing perfectionism. It is not that they fail to be able to learn, to remember, and to excel – usually in some artistic endeavour which reflects the sensory counterpart of their essentially oral fixation. It is that they cannot integrate it all: their ego is impotent.

You will want to know how Jean fared. As the child grew more mature, the discrepancy between her age and her behaviour became so marked that associations with children anywhere near her age level became impossible. Other difficulties arose which made at least an interval in a special school mandatory. There she quickly lost what she had gained in the years of her mother's heroic effort. Her treatment has since been resumed under the best residential circumstances and under the guidance of one of the most devoted and most imaginative child psychiatrists in this particular field.

The role which 'maternal rejection' or special circumstances of abandonment play in cases such as Jean's is still debatable. I think one should consider that these children may very early and subtly fail to return the mother's glance, smile, and touch; an initial reserve which makes the mother, in turn, unwittingly withdraw. The truism that the original problem is to be found in the mother–child relationship holds only in so far as one considers this relationship an emotional pooling which may multiply well-being in both but which will endanger both partners when the communication becomes jammed or weakened. In those cases of infantile schizophrenia which I have seen, there was a clear deficiency in 'sending power' in the child.[1] Because of the very early failure of communication, however, the child may only betray in more malignant form a frailty of affective contact which already exists in the parent(s), although in them it may be compensated for – at least in other relationships – by a special character make-up or by superior intellectual endowment.

As to the procedure described in this chapter, it should be clear that Jean's mother was capable of that exceptional curative effort which is a prerequisite for all experimentation on this frontier of human trust.

[1] In the First Edition, the wording was ' . . . the primary deficiency in "sending power" was in the child'. This referred only to those few cases that I had seen; and such cases were rare then in psychoanalytic practice. My statement was intended to counter certain facile interpretations then in vogue which claimed that rejecting mothers could cause such malignancy in their offspring. In the meantime, my statement has been quoted out of context in support of a strictly constitutional etiology of infantile psychosis. The careful reader of Chapter I, however, and of Jean's history, will see that in the case fragments presented in this book I am not trying to isolate first causes and therapeutic effects, but to delineate a new conceptual area encompassing both the struggles of the ego and of social organization. This approach, no doubt, bypasses details in parent–child interaction in which constitutional and environmental defects aggravate each other malignantly. But first causes can be isolated (or ruled out) only where rigorous diagnosis criteria exist and where anamneses in quantity permit comparison. Such work can be found in the growing literature of psychoanalytic child psychiatry.

E.H.E.

6   Toys and Reasons

Paraphrasing Freud, we have called play the royal road to the understanding of the infantile ego's efforts at synthesis. We have observed an example of a failure of such synthesis. We shall now turn to childhood situations which illustrate the capacity of the ego to find recreation and self-cure in the activity of play; and to therapeutic situations in which we were fortunate enough to be able to help a child's ego to help itself.

PLAY, WORK, AND GROWTH

Let us take as our text for the beginning of this more reassuring chapter a play episode described by a rather well-known psychologist. The occasion, while not pathological, is nevertheless a tragic one: a boy named Tom Sawyer, by verdict of his aunt, must whitewash a fence on an otherwise faultless spring morning. His predicament is intensified by the appearance of an age mate named Ben Rogers, who indulges in a game. It is Ben, the man of leisure, whom we want to observe with the eyes of Tom, the working man.

He took up his brush and went tranquilly to work. Ben Rogers hove in sight presently – the very boy, of all boys, whose ridicule he had been dreading. Ben's gait was the hop-skip-and-jump – proof enough that his heart was light and his anticipation high. He was eating an apple, and giving a long, melodious whoop, at intervals, followed by a deep-toned ding-dong-dong, ding-dong-dong, for he was personating a steamboat. As he drew near, he slackened speed, took the middle of the street, leaned far over to starboard and rounded to ponderously and with laborious pomp and circumstance – for he was personating the *Big Missouri*, and considered himself to be drawing nine feet of water. He was boat and captain and engine-bells combined, so he had to imagine himself standing on his own hurricane-deck giving the orders and executing them:

... 'Stop the stabboard! Ting-a-ling-ling! Stop the labboard! Come ahead on the stabboard! Stop her! Let your outside turn over slow! Ting-a-ling-ling! Chow-ow-ow! Get out that head-line! *Lively* now! Come – out with your spring-line – what're you about there! Take a turn round that stump with the bight of it! Stand by that stage, now – let her go! Done with the engines, sir! Ting-a-ling-ling! *Sh't! sh't! sh't!*' (trying the gauge-cocks).

Tom went on whitewashing – paid no attention to the steamboat. Ben stared a moment, and then said:

'Hi-*yi*! *You're* up a stump, ain't you! ... You got to work, hey?'

My clinical impression of Ben Rogers is a most favourable one, and this on all three counts: organism, ego, and society. For he takes care of the body by munching an apple; he simultaneously enjoys imaginary control over a number of highly conflicting items (being a steamboat and parts thereof, as well as being the captain of said steamboat, and the crew obeying said captain); while he loses not a moment in sizing up social reality when, on navigating a corner, he sees Tom at work. By no means reacting as a steamboat would, he knows immediately how to pretend sympathy though he undoubtedly finds his own freedom enhanced by Tom's predicament.

Flexible lad, we would say. However, Tom proves to be the better psychologist: he is going to put Ben to work. Which shows that psychology is at least the second-best thing to, and under some adverse circumstances may even prove superior to, ordinary adjustment.

In view of Ben's final fate it seems almost rude to add interpretation to defeat, and to ask what Ben's play may mean. I presented this question to a class of psychiatric social-work students. Most of the answers were, of course, of the traumatic variety, for in what other way could Ben become accessible to 'case work'? Ben must have been a frustrated boy, the majority agreed, to take the trouble to play so strenuously. The possible frustrations ranged from oppression by a tyrannical father from whom he escapes in fantasy by becoming a bossy captain, to a bedwetting or toilet trauma of some kind which now made him want to be a boat drawing nine feet of water. Some answers concerned the more obvious circumstance that he wanted to be big, and this in the form of a captain, the idol of his day.

My contribution to the discussion consisted of the consideration that Ben is a growing boy. To grow means to be divided into different parts which move at different rates. A growing boy has trouble in mastering his gangling body as well as his divided mind. He wants to be good, if only out of expediency, and always finds he has been bad. He wants to rebel, and finds that almost against his will he has given in. As his time-perspective permits a glimpse of approaching adulthood he finds himself acting like a child. One 'meaning' of Ben's play could be that it affords his ego a temporary victory over his gangling body and self by making a well-functioning whole out of brain (captain), the nerves and muscles of will (signal system and engine), and the whole bulk of the body (boat). It permits him to be an entity within which he is his own boss, because he obeys himself. At the same time, he chooses his metaphors from the tool world of the young machine age, and anticipates the identity of the machine god of his day: the captain of the *Big Missouri*.

Play, then, is a function of the ego, an attempt to synchronize the bodily and the social processes with the self. Ben's fantasy could well contain a phallic and locomotor element: a powerful boat in a mighty stream makes a good symbol. A captain certainly is a fitting father image, and, beyond that, an image of well-delineated patriarchal power. Yet the emphasis, I think, should be on the ego's need to master the various areas of life, and especially those in which the individual finds his self, his body, and his social role wanting and trailing. To hallucinate ego mastery and yet also to practise it in an intermediate reality between fantasy and actuality is the purpose of play – but play, as we shall see presently, is the undisputed master of only a slim margin of existence. What is play – and what is it not? Let us consult language, and then return to children.

The sunlight playing on the waves qualifies for the attribute 'playful' because it faithfully remains within the rules of the game. It does not really interfere with the chemical world of the waves. It insists only on an intermingling of appearances. These patterns change with effortless rapidity and with a repetitiveness which promises pleasing phenomena within a predictable range without ever creating the same configuration twice.

When man plays he must intermingle with things and people in a similarly uninvolved and light fashion. He must do something which he has chosen to do without being compelled by urgent interests or impelled by strong passion; he must feel entertained and free of any fear or hope of serious consequences. He is on vacation from social and economic reality – or, as is most commonly emphasized: he *does not work*. It is this opposition to work which gives play a number of connotations. One of these is 'mere fun' – whether it is hard to do or not. As Mark Twain commented, 'constructing artificial flowers . . . is work, while climbing the Mont Blanc is only amusement'. In Puritan times and places, however, mere fun always connoted sin; the Quakers warned that you must 'gather the flowers of pleasure in the fields of duty'. Men of equally Puritan mind could permit play only because they believed that to find 'relief from moral activity is in itself a moral necessity'. Poets, however, place the emphasis elsewhere: 'Man is perfectly human only when he plays,' said Schiller. Thus play is a borderline phenomenon to a number of human activities and, in its own playful way, it tries to elude definition.

It is true that even the most strenuous and dangerous play is by definition not work; it does not produce commodities. Where it does, it 'goes professional'. But this fact, from the start, makes the comparison of adult and child's play somewhat senseless; for the adult is a commodity-producing and commodity-exchanging being, whereas the child is only preparing to become one. To the working adult, play is recreation. It permits a periodical stepping out from those forms of defined limitation which are his social reality.

Take *gravity*: to juggle, to jump, or to climb adds unused dimensions to the awareness of our body. Play here gives a sense of divine leeway, of excess space.

Take *time*: in trifling, in dallying, we lazily thumb our noses at this, our slave-driver. Where every minute counts, playfulness vanishes. This puts competitive sports on the borderline of play: they seem to make concessions to the pressure of space and time, only to defeat this very pressure by a fraction of a yard or of a second.

Take *fate* and *causality*, which have determined who and what we are, and where. In games of chance we re-establish equality before fate, and secure a virgin chance to every player willing to observe a few rules which, if compared with the rules of reality, seem arbitrary and senseless. Yet they are magically convincing, like the reality of a dream, and they demand absolute compliance.

Let a player forget that such play must remain his free choice, let him become possessed by the demon of gambling, and playfulness vanishes again. He is a gambler, not a player.

Take *social reality*, and our defined cubicles in it. In playacting we can be what in life we could not or would not be. But as the play-actor begins to believe in his impersonation he comes closer to a state of hysteria, if not worse; while if he tries, for purposes of gain, to make others believe in his 'role' he becomes an imposter.

Take our *bodily drives*. The bulk of the nation's advertising effort exploits our wish to play with necessity, to make us believe, for example, that to inhale and to eat are not pleasurable necessities, but a fanciful game with ever new and sensuous nuances. Where the need for these nuances becomes compulsive, it creates a general state of mild addiction and gluttony, which ceases to transmit a sense of abundance and, in fact, produces an undercurrent of discontent.

Last but not least, in *love life* we describe as sex play the random activities preceding the final act, which permit the partners to choose body part, intensity, and tempo ('what, and with which, and to whom', as the limerick has it). Sex play ends when the final act begins, narrowing choice, dictating tempo, and giving rein to 'nature'. Where one of the preparatory random acts becomes compelling enough to completely replace the final act, playfulness vanishes and perversion begins.

This list of playful situations in a variety of human endeavours indicates the narrow area within which our ego can feel superior to the confinement of space and time and to the definitiveness of social reality – free from the compulsions of conscience and from impulsions of irrationality. Only within these limitations, then, can man feel at one with his ego; no wonder he feels 'only human when he plays'. But this presupposes one more most decisive condition: he must play rarely and work most of the time. He must have a defined role in society. Playboys and gamblers are both envied and resented by the working man. We like to see them exposed or ridiculed, or we put them to worse than work by forcing them to live in luxurious cages.

The playing child, then, poses a problem: whoever does not work shall not play. Therefore, to be tolerant of the child's play the adult must invent theories which show either that childhood play is really work – or that it does not count. The most popular theory and the easiest on the observer is that the child is *nobody yet*, and that the nonsense of his play reflects it. Scientists have tried to find other explanations for the freaks of childish play by considering them representative of the fact that childhood is neither here nor there. According to Spencer, play uses up *surplus energy* in the young of a number of mammalians who do not need to feed or protect themselves because their parents do it for them. However, Spencer noticed that wherever circumstances permit play, tendencies are 'simulated' which are 'unusually ready to act, unusually ready to have their correlative feelings aroused'. Early psychoanalysis added to this the 'cathartic' theory, according to which play has a definite function in the growing being in that it permits him to work off pent up emotions and to find imaginary relief for past frustrations.

In order to evaluate these theories, let us turn to the game of another boy, Tom's junior. He lived near another mighty river, the Danube, and his play was recorded by another great psychologist, Sigmund Freud, who wrote:[1]

Without the intention of making a comprehensive study of these phenomena, I availed myself of an opportunity which offered of elucidating the first game invented by himself of a boy eighteen months old. It was more than a casual observation, for I lived for some weeks under the same roof as the child and his parents, and it was a considerable time before the meaning of his puzzling and continually repeated performance became clear to me.

The child was in no respect forward in his intellectual development; ... but he made himself understood by his parents and the maid-servant, and had a good reputation for behaving 'properly'. He did not disturb his parents at night; he scrupulously obeyed orders about not touching various objects and not going into certain rooms; and above all he never cried when his mother went out and left him for hours together, although the tie to his mother was a very close one: she had not only nourished him herself, but had cared for him and brought him up without any outside help. Occasionally, however, this well-behaved child evinced the troublesome habit of flinging into the corner of the room or under the bed all the little things he could lay his hands on, so that to gather up his toys was often no light task. He accompanied this by an expression of interest and gratification, emitting a loud, long-drawn-out 'O-o-o-oh' which in the judgment

[1] Sigmund Freud, *A General Selection*, edited by John Rickman, The Hogarth Press and the Institute of Psycho-Analysis, London, 1937.

of the mother (one that coincided with my own) was not an inter-jection but meant 'go away' [*fort*]. I saw at last that this was a game, and that the child used all his toys only to play 'being gone' [*fort sein*] with them. One day I made an observation that confirmed my view. The child had a wooden reel with a piece of string wound round it. It never occurred to him, for example, to drag this after him on the floor and so play horse and cart with it, but he kept throwing it with considerable skill, held by the string, over the side of his little draped cot, so that the reel disappeared into it, then said his significant 'O-o-o-oh' and drew the reel by the string out of the cot again, greeting its reappearance with a joyful '*Da*' [there]. This was therefore the complete game, disappearance and return, the first act being the only one generally observed by the onlookers, and the one untiringly repeated by the child as a game for its own sake, although the greater pleasure unquestion-ably attached to the second act . . . This interpretation was fully established by a further observation. One day when the mother had been out for some hours she was greeted on her return by the informa-tion 'Baby o-o-o-oh' which at first remained unintelligible. It soon proved that during his long lonely hours he had found a method of bringing about his own disappearance. He had discovered his reflection in the long mirror which nearly reached to the ground and had then crouched down in front of it, so that the reflection was '*fort*'.

To understand what Freud saw in this game we must note that at the time he was interested in (and, in fact, writing about) the strange phenomenon of the 'repetition compulsion' – i.e., the need to re-enact painful experiences in words or acts. We have all experienced the occasional need of talking incessantly about a painful event (an insult, a quarrel, or an operation) which one might be expected to want to forget. We know of traumatized individuals who, instead of finding recovery in sleep, are repeatedly awakened by dreams in which they re-experience the original trauma. We also suspect that it is not so innocently accidental that some people make the same mistakes over and over again; that they 'coincidentally' and in utter blindness marry the same kind of impossible partner from whom they have just been divorced; or that a series of analogous accidents and mishaps always must happen just to *them*. In all these cases, so Freud concluded, the individual unconsciously arranges for variations of an original theme which he has not learned either to overcome or to live with: he tries to master a situation which in its original form had been too much for him by meeting it repeatedly and of his own accord.

As Freud was writing about this, he became aware of the solitary play described and of the fact that the frequency of the main theme (something or somebody disappears and comes back) corresponded to the intensity of the life experience reflected – namely, the mother's leaving in the morning and her return at night.

This dramatization takes place in the play sphere. Utilizing his mastery over objects, the child can arrange them in such a way that they permit him to imagine that he is master of his life predicament as well. For when the mother had left him, she had removed herself from the sphere of his cries and demands; and she had come back only when it happened to suit her. In his game, however the little boy has the mother by a string. He makes her go away, even throws her away, and then makes her come back at his pleasure. He has, as Freud put it, *turned passivity into activity*; he plays at doing something that was in reality done to him.

Freud mentions three items which may guide us in a further social evaluation of this game. First, the child threw the object away. Freud sees in this a possible explanation of revenge – 'If you don't want to stay with me, I don't want you' – and thus an additional gain in active mastery by an apparent growth of emotional autonomy. In his second play act, however, the child goes further. He abandons the object altogether and, with the use of a full-length mirror, plays 'going away' from himself and returning to himself. He is now both the person who is being left and the person who leaves. He has become master by incorporating not only the person who, in life, is beyond his control, but the whole situation, with *both* its partners.

This is as far as Freud goes with his interpretation. But we may make a point of the fact that the child greets the returning mother with the information that he has learned to 'go away' from himself. The game alone, as reported by Freud, could have become the beginning of an increasing tendency on the child's part to take life experiences into a solitary corner and to rectify them in fantasy, and only in fantasy. Let us assume that at the mother's return the child were to show complete indifference, extending his revenge to the life situation and indicating that he, indeed, can now take care of himself, that he does not need her. This often happens after the mother's first excursions: she rushes back, eager to embrace her child, only to be met by a bland face. She may then feel rejected and turn against or away from the unloving child, who is thus easily made to feel that the vengeance in the game of throwing away and his subsequent boast has hit its mark too well, that he has indeed made the mother go away for good, whereas he has only tried to recover from being abandoned by her. Thus the basic problem of being left and leaving would not be improved by its solution in solitary play. Our little boy, however, told his mother of his play, and we may assume that she, far from being offended, demonstrated interest and maybe even pride in his ingenuity. He was then better off all around. He had adjusted to a difficult situation, he had learned to manipulate new objects, and he had received loving recognition for his method. All this is in 'child's play'.

But does the child's play – so a frequent question goes – always 'mean' something personal and sinister? What if ten children, in horse-and-buggy days, begin to play with reels on strings, pulling them behind themselves and playing horsie? Must it mean anything to one of them over and beyond what it seems to mean to all?

As we have said already, children, if traumatized, choose for their dramatizations play material which is available in their culture and manageable at their age. What is available depends on the cultural circumstances and is therefore common to all children who share these circumstances. Bens today do not play steamboat but use bicycles as more tangible objects of coordination – which does not prevent them from imagining, on the way to school or the grocery, that they are flying through the air and machine-gunning the enemy; or that they are the Lone Ranger himself on a glorious Silver. What is manageable, however, depends on the child's power of coordination, and therefore is shared only by those who have reached a certain level of maturation. What has a *common meaning* to all the children in a community (i.e., the idea of having a reel and string represent a living thing on a leash) may have a *special meaning* to some (i.e., all those who have just learned to manipulate reel and string and may thus be ready to enter a new sphere of participation and communal symbolization). Yet all of this may have, in addition, a *unique meaning* to individual children who have lost a person or an animal and therefore endow the game with a particular significance. What these children 'have by the string' is not just any animal – it is the personification of a particular, a significant, and a lost animal – or person. To evaluate play the observer must, of course, have an idea of what all the children of a given age in a given community are apt to play. Only thus can he decide whether or not the unique meaning transcends the common meaning. To understand the unique meaning itself requires careful observation, not only of the play's content and form, but also of accompanying words and visible effects, especially those which lead to what we shall describe in the next chapter as 'play disruption'.

In order to approach the problem of anxiety in play, let us consider the activity of building and destroying a tower. Many a mother thinks that her little son is in a 'destructive stage' or even has a 'destructive personality' because, after building a big, big tower, the boy cannot follow her advice to leave the tower for Daddy to see, but instead *must* kick it and make it collapse. The almost manic pleasure with which children watch the collapse in a second of the product of long play labour has puzzled many, especially since the child does not appreciate it at all if his tower falls by accident or by a helpful uncle's hand. He, the builder, must destroy it himself. This game, I should think, arises from the not so distant experience of sudden falls at the very time when standing upright on wobbly legs afforded a new and fascinating perspective on existence. The child who consequently learns to *make* a tower 'stand up' enjoys causing the same tower to waver and collapse: in addition to the active mastery over a previously passive event, it makes one feel stronger to know that there is somebody weaker – and towers, unlike little sisters, can't cry and call Mummy. But since it is the child's still precarious mastery over space which is thus to be demonstrated, it is understandable that watching somebody else kick one's tower may make the child see himself in the tower rather than in the kicker: all fun evaporates. Circus clowns later take over when they obligingly fall all over the place from mere ineptness, and yet continue to challenge gravity and causality with ever renewed innocence: there are, then, even big people who are funnier, dumber, and wobblier. Some children, however, who find themselves too much identified with the clown cannot stand his downfalls: to them they are 'not funny'. This example throws light on the beginning of many an anxiety in childhood, where anxiety around the child's attempt at ego mastery finds unwelcome 'support' from adults who treat him roughly or amuse him with exercises which he likes only if and when he himself has initiated them.

The child's play begins with and centres on his own body. This we shall call *autocosmic* play. It begins before we notice it as play, and consists at first in the exploration by repetition of sensual perceptions, of kinaesthetic sensations, of vocalizations, etc. Next, the child plays with available persons and things. He may playfully cry to see what wave-length would serve best to make the mother reappear, or he may indulge in experimental excursions on her body and on the protrusions and orifices of her face. This is the child's first geography, and the basic maps acquired in such interplay with the mother no doubt remain guides for the ego's first orientation in the 'world'. Here we call as a witness Santayana:[2]

Far, far in a dim past, as if it had been in another world or in a pre-natal condition, Oliver remembered the long-denied privilege of sitting in his mother's lap. It had been such a refuge of safety, of softness, of vantage: You were carried and you were enveloped in an amplitude of sure protection, like a king on his throne, with his faithful bodyguard many ranks deep about him; and the landscape beyond, with its messengers and its motley episodes, became the most entertaining of spectacles, where everything was unexpected and exciting, yet where nothing could go wrong; as if your mother herself had been telling you a story, and these pictures were only the illustrations to it which painted themselves in your listening mind.

The *microsphere* – i.e., the small world of manageable toys – is a harbour which the child establishes, to return to when he needs to overhaul his ego. But the thing-world has its own laws: it may resist reconstruction, or it may simply break to pieces; it may prove to belong to somebody else and be subject to confiscation by superiors. Often the microsphere seduces the child into an unguarded expression of dangerous themes and attitudes which arouse anxiety and lead to sudden play-disruption. This

[2] George Santayana, *The Last Puritan*, Charles Scribner's Sons, New York, 1936.

is the counterpart in waking life of the anxiety dream; it can keep children from trying to play just as the fear of night terror can keep them from going to sleep. If thus frightened or disappointed in the microsphere, the child may regress into the autosphere, daydreaming, thumb-sucking, masturbating. On the other hand, if the first use of the thing-world is successful and is guided properly, the pleasure of mastering toy things becomes associated with the mastery of the traumata which were projected on them, and with the prestige gained through such mastery.

Finally, at nursery-school age playfulness reaches into the *macrosphere*, the world shared with others. First these others are treated as things, are inspected, run into, or forced to 'be horsie'. Learning is necessary in order to discover what potential play content can be admitted only to fantasy or only to autocosmic play; what content can be successfully represented only in the microcosmic world of toys and things; and what content can be shared with others and forced upon them.

As this is learned, each sphere is endowed with its own sense of reality and mastery. For quite a while, then, solitary play remains an indispensable harbour for the overhauling of shattered emotions after periods of rough going in the social seas. This, and the fact that a child can be counted upon to bring into the solitary play arranged for him whatever aspect of his ego has been ruffled most, form the fundamental condition for our diagnostic reliance on 'play therapy', which will be discussed next.

What is infantile play, then? We saw that it is not the equivalent of adult play, that it is not recreation. The playing adult steps sideward into another reality; the playing child advances forward to new stages of mastery. I propose the theory that the child's play is the infantile form of the human ability to deal with experience by creating model situations and to master reality by experiment and planning. It is in certain phases of his work that the adult projects past experience into dimensions which seem manageable. In the laboratory, on the stage, and on the drawing-board, he relives the past and thus relieves leftover effects; in re-constructing the model situation, he redeems his failures and strengthens his hopes. He anticipates the future from the point of view of a corrected and shared past.

No thinker can do more and no playing child less. As William Blake puts it: 'The child's toys and the old man's reasons are the fruits of the two seasons.'

PLAY AND CURE

Modern play-therapy is based on the observation that a child made insecure by a secret hate against or fear of the natural protectors of his play in family and neighbourhood seems able to use the protective sanction of an understanding adult to regain some play peace. Grandmothers and favourite aunts may have played that role in the past; its professional elaboration of today is the play therapist. The most obvious condition is that the child has the toys and the adult for himself, and that sibling rivalry, parental nagging, or any kind of sudden interruption does not disturb the unfolding of his play intentions, whatever they may be. For to 'play it out' is the most natural self-healing measure childhood affords.

Let us remember here the simple, if often embarrassing, fact that adults, when traumatized, tend to solve their tension by 'talking it out'. They are compelled, repeatedly, to describe the painful event: it seems to make them 'feel better'. Systems designed to cure the soul or the mind make ritual use of this tendency by providing, at regular intervals, an ordained or otherwise sanctioned listener who gives his undivided attention, is sworn not to censure arbitrarily or to betray, and bestows absolution by explaining how the individual's problem makes sense in some larger context, be it sin, conflict, or disease. The method finds its limitations where this 'clinical' situation loses the detachment in which life can be reflected, and itself becomes a passionate conflict of dependence and hostility. In psycho-analytic terms, the limitation is set by the tendency (especially strong in neurotics) to transfer basic conflicts from their original infantile setting into every new situation, including the thera-peutic one. This is what Freud meant when he said that the treatment itself, at first, becomes a 'transference neurosis'. The patient who thus transfers his conflict in all its desperate immediacy becomes at the same time resistive to all attempts at making him see the situation in a detached way, at formulating its meaning. He is *in resistance*; in a war to end all wars, he becomes more deeply embroiled than ever. At this point, non-psychoanalytic therapeutic efforts often end; the patient, it is said, cannot or does not want to get well or is too inferior to comprehend his obligations in treatment. Therapeutic psychoanalysis, however, begins at this point. It makes systematic use of the knowledge that no neurotic is undivided in his wish to get well and of necessity transfers his dependences and hostilities to the treatment and the person of the therapist. Psychoanalysis acknowledges and learns from such 'resistances'.

This phenomenon of *transference* in the playing child, as well as in the verbalizing adult, marks the point where simple measures fail – namely, when an emotion becomes so intense that it defeats playfulness, forcing an immediate discharge into the play and into the relationship with the play observer. The failure is characterized by what is to be described here as *play disruption* – i.e., the sudden and complete or diffused and slowly spreading inability to play. We saw such play disruption occur, on my provocation, in Ann's case, when she had to leave me and my tempting toys in order to re-join her mother. Similarly, we saw Sam trapped by his overpowering emotions in the middle of a game. In both cases we used play observation as an incidental diagnostic tool. I shall now introduce a little girl who, although she came for diagnostic purposes only, led me through a full cycle of play disruption and play triumph, and thus offered a good example of the way in which the ego, flooded by fear, can regain its synthesizing power through playful involvement and disengagement.

Our patient is Mary. She is three years old. She is a somewhat pale brunette, but looks (and is) intelligent, pretty, and quite feminine. When disturbed, however, she is said to be stubborn, babyish, and shut-in. Recently she has enriched her inventory of expression by nightmares and by violent anxiety-attacks in the play group which she has recently joined. All that the play group teachers can say is that Mary has a queer way of lifting things and has a rigid posture: and that her tension seems to increase in connection with the routines of resting and going to the toilet. With this information at hand we invite Mary to our office.

Maybe a word should be said here about the thoroughly difficult situation which ensues when a mother brings a child for observation. The child has not chosen to come. He often does not feel sick at all in the sense that he has a symptom which he wishes to get rid of. On the contrary, all he knows is that certain things and, most of all, certain people make him feel uncomfortable and he wishes that we would do something about these things and people – not about him. Often he feels that something is wrong with his parents, and mostly he is right. But he has no words for this and, even if he did have, he has no reason to trust us with such weighty information. On the other hand, he does not know what the parents have told us about him – while God only knows what they have told the child about us. For the parents, helpful as they may wish to be and necessary as they are as initial informants, cannot be trusted in these matters: the initial history given is often distorted by the wish to justify (or secretly punish) themselves or to punish (and unconsciously justify) somebody else, perhaps the grandparents who 'told you so'.

In this case, my office was in a hospital. Mary had been told that she was coming to discuss her nightmares with me – a man whom she had never seen before. Her mother had consulted a paediatrician regarding these nightmares and Mary had heard the mother and the doctor argue over the possible indication for a tonsillectomy. I had hoped, therefore, that she would notice that the appointments of my office indicated a strictly non-medical affair and that she would give me a chance in simple and straightforward terms to acknowledge the purpose of her visit, to tell her that I was not a doctor and then to make clear that we were going to play together in order to get acquainted. Such explanations do not quite settle a child's doubts, but they may permit him to turn to the toys and do something. And as soon as he does *something* we can observe what he selects and repudiates in our standard inventory of toys. Our next step, then, will be guided by the meaning thus revealed.

Mary holds on to her mother as she enters my office. When she offers me her hand it is both rigid and cold. She gives me a brief smile, then turns to her mother, puts her arms around her, and holds her close to the still open door. She buries her head in her mother's skirt as if she wanted to hide in it, and responds to my advances only by turning her head to me – now with tightly closed eyes. Yet she *had* for a split moment looked at me with a smile that seemed to convey an interest – as if she wanted to see whether or not the new adult was going to understand fun. This makes her flight to her mother seem somewhat dramatic. The mother tries to encourage her to look at the toys, but Mary again hides her face in her mother's skirt and repeats in an exaggeratedly babyish voice, 'Mommy, mommy, mommy!' A dramatic young lady: I am not even quite sure that she is not hiding a smile. I decide to wait.

Mary does make a decision. Still holding on to her mother, she points to a (girl) doll and says several times quickly and babyishly, 'What that, what that?' After the mother has patiently explained that it is a dolly, Mary repeats 'Dolly, dolly, dolly', and suggests in words not understandable to me that the mother take off the dolly's shoes. The mother tries to make her perform this act herself, but Mary simply repeats her demand. Her voice becomes quite anxious, and it seems that we may have tears in a moment.

Now the mother asks if it is not time for her to leave the room and wait outside as she has told Mary she would. I ask Mary whether we can let her mother go now and she, unexpectedly, makes no objection, not even when she suddenly finds herself without anybody to lean on. I try to start a conversation about the name of the doll, which the mother has left in Mary's hand. Mary grasps it firmly around the legs and suddenly, smiling mischievously, she begins to touch various things in the room with the doll's head. When a toy falls from the shelf, she looks at me to see whether she has gone too far; when she sees me smile permissively she laughs and begins to push smaller toys, always with the doll's head, in such a way that they fall too. Her excitement increases. With special glee she stabs with the doll's head at a toy train which is on the floor in the middle of the room. She overturns all the cars with growing evidence of a somehow too exciting kind of fun. As the engine overturns she suddenly stops and becomes pale. She leans with her back against the sofa, holds the doll vertically over her lower abdominal region, and lets it drop on the floor. She picks it up again, holds it over the same region, and drops it again. While repeating this several times, she begins first to whine and then to yell, 'Mommy, mommy, mommy.'

The mother re-enters, sure that communication has failed, and asks Mary whether she wants to go. I tell Mary that she may go if she wishes but that I hope she will be back in a few days. Quickly calmed, she leaves with her mother, saying good-bye to the secretary outside as if she had had a pleasant visit.

Strangely enough, I too felt that the child had made a successful if interrupted communication. With small children, words are not always necessary at the beginning. I had felt that the play was leading up to a conversation; and at any rate the child had conveyed to me by counterphobic activity what her danger was. The fact of the mother's anxious interruption was, of course, as significant as the child's play disruption. Together, they probably explain the child's babyish anxiety. But what had she communicated with this emotional somersault, this sudden hilarity and flushed aggressiveness, and this equally sudden inhibition and pale anxiety?

The discernible mode-content had been *pushing* things, not with her hand but with the doll as an extension of her hand; and then *dropping* the same doll from the genital region.

The doll as an extension of the hand was, as it were, a pushing tool. This suggests that she may not dare to touch or push things with her bare hand and reminds me of her teachers' observation that she seemed to touch or lift things in her own special way. This, together with the general rigidity in her extremities, suggests that Mary may be worried about her hands, maybe as aggressive tools.

The transfer of the doll to the lower abdominal region followed by her strangely obsessive and repetitive dropping leads to the further suggestion that she was dramatizing the loss from that region of an aggressive tool, a pushing instrument. The attack-like state which overcame her at this point reminds me of something which I learned long ago: severe hysterical attacks in adult women have been interpreted as dramatizations representing both partners in an imagined scene. Thus, one hand in tearing off the patient's dress may dramatize an aggressor's approach, while the other, in clutching it, may represent the victim's attempt to protect herself. Mary's attack impressed me as being of such a nature: by dropping the doll several times, panicky and yet as if obsessed, she seemed to be inexorably driven to dramatize both the robbed and the robber.

But what was to be stolen from her? Here we would have to know which meaning is more relevant, the doll's use as an aggressive tool – or the doll as a baby. In this play hour the dropped doll had first been the prolongation of an extremity and a tool of (pushing) aggression, and then something lost in the lower abdominal region under circumstances of extreme anxiety. Does Mary consider a penis such an aggressive weapon, and does she dramatize the fact that she does not have one? From the mother's account it is entirely probable that on entering the nursery school Mary was given her first opportunity to go to the toilet in the presence of boys and visits to the toilet were said to be occasions for anxiety.

I am thinking of the mother when she raps on the door. She has left the child, now quite composed, outside to come back and add something to Mary's biography. Mary was born with a sixth finger which was removed when she was approximately six months old; there is a scar on her left hand. Just prior to the outbreak of her anxiety attacks, Mary had repeatedly and urgently asked about this scar ('What that, what that?') and had received the routine answer that it was 'just a mosquito bite'. The mother agreed that the child when somewhat younger could easily have been present when her congenital anomaly was mentioned. Mary, the mother adds, has recently been equally insistent in her sexual curiosity.

We can now understand better the fact that Mary feels uneasy about the aggressive use of her hand, which has been robbed of a finger, and that she may equate the scar on her hand and her genital 'scar', the lost finger and the absent penis. Such an association would also bring into juxtaposition the observation of sex differences in the play school and the immediate question of a threatening operation.

Before Mary's second visit, her mother offered this further information: Mary's sexual curiosity had recently received a specific blow when her father, irritable because of a regional increase in unemployment which threatened his means of livelihood, had shown impatience with her during her usual morning visit to him in the bathroom. In fact, he had shoved her out of the room. As he told me later, he had angrily repeated the words 'You stay out of here!' She had liked to watch the shaving process and had also on recent occasions (to his slight annoyance) asked about his genitals. A strict adherence to a routine in which she could do, say, and ask the same thing over and over again had always been a necessary condition for Mary's inner security. She was 'heartbroken' over the consequent exclusion from the father's toilet.

We also discussed the fact (which I have already mentioned) that Mary's disturbed sleep and foul breath had been attributed by a paediatrician to a bad condition of the tonsils, and that the mother and the physician had engaged in a discussion in front of Mary as to whether she needed an immediate operation or not. *Operation*, then, and *separation* are seen to be the common denominators: the actual operation on the finger, the anticipated operation of the tonsils, and the mythical operation by which boys become girls; the separation from her mother during play-school hours, and the estrangement from her father. At the end of the first hour of play observation, then, this was the closest we could come to meanings on which all of the play elements and biographic data seemed to converge.

The antithesis of play disruption is play satiation, play from which a child emerges refreshed as a sleeper from dreams which 'worked'. Disruption and satiation are very marked and very clear only in rare cases. More often they are diffused and must be ascertained by detailed study. But not so in Mary's case. During her second appointment she obliged me with a specimen of play satiation as dramatic as that of her play disruption.

At first Mary again smiles bashfully at me. Again she turns her head away, holding on to her mother's hand and insisting that the mother come with her into the room. Once in the room, however, she lets her mother's hand go and, forgetting about the mother's and my presence, she begins to play animatedly and with obvious determination and goal-mindedness. I quickly close the door and motion the mother to sit down, because I do not want to disturb the play.

Mary goes to the corner where the blocks are on the floor. She selects two blocks and arranges them in such a way that she can stand on them each time she comes to the corner to pick up more blocks. Thus, play begins again with an extension of extremities, this time her feet. She now collects a pile of blocks in the middle of the room, moving to the corner and back without hesitation. Then she kneels on the floor and builds a small house for a toy cow. For about a quarter of an hour she is completely absorbed in the task of arranging the house so that it is strictly rectangular and at the same time fits tightly about a toy cow. She then adds five blocks to one long side of the house and experiments with a sixth block until its positions satisfies her (see Figure 10).

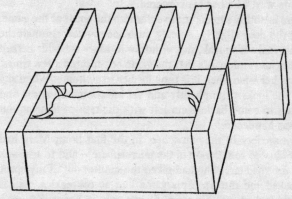

FIGURE 10

This time, then, the dominant emotional note is peaceful play concentration with a certain maternal quality of care and order. There is no climax of excitement, and the play ends on a note of satiation; she has built something, she likes it, now the play is over. She gets up with a radiant smile – which suddenly gives place to a mischievous twinkle. I do not realize the danger I am about to fall victim to, because I am too fascinated by the fact that the close-fitting stable looks like a hand – with a sixth finger. At the same time it expresses the 'inclusive' mode, a female-protective configuration, corresponding to the baskets and boxes and cradles arranged by little and big girls to give comfort to small things. Thus we see, so I muse, two restorations in one: the configuration puts the finger back on the hand and the happily feminine pattern belies the 'loss from the genital region' previously dramatized. The second hour's play thus accomplishes an expression of restoration and safety – and this concerning the same body parts (hand, genital region) which in the play disruption of the first hour had appeared as endangered.

But, as I said, Mary has begun to look teasingly at me. She now laughs, takes her mother's hand and pulls her out of the room, saying with determination, 'Mommy, come out.' I wait for a while, then look out into the waiting-room. A loud and triumphant, 'Thtay in there!' greets me. I strategically withdraw, whereupon Mary closes the door with a bang. Two further attempts on my part to leave my room are greeted in the same way. She has me cornered.

There is nothing to do but to enter into the spirit of the game. I open the door slightly, quickly push the toy cow through the opening, make it squeak, and withdraw it. Mary is beside herself with pleasure and insists that the game be repeated a few times. She gets her wish, then it is time for her to go home. When she leaves she looks triumphantly and yet affectionately at me and promises to come back. I am left with the task of figuring out what has happened.

From anxiety in the autosphere in the first hour, Mary had now graduated to satiation in the microsphere – and to triumph in the macrosphere. She had taken the mother out of my space and locked me into it. This game had as content: a man is teasingly locked into his room. It was only in connection with this playful superiority that Mary had decided to talk to me, and this in no uncertain terms. 'Thtay in there!' were the first words she had ever addressed to me! They were said clearly and in a loud voice, as if something in her had waited for the moment when she would be free enough to say them. What does that mean?

I think we have here the consummation of a play episode by way of a 'father transference'. It will be remembered that from the moment Mary came into my room at the beginning of the first contact she showed a somewhat coquettish and bashful curiosity about me, which she immediately denied by closing her eyes tightly. Since it can be expected that she would transfer to me (the man with toys) a conflict which disturbed her usually playful relationship with her father, it seems more than probable that in this game she was repeating with active mastery ('Thtay in there') and with some reversal of vectors (out–in) the situation of exclusion of which she had been a passive victim at home ('Stay out of here').

To some this may seem like a lot of complicated and devious reasoning for such a little girl. But here it is well to realize that these matters are difficult for rational thinking only. It would indeed be difficult to think up such a series of play tricks. It is even difficult to recognize and analyse it. But it happens, of course, unconsciously and automatically: here, never under-estimate the power of the ego – even of such a little girl.

This episode is presented to illustrate the self-curative trend in spontaneous play; for play therapy and play diagnosis must make systematic use of such self-curative processes. They may help the child to help himself – and they may help us to advise the parents. Where this fails, more complicated methods of treatment (child psychoanalysis)[3] must be initiated – methods which have not been discussed in this chapter. With advancing age, prolonged conversation would take the place of play. Here, however, it was my purpose to demonstrate that a few play-hours can serve to inform us of matters which the child could never verbalize. Trained observers, in the possession of numerous data, can see from a few play-contacts which of these data are acutely relevant to the child, and why. In Mary's case, her play disruption and her play satiation, if seen in the framework of all the known circumstances, strongly suggest that a variety of past and future, real and imagined, events had been incorporated into a system of mutually aggravating dangers. In her second play-hour, she disposed of them all: she restored her finger, reassured herself, reaffirmed her femininity – and told the big man off. Such play peace gained must, however, be sustained by new insight on the part of the parents.

Mary's parents accepted (and partly themselves suggested) the following recommendations. Mary's curiosity in regard to her scar, her genitals, and her operation required a truthful attitude. She needed to have other children, especially boys, visit her for play at her home. The matter of the tonsils called for the decision of a specialist, which could be candidly com-municated to the child. It did not seem wise to awaken and to restrain her during her nightmares; perhaps she needed to fight her dreams out, and there would be opportunity to hold her lightly and to comfort her when she awoke spontaneously. The child needed much activity; playful instruction in rhythmic motion might relax some of the rigidity in her extremities, which, whatever the initial cause, may have been at least aggravated by

[3] Anna Freud, *Psycho-Analytical Treatment of Children*, Imago Publishing Co., London, 1946.

fearful anticipation since hearing for the first time about the mysterious amputation of her finger.

When Mary, a few weeks later, paid me a short visit, she was entirely at home and asked me in a clear, loud voice about the colour of the train I had taken on my vacation. It will be remembered that she overturned a toy engine on the occasion of her first visit: now she could talk about engines. A tonsillectomy had proved unnecessary; the nightmares had ceased; Mary was making free and extensive use of the new play-companions provided in and near her home. There was a revived play-relationship with her father. He had intuitively made the most of Mary's sudden enraptured admiration for shining locomotives. He took her for regular walks to the railroad yards where they watched the mighty engines.

Here the symbolism which has pervaded this clinical episode gains a new dimension. In the despair of play disruption, the toy engine apparently had a destructive meaning in some context with phallic–locomotor anxiety: when Mary pushed it over, she apparently had that awesome 'Adam, where art thou' experience which we first observed in Ann. At the time, Mary's play relationship to her father had been disrupted, and this (as she could not know or understand) because of his worries over a possible disruption of his work status. This she seems to have interpreted entirely in terms of her maturational state and of her changes in status: and yet her reaction was not unrelated to the unconscious meaning of the father's actions. For threatened loss of status, threatened marginality, often result in an unconscious attempt by more stringent self-control and by purified standards to regain the ground lost or at least to keep from slipping any further. This, I believe, made the father react in a less tolerant way to the little girl's exploration, thus offending and frightening her in the general area which was already disturbed. It was, then, this area which appeared in her play in a condensed form, while she attempted, from the frightfulness of isolation, to work her way back to playful mutuality. Thus do children reflect and, where play fails, carry over into their own lives, the historical and economic crises of their parents.

Neither Mary's play nor the insight it provided could change the father's economic worries. But the moment he recognized the impact of his anxieties on his daughter's development, he realized that from a long-range point of view her anxieties mattered much more than the threatened change of his work status. In fact, actual developments did not confirm his apprehensions.

The father's idea of taking walks to the engine yards was felicitous. For the real engines now became symbols of power shared by father and daughter alike and sustained by the whole imagery of the machine culture in which this child is destined to become a woman.

Thus at the end of any therapeutic encounter with a child the parent must sustain what the adult patient must gain for himself: a realignment with the images and the forces governing the cultural development of his day, and from it an increased promise of a sense of identity.

But here, at last, we must try to come to a better description and definition of what we mean by identity.

THE BEGINNINGS OF IDENTITY

Play and Milieu

The emerging identity bridges the stages of childhood when the bodily self and the parental images are given their cultural connotations; and it bridges the stage of young adulthood, when a variety of social roles become available and, in fact, increasingly coercive. We will try to make this process more tangible, by looking first at some infantile steps towards identity and then at some cultural impediments to its consolidation.

A child who has just found himself able to walk, more or less coaxed or ignored by those around him, seems driven to repeat the act for the pure delight of functioning, and out of the need to master and perfect a newly initiated function. But he also acts under the immediate awareness of the new status and stature of 'one who can walk', with whatever connotation this happens to have in the coordinates of his culture's space–time – be it 'one who will go far', 'one who will be able to stand on his own feet', 'one who will be upright', 'one who must be watched because he might go too far'. The internalization of a particular version of 'one who can walk' is one of the many steps in child development which (through the coincident experience of physical mastery and of cultural meaning, of functional pleasure and of social prestige) contribute on each step to a more realistic self-esteem. This self-esteem grows to be a conviction that one is learning effective steps towards a tangible future, and is developing into a defined self within a social reality. The growing child must, at every step, derive a vitalizing sense of actuality from the awareness that his individual way of mastering experience (his ego synthesis) is a successful variant of a group identity and is in accord with its space–time and life plan.

In this children cannot be fooled by empty praise and condescending encouragement. They may have to accept artificial bolstering of their self-esteem in lieu of something better, but their ego identity gains real strength only from wholehearted and consistent recognition of real accomplishment – i.e., of achievement that has meaning in the culture. We have tried to convey this when discussing problems of Indian education, but yield to a more lucid statement:[4]

Dr Ruth Underhill tells me of sitting with a group of Papago elders in Arizona when the man of the house turned to his little three-year-old granddaughter and asked her to close the door. The door was heavy and hard to shut. The child tried, but it did not move. Several times the grandfather repeated: 'Yes, close the door.' No one jumped to the child's assistance. No one took the responsibility away from her. On the other hand there was no impatience, for after all the child was small. They sat gravely waiting until the child succeeded and her grandfather gravely thanked her. It was assumed that the task would not be asked of her unless she could perform it, and having been asked, the responsibility was hers alone just as if she were a grown woman.

The essential point of such child training is that the child is from infancy continuously conditioned to responsible social participation, while at the same time the tasks that are expected of it are adapted to its capacity. The contrast with our society is very great. A child does not make any contribution of labor to our industrial society except as it competes with an adult; its work is not measured against its own strength and skill but against high-geared industrial requirements. Even when we praise a child's achievements in the home, we are outraged if such praise is interpreted as being of the same order as praise of adults. The child is praised because the parent feels well disposed, regardless of whether the task is well done by adult standards or not and the child acquires no sensible standard by which to measure

[4] Ruth Benedict, 'Continuities and Discontinuities in Cultural Conditioning', *Psychiatry*, 1:161–67 (1938).

its achievement. The gravity of a Cheyenne Indian family ceremoniously making a feast out of a little boy's first snowbird is far removed from our behavior. At birth the little boy was presented with a toy bow and arrow, and from the time he could run about, serviceable bows and arrows suited to his stature were specially made for him by the man of the family. Animals and birds were brought to his awareness in a graded series beginning with those most easily taken, and as he brought in his first of each species his family duly made a feast of it, accepting his contribution as gravely as the buffalo his father brought. When he finally killed a buffalo, it was only the final step of his childhood conditioning, not a new adult role with which his childhood experience had been at variance.

It dawns on us, then, that the theories of play which are advanced in our culture and which take as their foundation the assumption that in children, too, play is defined by the fact that it is not work, are really only one of the many prejudices by which we exclude our children from an early source of a sense of identity.

But then, with primitives it is a different matter. Their cultures are exclusive. Their image of man begins and ends with their idea of a strong or clean Yurok or Sioux, in their defined segments of nature. In our civilization the image of man is expanding. As it becomes more individuated, it also tends to include untold millions in new regions, nations, continents, and classes. New syntheses of economic and emotional safety are sought in the formation of new national and social entities based on more inclusive identities.

Primitive tribes have a direct relationship with the sources and means of production. Their techniques are extensions of the human body; their magic is a projection of body concepts. Children in these groups participate in technical and magic pursuits. Body and environment, childhood and culture may be full of dangers, but they are all one world. This world may be small, but it is culturally coherent. The expansiveness of civilization, on the other hand, its stratification and specialization, make it impossible for children to include in their ego-synthesis more than segments of the society which is relevant to their existence. History itself has become a temporal environment to be adjusted to. Machines, far from remaining tools and extensions of man's physiological functions, destine whole organizations of people to be extensions of machinery. Child-hood, in some classes, becomes a separate segment of life, with its own folk-lore, its own literature.

The study of contemporary neuroses, however, points to the significance of this lag between child training and social actuality. Neuroses contain, so we find, unconscious and futile attempts to adjust to the heterogeneous present with the magic concepts of a more homogeneous past, fragments of which are still trans-mitted through child training. But mechanisms of adjustment which once made for evolutionary adaptation, tribal integration, caste coherence, national uniformity, etc., are at loose ends in an industrial civilization.

No wonder, then, that some of our troubled children con-stantly break out of their play into some damaging activity in which they seem to us to 'interfere' with our world; while analysis reveals that they only wish to demonstrate their right to find an identity in it. They refuse to become a speciality called 'child', who must play at being big because he is not given an opportunity to be a small partner in a big world.

Son of a Bombardier

During the last war a neighbour of mine, a boy of five, under-went a change of personality from a 'mother's boy' to a violent, stubborn, and disobedient child. The most disquieting symptom was an urge to set fires.

The boy's parents had separated just before the outbreak of war. The mother and the boy had moved in with some women cousins, and when the war began the father had joined the air force. The women cousins frequently expressed their disrespect for the father, and cultivated babyish traits in the boy. Thus, to be a mother's boy threatened to be a stronger identity-element than to be a father's son.

The father, however, did well in war; in fact, he became a hero. On the occasion of his first furlough the little boy had the experience of seeing the man he had been warned not to emulate become the much-admired centre of the neighbourhood's attention. The mother announced that she would drop her divorce plans. The father went back to war and was soon lost over Germany.

After the father's departure and death the affectionate and dependent boy developed more and more disquieting symptoms of destructiveness and defiance, culminating in fire setting. He gave the key to the change himself when, protesting against his mother's whipping, he pointed to a pile of wood he had set afire and exclaimed (in more childish words), 'If this were a German city, you would have liked me for it.' He thus indicated that in setting fires he fantasied being a bombardier like the father, who had told of his exploits.

We can only guess at the nature of the boy's turmoil. But I believe that we see here the identification of a son with his father, resulting from a suddenly increased conflict at the very close of the oedipus age. The father, at first successfully replaced by the 'good' little boy, suddenly becomes both a newly vitalized ideal and a concrete threat, a competitor for the mother's love. He thus devaluates radically the boy's feminine identifications. In order to save himself from both sexual and social disorientation, the boy must, in the shortest possible time, re-group his identifications; but then the great competitor is killed by the enemy – a fact which increases the guilt for the competitive feeling itself and compromises the boy's new masculine initiative which becomes maladaptive.

A child has quite a number of opportunities to identify himself, more or less experimentally, with habits, traits, occupations, and ideas of real or fictitious people of either sex. Certain crises force him to make radical selections. However, the historical era in which he lives offers only a limited number of socially meaningful models for workable combinations of identification fragments. Their usefulness depends on the way in which they simultaneously meet the requirements of the organism's maturational stage and the ego's habits of synthesis.

To my little neighbour the role of the bombardier may have suggested a possible synthesis of the various elements that comprise a budding identity: his temperament (vigorous); his maturational stage (phallic–urethral–locomotor); his social stage (oedipal) and his social situation; his capacities (muscular, mechanical); his father's temperament (a great soldier rather than a successful civilian); and a current historical prototype (aggressive hero). Where such synthesis succeeds, a most surprising coagulation of constitutional, temperamental, and learned reactions may produce exuberance of growth and unexpected accomplishment. Where it fails, it must lead to severe conflict, often expressed in unexpected naughtiness or delinquency. For should a child feel that the environment tries to deprive him too radically of all the forms of expression which permit him to develop and to integrate the next step in his identity, he will defend it with the astonishing strength encountered in animals who are suddenly forced to defend their lives. And indeed, in the social jungle of human existence, there is no feeling of being alive without a sense of ego identity. Deprivation of identity can lead to murder.

I would not have dared to speculate on the little bombardier's conflicts had I not seen evidence for a solution in line with our interpretation. When the worst of this boy's dangerous initiative had subsided, he was observed swooping down a hill on a bicycle, endangering, scaring, and yet deftly avoiding other children. They shrieked, laughed, and in a way admired him for it. In watching him, and hearing the strange noises he made, I could not help thinking that he again imagined himself to be an aeroplane on a bombing mission. But at the same time he gained in playful mastery over his locomotion; he exercised circumspection in his attack, and he became an admired virtuoso on a bicycle.

One should learn from such an example that re-education must seize upon the forces mobilized for playful integration. On the other hand, the desperate intensity of many a symptom must be understood as the defence of a step in identity development which to the child promises integration of the rapid changes taking place in all areas of his life. What to the observer looks like an especially powerful manifestation of naked instinct is often only a desperate plea for the permission to synthesize and sublimate in the only way possible. We can therefore expect our young patients to respond only to therapeutic measures which will help them to acquire the prerequisites for the successful completion of their identity. Therapy and guidance may attempt to substitute more desirable for less desirable items, but the total configuration of the developing identity elements soon becomes unalterable. It follows that therapy and guidance by professionals are doomed to failure where the culture refuses to provide an early basis for an identity and where opportunities for appropriate later adjustments are missing.

Our little son of a bombardier illustrates a general point. Psychosocial identity develops out of a gradual integration of all identifications. But here, if anywhere, the whole has a different quality from the sum of its parts. Under favourable circumstances children have the nucleus of a separate identity early in life; often they must defend it even against the necessity of over-identifying with one or both of their parents. These processes are difficult to study in patients, because the neurotic self has, by definition, fallen prey to over-identifications which isolate the small individual both from his budding identity and from his milieu.

Black Identity

But what if the milieu is determined to let live only at the expense of a permanent loss of identity?

Consider, for example, the chances for a continuity of identity in the American Negro child. I know a coloured boy who, like our boys, listens every night to Red Rider. Then he sits up in bed, imagining that he is Red Rider. But the moment comes when he sees himself galloping after some masked offenders and suddenly notices that in his fancy Red Rider is a coloured man. He stops his fantasy. While a small child, this boy was extremely expressive, both in his pleasures and in his sorrows. Today he is calm and always smiles; his language is soft and blurred; nobody can hurry him or worry him – or please him. White people like him.

Negro babies often receive sensual satisfactions which provide them with enough oral and sensory surplus for a lifetime, as clearly betrayed in the way they move, laugh, talk, sing. Their forced symbiosis with the feudal South capitalized on this oral–sensory treasure and helped to build a slave's identity: mild, submissive, dependent, somewhat querulous, but always ready to serve, with occasional empathy and childlike wisdom. But underneath a dangerous split occurred. The Negro's unavoidable identification with the dominant race, and the need of the master race to protect its own identity against the very sensual and oral temptations emanating from the race held to be inferior (whence came their mammies), established in both groups an association:

light – clean – clever – white, and dark – dirty – dumb – nigger. The result, especially in those Negroes who left the poor haven of their Southern homes, was often a violently sudden and cruel cleanliness training, as attested to in the autobiographies of Negro writers. It is as if by cleansing a whiter identity could be achieved. The attending disillusionment transmits itself to the phallic–locomotor stage, when restrictions as to what shade of girl one may dream of interfere with the free transfer of the original narcissistic sensuality to the genital sphere. Three identities are formed: (1) mammy's oral–sensual 'honey-child' – tender, expressive, rhythmical; (2) the evil identity of the dirty, anal–sadistic, phallic–rapist 'nigger'; and (3) the clean, anal–compulsive, restrained, friendly, but always sad 'white man's Negro'.

So-called opportunities offered the migrating Negro often only turn out to be a more subtly restricted prison which endangers his only historically successful identity (that of the slave) and fails to provide a reintegration of the other identity fragments mentioned. These fragments, then, become dominant in the form of racial caricatures which are underscored and stereotyped by the entertainment industry. Tired of his own caricature, the coloured individual often retires into hypochondriac invalidism as a condition which represents an analogy to the dependence and the relative safety of defined restriction in the South: a neurotic regression to the ego identity of the slave.

I have mentioned the fact that mixed-blood Indians in areas where they hardly ever see Negroes refer to their full-blood brothers as 'niggers', thus indicating the power of the dominant national imagery which serves to counterpoint the ideal and the evil images in the inventory of available prototypes. No individual can escape this opposition of images, which is all-pervasive in the men and in the women, in the majorities and in the minorities, and in all the classes of a given national or cultural unit. Psychoanalysis shows that the unconscious evil identity (the composite of everything which arouses negative identification – i.e., the wish not to resemble it) consists of the images of the violated (castrated) body, the ethnic out-group, and the exploited minority. Thus a pronounced he-man may, in his dreams and prejudices, prove to be mortally afraid of ever displaying a woman's sentiments, a Negro's submissiveness, or a Jew's intellectuality. For the ego, in the course of its synthesizing efforts, attempts to subsume the most powerful evil and ideal prototypes (the final contestants, as it were) and with them the whole existing imagery of superior and inferior, good and bad, masculine and feminine, free and slave, potent and impotent, beautiful and ugly, fast and slow, tall and small, in a simple alternative, in order to make one battle and one strategy out of a bewildering number of skirmishes.

While children may feel that coloured people have become dark by a dirtying process, coloured people may consider whites a bleached form of coloured man. In either case there is the idea of a washable layer.

All folks was born black, an' dem what's turnt white, dey jest had more sense. Angel of de Lord come down an' told de ontire bunch to meet on de fo'th Friday at de dark o' de moon an' wash deyselves in Jordan. He oxplained to 'em dat dey'd all turn white an' straighten de kinks outen deir hair. Angel kept preachin' an' preachin', but dem fool niggers didn't pay him no mind. Angel can't teach a nigger nothin'. When de fo'th Friday come a mighty little sprinklin' of 'em went down to de river an' commenced to scrub. Water was mighty low. 'Twarn't like Old Missip' – 'scusin' de Lord's river – 'twarn't no more'n a creek. You jest oughter seed dat crowd o' niggers settin' on de fence snickerin' at dem what went in washin'. Snickerin' an' throwin' slams. More niggers dan you ever see in Vicksburg on circus day.

Dem what went in de river kept scrubbin' and washin', special deir hair to git de kinks out. Old Aunt Grinny Granny – great-grand-mammy of all dem niggers – she sot on a log all day long, eatin' cheese and crackers and lowratin' dem what was washin'. When fust dark come, she jumped up and clapped her hands: 'Fore Gawd, dem niggers *is* gittin' white!' Grinny Granny jerked off her head hand-kercher an' went tumblin' down de bank to wash her hair, an' all dem fool niggers followed her. But de water was all used up, jest a tiny drap in de bottom, no more'n enough to moisten de palms o' deir hands and de soles o' deir feet. So dat's why a nigger is white in dem places.[5]

Folk-lore here makes use of a factor which racial prejudice (shared by black and white alike) has in common with sexual prejudice (also shared, deep down, by man and woman alike). The differentiating factor, whether it is the darker colour of the skin or the non-male form of the genitals, is assumed to have

[5] Members of the Federal Writers' Projects, *Phrases of the People*, The Viking Press, New York, 1937.

happened to the less-endowed, in the form of some oversight or punishment; and it is more or less outspokenly treated as a blemish.

The Negro, of course, is only the most flagrant case of an American minority which by the pressure of tradition and the limitation of opportunity is forced to identify with its own evil identity fragments, thus jeopardizing whatever participation in an American identity it may have earned.

What may be called an individual's ego space–time thus preserves the social topology of his childhood surroundings as well as the image of his own body, with its social connotations. To study both it is essential to correlate a patient's childhood history with the history of his family's sedentary residence in prototypal areas (East), in 'backward' areas (South), or in 'forward' areas (western and northern frontier), as these areas were gradually incorporated into the American version of the Anglo-Saxon cultural identity; his family's migration from, through, and to areas which at various periods may have represented the extreme sedentary or the extreme migratory pole of the developing American character; the family's religious conversions or digressions, with their class implications; abortive attempts at becoming standardized on a class level and the loss or abandonment of that level. Most important is that segment of the family's history which provided the last strong sense of cultural identity.

All of this impresses us with the dangers awaiting the minority-group American who, having successfully graduated from a marked and well-guided stage of autonomy, enters the most decisive stage of American childhood: that of initiative and industry. As indicated, minority groups of a lesser degree of Americanization are often privileged in the enjoyment of a more sensual early childhood. Their crisis comes when their mothers, losing trust in themselves and using sudden correctives in order to approach the vague but pervasive Anglo-Saxon ideal, create violent discontinuities; or where, indeed, the children themselves learn to disavow their sensual and overprotective mothers as temptations and a hindrance to the formation of a more American personality.

On the whole, it can be said that American schools successfully meet the challenge of training children of play-school age and of the elementary grades in a spirit of self-reliance and enterprise. Children of these ages seem remarkably free of prejudice and apprehension, preoccupied as they still are with growing and learning and with the new pleasures of association outside their families. This, to forestall the sense of individual inferiority, must lead to a hope for 'industrial association', for equality with all those who apply themselves wholeheartedly to the same skills and adventures in learning. Individual successes, on the other hand, only expose the now overly encouraged children of mixed backgrounds and of somewhat deviant endowments to the shock of American adolescence: the standardization of individuality and the intolerance of 'differences'.

A lasting ego-identity, we have said, cannot begin to exist without the trust of the first oral stage; it cannot be completed without a promise of fulfilment which from the dominant image of adulthood reaches down into the baby's beginnings and which, by the tangible evidence of social health, creates at every step of childhood and adolescence an accruing sense of ego strength. Thus, before entering further into identity problems of our time we must now recognize the place of identity in the human life cycle. What follows in the next chapter is a list of ego qualities which emerge from critical periods of development – criteria (identity is one) by which the individual demonstrates that his ego, at a given stage, is strong enough to integrate the timetable of the organism with the structure of social institutions.

7 Eight Ages of Man

BASIC TRUST v. BASIC MISTRUST

The first demonstration of social trust in the baby is the ease of his feeding, the depth of his sleep, the relaxation of his bowels. The experience of a mutual regulation of his increasingly receptive capacities with the maternal techniques of provision gradually helps him to balance the discomfort caused by the immaturity of homeostasis with which he was born. In his gradually increasing waking hours he finds that more and more adventures of the senses arouse a feeling of familiarity, of having coincided with a feeling of inner goodness. Forms of comfort, and people associated with them, become as familiar as the gnawing discomfort of the bowels. The infant's first social achievement, then, is his willingness to let the mother out of sight without undue anxiety or rage, because she has become an inner certainty as well as an outer predictability. Such consistency, continuity, and sameness of experience provide a rudimentary sense of ego identity which depends, I think, on the recognition that there is an inner population of remembered and anticipated sensations and images which are firmly correlated with the outer population of familiar and predictable things and people.

What we here call trust coincides with what Therese Benedek has called confidence. If I prefer the word 'trust', it is because there is more naïveté and more mutuality in it: an infant can be said to be trusting where it would go too far to say that he has confidence. The general state of trust, furthermore, implies not only that one has learned to rely on the sameness and continuity of the outer providers, but also that one may trust oneself and the capacity of one's own organs to cope with urges; and that one is able to consider oneself trustworthy enough so that the providers will not need to be on guard lest they be nipped.

The constant tasting and testing of the relationship between inside and outside meets its crucial test during the rages of the biting stage, when the teeth cause pain from within and when outer friends either prove of no avail or withdraw from the only action which promises relief: biting. Not that teething itself seems to cause all the dire consequences sometimes ascribed to it. As outlined earlier, the infant now is driven to 'grasp' more, but he is apt to find desired presences elusive: nipple and breast, and the mother's focused attention and care. Teething seems to have a prototypal significance and may well be the model for the masochistic tendency to assure cruel comfort by enjoying one's hurt whenever one is unable to prevent a significant loss.

In psychopathology the absence of basic trust can best be studied in infantile schizophrenia, while lifelong underlying weakness of such trust is apparent in adult personalities in whom withdrawal into schizoid and depressive states is habitual. The re-establishment of a state of trust has been found to be the basic requirement for therapy in these cases. For no matter what conditions may have caused a psychotic break, the bizarreness and withdrawal in the behaviour of many very sick individuals hides an attempt to recover social mutuality by a testing of the borderlines between senses and physical reality, between words and social meanings.

Psychoanalysis assumes the early process of differentiation between inside and outside to be the origin of projection and introjection which remain some of our deepest and most dangerous defence mechanisms. In introjection we feel and act as if an outer goodness had become an inner certainty. In projection, we experience an inner harm as an outer one: we endow significant people with the evil which actually is in us. These two mechanisms, then, projection and introjection, are assumed to be modelled after whatever goes on in infants when they would like to externalize pain and internalize pleasure, an intent which must yield to the testimony of the maturing senses and ultimately of reason. These mechanisms are, more or less normally, reinstated in acute crises of love, trust, and faith in adulthood and can characterize irrational attitudes towards adversaries and enemies in masses of 'mature' individuals.

The firm establishment of enduring patterns for the solution of the nuclear conflict of basic trust versus basic mistrust in mere existence is the first task of the ego, and thus first of all a task for maternal care. But let it be said here that the amount of trust derived from earliest infantile experience does not seem to depend on absolute quantities of food or demonstrations of love, but rather on the quality of the maternal relationship. Mothers create a sense of trust in their children by that kind of administration which in its quality combines sensitive care of the baby's individual needs and a firm sense of personal trustworthiness within the trusted framework of their culture's life style. This forms the basis in the child for a sense of identity which will later combine a sense of being 'all right', of being oneself, and of becoming what other people trust one will become. There are, therefore (within certain limits previously defined as the 'musts' of child care), few frustrations in either this or the following stages which the growing child cannot endure if the frustration leads to the ever renewed experience of greater sameness and stronger continuity of development, towards a final integration of the individual life-cycle with some meaningful wider belongingness. Parents must not only have certain ways of guiding by prohibition and permission; they must also be able to represent to the child a deep, an almost somatic conviction that there is a meaning to what they are doing. Ultimately, children become neurotic not from frustrations, but from the lack or loss of societal meaning in these frustrations.

But, even under the most favourable circumstances, this stage seems to introduce into psychic life (and become prototypical for) a sense of inner division and universal nostalgia for a paradise forfeited. It is against this powerful combination of a sense of having been deprived, of having been divided, and of having been abandoned that basic trust must maintain itself throughout life.

Each successive stage and crisis has a special relation to one of the basic elements of society, and this for the simple reason that the human life-cycle and man's institutions have evolved together. In this chapter we can do little more than mention, after the description of each stage, what basic element of social organization is related to it. This relation is two-fold: man brings to these institutions the remnants of his infantile mentality and his youthful fervour, and he receives from them – as long as they manage to maintain their actuality – a reinforcement of his infantile gains.

The parental faith which supports the trust emerging in the newborn has throughout history sought its institutional safeguard (and, on occasion, found its greatest enemy) in organized religion. Trust born of care is, in fact, the touchstone of the *actuality* of a given religion. All religions have in common the periodical childlike surrender to a Provider or providers who dispense earthly fortune as well as spiritual health; some demonstration of man's smallness by way of reduced posture and humble gesture; the admission in prayer and song of misdeeds, of misthoughts, and of evil intentions; fervent appeal for inner unification by divine guidance; and finally, the insight that individual trust must become a common faith, individual mistrust a commonly formulated evil, while the individual's restoration must become part of the ritual practice of many, and must become a sign of trustworthiness in the community.[1] We have illustrated how tribes dealing with one segment of nature develop a collective magic which seems to treat the Supernatural Providers of food and fortune as if they were angry and must be appeased by prayer and self-torture. Primitive religions, the most primitive layer in all religions, and the religious layer in each individual, abound with efforts at atonement which try to make up for vague deeds against a maternal matrix and try to restore faith in the goodness of one's strivings and in the kindness of the powers of the universe.

Each society and each age must find the institutionalized form of reverence which derives vitality from its world-image – from predestination to indeterminacy. The clinician can only observe that many are proud to be without religion whose children cannot afford their being without it. On the other hand, there are many who seem to derive a vital faith from social action or scientific pursuit. And again, there are many who profess faith, yet in practice breathe mistrust both of life and man.

[1] This is the communal and psychosocial side of religion. Its often paradoxical relation to the spirituality of the individual is a matter not to be treated briefly and in passing (see *Young Man Luther*). E.H.E.

In describing the growth and the crises of the human person as a series of alternative basic attitudes such as trust *v.* mistrust, we take recourse to the term a 'sense of', although, like a 'sense of health', or a 'sense of being unwell', such 'senses' pervade surface and depth, consciousness and the unconscious. They are, then, at the same time, ways of *experiencing* accessible to introspection; ways of *behaving*, observable by others; and unconscious *inner states* determinable by test and analysis. It is important to keep these three dimensions in mind, as we proceed.

Muscular maturation sets the stage for experimentation with two simultaneous sets of social modalities: holding on and letting go. As is the case with all of these modalities, their basic conflicts can lead in the end to either hostile or benign expectations and attitudes. Thus, to hold can become a destructive and cruel retaining or restraining, and it can become a pattern of care: to have and to hold. To let go, too, can turn into an inimical letting loose of destructive forces, or it can become a relaxed 'to let pass' and 'to let be'.

Outer control at this stage, therefore, must be firmly reassuring. The infant must come to feel that the basic faith in existence which is the lasting treasure saved from the rages of the oral stage, will not be jeopardized by this about-face of his, this sudden violent wish to have a choice, to appropriate demandingly, and to eliminate stubbornly. Firmness must protect him against the potential anarchy of his as yet untrained sense of discrimination, his inability to hold on and to let go with discretion. As his environment encourages him to 'stand on his own feet', it must protect him against meaningless and arbitrary experiences of shame and of early doubt.

The latter danger is the one best known to us. For if denied the gradual and well-guided experience of the autonomy of free choice (or if, indeed, weakened by an initial loss of trust) the child will turn against himself all his urge to discriminate and to manipulate. He will overmanipulate himself, he will develop a precocious conscience. Instead of taking possession of things in order to test them by purposeful repetition, he will become obsessed by his own repetitiveness. By such obsessiveness, of course, he then learns to repossess the environment and to gain power by stubborn and minute control, where he could not find large-scale mutual regulation. Such hollow victory is the infantile model for a compulsion neurosis. It is also the infantile source of later attempts in adult life to govern by the letter, rather than by the spirit.

Shame is an emotion insufficiently studied, because in our civilization it is so early and easily absorbed by guilt. Shame supposes that one is completely exposed and conscious of being looked at: in one word, self-conscious. One is visible and not ready to be visible; which is why we dream of shame as a situation in which we are stared at in a condition of incomplete dress, in night attire, 'with one's pants down'. Shame is early expressed in an impulse to bury one's face, or to sink, right then and there, into the ground. But this, I think, is essentially rage turned against the self. He who is ashamed would like to force the world not to look at him, not to notice his exposure. He would like to destroy the eyes of the world. Instead he must wish for his own invisibility. This potentiality is abundantly used in the educational method of 'shaming' used so exclusively by some primitive peoples. Visual shame precedes auditory guilt, which is a sense of badness to be had all by oneself when nobody watches and when everything is quiet – except the voice of the superego. Such shaming exploits an increasing sense of being small, which can develop only as the child stands up and as his awareness permits him to note the relative measures of size and power.

Too much shaming does not lead to genuine propriety but to a secret determination to try to get away with things, unseen – if, indeed, it does not result in defiant shamelessness. There is an impressive American ballad in which a murderer to be hanged on the gallows before the eyes of the community, instead of feeling duly chastened, begins to berate the onlookers, ending every salvo of defiance with the words, 'God damn your eyes.' Many a small child, shamed beyond endurance, may be in a chronic mood (although not in possession of either the courage or the words) to express defiance in similar terms. What I mean by this sinister reference is that there is a limit to a child's and an adult's endurance in the face of demands to consider himself, his body, and his wishes as evil and dirty, and to his belief in the infallibility of those who pass such judgement. He may be apt to turn things around, and to consider as evil only the fact that they exist: his chance will come when they are gone, or when he will go from them.

Doubt is the brother of shame. Where shame is dependent on the consciousness of being upright and exposed, doubt, so clinical observation leads me to believe, has much to do with a consciousness of having a front and a back – and especially a 'behind'. For this reverse area of the body, with its aggressive and libidinal focus in the sphincters and in the buttocks, cannot be seen by the child, and yet it can be dominated by the will of others. The 'behind' is the small being's dark continent, an area of the body which can be magically dominated and effectively invaded by those who would attack one's power of autonomy and who would designate as evil those products of the bowels which were felt to be all right when they were being passed. This basic sense of doubt in whatever one has left behind forms a substratum for later and more verbal forms of compulsive doubting; this finds its adult expression in paranoiac fears concerning hidden persecutors and secret persecutions threatening from behind (and from within the behind).

This stage, therefore, becomes decisive for the ratio of love and hate, cooperation and wilfulness, freedom of self-expression and its suppression. From a sense of self-control without loss of self-esteem comes a lasting sense of good will and pride; from a sense of loss of self-control and of foreign overcontrol comes a lasting propensity for doubt and shame.

If, to some reader, the 'negative' potentialities of our stages seem overstated throughout, we must remind him that this is not only the result of a preoccupation with clinical data. Adults, and seemingly mature and unneurotic ones, display a sensitivity concerning a possible shameful 'loss of face' and fear of being attacked 'from behind' which is not only highly irrational and in contrast to the knowledge available to them, but can be of fateful import if related sentiments influence, for example, interracial and international policies.

We have related basic trust to the institution of religion. The lasting need of the individual to have his will reaffirmed and delineated within an adult order of things which at the same time reaffirms and delineates the will of others has an institutional safeguard in the *principle of law and order*. In daily life as well as in the high courts of law – domestic and international – this principle apportions to each his privileges and his limitations, his obligations and his rights. A sense of rightful dignity and lawful independence on the part of adults around him gives to the child of good will the confident expectation that the kind of autonomy fostered in childhood will not lead to undue doubt or shame in later life. Thus the sense of autonomy fostered in the child and modified as life progresses, serves (and is served by) the preservation in economic and political life of a sense of justice.

INITIATIVE *v*. GUILT

There is in every child at every stage a new miracle of vigorous unfolding, which constitutes a new hope and a new responsibility for all. Such is the sense and the pervading quality of initiative. The criteria for all these senses and qualities are the same: a crisis, more or less beset with fumbling and fear, is resolved, in that the child suddenly seems to 'grow together' both in his person and in his body. He appears 'more himself', more loving, relaxed and brighter in his judgement, more activated and activating. He is in free possession of a surplus of energy which permits him to forget failures quickly and to approach what seems desirable (even if it also seems uncertain and even dangerous) with undiminished and more accurate direction. Initiative adds to autonomy the quality of undertaking, planning and 'attacking' a task for the sake of being active and on the move, where before self-will, more often than not, inspired acts of defiance or, at any rate, protested independence.

I know that the very word 'initiative', to many, has an American, and industrial, connotation. Yet, initiative is a necessary part of every act, and man needs a sense of initiative for whatever he learns and does, from fruit-gathering to a system of enterprise.

The ambulatory stage and that of infantile genitality add to the inventory of basic social modalities that of 'making', first in the sense of 'being on the make'. There is no simpler, stronger word for it; it suggests pleasure in attack and conquest. In the boy, the emphasis remains on phallic–intrusive modes; in the girl it turns to modes of 'catching' in more aggressive forms of snatching or in the milder form of making oneself attractive and endearing.

The danger of this stage is a sense of guilt over the goals contemplated and the acts initiated in one's exuberant enjoyment of new locomotor and mental power: acts of aggressive manipulation and coercion which soon go far beyond the executive capacity of organism and mind and therefore call for an energetic halt to one's contemplated initiative. While autonomy concentrates on keeping potential rivals out, and therefore can lead to jealous rage most often directed against encroachments by younger siblings, initiative brings with it anticipatory rivalry with those who have been there first and may, therefore, occupy with their superior equipment the field towards which one's initiative is directed. Infantile jealousy and rivalry, those often embittered and yet essentially futile attempts at demarcating a sphere of unquestioned privilege, now come to a climax in a final contest for a favoured position with the mother; the usual failure leads to resignation, guilt, and anxiety. The child indulges in fantasies of being a giant and a tiger, but in his dreams he runs in terror for dear life. This, then, is the stage of the 'castration complex', the intensified fear of finding the (now energetically erotized) genitals harmed as a punishment for the fantasies attached to their excitement.

Infantile sexuality and incest taboo, castration complex and superego all unite here to bring about that specifically human crisis during which the child must turn from an exclusive, pregenital attachment to his parents to the slow process of becoming a parent, a carrier of tradition. Here the most fateful split and transformation in the emotional powerhouse occurs, a split between potential human glory and potential total destruction. For here the child becomes forever divided in himself. The instinct fragments which before had enhanced the growth of his infantile body and mind now become divided into an infantile set which perpetuates the exuberance of growth potentials, and a parental set which supports and increases self-observation, self-guidance, and self-punishment.

The problem, again, is one of mutual regulation. Where the child, now so ready to overmanipulate himself, can gradually develop a sense of moral responsibility, where he can gain some insight into the institutions, functions, and roles which will permit his responsible participation, he will find pleasurable accomplishment in wielding tools and weapons, in manipulating meaningful toys – and in caring for younger children.

Naturally, the parental set is at first infantile in nature: the fact that human conscience remains partially infantile throughout life is the core of human tragedy. For the superego of the child can be primitive, cruel, and uncompromising, as may be observed in instances where children overcontrol and overconstrict themselves to the point of self-obliteration; where they develop an over-obedience more literal than the one the parent has wished to exact; or where they develop deep regressions and lasting resentments because the parents themselves do not seem to live up to the new conscience. One of the deepest conflicts in life is the hate for a parent who served as the model and the executor of the superego, but who (in some form) was found trying to get away with the very transgressions which the child can no longer tolerate in himself. The suspiciousness and evasiveness which is thus mixed in with the all-or-nothing quality of the superego, this organ of moral tradition, makes moral (in the sense of moralistic) man a great potential danger to his own ego – and to that of his fellow men.

In adult pathology, the residual conflict over initiative is expressed either in hysterical denial, which causes the repression of the wish or the abrogation of its executive organ by paralysis, inhibition, or impotence; or in overcompensatory showing off, in which the sacred individual, so eager to 'duck', instead 'sticks his neck out'. Then also a plunge into psychosomatic disease is now common. It is as if the culture had made a man over-advertise himself and so identify with his own advertisement that only disease can offer him escape.

But here, again, we must not think only of individual psychopathology, but of the inner powerhouse of rage which must be submerged at this stage, as some of the fondest hopes and the wildest fantasies are repressed and inhibited. The resulting self-righteousness – often the principal reward for goodness – can later be most intolerantly turned against others in the form of persistent moralistic surveillance, so that the prohibition rather than the guidance of initiative becomes the dominant endeavour. On the other hand, even moral man's initiative is apt to burst the boundaries of self-restriction, permitting him to do to others, in his or in other lands, what he would neither do nor tolerate being done in his own home.

In view of the dangerous potentials of man's long childhood, it is well to look back at the blueprint of the life-stages and to the possibilities of guiding the young of the race while they are young. And here we note that according to the wisdom of the ground plan the child is at no time more ready to learn quickly and avidly, to become bigger in the sense of sharing obligation and performance, than during this period of his development. He is eager and able to make things cooperatively, to combine with other children for the purpose of constructing and planning, and he is willing to profit from teachers and to emulate ideal prototypes. He remains, of course, identified with the parent of the same sex, but for the present he looks for opportunities where work-identification seems to promise a field of initiative without too much infantile conflict or oedipal guilt and a more realistic identification based on a spirit of equality experienced in doing things together. At any rate, the 'oedipal' stage results not only in the oppressive establishment of a moral sense restricting the horizon of the permissible; it also sets the direction towards the possible and the tangible which permits the dreams of early childhood to be attached to the goals of an active adult life. Social institutions, therefore, offer children of this age an *economic ethos*, in the form of ideal adults recognizable by their uniforms and their functions, and fascinating enough to replace the heroes of picture book and fairy tale.

INDUSTRY *v.* INFERIORITY

Thus the inner stage seems all set for 'entrance into life', except that life must first be school life, whether school is field or jungle or classroom. The child must forget past hopes and wishes, while his exuberant imagination is tamed and harnessed to the laws of impersonal things – even the three Rs. For before the child, psychologically already a rudimentary parent, can become a biological parent, he must begin to be a worker and potentia provider. With the oncoming latency period, the normally advanced child forgets, or rather sublimates, the necessity to 'make' people by direct attack or to become papa and mama in a hurry: he now learns to win recognition by producing things. He has mastered the ambulatory field and the organ modes. He has experienced a sense of finality regarding the fact that there is no workable future within the womb of his family, and thus becomes ready to apply himself to given skills and tasks, which go far beyond the mere playful expression of his organ modes or the pleasure in the function of his limbs. He develops a sense of industry – i.e., he adjusts himself to the inorganic laws of the tool world. He can become an eager and absorbed unit of a productive situation. To bring a productive situation to completion is an aim which gradually supersedes the whims and wishes of play. His ego boundaries include his tools and skills: the work principle (Ives Hendrick) teaches him the pleasure of work completion by steady attention and persevering diligence. In all cultures, at this stage, children receive some *systematic instruction*, although, as we saw in the chapter on American Indians, it is by no means always in the kind of school which literate people must organize around special teachers who have learned how to teach literacy. In preliterate people and in non-literate pursuits much is learned from adults who become teachers by dint of gift and inclination rather than by appointment, and perhaps the greatest amount is learned from older children. Thus the *fundamentals of technology* are developed, as the child becomes ready to handle the utensils, the tools, and the weapons used by the big people. Literate people, with more specialized careers, must prepare the child by teaching him things which first of all make him literate, the widest basic education for the greatest number of possible careers. The more confusing specialization becomes, however, the more indistinct are the eventual goals of initiative; and the more complicated social reality, the vaguer are the father's and mother's role in it. School seems to be a culture all by itself, with its own goals and limits, its achievements and disappointments.

The child's danger, at this stage, lies in a sense of inadequacy and inferiority. If he despairs of his tools and skills or of his status among his tool partners, he may be discouraged from identification with them and with a section of the tool world. To lose the hope of such 'industrial' association may pull him back to the more isolated, less tool-conscious familial rivalry of the oedipal time. The child despairs of his equipment in the tool world and in anatomy, and considers himself doomed to mediocrity or inadequacy. It is at this point that wider society becomes significant in its ways of admitting the child to an understanding of meaningful roles in its technology and economy. Many a child's development is disrupted when family life has failed to prepare him for school life, or when school life fails to sustain the promises of earlier stages.

Reagarding the period of a developing sense of industry, I have referred to *outer and inner hindrances* in the use of new capacities but not to aggravations of new human drives, nor to submerged rages resulting from their frustration. This stage differs from the earlier ones in that it is not a swing from an inner upheaval to a new mastery. Freud calls it the latency stage because violent drives are normally dormant. But it is only a lull before the storm of puberty, when all the earlier drives re-emerge in a new combination, to be brought under the dominance of genitality.

On the other hand, this is socially a most decisive stage: since industry involves doing things beside and with others, a first sense of division of labour and of differential opportunity, that is, a sense of the *technological ethos* of a culture, develops at this time. We have pointed in the last section to the danger threatening individual and society where the schoolchild begins to feel that the colour of his skin, the background of his parents, or the fashion of his clothes rather than his wish and his will to learn will decide his worth as an apprentice, and thus his sense of *identity* – to which we must now turn. But there is another, more fundamental danger, namely man's restriction of himself and constriction of his horizons to include only his work to which, so the Book says, he has been sentenced after his expulsion from Paradise. If he accepts work as his only obligation, and 'what works' as his only criterion of worthwhileness, he may become the conformist and thoughtless slave of his technology and of those who are in a position to exploit it.

IDENTITY *v*. ROLE CONFUSION

With the establishment of a good initial relationship to the world of skills and tools, and with the advent of puberty, childhood proper comes to an end. Youth begins. But in puberty and adolescence all samenesses and continuities relied on earlier are more or less questioned again, because of a rapidity of body growth which equals that of early childhood and because of the new addition of genital maturity. The growing and developing youths, faced with this physiological revolution within them, and with tangible adult tasks ahead of them are now primarily concerned with what they appear to be in the eyes of others as compared with what they feel they are, and with the question of how to connect the roles and skills cultivated earlier with the occupational prototypes of the day. In their search for a new sense of continuity and sameness, adolescents have to re-fight many of the battles of earlier years, even though to do so they must artificially appoint perfectly well-meaning people to play the roles of adversaries; and they are ever ready to install lasting idols and ideals as guardians of a final identity.

The integration now taking place in the form of ego identity. is, as pointed out, more than the sum of the childhood identifications. It is the accrued experience of the ego's ability to integrate all identifications with the vicissitudes of the libido, with the aptitudes developed out of endowment, and with the opportunities offered in social roles. The sense of ego identity, then, is the accrued confidence that the inner sameness and continuity of one's meaning for others, as evidenced in the tangible promise of a 'career'.

The danger of this stage is role confusion.[2] Where this is based on a strong previous doubt as to one's sexual identity, delinquent and outright psychotic episodes are not uncommon. If diagnosed and treated correctly, these incidents do not have the same fatal significance which they have at other ages. In most instances, however, it is the inability to settle on an occupational identity which disturbs individual young people. To keep themselves together they temporarily overidentify, to the point of apparent complete loss of identity, with the heroes of cliques and crowds. This initiates the stage of 'falling in love', which is by no means entirely, or even primarily, a sexual matter – except where the *mores* demand it. To a considerable extent adolescent love is an attempt to arrive at a definition of one's identity by

[2] See 'The Problem of Ego-Identity', *J. Amer. Psa. Assoc.*, 4:56–121.

projecting one's diffused ego-image on another and by seeing it thus reflected and gradually clarified. This is why so much of young love is conversation.

Young people can also be remarkably clannish, and cruel in their exclusion of all those who are 'different', in skin colour or cultural background, in tastes and gifts, and often in such petty aspects of dress and gesture as have been temporarily selected as *the* signs of an in-grouper or out-grouper. It is important to understand (which does not mean condone or participate in) such intolerance as a defence against a sense of identity confusion. For adolescents not only help one another temporarily through much discomfort by forming cliques and by stereotyping themselves, their ideals, and their enemies; they also perversely test each other's capacity to pledge fidelity. The readiness for such testing also explains the appeal which simple and cruel totalitarian doctrines have on the minds of the youth of such countries and classes as have lost or are losing their group identities (feudal, agrarian, tribal, national) and face world-wide industrialization, emancipation, and wider communication.

The adolescent mind is essentially a mind of the *moratorium*, a psychosocial stage between childhood and adulthood, and between the morality learned by the child, and the ethics to be developed by the adult. It is an ideological mind – and, indeed, it is the ideological outlook of a society that speaks most clearly to the adolescent who is eager to be affirmed by his peers, and is ready to be confirmed by rituals, creeds, and programmes which at the same time define what is evil, uncanny, and inimical. In searching for the social values which guide identity, one therefore confronts the problems of *ideology* and *aristocracy*, both in their widest possible sense which connotes that within a defined world image and a predestined course of history, the best people will come to rule and rule develops the best in people. In order not to become cynically or apathetically lost, young people must somehow be able to convince themselves that those who succeed in their anticipated adult world thereby shoulder the obligation of being the best. We will discuss later the dangers which emanate from human ideals harnessed to the management of super-machines, be they guided by nationalistic or international, communist or capitalist ideologies. In the last part of this book we shall discuss the way in which the revolutions of our day attempt to solve and also to exploit the deep need of youth to re-define its identity in an industrialized world.

INTIMACY *v*. ISOLATION

The strength acquired at any stage is tested by the necessity to transcend it in such a way that the individual can take chances in the next stage with what was most vulnerably precious in the previous one. Thus, the young adult, emerging from the search for and the insistence on identity, is eager and willing to fuse his identity with that of others. He is ready for intimacy, that is, the capacity to commit himself to concrete affiliations and partnerships and to develop the ethical strength to abide by such commitments, even though they may call for significant sacrifices and compromises. Body and ego must now be masters of the organ modes and of the nuclear conflicts, in order to be able to face the fear of ego loss in situations which call for self-abandon: in the solidarity of close affiliations, in orgasms and sexual unions, in close friendships and in physical combat, in experiences of inspiration by teachers and of intuition from the recesses of the self. The avoidance of such experiences because of a fear of ego-loss may lead to a deep sense of isolation and consequent self-absorption.

The counterpart of intimacy is distantiation: the readiness to isolate and, if necessary, to destroy those forces and people whose essence seems dangerous to one's own, and whose 'territory' seems to encroach on the extent of one's intimate relations. Prejudices thus developed (and utilized and exploited in politics and in war) are a more mature outgrowth of the blinder repudiations which during the struggle for identity differentiate sharply and cruelly between the familiar and the foreign. The danger of this stage is that intimate, competitive, and combative relations are experienced with and against the selfsame people. But as the areas of adult duty are delineated, and as the competitive encounter, and the sexual embrace, are differentiated, they eventually become subject to that *ethical sense* which is the mark of the adult.

Strictly speaking, it is only now that *true genitality* can fully develop; for much of the sex life preceding these commitments

237

is of the identity-searching kind, or is dominated by phallic or vaginal strivings which make of sex-life a kind of genital combat. On the other hand, genitality is all too often described as a permanent state of reciprocal sexual bliss. This, then, may be the place to complete our discussion of genitality.

For a basic orientation in the matter I shall quote what has come to me as Freud's shortest saying. It has often been claimed, and bad habits of conversation seem to sustain the claim, that psychoanalysis as a treatment attempts to convince the patient that before God and man he has only one obligation: to have good orgasms, with a fitting 'object', and that regularly. This, of course, is not true. Freud was once asked what he thought a normal person should be able to do well. The questioner probably expected a complicated answer. But Freud, in the curt way of his old days, is reported to have said: '*Lieben und arbeiten*' (to love and to work). It pays to ponder on this simple formula; it gets deeper as you think about it. For when Freud said 'love' he meant *genital* love, and genital *love*; when he said love *and* work, he meant a general work-productiveness which would not preoccupy the individual to the extent that he loses his right or capacity to be a genital and a loving being. Thus we may ponder, but we cannot improve on, 'the professor's' formula.

Genitality, then, consists in the unobstructed capacity to develop an orgastic potency so free of pregenital interference that genital libido (not just the sex products discharged in Kinsey's 'outlets') is expressed in heterosexual mutality, with full sensitivity of both penis and vagina, and with a convulsion-like discharge of tension from the whole body. This is a rather concrete way of saying something about a process which we really do not understand. To put it more situationally: the total fact of finding, via the climactic turmoil of the orgasm, a supreme experience of the mutual regulation of two beings in some way takes the edge off the hostilities and potential rages caused by the oppositeness of male and female, of fact and fancy, of love and hate. Satisfactory sex relations thus make sex less obsessive, overcompensation less necessary, sadistic controls superfluous.

Preoccupied as it was with curative aspects, psychoanalysis often failed to formulate the matter of genitality in a way significant for the processes of society in all classes, nations, and levels of culture. The kind of mutuality in orgasm which

238

psychoanalysis has in mind is apparently easily obtained in classes and cultures which happen to make a leisurely institution of it. In more complex societies this mutuality is interfered with by so many factors of health, of opportunity, and of temperament, that the proper formulation of sexual health would be rather this: a human being should be potentially able to accomplish mutuality of genital orgasm, but he should also be so constituted as to bear a certain amount of frustration in the matter without undue regression wherever emotional preference or considerations of duty and loyalty call for it.

While psychoanalysis has on occasion gone too far in its emphasis on genitality as a universal cure for society and has thus provided a new addiction and a new commodity for many who wished to so interpret its teachings, it has not always indicated all the goals that genitality actually should and must imply. In order to be of lasting social significance, the Utopia of genitality should include:

1. mutuality of orgasm
2. with a loved partner
3. of the other sex
4. with whom one is able and willing to share a mutual trust
5. and with whom one is able and willing to regulate the cycles of
   a. work
   b. procreation
   c. recreation
6. so as to secure to the offspring, too, all the stages of a satisfactory development.

It is apparent that such Utopian accomplishment on a large scale cannot be an individual or, indeed, a therapeutic task. Nor is it a purely sexual matter by any means. It is integral to a culture's style of sexual selection, cooperation, and competition.

The danger of this stage is isolation, that is, the avoidance of contacts which commit to intimacy. In psychopathology, this disturbance can lead to severe 'character-problems'. On the other hand, there are partnerships which amount to an isolation *à deux*, protecting both partners from the necessity to face the next critical development – that of generativity.

In this book the emphasis is on the childhood stages, otherwise the section on generativity would of necessity be the central one, for this term encompasses the evolutionary development which has made man the teaching and instituting as well as the learning animal. The fashionable insistence on dramatizing the dependence of children on adults often blinds us to the dependence of the older generation on the younger one. Mature man needs to be needed, and maturity needs guidance as well as encouragement from what has been produced and must be taken care of.

Generativity, then, is primarily the concern in establishing and guiding the next generation, although there are individuals who, through misfortune or because of special and genuine gifts in other directions, do not apply this drive to their own offspring. And indeed, the concept generativity is meant to include such more popular synonyms as *productivity* and *creativity*, which, however, cannot replace it.

It has taken psychoanalysis some time to realize that the ability to lose oneself in the meeting of bodies and minds leads to a gradual expansion of ego-interests and to a libidinal investment in that which is being generated. Generativity thus is an essential stage on the psychosexual as well as on the psychosocial schedule. Where such enrichment fails altogether, regression to an obsessive need for pseudo-intimacy takes place, often with a pervading sense of stagnation and personal impoverishment. Individuals, then, often begin to indulge themselves as if they were their own – or one another's – one and only child; and where conditions favour it, early invalidism, physical or psychological, becomes the vehicle of self-concern. The mere fact of having or even wanting children, however, does not 'achieve' generativity. In fact, some young parents suffer, it seems, from the retardation of the ability to develop this stage. The reasons are often to be found in early childhood impressions; in excessive self-love based on a too strenuously self-made personality; and finally (and here we return to the beginnings) in the lack of some faith, some 'belief in the species', which would make a child appear to be a welcome trust of the community.

As to the institutions which safeguard and reinforce generativity, one can only say that all institutions codify the ethics of generative succession. Even where philosophical and spiritual tradition suggests the renunciation of the right to procreate or to produce, such early turn to 'ultimate concerns', wherever instituted in monastic movements, strives to settle at the same time the matter of its relationship to the Care for the creatures of this world and to the Charity which is felt to transcend it.

If this were a book on adulthood, it would be indispensable and profitable at this point to compare economic and psychological theories (beginning with the strange convergencies and divergencies of Marx and Freud) and to proceed to a discussion of man's relationship to his production as well as to his progeny.

EGO INTEGRITY *v.* DESPAIR

Only in him who in some way has taken care of things and people and has adapted himself to the triumphs and disappointments adherent to being, the originator of others or the generator of products and ideas – only in him may gradually ripen the fruit of these seven stages. I know no better word for it than ego integrity. Lacking a clear definition, I shall point to a few constituents of this state of mind. It is the ego's accrued assurance of its proclivity for order and meaning. It is a post-narcissistic love of the human ego – not of the self – as an experience which conveys some world order and spiritual sense, no matter how dearly paid for. It is the acceptance of one's one and only life cycle as something that had to be and that, by necessity, permitted of no substitutions: it thus means a new, a different love of one's parents. It is a comradeship with the ordering ways of distant times and different pursuits, as expressed in the simple products and sayings of such times and pursuits. Although aware of the relativity of all the various life styles which have given meaning to human striving, the possessor of integrity is ready to defend the dignity of his own style against all physical and economic threats. For he knows that an individual life is the accidental coincidence of but one life cycle with but one segment of history; and that for him all human integrity stands or falls with the one style of integrity of which he partakes. The style of integrity developed by his culture or civilization thus becomes the 'patrimony of his soul', the seal of his moral paternity of himself (' . . . *pero el honor/Es patrimonio del alma*': Calderón). In such final consolidation, death loses its sting.

The lack or loss of this accrued ego integration is signified by fear of death: the one and only life cycle is not accepted as the ultimate of life. Despair expresses the feeling that the time is now short, too short for the attempt to start another life and to try out alternate roads to integrity. Disgust hides despair, if often only in the form of 'a thousand little disgusts' which do not add up to one big remorse: ' . . . *mille petits dégoûts de soi, dont le total ne fait pas un remords, mais un gêne obscur*': Rostand.

Each individual, to become a mature adult, must to a sufficient degree develop all the ego qualities mentioned, so that a wise Indian, a true gentleman, and a mature peasant share and recognize in one another the final stage of integrity. But each cultural entity, to develop the particular style of integrity suggested by its historical place, utilizes a particular combination of these conflicts, along with specific provocations and prohibitions of infantile sexuality. Infantile conflicts become creative only if sustained by the firm support of cultural institutions and of the special leader-classes representing them. In order to approach or experience integrity, the individual must know how to be a follower of image bearers in religion and in politics, in the economic order and in technology, in aristocratic living and in the arts and sciences. Ego integrity, therefore, implies an emotional integration which permits participation by followership as well as acceptance of the responsibility of leadership.

Webster's Dictionary is kind enough to help us complete this outline in a circular fashion. Trust (the first of our ego values) is here defined as 'the assured reliance on another's integrity', the last of our values. I suspect that Webster had business in mind rather than babies, credit rather than faith. But the formulation stands. And it seems possible to further paraphrase the relation of adult integrity and infantile trust by saying that healthy children will not fear life if their elders have integrity enough not to fear death.

In this book the emphasis is on the childhood stages. The foregoing conception of the life cycle, however, awaits systematic treatment. To prepare this, I shall conclude this chapter with a diagram. In this, as in the diagram of pregenital zones and modes, the diagonal represents the normative sequence of psychosocial gains made as at each stage one more nuclear conflict adds a new ego quality, a new criterion of accruing human strength. Below the diagonal there is space for the precursors of each of these solutions, all of which begin with the beginning; above the diagonal there is space for the designation of the derivatives of these gains and their transformations in the maturing and the mature personality.

The underlying assumptions for such charting are: (1) that the human personality in principle develops according to steps predetermined in the growing person's readiness to be driven towards, to be aware of, and to interact with, a widening social radius; and (2) that society, in principle, tends to be so constituted as to meet and invite this succession of potentialities for interaction and attempts to safeguard and to encourage the proper rate and the proper sequence of their enfolding. This is the 'maintenance of the human world'.

But a chart is only a tool to think with, and cannot aspire to be a prescription to abide by, whether in the practice of child-training, in psychotherapy, or in the methodology of child study. In the presentation of the psychosocial stages in the form of an *epigenetic chart* analogous to the one employed in Chapter 2 for an analysis of Freud's psychosexual stages, we have definite and delimited methodological steps in mind. It is one purpose of this work to facilitate the comparison of the stages first discerned by Freud as sexual to other schedules of development (physical, cognitive). But any one chart delimits one schedule only, and it must not be imputed that our outline of the psychosocial schedule is intended to imply obscure generalities concerning other aspects of development – or, indeed, of existence. If the chart, for example, lists a series of conflicts or crises, we do not consider all development a series of crises: we claim only that psychosocial development proceeds by critical steps – 'critical' being a characteristic of turning points, of moments of decision between progress and regression, integration and retardation.

It may be useful at this point to spell out the methodological implications of an epigenetic matrix. The more heavily-lined squares of the diagonal signify both a sequence of stages and a gradual development of component parts: in other words, the chart formalizes a progression through time of a differentiation

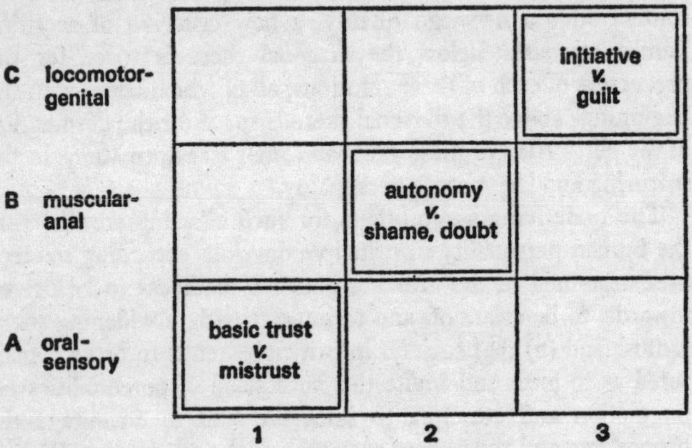

FIGURE II

of parts. This indicates (1) that each critical item of psychosocial strength discussed here is systematically related to all others, and that they all depend on the proper development in the proper sequence of each item; and (2) that each item exists in some form before its critical time normally arrives.

If I say, for example, that a favourable ratio of basic trust over basic mistrust is the first step in psychosocial adaptation, a favourable ratio of autonomous will over shame and doubt the second, the corresponding diagrammatic statement expresses a number of fundamental relations that exist between the two steps, as well as some facts fundamental to each. Each comes to its ascendance, meets its crisis, and finds its lasting solution during the stage indicated. But they all must exist from the beginning in some form, for every act calls for an integration of all. Also, an infant may show something like 'autonomy' from the beginning in the particular way in which he angrily tries to wriggle himself free when tightly held. However, under normal

	1	2	3	4	5	6	7	8
H maturity								ego integrity v. despair
G adulthood							generativity v. stagnation	
F young adulthood						intimacy v. isolation		
E puberty and adolescence					identity v. role confusion			
D latency				industry v. inferiority				
C locomotor-genital			initiative v. guilt					
B muscular-anal		autonomy v. shame, doubt						
A oral sensory	basic trust v. mistrust							

FIGURE 12

conditions, it is not until the second year that he begins to experience the whole *critical opposition of being an autonomous creature and being a dependent one*; and it is not until then that he is ready for a decisive encounter with his environment, an environment which, in turn, feels called upon to convey to him its particular ideas and concepts of autonomy and coercion in ways decisively contributing to the character and the health of his personality in his culture. It is this encounter, together with the resulting crisis, that we have tentatively described for each stage. As to the progression from one stage to the next, the diagonal indicates the sequence to be followed. However, it also makes room for variations in tempo and intensity. An individual, or a culture, may linger excessively over trust and proceed from AI over to A2 to B2, or an accelerated progression may move from AI over BI to B2. Each such acceleration or (relative) retardation, however, is assumed to have a modifying influence on all later stages.

An epigenetic diagram thus lists a system of stages dependent on each other; and while individual stages may have been explored more or less thoroughly or named more or less fittingly, the diagram suggests that their study be pursued always with the total configuration of stages in mind. The diagram invites, then, a thinking through of all its empty boxes: if we have entered Basic Trust in AI and Integrity in H8, we leave the question open, as to what trust might have become in a stage dominated by the need for integrity even as we have left open what it may look like and, indeed, be called in the stage dominated by a striving for autonomy (BI). All we mean to emphasize is that trust must have developed in its own right, before it becomes something more in the critical encounter in which autonomy develops – and so on, up the vertical. If, in the last stage (HI), we would expect trust to have developed into the most mature *faith* that an ageing person can muster in his cultural setting and historical period, the chart permits the consideration not only of what old age can be, but also what its preparatory stages must have been. All of this should make it clear that a chart of epigenesis suggests a global form of thinking and rethinking which leaves details of methodology and terminology to further study.[3]

[3] To leave this matter truly open, certain misuses of the whole conception would have to be avoided. Among them is the assumption that the sense of

trust (and all the other 'positive' senses postulated) is an *achievement*, secured once and for all at a given state. In fact, some writers are so intent on making an *achievement scale* out of these stages that they blithely omit all the 'negative' senses (basic mistrust, etc.) which are and remain the dynamic counterpart of the 'positive' ones throughout life. The assumption that on each stage a goodness is achieved which is impervious to new inner conflicts and to changing conditions is, I believe, a projection on child development of that success ideology which can so dangerously pervade our private and public daydreams and can make us inept in a heightened struggle for a meaningful existence in a new, industrial era of history. The personality is engaged with the hazards of existence continuously, even as the body's metabolism copes with decay. As we come to diagnose a state of relative strength and the symptoms of an impaired one, we face only more clearly the paradoxes and tragic potentials of human life.

The stripping of the stages of everything but their 'achievements' has its counterpart in attempts to describe or test them as 'traits' or 'aspirations' without first building a systematic bridge between the conception advanced throughout this book and the favourite concepts of other investigators. If the foregoing sounds somewhat plaintive, it is not intended to gloss over the fact that in giving to these strengths the very designations by which in the past they have acquired countless connotations of superficial goodness affected niceness, and all too strenuous virtue, I invited misunderstandings and misuses. However, I believe that there is an intrinsic relationship between ego and language and that despite passing vicissitudes certain basic words retain essential meanings.

I have since attempted to formulate for Julian Huxley's *Humanist Frame* (Allen and Unwin, 1961; Harper and Brothers, 1962) a blueprint of essential strengths which evolution has built both into the ground plan of the life stages and into that of man's institutions (an expanded discussion is offered in Chapter IV, 'Human Strength and the Cycle of Generations', of my *Insight and Responsibility* [W. W. Norton, 1964]. While I cannot discuss here the methodological problems involved (and aggravated by my use of the term 'basic virtues'), I should append the list of these strengths because they are really the lasting outcome of the 'favourable ratios' mentioned at every step of the chapter on psychosocial stages. Here they are:

Basic Trust *v.* Basic Mistrust: Drive and *Hope*
Autonomy *v.* Shame and Doubt: Self-Control and *Willpower*
Initiative *v.* Guilt: Direction and *Purpose*
Industry *v.* Inferiority: Method and *Competence*
Identity *v.* Role Confusion: Devotion and *Fidelity*
Intimacy *v.* Isolation: Affiliation and *Love*
Generativity *v.* Stagnation: Production and *Care*
Ego Integrity *v.* Despair: Renunciation and *Wisdom*

The italicized words are called *basic* virtues because without them, and their re-emergence from generation to generation, all other and more changeable systems of human values lose their spirit and their relevance. Of this list, I have been able so far to give a more detailed account only for Fidelity (see *Youth, Change and Challenge*, E. H. Erikson, editor, Basic Books, 1963). But here again, the list represents a total conception within which there is much room for a discussion of terminology and methodology.   E.H.E.

247

Part Four

Youth and the Evolution of Identity

Introduction to Part Four

With the attempt at formulating integrity as the mature quality accrued from all the ego states and libidinal phases, the scope of a book on childhood and society seems to have been overstepped – and with it, the range of psychoanalytic child psychology as now formulated. For psychoanalysis has consistently described the vicissitudes of instincts and of the ego only up to adolescence, at which time rational genitality was expected to absorb infantile fixations and irrational conflicts or to admit them to repeat performances under manifold disguises. The main recurrent theme thus concerned the shadow of frustration which falls from childhood on the individual's later life – and on his society. In this book we suggest that, to understand either childhood or society, we must expand our scope to include the study of the way in which societies lighten the inescapable conflicts of childhood with a promise of some security, identity, and integrity. In thus reinforcing the values by which the ego exists societies create the only condition under which human growth is possible.

Successive civilizations, while exploiting appropriate syndromes of infantile fears, can also be shown to raise the corresponding infantile ego value to highest collective endeavour. A religion, for example, may organize the nuclear conflict of sense of trust versus sense of evil, collectively cultivating trust in the form of faith and exploiting the sense of evil in the form of sin. Such an organization may have its era in history when it reinforces this particular ego value with a ceremonial power capable of infusing civilizations and of replenishing the communality of its followers in one form of human integrity. That organizations have a knack for outliving their historical ascendancy is another matter. As other ego values (i.e., autonomy) become the nuclei of collective endeavours, older organizations may increasingly depend on a ruthless exploitation of infantile fears. A church may have to take refuge in a system of indoctrination intended to convince people of the inescapable reality of a particular kind of evil in order to be able to announce that it alone possesses the key for the only door to salvation.

The history of societies records the rise and fall of upper classes, élites, and priesthoods which in their aristocratic aspirations cultivated one or the other of the ego values, giving true comfort and providing true progress, but then for the sake of the survival of their own petty hierarchies learned to exploit the infantile anxieties which they at first alleviated. Kings who, when great, were heroes in the drama of patriarchy have protected themselves and their rule by relying on the taboo against patricide. Feudal systems, which at their best are models for the apportioning of responsibility among leaders and led, have maintained themselves by predicting anarchy and threatening loss of face to dissidents. Political systems have thrived on the provocation of manifold and morbid doubt; economic systems on the guilty hesitation to initiate change. Yet political, economic, and technical élites, wherever they have accepted the obligation to perfect a new style of living at a logical point in history, have provided men with a high sense of identity and have inspired them to reach new levels of civilization. All in all, one may conclude that the price in concomitant misery has been too high; but this is a matter for purely philosophical deliberation.

These are impressions. I do not have the knowledge necessary to approach in any systematic fashion the relationship between ego qualities, social institutions, and historical eras. But, to repeat this in more dogmatic form, just as there is a basic affinity of the problem of basic trust to the institution of religion, the problem of autonomy is reflected in basic political and legal organization and that of initiative in the economic order. Similarly, industry is related to technology; identity to social stratification; intimacy to relationship patterns; generativity to education, art, and science; and integrity, finally, to philosophy. The study of society must concern itself with the relationship of these institutions to each other, and with the ascent and the decline of institutions as organizations. But I think that, in the long run, such study would forfeit one of its most fruitful considerations were it to overlook the way in which each generation can and must re-vitalize each institution even as it grows into it. I can pursue here only one specific direction suggested and confirmed by my own observations. I have focused on the problem of ego identity and on its anchoring in a cultural identity because I believe it to be that part of the ego which at the end of adolescence integrates the infantile ego stages and neutralizes the autocracy of the infantile superego. It is the only inner arrangement which prevents the superego's permanent alliance with the unreconstructed remnants of latent infantile rage.

I know very well that this shift in conceptual emphasis is dictated by historical accident – i.e., by the revolutions that are taking place in our lifetime, affecting our personal fortunes as well as the symptoms presented and the unconscious demands made on us by our patients. To condense it into a formula: the patient of today suffers most under the problem of what he should believe in and who he should – or, indeed, might – be or become; while the patient of early psychoanalysis suffered most under inhibitions which prevented him from being what and who he thought he knew he was. In this country especially, adult patients and the parents of prospective child patients often hope to find in the psychoanalytic system a refuge from the discontinuities of existence, a regression and a return to a more patriarchal one-to-one relationship.

As early as 1908[1] Freud pointed to the origin of the neuroses of his time, in the double standard for the two sexes and the excessive demands made by upper-class pretences on the wives and mothers in his urban environment. He acknowledged, as partially relevant, the damaging influence of rapid changes in social role suffered by individuals who moved from the country to the city or who climbed from the middle to the upper class. In all of this, however, he discerned as the mainspring of psychopathology a deep upset in the individual's sexual economy owing to the manifold hypocrisies and sexual repressions imposed on him.

To worthy subjects suffering from these arbitrary standards Freud offered the psychoanalytic method, a form of radical self-enlightenment, which soon burst the bounds of neuropsychiatry.

[1] Sigmund Freud, ' "Civilized" Sexual Morality and Modern Nervous Illness', *Standard Edition*, Vol. IX, The Hogarth Press, London, 1959.

For with it he found, in the depths of the inhibited individuals of his time, residues of and analogies to the taboos and conventions of all times. Beyond explaining the symptoms characteristic of its own period, psychoanalysis uncovered a timeless élite of brooding neurotics, successive versions of King Oedipus, Prince Hamlet, and the brothers Karamazov, and it undertook to deal with the spectacle of their tragic conflicts within a private method of self-enlightenment. Making their peace with the complexes emanating from the daemonic id, they would thereby gain not only health, but also a victory for reason, and individuation.

The history of civilization will record that Freud, in attempting to meet the demands of his neurological practice, inadvertently continued that revolution in human consciousness which in antiquity had lifted the tragic individual from the anonymous chorus of the archaic world and which had made self-conscious man the 'measure of all things'. The scientific inquiry which had then been directed towards 'all things' was re-directed by Freud to include human consciousness itself: we shall return, in the conclusion, to the dilemma caused by this re-application of the spirit of inquiry to its own organ and origin. In the meantime, the thematic affinity of the basic Freudian conflicts to the themes of Greek tragedy are obvious, in terminology as well as in spirit.

The spirit of Freud's work, then – in spite of terms and techniques connoting the physiological and physical laboratory of the nineteenth century – vastly antedates the World Wars, the world revolutions, and the rise of the first industrial culture in this country. Freud remained aloof from all of these developments. The Storm Troopers who searched his home (where he had surrounded himself with many choice little statues from the pre-tragic, the pre-selfconscious days of archaic antiquity) only seemed to confirm his original approach to group psychology, which led him to conclude that any organized group was a latent mob and a potential enemy to the spirit of individuation and reason.

The crowning value of what Freud called the 'primacy of the intellect' was the cornerstone of the early psychoanalyst's identity, giving him a firm foothold in the era of enlightenment, as well as in the ripe intellectuality of his own race. Only once, in a letter to a Jewish lodge, did Freud acknowledge this *Heimlichkeit der gleichen inneren Konstruktion*[2] – an untranslatable turn of phrase which, I feel, contains what we try to formulate in the term 'identity' – and indeed, Freud uses the term in this context.

Safely relying, then, on the basic premise of intellectual integrity, Freud could take certain fundamentals of morality for granted; and with morality, cultural identity. To him the ego stood like a cautious and sometimes shrewd patrician, not only between the anarchy of primeval instincts and the fury of the archaic conscience, but also between the pressure of upper-class convention and the anarchy of mob spirit. The bearer of such an identity could turn with dignified horror from mass developments which threatened to throw doubt upon the self-determination of his ego. Thus, preoccupied with symptoms which characterized the defined ego's defences, psychoanalysis had, at first, little to say about the way in which the ego's synthesis grows – or fails to grow – out of the soil of social organization.

The founders and early practitioners of psychoanalysis focused on one single endeavour – introspective honesty in the service of self-enlightenment. Since this became the ruling tenet of the psychoanalytic method and the acid test for its disciples and patients everywhere, remarkably little became known of the particular virtues of living which offered the little Oedipus and Electra of other cultural milieux zestful participation in a style of life. The alliance of the superego with a high sense of cultural identity remained neglected: ways by which a given environment permits and cultivates self-abandon in forms of passion or reason, ferocity or reserve, piety or scepticism, bawdiness or propriety, gracefulness or sternness, charity or pride, shrewdness or fair play. In fact, all pronounced varieties of cultural expression except those pertaining to intellectual *Bildung* of which psychoanalysis was a part became suspect as transparently hypo-

[2] Literally, 'the secret familiarity of identical psychological construction'. Sigmund Freud, 'Ansprache an die Mitglieder des Vereins B'nai B'rith (1926)', *Gesammelte Werke*, Vol. XVI, Imago Publishing Co., Ltd, London, 1941. In this speech Freud discussed his relationship to Jewry and discarded religious faith and national pride as 'the prime bonds'. He then pointed, in poetic rather than scientific terms, to an unconscious as well as a conscious attraction in Jewry: powerful, unverbalized emotions (*viele dunkle Gefühlsmächte*), and the clear consciousness of an inner identity (*die klare Bewusstheit der inneren Identität*). Finally, he mentioned two traits which he felt he owed his Jewish ancestry: freedom from prejudices which narrow the use of the intellect, and the readiness to live in opposition.

critical disguises or defences, all too costly bulwarks against the id and (like the superego) akin to and dangerously in league with the id. While it is true, of course, that those guiding values have all at times allied themselves with brutality and narrow-mindedness, they nevertheless have inspired what cultural development man has had and they cannot be omitted from the psychological balance sheet, past, present, or future.

And so it comes about that we begin to conceptualize matters of identity at the very time in history when they become a problem. For we do so in a country which attempts to make a super-identity out of all the identities imported by its constituent immigrants; and we do so at a time when rapidly increasing mechanization threatens these essentially agrarian and patrician identities in their lands of origin as well.

The study of identity, then, becomes as strategic in our time as the study of sexuality was in Freud's time. Such historical relativity in the development of a field, however, does not seem to preclude consistency of ground plan and continued closeness to observable fact. Freud's findings regarding the sexual etiology of the neurotic part of a mental disturbance are as true for our patients as they were for his; while the burden of identity loss which stands out in our considerations probably burdened Freud's patients as well as ours, as re-interpretations would show.[3] Different periods thus permit us to see in temporary exaggeration different aspects of essentially inseparable parts of personality.

In this fourth and last part I shall explore problems of identity connected with the entry into the industrial revolution of three great countries: America, Germany, and Russia. Our special focus will be on the need, in the youth of all of these countries, for a new, a fraternal conscience and a more inclusive, and necessarily industrial, identity.

I shall begin with this country, although I do so only with deep hesitation. In recent years a great many books and articles on the character structure of nations have shown rather clearly that this is still a most precarious subject in general and a nearly forbidding one in the case of this country.

The point is that it is almost impossible (except in the form of fiction) to write *in* America *about* America *for* Americans. You

[3] See 'Reality and Actuality', *J. Amer. Psa. Assoc.*, 10:45.1–473.

can, as an American, go to the South Sea Islands and write upon your return; you can, as a foreigner, travel in America and write upon taking leave; you can, as an immigrant, write as you get settled; you can move from one section of this country or from one 'class' of this country to another, and write while you still have one foot in each place. But in the end you always write about the way it feels to arrive or to leave, to change or to get settled. You write about a process of which you are a more or less willing, but always pleasurably harassed, part, and your style soon runs away with you in the high gear of dithyrambic or outraged expression.

The only healthy American way to write about America for Americans is to vent a gripe and to overstate it. This, however, calls for a delicate gift and for a particular intellectual ancestry, neither of which is easily acquired.

I shall restrict myself, then, to stating from the point of view of one who has practised and taught psychoanalysis in this country what kind of sense of identity and what kind of loss of identity seems to reveal itself in American patients, big and little.

8   Reflections on the American Identity

It is a commonplace to state that whatever one may come to consider a truly American trait can be shown to have its equally characteristic opposite. This, one suspects, is true of all 'national characters', or (as I would prefer to call them) national identities – so true, in fact that one may begin rather than end with the proposition that a nation's identity is derived from the ways in which history has, as it were, counterpointed certain opposite potentialities; the ways in which it lifts this counterpoint to a unique style of civilization, or lets it disintegrate into mere contradiction.

This dynamic country subjects its inhabitants to more extreme contrasts and abrupt changes during a lifetime or a generation than is normally the case with other great nations. Most of her inhabitants are faced, in their own lives or within the orbit of their closest relatives, with alternatives presented by such polarities as: open roads of immigration and jealous islands of tradition; outgoing internationalism and defiant isolationism; boisterous competition and self-effacing cooperation; and many others. The influence of the resulting contradictory slogans on the development of an individual ego probably depends on the coincidence of nuclear ego-stages with critical changes in the family's geographic and economic vicissitudes.

The process of American identity formation seems to support an individual's ego identity as long as he can preserve a certain element of deliberate tentativeness of autonomous choice. The individual must be able to convince himself that the next step is up to him and that no matter where he is staying or going he always has the choice of leaving or turning in the opposite direction if he chooses to do so. In this country the migrant does not want to be told to move on, nor the sedentary man to stay where he is; for the life style (and the family history) of each contains the opposite element as a potential alternative which he wishes to consider his most private and individual decision.

Thus the functioning American, as the heir of a history of extreme contrasts and abrupt changes, bases his final ego-identity on some tentative combination of dynamic polarities such as migratory and sedentary, individualistic and standardized, competitive and cooperative, pious and freethinking, responsible and cynical, etc.

While we see extreme elaborations of one or the other of these poles in regional, occupational, and characterological types, analysis reveals that this extremeness (of rigidity or of vacillation) contains an inner defence against the always implied, deeply feared, or secretly hoped-for, opposite extreme.

To leave his choices open, the American, on the whole, lives with two sets of 'truths': a set of religious principles or religiously pronounced political principles of a highly puritan quality, and a set of shifting slogans which indicate what, at a given time, one may get away with on the basis of not more than a hunch, a mood, or a notion. Thus, the same child may have been exposed in succession or alternately to sudden decisions expressing the slogans 'Let's get the hell out of here' and again, 'Let's stay and keep the bastards out' – to mention only two of the most sweeping ones. Without any pretence of logic or principle, slogans are convincing enough to those involved to justify action whether within or just outside of the lofty law (in so far as it happens to be enforced or forgotten, according to changing local climate). Seemingly shiftless slogans contain time and space perspectives as ingrained as those elaborated in the Sioux or Yurok system; they are experiments in collective time–space to which individual ego-defences are coordinated. But they change, often radically, during one and the same childhood.

A true history of the American identity would have to correlate Parrington's observations on the continuity of formulated thought with the rich history of discontinuous American slogans which pervade public opinion in corner stores and in studies, in the courts and in the daily Press. For in principles and concepts too, an invigorating polarity seems to exist on the one hand between the intellectual and political aristocracy which, always mindful of precedent, guards a measure of coherent thought and indestructible spirit, and, on the other hand, a powerful mobo-cracy which seems to prefer changing slogans to self-perpetuating principles. This native polarity of aristocracy and mobocracy (so admirably synthesized in Franklin D. Roosevelt) pervades American democracy more effectively than the advocates and the critics of the great American middle class seem to realize. This American middle class, decried by some as embodying an ossification of all that is mercenary and philistine in this country, may represent only a transitory series of overcompensatory attempts at settling tentatively around some Main Street, fireplace, bank account, and make of car; it does not, as a class should, preclude high mobility and a cultural potential unsure of its final identity. Status expresses a different relativity in a more mobile society: it resembles an escalator more than a platform; it is a vehicle, rather than a goal.

All countries, and especially large ones, complicate their own progress in their own way with the very premises of their beginnings. We must try to formulate the way in which self-contradictions in American history may expose her youth to an emotional and political short circuit and thus endanger her dynamic potential.

'MOM'

In recent years the observations and warnings of the psychiatric workers of this country have more and more converged on two concepts: the 'schizoid personality' and 'maternal rejection'. Essentially this means not only that many people fall by the wayside as a result of psychotic disengagements from reality, but also that all too many people, while not overtly sick, never-theless seem to lack a certain ego-tonus and a certain mutuality in social intercourse. One may laugh at this suggestion and point to the spirit of individualism and to the gestures of animation and of jovial friendliness characterizing much of the social life in this country; but the psychiatrists (especially after the shocking experience during the last war, of being forced to reject or to send home hundreds of thousands of 'psychoneurotics') see it differently. The streamlined smile within the perfectly tuned countenance and within the standardized ways of exhibiting self-control does not always harbour that true spontaneity which alone would keep the personality intact and flexible enough to make it a going concern.

For this the psychiatrists tend to blame 'Mom'. Case history after case history states that the patient had a cold mother, a dominant mother, a rejecting mother – or a hyperpossessive, over-protective one. They imply that the patient, as a baby, was not made to feel at home in this world except under the condition that he behave himself in certain definite ways, which were inconsistent with the timetable of an infant's needs and potentialities, and contradictory in themselves. They imply that the mother dominated the father, and that while the father offered more tenderness and understanding to the children than the mother did, he disappointed his children in the end because of what he 'took' from the mother. Gradually what had begun as a spontaneous movement in thousands of clinical files has become a manifest literary sport in books decrying the mothers of this country as 'Moms' and as a 'generation of vipers'.

Who is this 'Mom'? How did she lose her good, her simple name? How could she become an excuse for all that is rotten in the state of the nation and a subject of literary temper-tantrums? *Is* 'Mom' really to blame?

In a clinical sense, of course, to blame may mean just to point to what the informed worker sincerely considers the primary cause of the calamity. But there is in much of our psychiatric work an undertone of revengeful triumph, as if a villain had been spotted and cornered. The blame attached to the mothers in this country (namely, that they are frigid sexually, rejective of their children, and unduly dominant in their homes) has in itself a specific moralistic punitiveness. No doubt both patients and psychiatric workers were blamed too much when they were children; now they blame all mothers, because all causality has become linked with blame.

It was, of course, a vindictive injustice to give the name of 'Mom' to a certain dangerous type of mother, a type apparently characterized by a number of fatal contradictions in her motherhood. Such injustice can only be explained and justified by the journalistic habit of sensational contraposition – a part of the publicist folkways of our day. It is true that where the 'psychoneurotic' American soldier felt inadequately prepared for life, he often implicitly and more often unconsciously blamed his mother; and that the expert felt compelled to agree with him. But it is also true that the road from Main Street to the foxhole was longer – geographically, culturally, and psychologically – than was the road to the front lines from the home towns of nations which were open to attack and had been attacked, or which had prepared themselves to attack other people's homelands and now feared for their own. It seems senseless to blame the American family for the failures, but to deny it credit for the gigantic human achievement of overcoming that distance.

'Mom', then, like similar prototypes in other countries – see the 'German father', to be discussed in the next chapter – is a composite image of traits, none of which could be present all at once in one single living woman. No woman consciously aspires to be such a 'Mom', and yet she may find that her experience converges on this *Gestalt*, as if she were forced to assume a role. To the clinical worker, 'Mom' is something comparable to a 'classical' psychiatric syndrome which you come to use as a yardstick although you have never seen it in pure form. In cartoons she becomes a caricature, immediately convincing to all. Before analysing 'Mom', then, as a historical phenomenon, let us focus on her from the point of view of the pathogenic demands which she makes on her children and by which we recognize her presence in our clinical work:

1. 'Mom' is the unquestioned authority in matters of *mores* and morals in her home, and (through clubs) in the community; yet she permits herself to remain, in her own way, vain in her appearance, egotistical in her demands, and infantile in her emotions.

2. In any situation in which this discrepancy clashes with the respect which she demands from her children, she blames her children; she never blames herself.

3. She thus artificially maintains what Ruth Benedict would call the discontinuity between the child's and the adult's status without endowing this differentiation with the higher meaning emanating from superior example.

4. She shows a determined hostility to any free expression of the most naïve forms of sensual and sexual pleasure on the part of her children, and she makes it clear enough that the father, when sexually demanding, is a bore. Yet as she grows older she seems unwilling to sacrifice such external signs of sexual com-

petition as too youthful dresses, frills of exhibitionism, and 'make-up'. In addition, she is avidly addicted to sexual display in books, movies, and gossip.

5. She teaches self-restraint and self-control, but she is unable to restrict her intake of calories in order to remain within the bounds of the dresses she prefers.

6. She expects her children to be hard on themselves, but she is hypochondriacally concerned with her own well-being.

7. She stands for the superior values of tradition, yet she herself does not want to become 'old'. In fact, she is mortally afraid of that status which in the past was the fruit of a rich life, namely the status of the grandmother.

This will be sufficient to indicate that 'Mom' is a woman in whose life-cycle remnants of infantility join advanced senility to crowd out the middle range of mature womanhood, which thus becomes self-absorbed and stagnant. In fact, she mistrusts her own feelings as a woman and mother. Even her over-concern does not provide trust, but lasting mistrust. But let it be said that this 'Mom' – or, better, any woman who reminds herself and others of the stereotype Mom – is not happy; she does not like herself; she is ridden by the anxiety that her life was a waste. She knows that her children do not genuinely love her, despite Mother's Day offerings. 'Mom' is a victim, not a victor.

Assuming, then, that this is a 'type', a composite image of sufficient relevance for the epidemiology of neurotic conflict in this country: to explain it would obviously call for the collaboration of historian, sociologist, and psychologist, and for a new kind of history, a kind which at the moment is admittedly in its impressionistic and sensational stages. 'Mom', of course, is only a stereotyped caricature of existing contradictions which have emerged from intense, rapid, and as yet unintegrated changes in American history. To find its beginning, one would probably have to retrace this history back to the time when it was up to the American woman to evolve one common tradition, on the basis of many imported traditions, and to base on it the education of her children and the style of her home life; when it was up to her to establish new habits of sedentary life on a continent originally populated by men who in their countries of origin, for one reason or another, had not wanted to be 'fenced in'. Now, in fear of ever again acquiescing to an outer or inner autocracy, these men insisted on keeping their new cultural identity tentative to a point where women had to become autocratic in their demands for some order.

The American woman in frontier communities was the object of intense rivalries on the part of tough and often desperate men. At the same time, she had to become the cultural censor, the religious conscience, the aesthetic arbiter, and the teacher. In that early rough economy hewn out of hard nature it was she who contributed the finer graces of living and that spirituality without which the community falls apart. In her children she saw future men and women who would face contrasts of rigid sedentary and shifting migratory life. They must be prepared for any number of extreme opposites in milieu, and always ready to seek new goals and to fight for them in merciless competition. For, after all, worse than a sinner was a sucker.

We suggested that the mothers of the Sioux and of the Yurok were endowed with an instinctive power of adaptation which permitted them to develop child-training methods appropriate for the production of hunters and hunters' wives in a nomadic society, and of fishermen and acorn gatherers in a sedentary valley society. The American mother, I believe, reacted to the historical situation on this continent with similar unconscious adjustment when she further developed Anglo-Saxon patterns of child training which would avoid weakening potential frontiersmen by protective maternalism. In other words, I consider what is now called the American woman's 'rejective' attitude a modern fault based on a historical virtue designed for a vast new country, in which the most dominant fact was the frontier, whether you sought it, or avoided it, or tried to live it down.

From the frontier, my historian–sociologist and I would have to turn to puritanism as a decisive force in the creation of American motherhood and its modern caricature, 'Mom'. This much-maligned puritanism, we should remember, was once a system of values designed to check men and women of eruptive vitality, of strong appetites, as well as of strong individuality. In connection with primitive cultures we have discussed the fact that a living culture has its own balances which make it durable and bearable to the majority of its members. But changing history endangers the balance. During the short course of American history rapid developments fused with puritanism in such a way that they contributed to the emotional tension of mother and child. Among these were the continued migration of the native population, unchecked immigration, industrialization, urbanization, class stratification, and female emancipation. These are some of the influences which put puritanism on the defensive – and a system is apt to become rigid when it becomes defensive. Puritanism, beyond defining sexual sin for full-blooded and strong-willed people, gradually extended itself to the total sphere of bodily living, compromising all sensuality – including marital relationships – and spreading its frigidity over the tasks of pregnancy, childbirth, nursing, and training. The result was that men were born who failed to learn from their mothers to love the goodness of sensuality before they learned to hate its sinful uses. Instead of hating sin, they learned to mistrust life. Many became puritans without faith or zest.

The frontier, of course, remained the decisive influence which served to establish in the American identity the extreme polarization which characterizes it. The original polarity was the cultivation of the sedentary and migratory poles. For the same families, the same mothers, were forced to prepare men and women who would take root in the community life and the gradual class stratification of the new villages and towns and at the same time to prepare these children for the possible physical hardships of homesteading on the frontiers. Towns, too, developed their sedentary existence and oriented their inward life to work bench and writing desk, fireplace and altar, while through them, on the roads and rails, strangers passed bragging of God knows what greener pastures. You had either to follow – or to stay behind and brag louder. The point is that the call of the frontier, the temptation to move on, forced those who stayed to become defensively sedentary, and defensively proud. In a world which developed the slogan, 'If you can see your neighbour's chimney, it is time to move on', mothers had to raise sons and daughters who would be determined to ignore the call of the frontier – but who would go with equal determination once they were forced or chose to go. When they became too old, however, there was no choosing, and they remained to support the most sectarian, the most standardized adhesiveness. I think that it was the fear of becoming too old to choose which gave old age and death a bad name in this country. (Only recently have old couples found a solution, the national trailer system, which permits them to settle down to perpetual travelling and to die on wheels.)

We know how the problems of the immigrant and of the migrant, of the émigré and of the refugee, became superimposed on one another, as large areas became settled and began to have a past. To the new American, with a regional tradition of stratification, newcomers increasingly came to be characterized by the fact that they had escaped from something or other, rather than by the common values they sought; and then there were also the masses of ignorant and deceived chattels of the expanding industrial labour market. For and against all of these latter Americans, American mothers had to establish new moral standards and rigid tests of social ascendancy.

As America became the proverbial melting-pot, it was the Anglo-Saxon woman's determination which assured that of all the ingredients mixed, puritanism – such as it then was – would be the most pervasive streak. The older, Anglo-Saxon type became ever more rigid, though at the same time decent and kind in its way. But the daughters of immigrants, too, frantically tried to emulate standards of conduct which they had not learned as small children. It is here, I think, that the self-made personality originated as the female counterpart of the self-made man; it is here that we find the origin of the popular American concept of a fashionable and vain 'ego' which is its own originator and arbiter. In fact, the psychoanalysis of the children of immigrants clearly reveals to what extent they, as the first real Americans in their family, become their parents' cultural parents.

This idea of a self-made ego was in turn reinforced and yet modified by industrialization and by class stratification. Industrialization, for example, brought with it mechanical child-training. It was as if this new man-made world of machines, which was to replace the 'segments of nature' and the 'beasts of prey', offered its mastery only to those who would become like it, as the Sioux 'became' buffalo, the Yurok salmon. Thus, a movement in child-training began which tended to adjust the human organism from the very start to clocklike punctuality in order to make it a standardized appendix of the industrial world. This movement is by no means at an end either in this country or in countries which for the sake of industrial production want to become like us. In the pursuit of the adjustment to and mastery over the machine, American mothers (especially of the middle class) found themselves standardizing and overadjusting children who later were expected to personify that very virile individuality which in the past had been one of the outstanding characteristics of the American. The resulting danger was that of creating, instead of individualism, a mass-produced mask of individuality.

As if this were not enough, the increasing class-differentiation in some not large but influential classes and regions combined with leftovers of European aristocratic models to create the ideal of the lady, the woman who not only does not need to work, but who, in fact, is much too childlike and too determinedly uninformed to even comprehend what work is all about. This image, in most parts of the country, except the South, was soon challenged by the ideal of the emancipated woman. This new ideal seemed to call for equality of opportunity; but it is well known how it came, instead, to represent often enough a pretence of sameness in equipment, a right to mannish behaviour.

In her original attributes, then, the American woman was a fitting and heroic companion to the post-revolutionary man, who was possessed with the idea of freedom from any man's autocracy and haunted by the fear that the nostalgia for some homeland and the surrender to some king could ever make him give in to political slavery. Mother became 'Mom' only when Father became 'Pop' under the impact of the identical historical discontinuities. For, if you come down to it, Momism is only misplaced paternalism. American mothers stepped into the role of the grandfathers as the fathers abdicated their dominant place in the family, in the field of education, and in cultural life. The post-revolutionary descendants of the Founding Fathers forced their women to be mothers *and* fathers, while they continued to cultivate the role of freeborn sons.

I cannot try to appraise the quantity of emotional disturbance in this country. Mere statistics on severe mental disorders do not help. Our improved methods of detection and our missionary zeal expand together as we become aware of the problem, so that it would be hard to say whether today this country has bigger and better neuroses, or bigger and better ways of spotlighting them – or both. But I would, from my clinical experience, dare to formulate a specific *quality* in those who are disturbed. I would say that underneath his proud sense of autonomy and his exuberant sense of initiative the troubled American (who often looks the least troubled) blames his mother for having let him down. His father, so he claims, had not much to do with it – except in those rare cases where the father was an extraordinarily stern man on the surface, an old-fashioned individualist, a foreign paternalist, or a native 'boss'. In the psychoanalysis of an American man it usually takes considerable time to break through to the insight that there was a period early in life when the father did seem bigger and threatening. Even then, there is at first little sense of that specific rivalry for the mother as stereotyped in the oedipus complex. It is as if the mother had ceased to be an object of nostalgia and sensual attachment before the general development of initiative led to a rivalry with the 'old man'. Behind a fragmentary 'oedipus complex', then, appears that deep-seated sense of having been abandoned and let down by the mother, which is the silent complaint behind schizoid withdrawal. The small child felt, it seems, that there was no use regressing, because there was nobody to regress to, no use investing feelings because the response was so uncertain. What remained was action and motion right up to the breaking-point. Where action, too, failed, there was only withdrawal and the standardized smile, and later, psychosomatic disturbance. But wherever our methods permit us to look deeper, we find at the bottom of it all the conviction, the mortal self-accusation, that it was *the child who abandoned the mother*, because he had been in such a hurry to become independent.

American folk-lore highlights this complex in its original power, in the saga of the birth of John Henry, a coloured spiker, who, according to the widely known ballad, later died in an attempt to show that a he-man is the equal of any machine. The saga, not equally well known, goes as follows:[1]

Now John Henry was a man, but he's long dead.

The night John Henry was born the moon was copper-colored and the sky was black. The stars wouldn't shine and the rain fell hard. Forked lightning cleaved the air and the earth trembled like a leaf. The panthers squalled in the brake like a baby and the Mississippi River ran upstream a thousand miles. John Henry weighed forty-four pounds.

They didn't know what to make of John Henry when he was born. They looked at him and then went and looked at the river.

[1] Roark Bradford, *John Henry*, Harper Bros, New York, 1931.

'He got a bass voice like a preacher,' his mamma said.

'He got shoulders like a cotton-rollin' rousterbout,' his papa said.

'He got blue gums like a conjure man,' the nurse woman said.

'I might preach some,' said John Henry, 'but I ain't gonter be no preacher. I might roll cotton on de boats, but I ain't gonter be no cotton-rollin' rousterbout. I might got blue gums like a conjure man, but I ain't gonter git familiar wid de spirits. 'Cause my name is John Henry, and when folks call me by my name, dey'll know I'm a natchal man.'

'His name is John Henry,' said his mamma. 'Hit's a fack.'

'And when you calls him by his name,' said his papa, 'he's a natchal man.'

So about that time John Henry raised up and stretched. 'Well,' he said, 'ain't hit about supper-time?'

'Sho hit's about supper-time,' said his mamma.

'And after,' said his papa.

'And long after,' said the nurse woman.

'Well,' said John Henry, 'did de dogs had they supper?'

'They did,' said his mamma.

'All de dogs,' said his papa.

'Long since,' said the nurse woman.

'Well, den,' said John Henry, 'ain't I as good as de dogs?'

And when John Henry said that he got mad. He reared back in his bed and broke out the slats. He opened his mouth and yowled, and it put out the lamp. He cleaved his tongue and spat, and it put out the fire. 'Don't make me mad!' said John Henry, and the thunder rumbled and rolled. 'Don't let me git mad on de day I'm bawn, 'cause I'm skeered of my ownse'f when I gits mad.'

And John Henry stood up in the middle of the floor and he told them what he wanted to eat. 'Bring me four ham bones and a pot full of cabbages,' he said. 'Bring me a bait of turnip greens tree-top tall, and season hit down wid a side er middlin'. Bring me a pone er cold cawn bread and some hot potlicker to wash hit down. Bring me two hog jowls and a kittleful er whippowill peas. Bring me a skilletful er red-hot biscuits and a big jugful er cane molasses. 'Cause my name is John Henry, and I'll see you soon.'

So John Henry walked out of the house and away from the Black River Country where all good rousterbouts are born.

There are, of course, analogous stories in other countries, from Hercules to Buslaev. Yet there are specific points in this story which I feel are thoroughly American. To characterize the kind of humour employed here would demand an objective approach beyond my present means. But what we must keep in mind, for further reference, is the fact that John Henry begins with a gigantic gripe: he is thwarted in his enormous appetite; he begs, 'Don't let me git mad on de day I'm bawn'; he solves the dilemma by jumping on his own feet and by boasting of the capacity of his gut; he will not commit himself to any identity as predetermined by the stigmata of birth; and he leaves to become a man who is nothing but a man before any attempt is made to provide him with what he has demanded.

JOHN HENRY

This same John Henry is the hero of a legend which reports how, in his very death, he demonstrated the triumph of flesh over machine:

> Cap'n says to John Henry,
> 'Gonna bring me a steam drill 'round,
> Gonna take that steam drill out on the job,
> Gonna whop that steel on down,
> Lawd, Lawd, gonna whop that steel on down.'
> John Henry told his cap'n,
> Said, 'A man ain't nothin' but a man,
> And befo' I'd let that steam drill beat me down
> I'd die with this hammer in my hand,
> Lawd, Lawd, I'd die with the hammer in my hand.'[2]

The tune of this ballad, according to the Lomaxes, 'is rooted in a Scottish melody, its devices are those of medieval balladry, but its content is the courage of the common man' who believes to the end that a man counts only as a man.

John Henry thus is one of the occupational models of the stray men on the expanding frontier who faced new geographic and technological worlds as men and without a past. The last remaining model seems to be the cowboy, who inherited their boasts, their gripes, their addiction to roaming, their mistrust of personal ties, their libidinal and religious concentration on the limits of endurance and audacity, their dependence on 'critters' and climates.

These workmen developed to its very emotional and societal limits the image of the man without roots, the motherless man, the womanless man. Later in this book we shall maintain that

[2] J. A. Lomax and A. Lomax (Eds.), *Folksong U.S.A.*, Duell, Sloan and Pearce, New York, 1947.

this image is only one of a particular variety of new images existing over the whole world; their common denominator is the freeborn child who becomes an emancipated adolescent and a man who refutes his father's conscience and his nostalgia for a mother, bowing only to cruel facts and to fraternal discipline. They bragged as if they had created themselves tougher than the toughest critters and harder than any forged metal:

Raised in the backwoods, suckled by a polar bear, nine rows of jaw teeth, a double coat of hair, steel ribs, wire intestines, and a barbed wire tail, and I don't give a dang where I drag it. Whoopee-whee-a-ha![3]

They preferred to remain anonymous so that they could be the condensed product of the lowest and the highest in the universe.

I'm shaggy as a bear, wolfish about the head, active as a cougar, and can grin like a hyena, until the bark will curl off a gum log. There's a sprinkling of all sorts in me, from the lion down to the skunk; and before the war is over, you will pronounce me an entire zoological institute, or I miss a figure in my calculation.[4]

If there is totemism in this, taken over from the Indians, there is also a commitment of tragic incongruity: for you can meet a 'segment of nature' by identifying with it, but if you try to be colder and harder than machines, if you aspire to wire guts, your intestines may let you down.

When discussing two American Indian tribes, we concluded that their particular forms of early training were well synchronized with their world images and their economic roles in them. Only in their myths, in their rituals, and in their prayers did we find references to what their particular form of expulsion from infantile paradise had cost them. In a great and diverse nation like America, is there any form of folk life which would be apt to reflect typical trends in the early relationship to the mother?

I think that the folk song is the psychological counterpart in agricultural lands to the communal prayer chants of the primitives. The primitives' songs, as we saw, are songs addressed to the Supernatural Providers: these people put all the nostalgia for

[3] Alfred Henry Lewis, *Wolfville Days*, Frederic A. Stokes Co., New York, 1902. Quoted in B. A. Botkin, *A Treasury of American Folklore*, Crown Publishers, New York, 1944.
[4] *Colonel Crockett's Exploits and Adventures in Texas*, Written by Himself, 1836.

the lost paradise of infancy into their songs in order to make them convincing through the magic of tears. Folk songs, however, express the nostalgia of the working-men who have learned to coerce the soil with harsh tools wielded in the sweat of their brow. Their longing for a restored home is sung as recreation after work – and often as an accompaniment to it, if not as an auxiliary tool, in their work songs.

In its 'old-time love songs' American song has inherited much of the quiet depth of the European folk song: 'Black, black, black is the color of my true love's hair.' But it is primarily in the melodies that the memory of the old world's deep valleys, quiet mills, and sweet lassies survives. In its changing words the folk song in this country deliberately cultivates that 'split personality' which much later enters melody in the era of jazz. As a discrepancy between melody and word it is already attested to in the supposedly oldest American song, 'Springfield Mountain'. The sweetest melodies may serve both the goriest and the most disrespectful verses; even the love songs have a tendency to dissipate deep sentiment. 'If you look between the lines,' so the Lomaxes say, 'you cannot help but be struck by two repeatedly expressed attitudes towards love . . . Love is dangerous – "It ain't nothing but a notion that is gone with the wind." . . . Love is for laughter, and courtship is a comedy. Apparently these people who weren't afraid of Indians, or loneliness, or the varmints, or the woods, or freedom, or wild horses, or prairie fires, or drought, or six-guns, were afraid of love.'[5]

It is, then, in the very love songs, that we find not only the sorrow of having been abandoned (an international theme) but also the fear of committing yourself to deep emotions, lest you get caught, and hurt, by 'keerless love'.

Instead of romanticism there is in much of American song a stubborn clinging to the ugly facts of poverty, loneliness, and toil on a continent that punished as it challenged. There is a special emphasis on animals which are of immediate and constant nuisance value: 'June bugs, possums, coons, roosters, geese, hound dogs, mocking birds, rattlesnakes, billy goats, razor-back hogs, liver lipped mules.' The use of animals particularly serves the class of nonsense songs and fancy word-play which must half hide from the severe elders and half reveal to the young folk

[5] Lomax and Lomax, op. cit.

some kind of erotic allusions, when at 'innocent' play-parties dance steps had to be avoided and yet approximated in 'play steps':

> And it's ladies to the center and it's gents around the row,
> And we'll rally round the canebrake and shoot the buffalo.
> The girls will go to school, the boys will act the fool,
> Rally round the barnyard and chase the old gray mule.
> Oh, the hawk shot the buzzard and the buzzard shot the crow
> And we'll rally round the canebrake and shoot the buffalo. [6]

Nonsense becomes most irreverent in its dealings with the decline and end of expendable old things. These are mostly animals – 'the old gray mare', who 'ain't what she used to be', or 'the old red rooster', who 'can't crow like he uster', or Aunt Nancy's grey goose:

> Go tell Aunt Nancy
> Her old gray goose is dead.
>
> The one she's been savin'
> To make her feather bed.
>
> The goslin's are mournin'
> 'Cause their mammy's dead.
>
> She only had one fe-eather,
> A-stickin' in her head. [7]

The bitter and yet gay irony in this last verse refers to the days when, according to the Lomaxes, 'a goosefeather bed was the very prime in sleeping, because it cradled you and cuddled you and almost covered you at the same time'. Sometimes, however, the gay good riddance applies undisguisedly to people:

> My wife, she died, O then, O then,
> My wife, she died, O then,
> My wife, she died,
> And I laughed till I cried,
> To think I was single again. [8]

It fits the free expression of these sentiments of 'to hell with the worn-out' and of 'don't take yourself too seriously' that so much of American song must be walked, danced, and run to, to reveal

[6] ibid.   [7] ibid.   [8] ibid.

273

its true spirit. Here perpetual action fuses with gay references to everyday work-techniques expressing the American creed, the faith in magic liberation by going places and by doing things.

Cowboy songs, reflecting one of the last forms of the unique and deviant ways of the highly specialized workmen of the frontier, show an exquisite synthesis of work pattern and emotional expression. While trying to tire a bucking bronco, careful lest he let his muscular calm be sabotaged by fear or rage, or while shoving his animals along the hot and dusty trail, careful lest he hasten or upset the cattle which must be delivered in the pink of well-fed condition, the cowboy engaged in the sing-song out of which came the purified versions of popular song. Throughout, the rhyme and reason of the 'cowboy's lament' remains the fact that for him there is no way back. There are the well-known tear-jerkers of the cowboy who will never see his mother again, nor his 'darling sister'; or who will return to a sweetheart only to find himself deceived once more. But more genuinely pervading is the strange fact that this man's man in his songs becomes something of a mother and a teacher and a nurse-maid to the dogies whom he delivers to their early death:

> Your mother was raised away down in Texas
> Where the jimpson weed and the sand-burrs grow,
> So we'll fill you up on cactus and cholla,
> Until you are ready for Idaho.[9]

He sings lullabies to his dogies as they move through the early prairie night on a thousand little hoofs:

> Go slow, little dogies, stop milling around,
> For I'm tired of your roving all over the ground,
> There's grass where you're standin',
> So feed kind o' slow,
> And you don't have forever to be on the go,
> Move slow, little dogies, move slow.[10]

And although he protests, 'It's your misfortune and none of my own', he feels identified with these little steers whom he has branded, castrated, and nursed along until they were ready to be shipped and slaughtered:

[9] M. and T. Johnson, *Early American Songs*, Associated Music Publishers, Inc., New York, 1943.
[10] From *Singing America*, used by permission of the National Recreation Association, copyright owners, and C. C. Birchard and Co., publishers.

> You ain't got no father, you ain't got no mother,
> You left them behind when first you did roam,
> You ain't got no sister, you ain't got no brother,
> You're just like a cowboy, a long way from home.[11]

American song, then, in its melodies affirms the nostalgia for the old, even while in its words it often expresses a deliberate and stubborn paradox, a denial of trust in love, a denial of a need for trust. It thus becomes a more intimate declaration of independence.

In this country the image of the freeman is founded on that northern European who, having escaped feudal and religious laws, disavowed his motherland and established a country and a constitution on the prime principle of preventing the resurgence of autocracy. This image, of course, later developed along lines which were quite unforeseeable to those original settlers who merely wanted to reinstate on this continent a new England, an England with equally quaint villages, but with more elbow-room for free thought. They could not foresee the persistent wild call of a continent which had never been anybody's motherland and which, with all its excessive rigours, became an autocratic tempter. In America nature is autocratic, saying, 'I am not arguing, I am telling you.' The size and rigour of the country and the importance of the means of migration and transportation helped to create and to develop the identity of autonomy and initiative, the identity of him who is 'going places and doing things'. Historically the overdefined past was apt to be discarded for the undefined future; geographically, migration was an ever-present fact; socially, chances and opportunities lay in daring and luck, in taking full advantage of the channels of social motility.

It is no coincidence, then, that psychological analyses should find at the bottom of much specific mental discomfort the complex of having abandoned the mother and of having been abandoned by her. In general, Americans do not experience 'this country' as a 'motherland' in the soft, nostalgic sense of 'the old country'. 'This country' is loved almost bitterly and in a remarkably unromantic and realistic way. Oratory may emphasize localities; deeper loyalties are attached to voluntary associations and opportunities, signifying level of achievement rather than local belonging. Today when there is so much demand for homes

[11] Johnson, op. cit.

275

in defensively overdefined, overly standardized, and over-restricted neighbourhoods, many people enjoy their most relaxed moments at crossroads counters, in bars, in and around automotive vehicles, and in camps and cabins, playing that they are unconfined and free to stay, free to move on. No country's population travels farther and faster. After the war, more veterans of this than of any other nation chose to start their new lives in places other than the home town they had dreamed of in the front lines. To many Americans, then, while there is 'no place like home', it is important that you should be able to take it with you or find its facsimile a thousand miles away. Those with the best places to stay in probably travel the most.

But in thus mastering with a vengeance the expanses of a vast continent, Americans also learned to control the second autocrat, which was unexpectedly met with by the free sons: the machine.

The autocracy of the continent and the autocracy of the machine must be understood when one undertakes to study or criticize American child-training methods which tend to make a child slightly nostalgic and yet faithful, autonomous and yet reliable, individualistic and yet predictable. That such methods begin with systematic maternal 'rejection' is in itself folk-lore, which must be traced to facts, born of necessity, and to fancy, born of need; for the man and the woman who would fit into the image of the self-made man and the self-made personality, and who would create and 'adjust' their ego identity as they went along, did not have much use for protective mother love. Indeed, where they received it as children, they had to repudiate it later. Where 'Mom' did not exist, she had to be invented: for such is the historical importance of 'griping' in this country that a man, to stand on his own feet in a powerfully changing world, must keep himself up by his own gripes.

Because John Henry was born after the dogs had been fed, he jumped on his feet before he had his first meal. In view of the continent before him, and of the tasks required of him, his first hours in this world were meaningful, although admittedly extreme. But what will John Henry do in a double-breasted business suit? What will happen to his 'wire guts' when he must serve machines and finds himself caught in the impersonal machinery of modern life?

Adolescence is the age of the final establishment of a dominant positive ego-identity. It is then that a future within reach becomes part of the conscious life plan. It is then that the question arises whether or not the future was anticipated in earlier expectations.

The problem posed by physiological maturation has been stated forcefully by Anna Freud.[12]

The physiological process which marks the attainment of physical sexual maturity is accompanied by a stimulation of the instinctual processes . . . Aggressive impulses are intensified to the point of complete unruliness, hunger becomes voracity and the naughtiness of the latency-period turns into the criminal behavior of adolescence. Oral and anal interests, long submerged, come to the surface again. Habits of cleanliness, laboriously acquired during the latency-period, give place to pleasure in dirt and disorder, and instead of modesty and sympathy we find exhibitionistic tendencies, brutality and cruelty to animals. The reaction-formations, which seemed to be firmly established in the structure of the ego, threaten to fall to pieces. At the same time, old tendencies which had disappeared come into consciousness. The Oedipus wishes are fulfilled in the form of phantasies and day-dreams, in which they have undergone but little distortion; in boys ideas of castration and in girls penis-envy once more become the center of interest. There are very few new elements in the invading forces. Their onslaught merely brings once more to the surface the familiar content of the early infantile sexuality of little children.

This is the picture in terms of the individual ego, which appears to be invaded by a newly mobilized and vastly augmented id as though from a hostile innerworld, an inner outerworld. Our interest is directed towards the quantity and quality of support the adolescent ego, thus set upon, may expect from the outer outerworld; and towards the question of whether ego defences as well as identity fragments developed in earlier stages receive the necessary additional sustenance. What the regressing and growing, rebelling and maturing youths are now primarily concerned with is who and what they are in the eyes of a wider circle of significant people as compared with what they themselves have come to feel they are; and how to connect the dreams, idio-

---

[12] Anna Freud, *The Ego and the Mechanisms of Defence*, The Hogarth Press and the Institute of Psycho-Analysis, London, 1937.

syncrasies, roles, and skills cultivated earlier with the occupational and sexual prototypes of the day.

The danger of this stage is role diffusion; as Biff puts it in *Death of a Salesman*: 'I just can't take hold, Mom, I can't take hold of some kind of a life.' Where such a dilemma is based on a strong previous doubt as to one's ethnic and sexual identity, delinquent and outright psychotic incidents are not uncommon. Youth after youth, bewildered by his assumed role, a role forced on him by the inexorable standardization of American adolescence, runs away in one form or another: leaves schools and jobs, stays out at night, or withdraws into bizarre and inaccessible moods. Once he is 'delinquent', his greatest need and often his only salvation is the refusal on the part of older youths, of advisers, and of judiciary personnel to type him further by pat diagnoses and social judgements which ignore the special dynamic conditions of adolescence. Their greatest service may be the refusal to 'confirm' him in his criminality.[13]

Among young Americans with early defined identities, there is a type of teen-age boy whom I will try to sketch in the setting of his milieu. My method is the clinical description of a 'type': but the boy is not a patient, far from it. In fact, he has no use for 'headshrinkers'. Maybe for this very reason, one should find a means of studying him thoughtfully: for to restrict our understanding to those who need us desperately would mean to limit our view unduly.

The family is Anglo-Saxon, mildly Protestant, of the white-collar class. This type of boy is tall, thin, muscular in his body build. He is shy, especially with women, and emotionally retentive, as if he were saving himself for something. His occasional grin, however, indicates a basic satisfaction with himself. Among his peers, he can be rowdy and boisterous; with younger children, kind and circumspect. His goals are vaguely defined. They have something to do with action and motion. His ideal prototypes in the world of sports seem to fulfil such needs as disciplined locomotion; fairness in aggression; calm exhibitionism; and dormant masculine sexuality. Neurotic anxiety is avoided by concentration on limited goals with circumscribed laws. Psycho-

[13] See E. H. and K. T. Erikson, 'The Confirmation of the Delinquent', *Chicago Review*, Winter 1957.

analytically speaking, the dominant defence-mechanism is self-restriction.

His mother is somewhat of a 'Mom'. She can be harsh, loud-voiced, and punitive. More likely than not she is sexually rather frigid. His father, while exhibiting the necessary toughness in business, is shy in his intimate relationships and does not expect to be treated with much consideration at home. Such parents in our case histories are still noted down as pathogenic, while it is quite clear that they represent a cultural pattern. What they will do to a child depends on variables not covered by the existing clinical terms. As for the mother, who shows a certain contempt for male weakness, her bark is worse than her bite. She has a male ideal, derived from the history of her family; it usually comes from her father's side, and she indicates to the son that she believes that he has a chance to come close to this ideal. She is wise enough (sometimes lazy or indifferent enough) to leave it to him whether he wants to live up to this ideal or not. Most important, she is not overprotective. Unlike mothers who drive on but cannot let go (they are the pathogenic, the 'overprotective' ones), she does not overly tie the boy to herself. She gives her teen-age children the freedom of the street, of the playground, and of parties, even into the night. The father is prevailed upon not to worry and to lend his car, or rather 'the car'. It must be admitted that this mother is sure of how far the boy will go in sexual matters, because unconsciously she knows that she starved some of the original devil out of him when he was small. In his early childhood she deliberately understimulated him sexually and emotionally.

I have indicated how far a certain determined lack of maternalism in such mothers may be historically founded, not only in religious puritanism, but in unconscious continuation of historical conditions which made it dangerous for a son to believe more in the past than in the future; dangerous to base his identity on the adherence to his childhood home and on the exclusion of possible migration in pursuit of a better chance; dangerous ever to appear to be a 'sissy' instead of one who has learned to tolerate a certain amount of deprivation and loneliness.

We have discussed the development of the basic body feeling out of the mutual regulation of mother and infant. Parts of the body feel like 'mine' and feel 'good' to the degree in which early surroundings first took them in trust and then, with proper connotations, gradually released them to the child's own care. Areas of greatest conflict remain areas abruptly disconnected from the body feeling, and later from one's identity. They remain disturbing areas in the fast-growing body of the adolescent who will be overly concerned and self-conscious about them and suffer periods of a loss of contact with his own body parts. There is no doubt that this adolescent in his most intimate feelings is detached from his genitals; they have been called 'private' all along, and this not in the sense that they were his private property, but rather that they were too private even for him to touch. He has been threatened – early and almost casually – with the loss of his genitals; and in accord with the general ego-restriction which is his favourite defence mechanism, he has detached himself from them. Of this he is, of course, unconscious. Vigorous exercise helps to keep his body image intact and permits him to live out his intrusiveness in the goal-mindedness of sports.

The ego quality of autonomy, as we have said, depends on a consistent definition of individual privilege and obligation in the nursery. In the wake of recent developments, which involve our adolescent, all kinds of influences have weakened the bonds of privileges and obligations, with and against which the child may develop his autonomy. Among these are the decrease in the size of our families, and early bowel-training. A large group of siblings can see to it, and does, that there is feasible equality in the apportioning of privileges and obligations to the 'too young' and the 'already old enough'. A large family, if utilized for this purpose, is a good school for democracy, especially if the parents gradually learn to restrict themselves to a firm advisory capacity. Small families accentuate diversities such as sex and age. In the wake of the demand for early training in cleanliness, orderliness, and punctuality, individual mothers, in small families, often face one child at a time in a guerrilla war of wits and endurance. Our mother, then, has unhesitatingly subscribed to the scientific slogan that it is best to 'condition' the child as early as possible, *before* the matter can become an issue of his muscular ambivalence. It makes sense to her to expect that very early training will lead to automatic compliance and maximum efficiency, with a minimum of friction. After all, the method works with dogs.

With the 'behaviourist' psychology of her day, she failed to consider the fact that dogs are trained to serve and die; that they will not be forced to represent to their young what their masters represented to them. Children must eventually train their own children, and any impoverishment of their impulse life, for the sake of avoiding friction, must be considered a possible liability affecting more than one lifetime. Generations will depend on the ability of every procreating individual to face his children with the feeling that he was able to save some vital enthusiasm from the conflicts of his childhood. Actually, such early training principles fail to work smoothly from the start because they demand too constant effort on the part of the parent: they become parent training rather than child training.

Our boy thus became 'regular', but he also learned to associate both meals and bowels with worry and haste. His belated campaign for somatic autonomy thus started under bewildering circumstances, and this with a definite initial deficit in the boy's ability to make choices because his area of control had been invaded before he could either object or comply by reasonably free choice. I would like to suggest in all seriousness that early bowel-training and other arrangements invented to condition the child in advance of his ability to regulate himself may be a very questionable practice in the upbringing of individuals who later on are supposed to exert vigorous and free choice as citizens. It is here that the machine ideal of 'functioning without friction' invaded the democratic milieu. Much political apathy may have its origin in a general feeling that, after all, matters of apparent choice have probably been fixed in advance – a state of affairs which becomes fact, indeed, if influential parts of the electorate acquiesce in it because they have learned to view the world as a place where grown-ups talk of choice, but 'fix' things so as to avoid overt friction.

As for the so-called oedipus stage when 'the child identifies with the superego of the parents', it is most important that this superego should make a maximum of collective sense in terms of the ideals of the day. The superego is bad enough as a mere institution, because it perpetuates internally the relation of the big-and-angry adult and the small-but-bad child. The patriarchal era exploited the universal evolutionary fact of an internalized and unconscious moral 'governor' in certain definite ways, while other eras have exploited it in other ways. The paternal exploitation apparently leads to suppressed guilt-feelings and fear of castration as a result of rebellion against the father; the maternal one focuses on feelings of mutual destruction and mutual abandonment of mother and child. Each age, then, must find its own way of dealing with the superego as a universally given potentiality for the inner, automatic survival of a universal outer chasm between adult and child. The more idiosyncratic this relationship and the less adequate the parent in reflecting changing cultural prototypes and institutions, the deeper the conflict between ego identity and superego will be.

Self-restriction, however, saves our boy much moral wear and tear. He seems to be on reasonably good terms with his superego and remains so in puberty and adolescence because of an ingenious arrangement in American life which diffuses the father ideal. The boy's male ideal is rarely attached to his father, as lived with in daily life. It is usually an uncle or friend of the family, if not his grandfather, as presented to him (often unconsciously) by his mother.

The grandfather, a powerful and powerfully driven man – according to a once widely prevailing American pattern, another composite of fact and myth – sought new and challenging engineering tasks in widely separated regions. When the initial challenge was met, he handed the task over to others, and moved on. His wife saw him only for an occasional impregnation. His sons could not keep pace with him and were left as respectable settlers by the wayside; only his daughter was and looked like him. Her very masculine identification, however, did not permit her to take a husband as strong as her powerful father. She married what seemed, in comparison, a weak but safe man and settled down. In many ways, however, she talks like the grandfather. She does not know how she persistently belittles the sedentary father and decries the family's lack of mobility, geographic and social. Thus she establishes in the boy a conflict between the sedentary habits which she insists on, and the reckless habits she dares him to develop. At any rate, the early 'oedipus' image, the image of the overpoweringly bigger and greater father and possessor of the mother, who must be emulated or defeated, becomes associated with the myth of the grandfather. Both become deeply unconscious and remain so under the dominant necessity of learning how to be a fair brother, restricted and restricting, and yet healthy and encouraging. The father goes relatively free of his boys' resentment, unless, of course, he happens to be 'old-fashioned', obviously alien, or a man of the 'boss type'. Otherwise he too becomes more of a big brother. Much of sexual rivalry, like sexuality in general, has been excluded from awareness.

The boys I have in mind, already in early adolescence, are tall, often taller than their fathers. About this they make slightly condescending jokes. In fact, it seems that something akin to the Indians' 'joking relationship' is developing between father and son in this country. This joking is often applied to that marginal area where one may hope 'to get away with something' – i.e., elude the mother's watchful eye. This establishes a mutual identification which helps to avoid any direct opposition, and any clear conflict of wills. The boys' dreams indicate that their physical prowess and their independent identity arouses anxiety in them: for once, when they were small boys, they were afraid of these same fathers who then seemed so wise and so potent. It is as if these boys were balancing on a tightrope. Only if they are stronger than or different from the real father will they live up to their secret ideals, or indeed, to their mother's expectations; but only if they somehow demonstrate that they are weaker than the omnipotent father (or grandfather) image of their childhood will they be free of anxiety. Thus, while they become boastful and ruthless in many respects, they can be astonishingly kind and apologetic in others.

Where the son's initiative is concerned, convention urges the father, too, to restrain any tendency he may have to challenge the son. To this purpose the future is emphasized as against the past. If the sons in their group behaviour seem to be organized in the pursuit of one further degree of Americanization it is the fatherly obligation to let the children proceed in their own way. In fact, because of their greater affinity with the tempo and with the technical problems of the immediate future, the children are in a sense 'wiser' than the parents; and indeed, many children are more mature in their outlook on problems of daily living. The father of such boys does not hide his relative weakness behind a mask of inflated patriarchal claims. If he shares with the son an admiration for an ideal type, be he baseball player or industrial leader, comedian, scientist, or rodeo artist, the need to become like the ideal is emphasized without burdening it with a problem of the father's defeat. If the father plays baseball with his son, it is not in order to impress him with the fact that he, the father, comes closer to the perfection of a common ideal type – for he probably does not – but rather that they play together at identifying with that type, and that there is always the chance, hoped for by both, that the boy may more nearly approach the ideal than the father did.

All of this by no means excludes the fact that the father is potentially quite a man, but he shows it more away from home, in business, on camping trips, and in his club. As the son becomes aware of this, a new, almost astonished respect is added to his affection. There are real friendships between fathers and sons.

Fraternal images, boldly or gingerly, thus step into the gaps left by decaying paternalism; fathers and sons are unconsciously working on the development of a fraternal pattern which will forestall the reactionary return of more patriarchal oedipus patterns without, on the other hand, leading to a general impoverishment of the father–son relationship.[14]

How does his home train this boy for democracy? If taken too literally, one may hardly dare to ask that question. The boy has no political sense whatsoever. The 'dignity of man' has never occurred to him. In fact, he does not even know any kind of indignation in the positive sense of becoming acutely aware of the violation of a principle, with the exception of *unfairness*. In early life this takes the form of feeling cheated out of a birthright, when bigger and smaller siblings, on the basis of their superiority or inferiority, demand special privileges. Painfully learning a measure of obligation and privilege as related to strength and weakness, he becomes an advocate of fairness – unfairness, primarily in sports, is probably the only subject which would

[14] In psychoanalytic patients the overwhelming importance of the grandfather is often apparent. He may have been a blacksmith of the old world or a railroad builder of the new, an as yet proud Jew or an unreconstructed Southerner. What these grandfathers have in common is the fact that they were the last representatives of a more homogeneous world, masterly and cruel with good conscience, disciplined and pious without loss of self-esteem. Their world invented bigger and better machinery like gigantic playthings which were not expected to challenge the social values of the men who made them. Their mastery persists in their grandsons as a stubborn, an angry sense of superiority. Overtly inhibited, they yet can accept others only on terms of prearranged privilege.

cause a facsimile of indignation – and then, of course, bossiness of any kind. 'No one can do this to me' is the slogan of such indignation. It is the counterpart of other countries' more heroic honour or *honneur*, *droit* or fair play. While this boy may grin-ningly join in some casual references to a lower race or class, he is not really intolerant: for the most part his life is too protected and 'restricted' to bring him up against an individual decision in this matter. Where he is up against it, he decides on the basis of friendship, not citizenship. It is his privilege, not his duty, to accept a pal of whatever kind. As far as 'general citizenship' is concerned, he catches on to the school's concept of behaviour which goes by this name, but he does not connect it with politics. Otherwise, he more or less somnambulistically moves in a maze of undefined privileges, licences, commitments, and responsibili-ties. He wants a vague, general success, and he is glad if he can get it in fairness, or while being unaware of unfairness. In this connection it must be said that our boy, mostly by default and because of restricted vision, and often out of carelessness, causes great harm to his less fortunate age-mates of darker shades, whom he excludes from his home, his clique, and himself, because to see and to face them as actual human beings might cause vague discomfort. He ignores them, although he might have furthered their participation in the American identity by taking more seri-ously the simple social principle that what nobody can do to me, nobody should do to anybody else either.

But I submit that this boy's family life harbours more de-mocracy than meets the eye. It may not reflect the democracy of the history books and the newspaper editorials, but it reflects a number of trends characterizing, for better or worse, the demo-cratic process as it is, and as it must expand. I must point here to one of those configurational analogies between family life and national *mores* which are hard to fit into a theoretical pattern but seem of utmost relevance:

Now it is an unwritten but firm rule of Congress that no important bloc shall ever be voted down – under normal circumstances – on any matter which touches its own vital interests.[15]

This statement refers, of course, to political interest groups (the farm bloc, the silver bloc, the friends of labour, etc.) which

[15] John Fischer, 'Unwritten Rules of American Politics', *Harper's Magazine*, 197: 27–36, November, 1948.

utilize in a powerful, yet unofficial way, the official two-party polarization – and are utilized by it. At times they contribute positive legislation, but more often – and what is sometimes more important – they prevent unwelcome legislation. What ensues of positive legislation may be good legislation, but it must, first of all, not be unacceptable to any of the major blocs (just as a candidate for president *may* be a potentially great man, but *must* be a man not unacceptable to any large block of voters). This principle not only keeps any one group from complete domination, but it also saves each group from being completely dominated.

The American family, similarly, tends to guard the right of the individual member – parents included – not to be dominated. In fact, each member, as he grows and changes, reflects a variety of outside groups and their changing interests and needs: the father's occupational group, the mother's club, the adolescent's clique, and the children's first friends. These interest groups determine the individual's privileges in his family; it is they who judge the family. The sensitive receptor of changing styles in the community and the sensitive arbiter of their clash within the home is, of course, the mother; and I think that this necessity to function as arbiter is one more reason why the American mother instinctively hesitates to lavish on her children the kind of naïve animal-love which, in all its naïveté, can be so very selective and unjust; and which, above all, may weaken the child in his determination to seek in his peers what the family cannot and should not give him. The mother remains, in a sense, above the parties and interests; it is as if she had to see to it that each party and interest develops as vigorously as possible – up to the point where she must put in a veto in the interest of another individual or of the family as a whole. Here, then, we must expect to find the inner rationale for a variety of activities and inactivities: they represent not so much what everybody wants to do, but rather what, of all the available things to do, is least unacceptable to anybody concerned. Such an inner arrangement, of course, is easily upset by any show of vested interest, or special interest, or minority interest: and it is for this reason that there is a great amount of apparently petty bickering whenever interests clash. The family is successful if the matter is settled to the point of 'majority concurrence', even if this is reluctantly given; it is gradually undermined by frequent decisions in favour of one interest group, be it the parents or the babies. This give-and-take cuts down to an extraordinary degree the division of the family into unequal partners who can claim privileges on the basis of age, strength, weakness, or goodness. Instead, the family becomes a training ground in the tolerance of different *interests* – not of different *beings*; liking and loving has little to do with it. In fact, both overt loving and overt hating are kept on a low key, for either might weaken the balance of the family and the chances of the individual member: for the over-all important thing is to accrue claims for future privilege justifiable on the basis of one's past concessions.

The meaning of it all is, of course, an automatic prevention of autocracy and inequality. It breeds, on the whole, undogmatic people, people ready to drive a bargain and then to compromise. It makes complete irresponsibility impossible, and it makes open hate and warfare in families rare. It also makes it quite impossible for the American adolescent to become what his brothers and sisters in other large countries become so easily: uncompromising ideologists. Nobody can be sure he is right, but everybody must compromise – for the sake of his future chance.

The analogy here to the two-party system is clear: American politics is not, as is that of Europe, 'a prelude to civil war'; it cannot become either entirely irresponsible or entirely dogmatic; and it must not try to be logical. It is a rocking sea of checks and balances in which uncompromising absolutes must drown. The danger is that such absolutes may be drowned in all-around acceptable banalities, rather than in productive compromise.

In the family, the corresponding danger is that the interests which are not unacceptable to the whole family become areas so devoid of real issues that family life becomes an institution for parallel daydreaming where each member is tuned in on his favourite radio programme, or withdrawn behind the magazine representing his interests. A general low tonus of mutual responsibility may empty the pattern of majority concurrence of its original indignation, and thus of its dignity.

Where in Europe, then, adolescence would lead to a conflict with the father, and the necessity of either rebelling or submitting (or, as we shall see in the chapter on Germany, first rebelling and then submitting) there is, on the whole, no necessity for such exertion in the American family. The adolescent swings of the American youth do not overtly concern the father, nor the matter of authority, but focus rather on his peers. The boy has a delinquent streak, as had his grandfather in the days when laws were absent or not enforced. This may express itself in surprising acts of dangerous driving or careless destruction and waste, an individual counterpart to the mass plundering of the continent. This stands in surprising contrast to the defence mechanisms of ascetic self-restriction – until one realizes that occasional utter carelessness is the necessary counterpart and safety-valve of self-restriction. Both carelessness and self-restriction 'feel' self-initiated; they underscore the fact that there is no boss – and that there need be little thought.

Our boy is anti-intellectual. Anybody who thinks or feels too much seems 'queer' to him. This objection to feeling and thinking is, to some extent, derived from an early mistrust of sensuality. It signifies some atrophy in this sphere, and then again, it is representative of a general tentativeness, of a wish not to meditate and not to make up his mind until the free exploration by action of a number of chances may force him to think.

If this boy attends church, and as I suggested he is Protestant, he finds a milieu which makes no great demands on his ability to surrender to moods of damnation or salvation or even of simple piety. In church life he must prove himself by overt behaviour which demonstrates discipline by self-restriction, thus earning the fellowship of all those whose good and fair fortunes on earth God obviously legitimizes. Church membership, then, makes things ever so much easier, since at the same time it provides a clearer definition of one's social and credit status in the community. Here again, sociologists, in their somewhat naïve and literal criticism of the 'American class system', seem sometimes to overlook the historic necessity in America of finding in community and church life a scope for activities which are acceptable to all the individuals concerned. This calls for some initial principle of selection, for some uniformity. Without it, democracy would not have begun to work in this country. But the sociologists are right in pointing out that all too often membership of lesser or greater exclusiveness, sectarianism, and faddism leads to a mere shell of fraternal congregation where the habits of family life are further indulged rather than brought to any political or spiritual fruit. The church community becomes a frigid and punitive Mom; God a Pop who in view of public pressure cannot avoid providing for those of his children who prove worthy by self-restricted conduct and proper appearance; while the brethren have the prime obligation of proving their credit-worthiness by being moderate in dealing with one another and by diverting more energetic tactics to 'outsiders'.

The type of adolescent I am discussing here is not and will never be a true individualist. But then it would be hard to point out any true individualist within the orbit of his experience – unless it be the myth of the mother's father. But this image becomes buried in self-constriction or is, at the most, held in abeyance for the day when, as grown men, they may become the 'bosses' of something or other.

With this individualistic core in him, complicated as it is by the transmission through the mother, our adolescent is allergic to the professional kinds of individualism displayed by writers and politicians. He mistrusts both – they make him feel uncomfortable, as if they reminded him that there is something that he should be or should do but that he cannot remember. He has experienced, or rather faced, no autocracy except that of his mother, who by now has become Mom, in the original and kinder sense, to him. If he resents her he tries to forget it.

He is aware that his older sister, slim, trim, and poised, on occasion seems to get almost physically upset in the mother's presence. The boy cannot see why; but then, this belongs to the general area of women's whims which he carefully circumnavigates. He does not know, he does not want to know, the burden which the sister must carry in becoming a woman and a mother without becoming like the woman who is her mother. For she must be the self-made woman of *her* period; she must work on herself, in competitive companionship with all the other girls who make and are made by the new standards. Margaret Mead has impressively described the difficult job which these girls share, namely, the necessity of saving a full measure of warmth and sexual responsiveness through the years of calculated appearances when even naturalness on occasion must be affected.[16] The sister's crisis will come when she becomes a mother and when the

[16] Margaret Mead, *Male and Female*, William Morrow and Co., New York, 1949.

vicissitudes of child training will perforce bring to the fore the infantile identification with her mother. There is much less of 'Mom' in her than there was in her mother; whether this remnant will be decisive depends on region, class, and kind of husband.

This American adolescent, then, is faced, as are the adolescents of all countries who have entered or are entering the machine age, with the question: freedom for what, and at what price? The American feels so rich in his opportunities for free expression that he often no longer knows what it is he is free from. Neither does he know where he is not free; he does not recognize his native autocrats when he sees them. He is too immediately occupied with being efficient and being decent.

This adolescent will make an efficient and decent leader in a circumscribed job, a good manager or professional worker and a good officer, and will most enjoy his recreation with 'the boys' in the organizations to which he belongs. As a specimen, he illustrates the fact that in war or in peace the fruit of American education is to be found in a combination of native mechanical ability, managerial autonomy, personalized leadership, and unobtrusive tolerance. These young men truly are the backbone of the nation.

But are they, as men, not strangely disinterested in the running of the nation? Are these freeborn sons not apt to be remarkably naïve, overly optimistic, and morbidly self-restrained in their dealings with the men who run them? They know how to accept a circumscribed task; they can be boisterous when on a spree; but on the whole, they respectfully shy away from all bigness, whether it is dollars or loud words. They (theoretically) hate autocrats, but they tolerate bossism because they usually cannot differentiate between a boss and 'bosses'. We have repeatedly mentioned this category of 'boss', and it is time to state explicitly that there is a boss and a 'boss', just as there is a Mom and a 'Mom'. We use both words without quotation marks in their more colloquial and more affectionate sense, in the sense of *my Mom*, and *my boss*; while we designate with quotation marks the 'Moms' who make for Momism as discussed above and the 'bosses' that constitute the bossism to which we must now make reference.

For the old autocrats have disappeared, and the new ones know how to hide behind the ambiguity of language, which fills the legislatures and the daily Press, industrial strife and organized entertainment. 'Bosses' are self-made autocrats and, therefore, consider themselves and one another the crown of democracy. As far as is necessary, a 'boss' stays within the law, and as far as is possible he enters boldly into the vacuum left by the emancipated sons in their endeavour to restrict themselves in fairness to others. He looks for areas where the law has been deliberately uncharted (in order to leave room for checks, balances, and amendments) and tries to use it and abuse it for his own purposes. He is the one who – to speak in highway terms – passes and cuts in where others leave a little space for decency's and safety's sake.

Here it is not a matter of taste or mere principle which makes me join those who decry the danger of bossism. I approach the matter from the point of view of psychological economy. 'Bosses' and 'machines', I have learned, are a danger to the American identity, and thus to the mental health of the nation. For they present to the emancipated generations, to the generations with tentative identities, the ideal of an autocracy of irresponsibility. In them is seen the apparently successful model, 'he who measures himself solely by what "works", by what he can get away with and by what he can appear to be'. They make 'functioning' itself a value above all other values. In their positions of autocratic power in legislation, in industry, in the Press, and in the entertainment world, they knowingly and unknowingly use superior machinery to put something over on the naïve sons of democracy. They thrive on the complication of 'machinery' – a machinery kept deliberately complicated in order that it may remain dependent on the hard-bitten professional and expert of the 'inside track'. That these men run themselves like machinery is a matter for their doctor, psychiatrist, or undertaker. That they view the world and run the people as machinery becomes a danger to man.

Consider our adolescent boy. In his early childhood he was faced with a training which tended to make him machine-like and clock-like. Thus standardized, he found chances, in his later childhood, to develop autonomy, initiative, and industry, with the implied promise that decency in human relations, skill in technical details, and knowledge of facts would permit him freedom of choice in his pursuits, that the identity of free choice would balance his self-coercion. As an adolescent and man, however, he finds himself confronted with superior machines, complicated, incomprehensible, and impersonally dictatorial in their power to standardize his pursuits and tastes. These machines do their powerful best to convert him into a consumer idiot, a fun egotist, and an efficiency slave – and this by offering him what he seems to demand. Often he remains untouched and keeps his course: this will largely depend on the wife whom he – as the saying goes – chooses. Otherwise, what else can he become but a childish joiner, or a cynical little boss, trying to get in on some big boss's 'inside track' – or a neurotic character, a psychosomatic case?

For the sake of its emotional health, then, a democracy cannot afford to let matters develop to a point where intelligent youth, proud in its independence, and burning with initiative, must leave matters of legislation, law, and international affairs, not to speak of war and peace, to 'insiders' and 'bosses'. American youth can gain the full measure of its identity and of its vitality only by being fully aware of autocratic trends in this and in any other land as they repeatedly emerge from changing history. And this not only because political conscience cannot regress without catastrophic consequences, but also because political ideals are part and parcel of an evolution in conscience-structure which, if ignored, must lead to illness.

As we consider what consequences must arise from the particular dangers threatening the emotional state of the nation, our attention is drawn to Momism and to bossism, the two trends which have usurped the place of paternalism: Momism in filiance with the autocratic rigour of a new continent, and bossism with the autocracy of the machine and the 'machines'.

Psychiatric enlightenment has begun to debunk the superstition that to manage a machine you must become a machine, and that to raise masters of the machine you must mechanize the impulses of childhood. But let it be clear that the humanization of early childhood – as pioneered by enlightened obstetricians and paediatricians – must have its counterpart in a political rejuvenation. Men and women in power must make a concerted effort to overcome the rooted conception that man, for his own good, must be subject to 'machines' either in politics, business, education, or entertainment. American adolescents believe deeply in truly free enterprise; they prefer one big chance in a hundred little ones to an average-sized certainty. The very fact that for this same reason they do not contemplate rebellion (as those seem to fear who would gag their sources of information) obliges us to protect youth against a state of affairs which may make their gestures of free men seem hollow and their faith in man illusory and ineffective.

The question of our time is, How can our sons preserve their freedom and share it with those whom, on the basis of a new technology and of a more universal identity, they must consider equals? This makes it necessary for men and women in power to give absolute priority over precedent and circumstance, convention and privilege, to the one effort which can keep a democratic country healthy: the effort to 'summon forth the potential intelligence of the younger generation' (Parrington).

I have sketched some of the dilemma of the grandsons of self-made men, themselves the grandsons of rebels. In other countries youth is still involved in the first phases of revolution against autocracy. Let us turn to some of their historical problems.[17]

[17] What did I dread in some of the now more obscure passages of this chapter? I think it is the inner split between the morality of daily existence, the ideologies of political life, and the neutral dictates of modern super-organization. The bosses are, at least in this country, about to be absorbed in the smoother teams of managerial power. In other and newer nation states (which repeat a century of our history in decades), a variety of revolutionary ideologies are bringing to power the bosses of party machines, of military and industrial machineries, of labour organizations, etc. The frequent display of the ethical bewilderment of middle age charged with the management of unforeseen changes forces much of youth into apathetic conformity or cynical detachment. The moral is that the identity gain of successful revolts against ageing systems does not in itself guarantee the generative values necessary for an ethics of mature power. If man permits his ethics to depend on the machineries he can set in motion, forgetting to integrate childhood and society, he may find himself helplessly harnessed to the designs of total destruction along with those of total production. (For a discussion of the moral, the ideological, and the ethical sense in human development, see 'The Golden Rule and the Cycle of Life', *Harvard Medical Alumni Bulletin*, December, 1962.) E.H.E.

9 The Legend of Hitler's Childhood

The most ruthless exploiters of any nation's fight for a safe identity have been Adolf Hitler and his associates, who for a decade were the undisputed political and military masters of a great, industrious, and studious people. To stop these experts of the cheap word from becoming a threat to the whole of Western civilization the combined resources of the industrial nations of the world were mobilized.

The West would now prefer to ignore the question mark which thus challenges the idea of unilinear progress. It hopes that, after some feeding and policing by occupation troops, these same Germans will once more emerge as good customers, easily domesticated; that they will return to the pursuit of *Kultur*, and forever forget the martial foolishness they were once more trapped into.

Men of good will must believe in psychological as well as in economic miracles. Yet I do not think that we are improving the chances of human progress in Germany or anywhere else by forgetting too soon what happened. Rather, it is our task to recognize that the black miracle of Nazism was only the German version – superbly planned and superbly bungled – of a universal contemporary potential. The trend persists; Hitler's ghost is counting on it.

For nations, as well as individuals, are not only defined by their highest point of civilized achievement, but also by the weakest one in their collective identity: they are, in fact, defined by the distance, and the quality of the distance, between these points. National Socialist Germany has provided a clear-cut illustration of the fact that advancing civilization is potentially endangered by its own advance, in that it splits ancient conscience, endangers incomplete identities, and releases destructive forces which now can count on the cold efficiency of the super-managers. I shall therefore go back this one step in our history and re-state here a few formulations written for a U.S. government agency at the beginning of the Second World War, in preparation for the arrival of the – oh, so arrogant – first Nazi prisoners. Some of these formulations may already sound dated. Yet the psychological problems presented here do not vanish overnight either from Germany proper, or from the continent of which she is the centre. At any rate, history only teaches those who are not over-eager to forget.

I shall take as my text the Brown Piper's sweetest, most alluring tune: the account of his childhood, in *Mein Kampf*.

In this little town on the river Inn, Bavarian by blood and Austrian by nationality, gilded by the light of German martyrdom, there lived, at the end of the eighties of last century, my parents: the father a faithful civil servant, the mother devoting herself to the cares of the household and looking after her children with eternally the same loving care.[1]

The sentence structure, the tone quality, indicate that we are to hear a fairy tale; and indeed we shall analyse it as part of a modern attempt to create a myth. But a myth, old or modern, is not a lie. It is useless to try to show that it has no basis in fact; nor to claim that its fiction is fake and nonsense. A myth blends historical fact and significant fiction in such a way that it 'rings true' to an area or an era, causing pious wonderment and burning ambition. The people affected will not question truth or logic; the few who cannot help doubting will find their reason paralysed. To study a myth critically, therefore, means to analyse its images and themes in their relation to the culture area affected.

GERMANY

'This little town . . . Bavarian by blood and Austrian by nationality, gilded by the light of German martyrdom . . .'

Hitler was born in the Austrian town of Braunau, near the German border. He thus belonged to the Austrian Empire's German minority.

It had been in Braunau, he records, that a man named Palm was shot by Napoleon's soldiers for printing a pamphlet: *In the*

[1] Adolf Hitler, *Mein Kampf*, Reynal & Hitchcock edition, New York, 1941, by arrangement with Houghton Mifflin Company.

Hour of Germany's Deepest Humiliation. Palm's memorial stands in the centre of the town.

There was, of course, no German Reich in Palm's time. In fact, some of the German states were Napoleon's military allies. But having used the all-inclusive, the magic term 'Germany', Palm, when delivered to Napoleon by the Austrian police, became the idol of the nationalist movement calling for a greater Germany.

Having pointed to Palm's resistance to and martyrdom under the sinister *Bonaparte*, the story proceeds to describe young Adolf's heroic opposition to his *father*, and tells of the German minority's hatred of the Austrian *emperor*. Little Adolf belonged, so he says, to 'those who in painful emotion long for the hour that will allow them to return to the arms of the beloved mother' – Germany.

It is here that his imagery begins to involve terms of family relations which openly identify his 'oedipus' situation with his country's national problems. He complains that this 'beloved mother, . . . the *young* Reich,' by her 'tragic alliance with the *old Austrian sham state* . . . herself sanctioned the slow extermination of the German nationality'.

Hitler's mother was twenty-three years younger than his father; and, as we shall see, the mother, as a good woman of her day, valiantly stood up for the man who beat her. The father was a drunkard and a tyrant. The equation suggests itself that in Hitler's national as well as domestic imagery, the young mother betrays the longing son for a senile tyrant. Little Adolf's personal experience thus blends with that of the German minority which refuses to sing 'God Save Emperor Francis', when the Austrian anthem is sung and substitutes for it 'Germany over All'. Hitler continues:

The direct result of this period was: first, I became a nationalist; second, I learned to grasp and to understand the meaning of history . . . so that at fifteen, I already understood the difference between dynastic patriotism and popular nationalism.

Such seemingly naïve coincidence of themes lends itself easily – much too easily – to a psychoanalytic interpretation of the first chapter of *Mein Kampf* as an involuntary confession of Hitler's oedipus complex. This interpretation would suggest that in Hitler's case the love for his young mother and the hate for his

296

old father assumed morbid proportions, and that it was this conflict which drove him to love and to hate and compelled him to save or destroy people and peoples who really 'stand for' his mother and his father. There have been articles in psychoanalytic literature which claim such simple causality. But it obviously takes much more than an individual complex to make a successful revolutionary. The complex creates the initial fervour; but if it were too strong it would paralyse the revolutionary, not inspire him. The striking use of parental and familial images in Hitler's public utterances has that strange mixture of naïve confession and shrewd propaganda which characterizes the histrionic genius. Goebbels knew this and he guided his barking master well – until very close to the end.

I shall not now review the psychiatric literature which has described Hitler as a 'psychopathic paranoid', an 'amoral sadistic infant', an 'overcompensatory sissy', or 'a neurotic labouring under the compulsion to murder'. At times, he undoubtedly was all of that. But, unfortunately, he was something over and above it all. His capacity for acting and for creating action was so rare that it seems inexpedient to apply ordinary diagnostic methods to his words. He was first of all an adventurer, on a grandiose scale. The personality of the adventurer is akin to that of an actor, because he must always be ready to personify, as if he had chosen them, the changing roles suggested by the whims of fate. Hitler shares with many an actor the fact that he is said to have been queer and unbearable behind the scenes, to say nothing of in his bedroom. He undoubtedly had hazardous borderline traits. But he knew how to approach the borderline, to appear as if he were going too far, and then to turn back on his breathless audience. Hitler knew how to exploit his own hysteria. Medicine-men, too, often have this gift. On the stage of German history, Hitler sensed to what extent it was safe to let his own personality represent with hysterical abandon what was alive in every German listener and reader. Thus the role he chose reveals as much about his audience as about himself; and precisely that which to the non-German looked queerest and most morbid became the Brown Piper's most persuasive tune for German ears.

'. . . the father a faithful civil servant . . .'

Despite this sentimental characterization of the father, Hitler spends a heated portion of his first chapter in reiterating the assertion that neither his father nor 'any power on earth could make an official' out of him. He knew already in earliest adolescence that the life of an official had no appeal for him. How different he was from his father! For though his father, too, had rebelled in early adolescence and at the age of thirteen had run away from home to become 'something "better"', he had, after twenty-three years, returned home – and become a minor official. And 'nobody remembered the little boy of long ago'. This futile rebellion, Hitler says, made his father old early. Then, point for point, Hitler demonstrates a rebellious technique superior to that of his father.

Is this the naïve revelation of a pathological father-hate? Or if it is shrewd propaganda, what gave this Austrian German the right to expect that the tale of his boyhood would have a decisive appeal for masses of Reichs-Germans?

Obviously, not all Germans had fathers of the kind Hitler had, although many undoubtedly did. Yet we know that a literary theme, to be convincing, need not be true: it must sound true, as if it reminded one of something deep and past. The question, then, is whether the German father's position in his family made him act -- either all of the time, or enough of the time, or at memorable times – in such a way that he created in his son an *inner* image which had some correspondence to that of the older Hitler's publicized image.

Superficially, the position in his family of the German middle-class father of the late nineteenth and the early twentieth century may have been quite similar to other Victorian versions of 'life with Father'. But patterns of education are elusive. They vary in families and persons; they may remain latent only to appear during memorable crises; they may be counteracted by determined attempts to be different.

I shall present here an impressionistic version of what I consider one pattern of German fatherhood. It is representative in the sense in which Galton's blurred composites of photography are representative of what they are supposed to show.

When the father comes home from work, even the walls seem to pull themselves together (*'nehmen sich zusammen'*). The mother – although often the unofficial master of the house – behaves differently enough to make a baby aware of it. She hurries to fulfil the father's whims and to avoid angering him. The children hold their breath, for the father does not approve of 'nonsense' – that is, neither of the mother's feminine moods nor of the children's playfulness. The mother is required to be at his disposal as long as he is at home; his behaviour suggests that he looks with disfavour on that unity of mother and children in which they had indulged in his absence. He often speaks to the mother as he speaks to the children, expecting compliance and cutting off any answer. The little boy comes to feel that all the gratifying ties with his mother are a thorn in the father's side, and that her love and admiration – the model for so many later fulfilments and achievements – can be reached only without the father's knowledge, or against his explicit wishes.

The mother increases this feeling by keeping some of the child's 'nonsense' or badness from the father – if and when she pleases; while she expresses her disfavour by telling on the child when the father comes home, often making the father execute periodical corporal punishment for misdeeds, the details of which do not interest him. Sons are bad, and punishment is always justified. Later, when the boy comes to observe the father in company, when he notices his father's subservience to superiors, and when he observes his excessive sentimentality when he drinks and sings with his equals, the boy acquires that first ingredient of *Weltschmerz*: a deep doubt of the dignity of man – or at any rate of the 'old man'. All this, of course, exists concurrently with respect and love. During the storms of adolescence, however, when the boy's identity must settle things with his father-image, it leads to that severe German *Pubertät* which is such a strange mixture of open rebellion and 'secret sin', cynical delinquency and submissive obedience, romanticism and despondency, and which is apt to break the boy's spirit, once and for all.

In Germany, this pattern had traditional antecedents. It always just happened to happen, although it was, of course, not 'planned'.

Indeed, some fathers who had resented the pattern deeply during their own boyhood wished desperately not to inflict it on their boys. But this wish again and again traumatically failed them in periods of crisis. Others tried to repress the pattern, only to augment both their and their children's neuroticisms. Often the boy sensed that the father himself was unhappy about his inability to break the vicious circle; for this emotional impotence the boy felt pity and disgust.

What, then, made this conflict so universally fateful? What differentiates – in an unconscious but decisive way – the German father's aloofness and harshness from similar traits in other Western fathers? I think the difference lies in the German father's essential lack of true inner authority – that authority which results from an integration of cultural ideal and educational method. The emphasis here definitely lies on *German* in the sense of *Reichs-German*. So often when discussing things German, we think and speak of well-preserved German *regions*, and of 'typical' yet isolated instances where the German father's inner authority seemed deeply justified, founded as it was on old rural and small urban *Gemütlichkeit*; on urban *Kultur*; on Christian *Demut*; on professional *Bildung*; or on the spirit of social *Reform*. The important point is that all of this did not assume an integrated meaning on a national scale as the imagery of the Reich became dominant and industrialization undermined the previous social stratification.

Harshness is productive only where there is a sense of obligation in command, a sense of dignity in voluntary obedience. This, however, only an integrating cause can provide: a cause that unites past and present in accord with changes in the economic, political, and spiritual institutions.

The other Western nations had their democratic revolutions. They, as Max Weber demonstrated, by gradually taking over the privileges of their aristocratic classes, had thereby identified with aristocratic ideals. There came to be something of the French chevalier in every Frenchman, of the Anglo-Saxon gentleman in every Englishman, and of the rebellious aristocrat in every American. This something was fused with revolutionary ideals and created the concept of 'free man' – a concept which assumes inalienable rights, indispensable self-denial, and unceasing revolutionary watchfulness. For reasons which we shall discuss presently, in connection with the problem of *Lebensraum*, the German identity never quite incorporated such imagery to the extent necessary to influence the unconscious modes of education. The average German father's dominance and harshness was not blended with the tenderness and dignity which comes from participation in an integrating cause. Rather, the average father, either habitually or in decisive moments, came to represent the habits and the ethics of the German top-sergeant and petty official who – 'dress'd in a little brief authority' – would never be more but was in constant danger of becoming less; and who had sold the birthright of a free man for an official title or a life pension.

In addition, there was the breakdown of the cultural institution which had taken care of the adolescent conflict in its traditional – and regional – forms. In the old days, for example, the custom of *Wanderschaft* existed. The boy left home in order to be an apprentice in foreign lands at about the age – or a little later – at which Hitler announced his opposition, and at which Hitler's father had run away from home. In the immediate pre-Nazi era, some kind of break either still took place, with paternal thunder and maternal tears; or it was reflected in more moderate conflicts which were less effective because more individualized and often neurotic; or it was repressed, in which case not the father–boy relation, but the boy's relation to himself, was broken. Often the – exclusively male – teachers had to bear the brunt of it; while the boy extended his idealistic or cynical hostility over the whole sphere of *Bürgerlichkeit* – the German boy's contemptible world of 'mere citizens'. The connotation of this word *Bürger* is hard to transmit. It is not identical with the solid burgher; nor with the glutted *bourgeois* of the class-conscious revolutionary youth; and least of all with the proud *citoyen* or the responsible citizen, who, accepting his equal obligations, asserts his right to be an individual. Rather it means a kind of adult who has betrayed youth and idealism, and has sought refuge in a petty and servile kind of conservatism. This image was often used to indicate that all that was 'normal' was corrupt, and that all that was 'decent' was weak. As 'Wanderbirds', adolescent boys would indulge in a romantic unity with Nature, shared with many co-rebels and led by special types of youth leaders, professional and confessional adolescents. Another type of adolescent, the 'lone genius', would write diaries, poems, and treatises; at fifteen he would lament with Don Carlos's most German of all adolescent complaints: 'Twenty years old, and as yet nothing done for immortality!' Other adolescents would form small bands of intellectual cynics, of delinquents, of homosexuals, and of race-conscious chauvinists. The common feature of all these activities, however, was the exclusion of the individual fathers as an influence and the adherence to some mystic-romantic entity: Nature, Fatherland, Art, Existence, etc., which were super-images of a pure mother, one who would not betray the rebellious boy to that ogre, the father. While it was sometimes assumed that the mother would openly or secretly favour, if not envy, such freedom, the father was considered its mortal foe. If he failed to manifest sufficient enmity, he would be deliberately provoked: for his opposition was the life of the experience.

At this stage, the German boy would rather have died than be aware of the fact that this misguided, this excessive initiative in the direction of utter Utopianism would arouse deep-seated guilt and at the end lead to stunned exhaustion. The identification with the father which in spite of everything had been well established in early childhood would come to the fore. In intricate ways treacherous Fate (= reality) would finally make a *Bürger* out of the boy – a 'mere citizen' with an eternal sense of sin for having sacrificed genius for Mammon and for a mere wife and mere children such as anyone can have.

Naturally, this account is made typical to the point of caricature. Yet I believe that both the overt type and the covert pattern existed, and that, in fact, this regular split between precocious individualistic rebellion and disillusioned, obedient citizenship was a stronger factor in the political immaturity of the German: this adolescent rebellion was an abortion of individualism and of revolutionary spirit. It is my belief that the German fathers not only did not oppose this rebellion, but, indeed, unconsciously fostered it, as one sure way of maintaining their patriarchal hold over youth. For once a patriarchal superego is firmly established in early childhood, you can give youth rope: they cannot let themselves go far.

In the Reichs-German character, this peculiar combination of idealistic rebellion and obedient submission led to a paradox. The German conscience is self-denying and cruel; but its ideals are shifting and, as it were, homeless. The German is harsh with himself and with others; but extreme harshness without inner authority breeds bitterness, fear, and vindictiveness. Lacking coordinated ideals, the German is apt to approach with blind conviction, cruel self-denial, and supreme perfectionism many contradictory and outright destructive aims.

After the defeat and the revolution of 1918 this psychological conflict was increased to the point of catastrophe in the German middle classes; and the middle classes anywhere significantly include the worker class in so far as it aspires to become middle-class. Their servility towards the upper class, which had lost the war, was now suddenly robbed of any resemblance to a meaningful subordination. The inflation endangered pensions. On the other hand, the groping masses were not prepared to anticipate or usurp either the role of free citizens or that of class-conscious workers. It is clear that only under such conditions could Hitler's images immediately convince so many – and paralyse so many more.

I shall not claim, then, that Hitler's father, as described in derogatory accounts, was, in his manifestly rude form, a typical German father. It frequently happens in history that an extreme and even atypical personal experience fits a universal latent conflict so well that a crisis lifts it to a representative position. In fact, it will be remembered here that great nations are apt to choose somebody from just beyond the borders to become their leader: as Napoleon came from Corsica, Stalin came from Georgia. It is a universal childhood pattern, then, which is the basis for the deep wonderment which befell the German man who read about Hitler as a youth. 'No matter how firm and determined my father might be . . . his son was just as stubborn and obstinate in rejecting an idea which had little or no appeal for him. I did not want to become an official.' This combination of personal revelation and shrewd propaganda (together with loud and determined action) at last carried with it that universal conviction for which the smouldering rebellion in German youth had been waiting: that no old man, be he father, emperor, or god, need stand in the way of his love for this mother Germany. At the same time it proved to the grown-up men that by betraying their rebellious adolescence they had become unworthy of leading Germany's youth, which henceforth would 'shape its own destiny'. Both fathers and sons now could identify with the Führer, an adolescent who never gave in.

Psychologists overdo the father-attributes in Hitler's historical image; Hitler the adolescent who refused to become a father by any connotation, or, for that matter, a Kaiser or a president. He did not repeat Napoleon's error. He was the Führer: a glorified older brother, who took over prerogatives of the fathers without overidentifying with them: calling his father 'old while still a child', he reserved for himself the new position of the one who remains young in possession of supreme power. He was the unbroken adolescent who had chosen a career apart from civilian happiness, mercantile tranquillity, and spiritual peace: a gang leader who kept the boys together by demanding their admiration, by creating terror, and by shrewdly involving them in crimes from which there was no way back. And he was a ruthless exploiter of parental failures.

'The question of my career was to be settled more quickly than I had anticipated . . . When I was thirteen my father died quite suddenly. My mother felt the obligation to continue my education for the career of an official.' Thus thwarted, Hitler developed a severe pulmonary illness, and 'all that I had fought for, all that I had longed for in secret, suddenly became reality . . .' His mother had to grant the sick boy what she had denied the healthy and stubborn one: he could now go and prepare to be an artist. He did – and failed the entrance examination to the national art-school. Then his mother died, too. He was now free – and lonely.

Professional failure followed that early school failure which in retrospect is rationalized as character strength and boyish toughness. It is well known how in picking his sub-leaders Hitler later redeemed similar civilian failures. He got away with this only because of the German habit of gilding school failure with the suspicion of hidden genius: 'humanistic' education in Germany suffered all along from the severe split of fostering duty and discipline while glorifying the nostalgic outbreak of poets.

In dealings with the 'old' generation inside or outside Germany, Hitler consequently played a role as stubborn, as devious, and as cynical as he reports his to have been in relation to his father. In fact, whenever he felt that his acts required public justification and apology, he was likely to set the stage as he did in the first chapter of *Mein Kampf*. His tirades were focused on one foreign leader – Churchill or Roosevelt – and described him as a feudal tyrant and a senile fool. He then created a second image, that of the slick, rich son and decadent cynic: Duff-Cooper and Eden, of all men, are the ones he selected. And, indeed, Germans acquiesced to his broken pledges, as long as Hitler, the tough adolescent, seemed merely to be taking advantage of other men's senility.

MOTHER

. . . the mother devoting herself to the cares of the household and looking after her children with eternally the same loving care.'

Beyond this continuation of his fairy tale, Hitler says little of his mother. He mentions that she was sometimes lovingly worried about the fights he, the boy hero, got into; that after the father's death, she felt 'obliged' – out of duty rather than inclination – to have him continue his education; and that soon she, too, died. He had respected his father, he says, but loved his mother.

Of 'her children' there is no further word. Hitler never was the brother of anyone.

That Hitler, the histrionic and hysterical adventurer, had a pathological attachment to his mother, there can be little doubt. But this is not the point here. For, pathological or not, he deftly divides his mother image into the two categories which are of the highest propagandistic value: the loving, childlike, and slightly martyred cook who belongs in the warm and cosy background – and the gigantic marble or iron virgin, the monument to the ideal. In contrast to the sparsity of reference to his personal mother, then, there is an abundance of superhuman mother-figures in his imagery. His Reichs-German fairy tale does not simply say that Hitler was born in Braunau because his parents lived there; no, it was 'Fate which designated my birthplace'. This happened when it happened not because of the natural way of things; no, it was an 'unmerited mean trick of Fate' that he was 'born in a period between two wars, at a time of quiet and order'. When he was poor, 'Poverty clasped me in her arms'; when sad, 'Dame Sorrow was my foster mother'. But all this 'cruelty of Fate' he later learned to praise as the 'wisdom of Providence', for it hardened him for the service of Nature, 'the cruel Queen of all wisdom'.

When the World War broke out, 'Fate graciously permitted' him to become a German foot-soldier, the same 'inexorable Goddess of Fate, who uses wars to weigh nations and men'. When after the defeat he stood before a court defending his first revolutionary acts, he felt certain 'that the Goddess of History's eternal judgement will smilingly tear up' the jury's verdict.

Fate, now treacherously frustrating the hero, now graciously catering to his heroism and tearing up the judgement of the bad old men: this is the infantile imagery which pervades much of German idealism; it finds its most representative expression in the theme of the young hero who becomes great in a foreign country and returns to free and elevate the 'captive' mother: the romantic counterpart to the saga of King Oedipus.

Behind the imagery of superhuman mothers there thus lurks a two-faced image of maternity: the mother at one time appears playful, childlike, and generous; and at another, treacherous, and in league with sinister forces. This, I believe, is a common set of images in patriarchal societies where woman, in many ways kept irresponsible and childlike, becomes a go-between and an inbetween. It thus happens that the father hates in her the elusive children, and the children hate in her the aloof father. Since 'the mother' regularly becomes and remains the unconscious model for 'the world', under Hitler the ambivalence towards the maternal woman became one of the strongest features of German official thinking.

The Führer's relationship to motherhood and family remained ambiguous. In elaboration of a national fantasy he saw in himself a lonely man fighting and pleasing superhuman mother-figures which now try to destroy him, now are forced to bless him. But he did not acknowledge women as companions up to the bitter end, when he insisted on making an honest woman out of Eva Braun, whom he presently shot with his own hands – or so the legend ends. But the wives of other men gave birth to their children in the shelter of the chancellery, while he himself, according to his official biographer, 'is the embodiment of the national will. He does not know any family life; neither does he know any vice.'

Hitler carried this official ambivalence towards women over into his relationship to Germany as an image. Openly despising the masses of his countrymen, who, after all, constitute Germany, he stood frenziedly before them, and implored them with his fanatical cries of 'Germany, Germany, Germany' to believe in a mystical national entity.

But then, the Germans have always been inclined to manifest a comparable attitude of ambivalence towards mankind and the world at large. That the world is essentially perceived as an 'outer world' is true for most tribes or nations. But for Germany the world is constantly changing its quality – and always to an extreme. The world is experienced either as vastly superior in age and wisdom, the goal of eternal longing and *Wanderlust*; or as a mean, treacherous, encircling encampment of enemies living for one aim – namely, the betrayal of Germany; or as a mysterious *Lebensraum* to be won by Teutonic courage and to be used for a thousand years of adolescent aggrandizement.

ADOLESCENT

In this country, the word 'adolescence', to all but those who have to deal with it professionally, has come to mean, at worst, a no-man's-land between childhood and maturity, and at best, a 'normal' time of sports and horse-play, of gangs and cliques and parties. The adolescent in this country offers less of a problem and feels less isolated because he has, in fact, become the cultural arbiter; few men in this country can afford to abandon the gestures of the adolescent, along with those of the freeman forever dedicated to the defeat of autocrats.

From here, then, it is hard to see what adolescence may mean in other cultures. In the primitive past, dramatic and bizarre adolescence-rites were performed in an endeavour to modify and sublimate the adolescent's budding manhood. In primitive rituals the adolescent was forced to sacrifice some of his blood, some of his teeth, or a part of his genitals; in religious ceremonies he is taught to admit his sinfulness and bow his knee. Ancient rites confirmed the boy's intention of becoming a man in his father's world but at the same time of remaining eternally the modest son of a 'Great Father'. Leaders of the ritual dance, redeemers, and tragic actors were the representatives of guilt and expiation. Germany's adolescent rebellion was a climactic step in a universal psychological development which parallels the decline of feudalism: the inner emancipation of the sons. For while there are close parallels between primitive adolescence-rites and those of National Socialism, there is one most significant difference. In Hitler's world, the adolescent marched with his emancipated equals. Their leader had never sacrificed his will to any father. In fact, he had said that conscience is a blemish like circumcision, and that both are Jewish blemishes.

Hitler's horror of Jewry – an 'emasculating germ' represented by less than one per cent of his nation of seventy million – is clothed in the imagery of phobia; he describes the danger emanating from it as a weakening infection and a dirtying contamination. Syphilophobia is the least psychiatry can properly diagnose in his case. But here again, it is hard to say where personal symptom ends and shrewd propaganda begins. For the idealistic adolescent's imagery is typically one of purest white and blackest black. His constant preoccupation is with the attainment of what is white, and the phobic avoidance and extirpation of everything black, in others and in himself. Fears of sexuality, especially, make the adolescent suggestible to words like these: 'Alone the loss of purity of the blood destroys the inner happiness forever; it eternally lowers man, and never again can its consequences be removed from body and mind.'[2]

The pre-Nazi German adolescent was passionately cruel with himself; it was not in order to indulge himself that he opposed his father. When he 'fell', his guilt was great. Hitler, so this adolescent was made to feel, was the man who had the right to be cruel against black everywhere because he was not lenient with himself. What aroused suspicions in sensible non-Germans – namely, Hitler's proclaimed abstinence from meat, coffee, alcohol, and sex – here counted as a heavy propaganda factor. For Hitler thus proved his moral right to free the Germans from their postwar masochism and to convince them that they, in turn, had a right to hate, to torture, to kill.

[2] ibid.

In the children, Hitler tried to replace the complicated conflict of adolescence as it pursued every German, with simple patterns of hypnotic action and freedom from thought. To do so he established an organization, a training, and a motto which would divert all adolescent energy into National Socialism. The organization was the Hitler Youth; the motto, 'Youth shapes its own destiny'.

God no longer mattered: 'At this hour when the earth is consecrating itself to the sun, we have only one thought. Our sun is Adolph Hitler.'[3] Parents did not matter: 'All those who from the perspective of their "experience", and from that alone combat our method of letting youth lead youth, must be silenced ...'[4] Ethics did not matter: 'An entirely fresh, new-born generation has arisen, free from the preconceived ideas, free from compromises, ready to be loyal to the orders which are its birthright.'[5] Brotherhood, friendship did not matter: 'I heard not a single song expressing any tender emotion of friendship, love of parents, love for fellow-man, joy of living, hope for future life.'[6] Learning did not matter: 'National Socialist ideology is to be a sacred foundation. It is not to be degraded by detailed explanation.'[7]

What mattered was: to be on the move without looking backward. 'Let everything go to pieces, we shall march on. For today Germany is ours; tomorrow, the whole world.'

On such a foundation Hitler offered a simple radical dichotomy of cosmic dimensions: the German (soldier) versus the Jew. The Jew is described as small, black, and hairy all over; his back is bent, his feet are flat; his eyes squint, and his lips smack; he has an evil smell, is promiscuous, and loves to deflower, impregnate, and infect blonde girls. The Aryan is tall, erect, light, without hair on chest and limbs; his glance, walk, and talk are *stramm*, his greeting the outstretched arm. He is passionately clean in his habits. He would not knowingly touch a Jewish girl – except in a brothel.

[3] Quoted in G. Ziemer, *Education for Death*, Oxford University Press, New York, 1941.
[4] Quoted in Hans Siemsen, *Hitler Youth*, Lindsay Drummond, London, 1941.
[5] Quoted in Ziemer, op. cit.
[6] Ziemer, op. cit.
[7] Quoted in Ziemer, op. cit.

This antithesis is clearly one of ape man and superman. But while in this country such imagery may have made the comics, in Germany it became official food for adult minds. And let us not forget (for the Germans will not forget) that for long years German youth and the German army seemed to indicate a success for Hitler's imagery. Healthy, hard, calm, obedient, fanatic, they 'challenge everything that is weak in body, in intensity, and in loyalty'.[8] They were arrogant in the extreme; and it was only in their sneering arrogance that the old German fear of succumbing to foreign 'cultured' influence could be recognized.

In women, too, National Socialist race consciousness established a new pride. Girls were taught to accept joyfully the functions of their bodies if mated with selected Aryans. They received sexual enlightenment and encouragement. Childbirth, legitimate or illegitimate, was promoted by propaganda, by subsidies, by the institution of 'State children', who were born 'for the *Führer*'. Breast feeding was advocated; what American psychiatrists at that time dared suggest only in professional journals, the German state decreed: '*Stillfähigkeit ist Stillwille*' – ability to nurse is the will to nurse. Thus German babyhood was enriched for the sake of the race and of the Führer.

In his imagery no actor and no effective innovator is really independent, nor can he dare to be entirely original: his originality must consist in the courage and singular concentration with which he expresses an existing imagery – at the proper time. If he does so, however, he is convincing to himself and to others – and paralyses his adversaries, in so far as they unconsciously partake of his imagery, so that they will wait, become insecure, and finally surrender.

In Germany, then, we saw a highly organized and highly educated nation surrender to the imagery of ideological adolescence. We have indicated that we cannot lay the blame for this on the power of the leaders' individual neuroses. Can we blame the childhood patterns of the led?

[8] Ziemer, op. cit.

The mere impressionistic comparison of a nation's familial imagery with her national and international attitudes can easily become absurd. It seems to lead to the implication that one could change international attitudes by doctoring a nation's family patterns. Yet nations change only when their total reality changes. In America, the sons and daughters of all nations become Americans, although each remains beset by their specific conflict: and I dare say that many a German-American reader will have recognized some of his own father's problems in this chapter. He will recognize it because there is a lag between his father's world and his: his father lives in a different space–time.

The very ease with which comparisons between childhood patterns and national attitudes can be drawn, and the very absurdity to which they can lead, obscures the important truth which is, nevertheless, involved. We shall therefore use this chapter to illustrate the way in which historical and geographic reality amplify familial patterns and to what extent, in turn, these patterns influence a people's interpretation of reality. It is impossible to characterize what is German without relating Germany's familial imagery to her central position in Europe. For, as we saw, even the most intelligent groups must orient themselves and one another in relatively simple sub-verbal, magic design. Every person and every group has a limited inventory of historically determined spatial–temporal concepts, which determine the world image, the evil and ideal prototypes and the unconscious life plan. These concepts dominate a nation's strivings and can lead to high distinction; but they also narrow a people's imagination and thus invite disaster. In German history, such outstanding configurations are encirclement versus *Lebensraum*; and disunity versus unity. Such terms are, of course, so universal that they seem unspecific; the observer who realizes the weight which these words carry in German thinking must suspect them of being insincere propaganda. Yet nothing can be more fatal in international encounters than the attempt to belittle or to argue another nation's mythological space–time. The non-German does not realize that in

311

Germany these words carried a conviction far beyond that of ordinary logic.

The official version of *Lebensraum* stated that the Nazi state must assure, within Europe, military hegemony and armaments monopoly, economic preponderance, and intellectual leadership. Beyond this, *Lebensraum* had an essentially magic meaning. What is this meaning?

At the end of the First World War Max Weber wrote that destiny had decreed [even a realistic German says 'destiny', not 'geography' or 'history'] that Germany alone should have as its immediate neighbours three great land-powers and the greatest sea-power and that it should stand in their way. No other country on earth, he said, was in this situation.[9]

As Weber saw it, the necessity to create national greatness and security in a thoroughly encircled and vulnerable position left two alternatives: Germany might retain its regional quality and become a modern federation like Switzerland – likeable and useful to everybody and a danger to nobody; or it might quickly develop a Reich, fashioned out of quite unfavourable political characteristics, a Reich as mature and powerful as that of England or France, capable of playing power politics, in order to build with the West a cultural and military defence unit against the East. But Weber was a 'realist', which meant he considered only what, according to the considered thinking of his conservative mind, seemed 'reasonable'.[10] He did not dream

[9] Max Weber, *Gesammelte Politische Schriften*, Drei Masken Verlag, Munich, 1921.

[10] The publication in this country of (H. H. Gerth and C. Wright Mills, *From Max Weber: Essays in Sociology*, Oxford University Press, New York, 1946, pp. 28–9) gives an account of certain events in Weber's life which will be quoted here because they strikingly illustrate the familial patterns under discussion:

'His strong sense of chivalry was, in part, a response to the patriarchal and domineering attitude of his father, who understood his wife's love as a willingness to serve and to allow herself to be exploited and controlled by him. This situation came to a climax when Weber, at the age of 31, in the presence of his mother and his wife, saw fit to hold judgment over his father: he would remorselessly break all relations with him unless he met the son's condition: the mother should visit him "alone" without the father. We have noted that the father died only a short time after this encounter and that Weber came out of the situation with an ineffaceable sense of guilt. One may certainly infer an inordinately strong Oedipus situation.

'Throughout his life, Weber maintained a full correspondence with his mother, who once referred to him as "an older daughter". She eagerly sought

that within a few years a man would stand up and proclaim, even bring to near fulfilment, a third alternative – namely, that Germany would become a nation so powerful and so shrewdly led that the whole encircling combination of Paris, London, Rome, and Moscow could one by one be overrun and occupied long enough to be emasculated 'for a thousand years'.

This plan still appears fantastic to the non-German. He wonders how such a scheme could live together in one and the same national mind with the simple kindness and the cosmopolitan wisdom representative of the 'real' German culture. But, as pointed out, the world meant regional, not national, virtues when it spoke of German culture. It persistently underestimated the desperate German need for unity which, indeed, cannot be appreciated by peoples who in their own land take such unity for granted. The world is apt once more to underestimate the force with which the question of national unity may become a matter of the *preservation of identity*, and thus a matter of (human) life and death, far surpassing the question of political systems.

Throughout her history, the area of Germany has been subjected, or has been potentially vulnerable, to sweeping invasions. It is true that in a hundred-odd years her vital centres had not been occupied by an enemy; but she remained conscious of her vulnerable position, both rationally and irrationally.

The threat of military invasion, however, is not the only one. Whether invading or being invaded by different countries, Germany has been impressed by *foreign values*. Her attitude towards these values, and their relation to her own cultural diversity, constitute a clinical problem hard to define. But one may say that no other young nation of similar size, density, and historical diversity of population, with a similar lack of natural frontiers, is exposed to cultural influences as

counsel with him, her first-born, rather than with her husband, in matters concerning the demeanor of her third son. One should also pay heed to what was, to be sure, a passing phase of young Weber's aspiration: his desire to become a real he-man at the university. After only three semesters, he succeeded in changing externally from a slender mother's boy to a massive, beer-drinking, duel-marked, cigar-puffing student of Imperial Germany, whom his mother greeted with a slap in the face. Clearly, this was the father's son. The two models of identification and their associated values, rooted in mother and father, never disappeared from Max Weber's inner life . . .'

divergent in their nature and as disturbing in their succession as the influences emanating from Germany's neighbours. As is true for the elements which make for individual anxiety, it is the consistent mutual aggravation of all these items which has never allowed German identity to crystallize or to assimilate economic and social evolution in gradual and logical steps.

The German image of disunity is based on a historical feeling of discomfort which may be called the 'Limes complex'. The Limes Germanicus was a wall – comparable to the Chinese wall – built by the Romans through western and southern Germany to separate the conquered provinces from those which remained barbaric. This wall was destroyed long ago. But it was replaced by a cultural barrier which separated the area in the south influenced by the Church of Rome from that of Protestant northern Germany. Other empires (military, spiritual, cultural) have thus reached into Germany: from the west, sensual and rational France; from the east, illiterate, spiritual, and dynastic Russia; from the north and north-west, individualistic 'protestantism', and from the south-east, oriental easygoingness. All conflicts between east and west, north and south, were fought out in battle somewhere in Germany – and in the German mind.

Germany, from the beginning, was thus constantly disturbed by a traumatic sequence of divergent influences, which aggravated and kept acute a specific form of the universal conflict between suggestibility and defensive stubbornness. Hitler thus promised Germany not only the military conquest of the invasion centres surrounding the Reich, but also a victory of race consciousness over the 'bacterial' invasion of foreign aesthetics and ethics within the German mind. His aim was not only the eternal obliteration of Germany's military defeat in the First World War, but also a complete purge of the corrupt foreign values which had invaded German culture. To the tormented Germans this was real 'freedom'; other freedoms, in comparison, seemed vague and unessential.

Thus the appeal of Adolf Hitler's violent remedy was directed towards a Reich which was large and felt potentially great; but which at the same time felt vulnerable in its frontiers and undeveloped in its political core. It was directed towards a national mind with a great regional heritage and burning spiritual ambitions but with a morbid suggestibility and a deep insecurity in its basic values. Only an adversary who can fathom the effect of such a situation on the struggle for identity in a nation's youth can divine their danger – and his.

Germany's desperate paradoxes led to those extremes of German contradictions which – before Hitler – were considered to constitute two different Germanies. In reaction to the sense of cultural encirclement one type of Reichs-German became, as it were, too broad, while the other became too narrow. That other nations have analogous conflicts between cosmopolitanism and provincialism does not remove the necessity of understanding the German version of this dilemma. The 'too broad' type denied or hated the German paradox and embraced the whole encircling 'outer world'; he became cosmopolitan beyond recognition. The 'narrow' type tried to ignore foreign temptations and became 'German' to the point of caricature. The first was always glad to be mistaken for an Englishman, a Frenchman, or an American; the second arrogantly overdid the narrow inventory of his few genuine characteristics. The first felt and thought on an Olympian scale; the second became obedient and mechanical to the exclusion of all thought and feeling. The first often was a lifelong nostalgic, a voluntary exile, or a potential suicide or psychotic; the second remained at home, or wherever he went made himself at home and, gritting his teeth, remained a German.

The world admired the first type and sneered at the second; the world ignored, until it was too late, the fact that neither of these types led to a re-birth on a national level of that maturity and of that monumental dignity which at times had characterized the burghers and artisans of Germany's regions. The world ignored the fact that neither type felt sure in himself and safe in the world, that neither of them accepted a part in man's political emancipation.

It is a fatal error to assume that National Socialism came about *in spite* of Germany's intellectual greatness. It was the natural result of the particular social – or rather asocial – orientation of its great men.

We need not limit ourselves here to the consideration of such a lonely hater of man's realities as Nietzsche, who was fortunate enough to die demented and deluded instead of being forced to witness the stark reality of the uniformed supermen whom he had helped to create. No, we may think of men with an exquisite eye for realities, such as Thomas Mann, who during the First World War is reported to have encouraged the Germans by saying that, after all, the possession of a philosopher such as Kant more than compensated for the French Revolution, and that the *Critique of Pure Reason* was, in fact, a far more radical revolution than was the proclamation of the rights of man.[11]

I realize that this may well have been a great intellectual's way of saying the wrong thing at the right time, which is an intellectual's privilege during his nation's emergencies. But the statement illustrates the German's awe of overpowering, lonely, and often tragic greatness, and his readiness to sacrifice the individual's right in order to emancipate the greatness in his own heart.

Neither as aloof a cosmopolitan as Goethe, nor as aloof a statesman as Bismarck – then the dominant images in the German school's inventory of guiding images – had essentially contributed to a German image of democratic man.

The attempt, after the defeat of 1918, to create a republic led to a temporary dominance of the 'too broad' German. The leaders of that era could not prevent the merging of political immaturity and intellectual escapism which combined to create a myth of strange, almost hysterical passion: *Fate* had sent defeat to Germany in order to single her out from among the nations. *Fate* had elected her to be the first great country to accept defeat voluntarily, to shoulder moral blame completely, and to resign political greatness once and for all. Thus *Fate* had used all the Allied countries with all their soldiers, alive and dead, merely to elevate Germany to an exalted existence in an unlimited *spiritual Lebensraum*. Even in this very depth of masochistic self-abasement – impressively decried by Max Weber – world history was still a secret arrangement between the Teutonic spirit and the Goddess of Fate. Germany's basic relationship to history had not changed. The world seems to have been surprised when this spiritual chauvinism

[11] Janet Flanner, 'Goethe in Hollywood', *The New Yorker*, December 20, 1941.

316

gradually turned back into militarism, when it again employed sadistic rather than masochistic images and techniques. The Great Powers at this point failed in their responsibility to 're-educate' Germany in the only way in which one can re-educate peoples – namely, by presenting them with the incorruptible fact of a new identity within a more universal political framework. Instead, they exploited German masochism and increased her universal hopelessness. The too narrow German, in bitter hiding since defeat, now came forward to prepare the widest possible earthly *Lebensraum* for the narrowest type of German: Aryan world-domination.

Caught between the too narrow and the too broad, the few statesmen capable of dignity, realism, and vision broke under the strain or were murdered. The Germans, without work, without food, and without a new integrity, began to listen to Hitler's imagery, which, for the first time in Reichs-German history, gave political expression to the spirit of the German adolescent. There was magic weight in the words, 'I, however, resolved now to become a politician', with which the unbroken adolescent closes the seventh chapter of *Mein Kampf*.

When Hitler thus undertook to bring the adolescent imagery of his people to political dominance, a magnificent tool gradually became his – the German army. Book knowledge of the war of 1870-1 had been Hitler's 'greatest spiritual experience'. In 1914, when he had been permitted to become a Reichs-German soldier, he had moved into the full light of that heroic history. Then had come defeat. Hitler had denied with hysterical fanaticism – he himself had been blinded by gas, some say by emotional exertion – that the light had withdrawn from that image. He had appeared determined to redeem it. His enemies, inside and outside Germany, had shrugged their shoulders.

But here again it is necessary to look beyond the obsessive and to see the ingenious. From the First World War's Thomas Mann to the Second's Nazi philosopher, the German soldier was conceived of as a personification, or even the spiritualization, of what is German. He represented 'the Watch on the Rhine': the human wall replacing Germany's non-existent natural frontiers. In him unity through blind obedience proved itself and aspirations towards democratic diversity defeated themselves. It would be dangerous to overlook the fact that this position, exploited as it was by a noisy type of high-stepping young officer, also helped to develop an officer aristocracy which in true absorption of the aristocratic–revolutionary principles of other nations harboured one of the few politically mature European types in Germany. If Hitler, therefore, denied the defeat of this army with all the weapons of self-deception and falsehood, he saved for himself and for German youth the only integrated image that could belong to everybody.

The treaty of Versailles, cleverly exploited, proved helpful in the creation of a new streamlined German soldier. The small army became an army of specialists. Thus the oldest and least modified Reichs-German type was re-created with the insignia of the modern technician. A spirit of teamwork and of personal responsibility replaced that of blind obedience; maturity, instead of caste, became the mark of the officer. With such new material the blitzkrieg was prepared: not only a technical feat, but also a sweeping solution and salvation for the traumatized German people. For it promised a victory of movement over the Allied superiority in artillery power (and the industrial might behind it) which, during the First World War, had 'nailed down' the Germans until they became ready to trust Wilson, to break up, and to attend to higher things. Furthermore, Germany's youth, in the blitzkrieg, experienced 'finalities of a revolution reaching into spiritual, mental and material depths'.[12] It relieved the feeling of encirclement and of peripheral vulnerability. And, to quote a Nazi: 'The instinctive pleasure which youth finds in the power of engines here divines the expansions of mankind's limitations, which were so narrow from the start, and, on the whole, have not been widened by civilization.'[13] It would be fatal to brush aside such Nazi mysticism. To defeat motorized Germany, the youth of other countries also had to learn like modern centaurs to grow together with their fighting machines into new restless beings of passionate precision. Hitler tried to anticipate an age that would experience a motorized world as natural; and to fuse it with the image of a totalitarian 'state machine'. He took it as a personal insult when he saw the

[12] W. W. Backhaus, 'Überwindung der Materialschlacht', *Das Reich*, Berlin, July 13, 1941.
[13] ibid.

318

industries of the democracies go into high gear (*Gelump* – rubbish – he tried to call their output). When their fire-power came on wings right into his cities, and above all, when he saw that Anglo-Saxon youths could identify with their machines without losing their heads, he was incredulous. When he then saw the Russians perform miracles not only of defence but also of offence, his irrational fury knew no bounds, for in his inventory of images he had characterized them not only as unequal to his soldiers, but as people below any possible comparison: men of the mud (*Sumpfmenschen*), he called them, and subhuman. They thus became, towards the end, equivalent to the other subhumans, the Jews: only the more fortunate Russians had a country and an army.

It is obvious enough that much envy was hidden in Hitler's fantastic overestimation of the Jewish 'danger', embodied as it was in such a small part of the population, and a highly intellectualized one at that. But as we have said, the narrow German always felt endangered, denationalized, by information which exposed him to the relativity and diversity of cultural values. The Jew seemed to remain himself despite dispersion over the world, while the German trembled for his identity in his own country. In fact, these mysterious Jews seemed to be making of intellectual relativity a means of racial self-preservation. To some Germans, this was not understandable without assuming an especially devious chauvinism, a hidden Jewish pact with Fate.

A NOTE ON JEWRY

Oswald Spengler had already suspected that anti-Semitism was largely a matter of projection: which means that people see over-clearly in Jews what they wish not to recognize in themselves. A hidden pact with Fate, of the variety which would hide dreams of world conquest behind a 'chosen' sense of intellectual superiority, is an idea entirely akin to German chauvinism.

While projections are hostile and fearful distortions, however, they are commonly not without a kernel of profound meaning. True, the projector who sees a mote in his brother's eye overlooks the beam in his own, and the degree of distortion and the frightfulness of his reaction remain his responsibility. Yet there usually is something in the neighbour's eye which lends itself to specific magnification. It was by no means a coincidence that at this crucial moment in history (when 'one world' became a real image, two worlds an unavoidable reality) the most encircled of the civilized nations should be susceptible to propaganda which warned of the devilish powers of the most dispersed nation. We must therefore ask in passing what seems to make the Jew a favourite target of the most vicious projections – and this by no means only in Germany. In fact, in Russia, too, we have recently witnessed a violent campaign against 'cosmopolitan intellectuals'. Jewry is a singular example of an old entity which clings to its identity – be it racial, ethnic, religious, or cultural – in such a way that it is felt to be a danger to emerging identities.

Does the Jew remind the Western world of those sinister blood-rites (mentioned above) in which the father-god demands a token of the boy's sexual member, a tax on his masculinity, as a sign of the covenant? Psychoanalysts offer the explanation that the Jew arouses 'castration fear' in peoples who have not accepted circumcision as a hygienic measure. We saw how, in Germany, this fear could be extended to that more inclusive fear of giving in, of losing one's adolescent will. The fact that the Jews had left their homeland and sacrificed their national right of organized self-defence undoubtedly played a role here. Until this was heroically righted by Zionist youth, it seemed to the youth of other nations as though the Jews were in the habit of 'asking for it' on two scores: from their God and from their host-countries.

I think that the theory of psychosocial identity permits of another interpretation. The universal conflict of defensive rigidity and of adaptive flexibility, of conservatism and progressivism, in the Jews of the Diaspora expresses itself in the opposition of two trends: dogmatic orthodoxy, and opportunistic adaptability. These trends, of course, were favoured by centuries of dispersion. We may think here of types, such as the religiously dogmatic, culturally reactionary Jew, to whom change and time mean absolutely nothing: the Letter is his reality. And we may think of his opposite, the Jew to whom geographic dispersion and cultural multiplicity have become 'second nature': relativism becomes for him the absolute, exchange value his tool.

There are extreme types which can be seen as living caricatures: the bearded Jew in his caftan, and Sammy Glick. The psychoanalyst, however, knows that this same set of opposites, this conflict between the adherence to the Letter, and the surrender to the changing price of things pervades the unconscious conflicts of men and women of Jewish extraction who do not consider themselves, nor are considered by others, as 'Jewish' in a denominational or racial sense. Here the Letter may have become political or scientific dogma (socialism, Zionism, psychoanalysis) quite removed from the dogma of the Talmud, yet quoted and argued in a way not unlike the disputation of passages from the Talmud in the tradition of their ancestors; and exchange value may have become obsessive preoccupation with the comparative value – of values. Economically and professionally, later stages of history have exploited what earlier history initiated: the Jews were confined to what they did best, while they, of course, learned to perfect what they were permitted to do. Thus they have become not only the traditional traders of goods, but also the mediators in culture change, the interpeters in the arts and sciences, the healers of disease and of inner conflict. Their strength, in these fields, lies in a responsible sense of relativity. But this defines Jewish weakness as well: for where the sense of relativity loses its responsibility it can become cynical relativism.

Jewish genius, in turn, quietly possessed of the courage of the ages, lifts the matter of relative values to a plane on which known reality becomes relative to more inclusive orders. In the religious sphere we have observed that Christian ethics is based on a radical subordination of this world to 'the other world', of earthly empires to the Kingdom of God: when Hitler called conscience a Jewish blemish, he included Christianity and its doctrine of sin and salvation.

In modern times, man's freedom of will, of the conscious choice of his values, and of his power of judgement have been questioned by the theories of three Jews. The Marxian theory of historical determinism established the fact that our values unconsciously depend on the means by which we make a living. (As a psychological fact this is not entirely identical with the political doctrine of Marxism, which in a variety of countries has led to a variety of socialisms.) In psychology, Freud's theory of the unconscious showed abundantly that we are unaware of the worst and of the best in our motivations. Finally, it was Einstein's theory of relativity which gave modern reorientation the broad basis of changing physical theory. He showed that, indeed, our measuring-sticks are relative to the relationships which we measure.

It is clear that the theories of these men can each be shown to have emerged at the 'logical' moment in the history of their respective fields; and that these thinkers climaxed the cultural and scientific crisis of Europe not because they were Jews, but because they were Jews *and* Germans *and* Europeans. Yet the ingredients which go into radical innovations at the crossroads of any field have hardly been studied; [14] and we may well ask whether it is altogether mere historical accident that Marx, Freud, and Einstein, all men of German-Jewish ancestry, have come to formulate and, moreover, to *personify* radical redefinitions of the very ground man thought he stood on.

Strong eras and strong countries assimilate the contributions of strong Jews because their sense of identity is enhanced by progressive redefinitions. In times of collective anxiety, however, the very suggestion of relativity is resented, and this especially by those classes which are about to lose status and self-esteem. In their effort to find a platform of conservation, they cling with grim single-mindedness to the few absolutes which they hope will save them. It is at this point that paranoid antisemitism is aroused by agitators of many descriptions and purposes, who exploit mass cowardice and mass cruelty.

I think then, that insight into the deadly nature of the identity problem can throw some light on the fact that hundreds of thousands of Germans participated and millions acquiesced in the German 'solution of the Jewish problem'. These methods defy comprehension to such an extent that beyond abortive fits of revulsion, nobody – be he American, Jew, or German – can as yet maintain any consistent emotional reaction to them. This, then, was the climactic accomplishment of the perverse mythological genius of Nazism: to create a hell on earth which seems impossible even to those who know it to have been fact.

[14] See *Young Man Luther*.

The political and military machinery of National Socialism is crushed. The form of its defeat, however, carries within it the conditions for the emergence of new dangers. For again Germany has been divided against herself; the formation of a German political identity has again been delayed. Again German conscience finds itself the helpless pointer on the balance scales of two world moralities: tomorrow she may again claim to be the very arbiter who holds these scales in her hands. For total defeat, too, breeds a sense of total uniqueness, ready to be exploited once more by those who may seem to offer a sense of total power together with permanent unity, and a new sense of identity which redeems the now senseless past.

Whoever hopes and works for a change in Europe which will provide the Germans with a destiny of peace must first understand the historical dilemma of her youth and of the youth of other large areas in the world, where abortive national identities must find new alignments in an over-all industrial and fraternal identity. It is for this reason that I have gone back into the period preceding the last war. Until the forces then at work prove to have been harnessed in concerted efforts towards a truly new order, we cannot afford to forget.[15]

[15] While it would seem senseless to bring this chapter (or, indeed, the preceding and the following ones) 'up to date', I cannot leave unmentioned two developments of our day. By some eerie historical logic, there exists again in our nuclear age a simple wall concretely dividing Germans from Germans. On the other hand, the new economic empire of Europe includes one part of Germany. Neither her newly reinforced division nor the new field for her organizational genius seem to settle the problem of Germany's national identity or that of her hegemony over the continent of which she is the centre.

E.H.E.

10 The Legend of Maxim Gorky's Youth[1]

It is difficult today to learn much about Russia that is certain, relevant, and articulate at the same time. What little I know has recently been crystallized around the imagery of an old and yet vital Russian moving-picture, and especially around the countenance of a boy who is its hero.

The moving-picture tells the Bolshevik legend of Maxim Gorky's childhood. As before with the National Socialist version of Hitler's childhood, I shall analyse the imagery in relation to the geographic locus and the historical moment of its origin.[2] In some significant respects the two legends are not dissimilar. They both show a growing, self-willed youngster in bitter fight with a father who is a merciless tyrant yet himself a senile failure. Both Hitler and Gorky in adolescence fell mentally ill with the senselessness of existence and the futility of rebellion. They became intellectual proletarians, close to utter despair. It is an ironic coincidence that both were known on the police books of their respective countries as 'paperhangers'. But here the analogy ends.

Gorky became a writer, not a politician. True, after the Russian revolution he continued to remain an idol of the Soviet state. He returned to Russia, and he died there. Whether his death was mysterious or merely mystified for political reasons we

[1] This chapter developed out of my participation as occasional consultant in the Columbia University Research Project in Contemporary Cultures, sponsored by the Office of Naval Research. For facts and insights I owe thanks to the members of the Russian group in this project, especially to Sula Benet, Nicolas Calas, Geoffrey Gorer, Nathan Leites, and Bertram Schaffner; and above all to their seminar leader, Margaret Mead, who introduced me to the moving-picture reviewed here.
[2] According to a prospectus in the film library of the Museum of Modern Art in New York, the moving-picture discussed here was first shown in Moscow in 1938. The producer was a writer named Mark Donskoi, the firm Soyuztetfilm. I saw the picture in New York in March 1948.

do not know. At his bier Molotov compared his loss to that of Lenin himself. But the reason for this national stature certainly does not lie in doctrinaire fanaticism or in political astuteness on the part of Gorky. For he, the friend of Lenin, said: 'Differences of outlook ought not to affect sympathies; I never gave theories and opinions a prominent place in my relation to people.' In fact, one gathers that both Lenin and Stalin were exceptionally lenient with Gorky in ignoring certain acquaintances of his who were of questionable orthodoxy. The answer lies in the fact that Gorky, consciously and stubbornly, was a writer of and for the people. He, the 'vagrant' and the 'provincial', lived in a double exile, one from the Tsarist police and the other from the intellectual circles of his time. His *Reminiscences* show how calmly and deliberately he delineated himself even in the presence of such overpowering idols as Tolstoy.

Like Tolstoy, Gorky belongs to that epoch of Russian realism which made literate Russia so cruelly self-observant and so miserably self-conscious. But his writing did not surrender to the self-intoxication of misery which pervades that of his greater contemporaries. He did not end up in a fatal deadlock of good and evil, a final surrender to the demons of the past, as did Tolstoy and Dostoevsky. Gorky learned to observe and to write simply, because he saw 'the necessity of representing exactly certain – most rare and positive – phenomena of actuality'. The moving-picture portrays the growth of this frame of mind. Beyond that, it illustrates a Russian dilemma, a Bolshevik dilemma, and, as I shall try to show, the dilemma of a 'protestant' frame of mind belatedly emerging in the countries of the East.

The film is an old one. At first it makes impossible demands on American eyes and ears. But in content, it seems easy as a fairy tale. It flows along as a loose and sentimental narrative apparently designed to bring the hero, little Alyosha, close to the heart of audiences who recognize in it all their native Russia and their childhood, and who at the same time know that this Alyosha will some day be the great Gorky. In the Russians who saw the picture with me it left only nostalgic pensiveness, and no aftertaste of political controversy. The legend is its own propaganda.

At the beginning there is the Russian trinity: empty plains, Volga, balalaika. The vast horizons of central Russia reveal their dark emptiness; and immediately balalaika tunes rise to compassionate crescendos, as if they were saying, 'You are not alone, we are all here.' Somewhere along the Volga, broad river boats deliver bundled-up people into isolated villages and crowded towns.

The vastness of the land and the refuge of the small, gay community thus are the initial theme. One is reminded of the fact that 'mir', the word for village, also means world (and peace), and of the saying, 'Even death is good if you are in the mir'. A thousand years ago the Vikings called the Russians 'the people of the stockades' because they had found them huddling together in their compact towns, thus surviving winters, beasts, and invaders – and enjoying themselves in their own rough ways.

A bulky boat docks by a pier, which is crowded with festive friends. Among them, a group of relatives close in on two arrivals: Varvara, the widowed mother, and her boy, Alyosha. His handsome little face first appears, wide-eyed and open-mouthed, as he emerges from behind his mother's long full skirts, eyeing with awe the noisy relatives who embrace and engulf them. And indeed, as he dares to show more of his face, practical jokers test the stamina of his curiosity. A mischievous little cousin puts out his tongue and hoots at him; an uncle grasps his nose and gently presses it in synchronization with the ship's whistle. A handsome young man laughs loudly when he sees him, good-naturedly so, but one cannot be sure. Finally, the boy is clouted on the head and pushed into a small boat.

The family is then seen marching up the centre of the street tramping heavily in compact closeness, like a procession of pilgrims, or maybe a band of prisoners – or both. Undercurrents of hostile gossip become louder. Somebody whispers, 'They are still fighting over their shares of the old man's property.' Somebody suggests that Alyosha's widowed mother has come home to exact another dowry from her father. The grandmother, whose large frame leads the procession, whisperingly wails, 'Children, children', as if the measure of progeny were overflowing.

Now we see this large family at home, crowded into a small room and immersed in a sequence of strange moods. A balalaika suggests tentative tunes of misery and nostalgia. As if in lieu of a prayer before the meal which is laid out before them, these people indulge in musical self-commiseration, together and yet each in his own preoccupied way. Old Gregory expresses the theme most strikingly: in rhythm with the song he beats his own head. It is not clear which he is enjoying more, the rhythm or the beating.

But as if enough were enough, Uncle Yakov's expression suddenly changes. He takes a sip (of vodka?), he smells a whiff (of an onion?) and plays a gay and rhythmic tune, singing some nonsense of crickets and roaches. There is an immediate and electrifying crescendo, too fast for a Western mind to comprehend. Then we see Gypsy dance the squatting dance.

Gypsy is young and handsome; and as he loosens his sleeves, pulls his shirt tails out, and generally 'unties' himself, he gives the most relaxedly vigorous performance of the whole picture. He leaps in the air, slaps his heels, and kicks his legs out from under him. The whole crowded room responds, as if in a gay earthquake. The furniture rocks, dishes jiggle, even the water in the decanter sways.

This most manly performance somehow is then replaced with a scene of generous femininity. The grandmother herself is prevailed upon to dance. Grandmother is really an enormous old woman, heavily wrapped in clothing, with a square head and broad face, and with a smile like the dawn. This heavy creature manages to be first childishly shy, then girlishly pleased, and then to move her strong frame in a sincerely serene fashion suggesting utter charm and lightness. She does not move her feet much, her body remains straight and regal; but as she slowly turns, she extends first one, then both of her arms, lifting her heavy shawl, as if baring to everybody her broad breasts.

At this moment she suddenly stops, pales, and draws her shawl around her shoulders. The music stops, motion freezes. All eyes stare at the door; grandfather has entered. To be sure: we had not even missed him. Yet nothing could be stronger than the implication that it was only in his absence that grandmother could bare her heart and her body to her children.

327

These vigorous scenes mark a happy beginning, or rather the reference to a happy past. As Westerners we had better prepare ourselves for the fact that there is no happy ending in this movie: no love story, no success story. What we see at the beginning is the remembrance of things past; at the end there will be a future of which only one thing is certain: it will be bitter. 'Gorky' means 'bitter'.

For the grandfather has entered, and with him miserliness and the hate of men. His face is tense, his motions jerky; he is all secretive excitement. It seems that instead of joining them he left to buy a tablecloth, a white tablecloth. As he childishly shows it around, it becomes plain that to him the white table-cloth is a symbol of his status: he is trying to use the reception for an egotistic display of the fact that he is now rich enough to be able to afford a white tablecloth. He is the owner of a small dyeing establishment, yet exposed to proletarization.

Immediately whispers and shouts take up the question of his property. When is he going to retire, to distribute his wealth to his already nearly middle-aged sons?

As angry whispers increase, the grandfather shouts in a shrill, senile way: 'Silence! I give to no one!' His voice betrays the despair but also the last strength of a cornered animal. The grandfather's shouting is like a signal for murderous glances between his sons. Soon the sons roll on the floor fighting one another in drunken rage. The grandfather's coat gets entangled and his sleeve is torn. He (quite surprisingly) turns against his wife. 'Witch!' he whines. 'You gave birth to wild animals!' – a theme to be remembered.

As the guests disperse in panic, as the festive table becomes a ruin, poor little Alyosha flees to the top of the stove, the refuge of babies. He has seen enough for his first day. So far he has not said a word. What it all meant and what it will mean to him in the end can be seen only in the way he acts or indeed refrains from participating, as his position is elaborated in a sequence of encounters.

So that we may concentrate on the nature of these encounters, I shall briefly outline the whole story.

Alyosha's father, Maxim Pyeshkov, had left the house of his in-laws, the Kashirins, years ago. He has died in a faraway region. Varvara, his wife, and Alyosha are forced to return to her family. The Kashirins are a greedy lot. The uncles (Vanya and Yakov) want the senile grandfather to turn his dye factory over to them. He refuses. At first they get even with him in 'practical jokes'. He revenges himself by flogging his small grandsons. One of the uncles sets fire to the establishment, and the disintegration of the family begins. Alyosha's mother eventually finds refuge in a marriage to a petty official and moves to the city. Alyosha is left with his grandparents and must witness the grandfather's economic and mental decline. He finds friends outside of the family first among the servants, then among the children of the town. At home, there are old Gregory, the foreman who during the fire loses his eyesight, and Ivan ('Gypsy'), the apprentice, who later dies. In the streets Alyosha befriends a gang of homeless boys and a crippled youngster, Lyenka. Most decisive, however, is his encounter with a mysterious boarder, who is later arrested by the police as an 'anarchist'. At the end we see Alyosha, now perhaps twelve or fourteen, set a resolute face towards the horizon. He leaves decay behind. Little is said of what lies ahead.

Throughout these scenes Alyosha does not say or do much. He participates rarely, but he observes eagerly, and mostly he reacts by refraining from participation. Such dramatization by non-action is hardly a feature of what we Westerners consider a story.

By studying the omissions as much as the commissions, I gradually became convinced that the very meaning of these scenes is that of way-stations in the boy's resistance to temptation: temptations of a kind completely strange to us.

To translate it into terms of our radio announcements: will Alyosha submit to his grandmother's primitive fatalism? Will his mother's betrayal make him a pessimist? Will his grandfather's sadism provoke him into patricidal rage – and futile remorse? Will the fratricidal uncles induce him to share their crimes – and their drunken soul-baring? Will the blind and the crippled arouse paralysing pity and cheap charity in him? Will it all deflect him from becoming a new Russian – from becoming Gorky?

Each scene and each significant person thus represents a temptation to regress to the traditional morality and to the ancient folkways of his people, to remain bound by the traditional superego within and by serfdom without. On the positive side, Alyosha is seen to become sure of himself, as if he had taken a secret vow; and he seems to devote himself with deepening fidelity to an unformulated goal.

Westerners, of course, have learned to identify what we here call temptations with the quaintness of the Russian soul – and with its brand of Christianity. And we get angry if people do not stick to the brand of soul which they have advertised and which has become their easy label. But we must try to understand: Alyosha, by virtue of his fate as a displaced Pyeshkov among the Kashirins, demonstrates the way-stations of an emergent new Russian frame of mind, a Russian individualism. No Luther, no Calvin has shown him new recesses of the mind; and no founding fathers and pioneers have opened up uncharted continents where he might overcome his inner and his outer serfdom. By himself, and in secret agreement with kindred minds, he must learn to protest, and to develop – in the very widest sense – a 'protestant' morality.

THE MOTHERS

We have met with a display of grandmother's strength, charm, and generosity in the reception scene. By far the greatest temptation, and the one which accompanies Alyosha to the very end, is that of finding refuge in his grandmother's peace of mind (as – at the very beginning of the picture – he hid in his mother's full skirts) and becoming part of her calm conscience. This old woman seems to represent the matter-of-factness of the earth, the self-evident strength of the flesh, and the native stoutness of the heart. Her maternal generosity is boundless. Not only did she bear and nurse the Kashirin breed, whom she has learned to endure; she also found and fondled Gypsy, making the homeless boy free and happy.

It becomes increasingly clear to Alyosha that the grandmother is even nursing the wailing grandfather along. In the fatal matter of property distribution, her principles are simple if 'unprincipled': 'Give it away,' she says; 'you will feel better.' And in the face of the old man's horror she says, 'I'll go begging for you.' At the same time she lets the senile man beat her, simply going down on her knees as if he had actually been strong enough to push her down. Alyosha is bewildered. 'You are stronger than he!' he cries. 'Yes,' she acknowledges, 'but he is my husband.' Soon she becomes Alyosha's mother as well. For as Varvara leaves the grandmother says simply: 'I will be his grandmother *and* his mother.'

This woman seems to know no law but that of giving; no principles except the complete trust in her own inner endurance: in this she obviously symbolizes the primitive trust of the people, their ability to survive and to persist, and yet also their weakness in enduring what will ultimately enslave them.

Alyosha comes to accept the grandmother's grandiose endurance as something from another world. This world, it seems, is the oldest Russia and the deepest stratum of her – and his – identity. It is the primitive Russia which persisted through the early Christian era, when wooden images survived forced baptisms and naïve Christianizations. It is the peace of mind of the original stockade, the primitive mir which had found some organization close to the earth and some faith in animistic dealings with the wild forces in nature. Grandmother still uses animistic practices in secret. She remembers the old ballads and can say them simply and forcefully. She is not afraid of God or of the elements. She proves to be on quite good terms with fire, which throughout the picture symbolizes destructive passion.

During the great fire grandmother enters the burning house to remove a bottle of vitriol; and she easily calms the horse which is rearing and plunging. 'Did you really think I would let you burn in there?' she says, and the horse seems to be reassured. She accepts the passions of men as she accepts the fire: both are external if unavoidable evils. It is as if she had lived long before passions had made men ambitious, greedy, and, in turn, childishly repentant; and as if she expected to outlast it all.

Her passion, then, is compassion. Even when she prays to God, she is most intimate with Him, as if He really resided in the icon right in front of her. Her approach is that of equality, or even that of a mother asking something of a child of hers who had happened to become God. She does not need to be destructive in her passion, because her conscience is without cruelty. Thus she is a primitive Madonna, a mother of God and man, and of spirits, too.

The grandmother thus assumes that place in the boy's life which women in Russia play traditionally for 'anybody's' children: the role of the *babushka*, and that of the *nyanya*: women who are at home in this world because (and often only as long as) they make it a home for others. Like the big stove in the centre of the house, they can be relied upon eternally – a reliance of the kind which makes a people endure and permits it to wait, to wait so long that reliance becomes apathy and stamina becomes serfdom.

Alyosha must not only learn to leave his mothers, but more, to leave without a residue of sinfulness which makes a straying soul penitently hold on to mother-symbols: as if, in tearing himself away, he had destroyed his mother. For much of the morbid and unrestrained surrender of the soul had its source in the necessity of overcoming an overwhelming sense of having ravished and abandoned the maternal origin and of restoring by soul-fusion the earliest sense of home, of paradise.

That home, it seems, is not of necessity the real mother. There are series and degrees of motherhood in peasant Russia which prevent an exclusive mother-fixation and give the child a rich inventory of giving and frustrating mother-images. The *babushka* is and remains the representative of the mother-image of infancy, unmarred by the growing boy's oedipal jealousies.

In our picture Alyosha's 'real' mother becomes vague and almost without a will of her own; she gradually recedes, first as a source of strength and then as an object of affection. There is a moment at the beginning when this mother, to protect her child, proudly sails into one of the unkind uncles, kicking him over like a piece of furniture. At this point Alyosha gives in to temptation and says loudly, 'My mother is strong.' The poor boy has to eat these words later, when he is flogged by his grandfather, while his awe-stricken mother can only whimper, 'Don't do it, *papasha*.' '*Now* is your mother strong?' echoes the mean little cousin. The weakness of women is not physical. It is that they 'give in'.

While the grandmother is a law unto herself and is un-principled only because she antedates the principles of formulated morality, the mother chooses the hypocritical safety of petty officialdom. She sells herself in marriage to a uniformed lackey of a man, and explains to the boy that thus will she be able to buy freedom for him. This once, this single once, he acts violently, passionately. He insults the mother's suitor, throws himself on his bed, and cries as a child cries. As she leaves she immerses him once more in her physical presence, by enfolding him in her shawl. But there is no suggestion that he intends to follow her, to take advantage of her personal and social betrayal. 'It seems to be your fate to stay with me,' says old Kashirin. The boy is silent and grim.

One wonders: the traditional division and diffusion of motherhood in peasant Russia probably made the world a more reliable home, since mothering was not dependent on one frail relationship but was a matter of homogeneous atmosphere. And yet a bitter nostalgia was plainly related to the mother's turning to 'another man', or the mother's permitting herself otherwise to be degraded and destroyed – or so it sometimes seems in the literature. As to Alyosha's new father, remember that Hitler's father, too, was an official, a member of the servile and yet officious 'middling' class.

The Alyosha of the moving-picture determinedly swallows his nostalgia. What such 'swallowed nostalgia' did to the real Gorky we shall see later when discussing his fits of anger and contempt and his strange attempt at suicide in young manhood. His writing long suffered from nostalgia. Chekhov wrote to him: '[Your] lack of restraint is felt especially in the description of nature . . . in your description of women . . . and in your love scenes. You speak a great deal about waves . . .'[3] Gorky worked hard to overcome this weakness.

SENILE DESPOT AND CURSED BREED

The grandfather is a little man with 'reddish beard, green eyes, and hands that seemed to be smeared with blood, the dye had so eaten into the skin. His abuse and prayers, his jests and moralizing, all merged in some strange way into a rasping, caustic whine

[3] A. Roskin, *From the Banks of the Volga*, Philosophical Library, New York, 1946.

that ate like rust into one's heart.'[4] The movie reflects this description faithfully. The grandfather is depicted as the destroyer of all boyish gaiety. He is a man dependent to the point of childishness on his money and on his wife's strength. A sadistic–retentive miser, he gradually regresses to the dependence of a beggar.

The variables of his character become most apparent in the flogging scene. The anger of the man, which flared up at the violent end of the reception scene, smoulders on. We become acquainted with the dye establishment where the uncles, hunched over their sewing, furtively think of mean revenge. Practical jokes again precede more direct destruction. The uncles make Sasha heat grandfather's thimble over a flame and put it back in place. As he puts his outstretched finger into it, he 'nearly goes through the ceiling' with pain. But the grandfather's very core is invaded when Alyosha, in his only boyish prank, is led by the other boys to dye the new tablecloth, to destroy its whiteness. The grandfather decides to flog the boys – on the Sabbath, after church.

The flogging is shown in slow detail: the grandfather's cold preparations; the women's dramatic but impotent intervention; the whining of the whip and the writhing of the small bodies. Gypsy must hold them down on the bench of torture.

After the flogging Alyosha lies in bed – on his face, for his back is marked with long, thin welts. Suddenly the grandfather enters. The boy views him first suspiciously, then angrily. But the grandfather dangles nicely shaped cookies before his eyes. The boy kicks him; the old man ignores it. Kneeling down by the boy's bed, he pleads with him: 'You are not suffering for nothing, it will all add up.' The sadist thus introduces the masochistic theme that suffering is good for salvation, that as we suffer we stack up credit for ourselves on a heavenly board of accounting. But he goes further. He speaks of his own sufferings as a Volga boatman, in his youth. When you draw barges in bare feet along river beaches with sharp stones, 'your eyes fill, your soul weeps, your tears drop,' he says with deep emotion. Again, the implication is that a man's suffering explains and excuses his imparting further suffering on those weaker than himself, a

[4] Maxim Gorky, *Reminiscences of Tolstoy, Chekhov and Andreyev*, The Viking Press, Inc., New York, 1959.

Russian form of saying, 'What was good enough for me is good enough for you.' The boy does not seem moved. He makes no gesture of peace; nor does he repay the outpouring of the grandfather's soul with an exchange of commiseration. The grandfather is called away.

Another temptation has passed: that of acquiring in a moment of torment an identification with the tormentor and with his sado-masochistic reasoning. If the boy had permitted his anger at this moment to turn into pity, if he had let his soul pour out to the tormentor who was opening his own soul to him, he would have acquired that pattern of masochistic identification with authority which apparently has been a strong collective force in the history of Russia. The Tsar, as the little white father, was just such a symbol of pitied autocracy. Even the man whom history called Ivan the Terrible was to his people only Ivan the Severe, for he claimed that as a child he had suffered under the cruelty of the court oligarchy.

The grandfather's sado-masochistic mood-swings are illustrated in other scenes. As his property slips away from him he wails before the icon, 'Am I a worse sinner than the others?' The icon does not answer. But the grandmother takes him into her arms, almost on her lap. She calms him and promises to go begging for him. He collapses on her in foolish fondness, only to rally suddenly and to knock her down in a rage of jealousy, for he claims she loves the cursed breed more than she loves him. The implication is obvious that his wife is his property and his property is a kind of substitute mother without whom he cannot live. The 'privileged owner's' utter defeat in the oedipal game is, of course, one of the implicit propagandistic notes of the picture – just as the defeat of Hitler's father was a necessary note in his imagery. The grandfather becomes more and more senile, and becomes useless as a provider.

In one of the final scenes Alyosha brings his fight with his grandfather to victorious conclusion. He has just given grandmother a coin which he has earned; she looks tenderly at him. At this point Alyosha becomes aware of his grandfather's eyes, which are narrowed down with hate. Alyosha takes on the challenge and a duel of the eyes ensues. The boy's eyes become thin as razor blades and it is as if the two wanted to pierce and cut one another with their glances. They both know that this is the end, and that the boy must leave. But he leaves undefeated.

This cutting of eye by eye is an impressive encounter. Yet there is something Russian about this particular use of the eye as an aggressive and defensive weapon. In Russian literature there is endless variation in the use of the eye as a soulful receptor, as an avid grasper, and as the very organ for mutual soulful surrender. In regard to the great models of political and literary life, however, the emphasis is on the eye as an incorruptible instrument for the manipulation of the future. Gorky's description of Tolstoy is typical: 'With sharp eyes, from which neither a single pebble nor a single thought could hide itself, he looked, measured, tested, compared.' Or again, his eyes are 'screwed up as though straining to look into the future'.

Equally typical is Trotsky's description of Lenin:

When Lenin, his left eye narrowed, receives a wireless containing a speech he resembles a devilishly clever peasant who does not let himself be confused by any words, or deluded by any phrases. That is highly intensified peasant shrewdness, lifted to the point of inspiration.[5]

The scene of the grandfather sitting by the bedside of his bruised grandson, in that shabby hut, begging his forgiveness, somehow reminded me of a famous Russian painting showing a similar scene in a palace: Ivan the Terrible sits by the corpse of his oldest son, whom he has murdered. Paternal violence à la Kashirin characterizes Russia's leading families from the beginning of history, and it permeates the literature of the pre-revolutionary epoch. In both it developed to heights of crude violence unknown in comparable regions and periods of history. The coincidence of these two scenes invites a digression into history.

The original Slavs were peaceful and prolific peasants, hunters, and stockade dwellers. About a thousand years ago they asked Rurik, a Viking, to undertake their protection against nomadic invaders from the south. They apparently thought to buy, against reasonable concessions, peace and the permission to maintain the *status quo* of hunting with primitive weapons, of

[5] Leon Trotsky, 'The Russian in Lenin', *Current History Magazine*, March 1924.

cultivating the soil with their crude wooden tools, and of worshipping their wooden idols and nature gods. Whatever forced them to surrender their autonomy to those shiningly armoured, light-skinned warriors of the north, they received more protection than they had bargained for. The protectors begot sons who wanted to be in on the protection business. 'Foreigners' muscled in. Soon, protecting the people against other protectors became an established occupation. The first prince initiated the grand-prince system, a kind of rank-order of residences for his sons which led to endless feuds over the cities which first emerged: Kiev and Novgorod. Such feuds were repeated over and over in smaller and larger segments of the land, making the people at last wish and pray for the one 'strong father', the central authority who would unite the various sons even if he had to murder them all. Thus in early Russian history the stage was set for the interplay of the people who needed guidance and protection against enemies; the oligarchic protectors who became petty tyrants; and the central super-tyrant who was a captive of the oligarchy and a secret redeemer.

The protectors forcibly introduced Christianity (of the Byzantine variety) and with it another hierarchy which forever remained locked in conflict with itself and with the worldly princes. While both the princes and the priests had their cultural and often their ethnic origins in a variety of other lands, they gradually began to perform the spectacle which the books call Russian history: a sequence of dynastic struggles which not only survived the terrible Tartar invasion but gained in violent momentum and national scope. By way of counterpoint, these led to the establishment of a nation, of a Russian Christianity, and of a Russian tsardom: in the fifteenth century Moscow became 'the third Rome' and Ivan III the first ruler of all the Russians and the Protector of the True Faith. He made ancient Russia into a national state; his son expanded this Russian state over its numerous and varied neighbours.

With Ivan the Terrible the tradition, existing since the tenth century, of 'quarrelsome and murderous sons' reached its climax. Patricide had abounded in high circles for centuries. But Ivan, whom history calls 'the Terrible', slew his oldest, his favourite, son with his own hands. He (like old Kashirin at bruised Alyosha's bedside) blamed his sufferings as a boy for the cruel madness of his manhood. The people agreed. As I have pointed out, they did not call him the Terrible, as did history; they called him the Severe. For had he not been the victim of the oligarchic aristocracy – his enemies, and the people's – who had made his boyhood miserable? And indeed this first Tsar had turned in his saner moments to the people, had permitted them to petition him, had initiated judiciary reforms and introduced printing. In his insaner states he continued to gloat over lists of murdered aristocrats, only to indulge, in turn, in the most abject remorse. The people idolized and gladly strengthened the authority of this Tsar in order to keep the princes, aristocrats, and middle classes in check.

As centralization progressed and national organization developed, the paradoxes of Russian history became self-perpetuating. For one: with every step towards organized and centralized statehood in this immense land, the number of middlemen increased. They governed and policed 'for the Tsar', they taught school and collected taxes, and they extorted and corrupted. It is an old theme in Russia that every progress on a national scale is paid for with new power to a bureaucracy – which explains an 'inborn' hostile indifference of the people both to progress in general and to the contemporary oligarchy in particular.

Secondly, every step towards Westernization and enlightenment led to increased serfdom. Ivan, in pursuit of his holy 'severity', robbed the peasants of their right to change masters on St George's day. Catherine, friend and enlightened correspondent of Voltaire, gave away 800,000 crown slaves to be tortured and sold at will by individual aristocratic owners. And when much later Alexander II liberated twenty million slaves, because he feared that they might liberate themselves, he only exposed them to landlessness, proletarization, and at best the necessity of tilling with antiquated tools small portions of land to be paid for in instalments.

But what interests us here is the third paradox: the people's tacit permission for these tsars to behave in a grandiosely irrational way. Peter the Great, a precocious boy and impetuous like Ivan, was Russia's first emperor and the greatest of Russia's monarchic reformers. He, too, murdered his oldest son, although with progressing civilization he used his secret police, not a club in his own hands. In addition to such outright family murders, there were in Russian history all kinds of strange regency arrangements. There were mysterious and immensely popular pretenders, alleged sons of murdered tsars, who, like Alyosha, came back to challenge the evildoers; and who were almost holy by mere virtue of not belonging to the dominant 'cursed breed'. Maybe the height of oedipal atrocity was reached when near-demented Tsar Paul (the people called him the Poor), at the death of his mother Catherine, had his father (whom she had murdered) exhumed and put beside her. He forced her numerous lovers to stand splendid military guard over the decomposition of the imperial corpses.

Historians take it for granted that such is 'history'. But how explain not only a people's passive consent to but passionate altruistic identification with such imperial tragedies and comedies? Why should a sturdy and prolific people have bowed to foreign protectors? Why did it admit their system into its national life, involving its very life style ever deeper in a relationship of mutual possessedness? Is the explanation to be sought first in the superiority of murderous nomads and wild beasts, and then in the impotence of this immense population against the armed oligarchy?

The answer is probably that forms of leadership are defined not only by the historical dangers to be warded off by their work of organization; they must also serve the public display of popular fantasies and anticipations. Monarchs, even if foreign (and often, because they are foreign) become visible safeguards of a people's weak inner moral forces; aristocratic élites, personifications of dimly perceived new ideals. It is for this purpose that monarchs and aristocrats may and must play out on the stage of history the full cycle of irrational conflict: they must sin more defiantly and atone more deeply, and finally emerge with increased personal and public stature. While they try to accomplish this cycle, the people will gladly serve as their whispering chorus and their sacrificial animals. For the grandiose sin of a few promises total salvation to all.

This, then, is more than a 'projection' either of inner badness (the id) or of inexorable conscience. I think it has also a collective ego function; it serves the development of a better-defined national and moral identity. Ivan and Peter are great, not in spite of the tragic passions which seemingly marred their stature as leaders, but because they could display on a gigantic scale the tragedy of early patriarchal organization and its inner counterpart, the superego; and because in doing so, they advanced national consciousness and national conscience, each by a decisive step. Maybe our concept of history must be expanded to include an analysis of the dynamic demands made by the governed masses on their most 'self-willed' masters who thus are forced to act out the conflicts of human evolution on the macrocosmic stage of history: in this sense, perhaps, kings are the toys of the people. In later stages of civilization their tragedies and comedies are transferred to a fictitious macrocosm, the stage, and finally, to the microcosm of fiction.

We can now see the historical mission of Russian realistic literature: it put the tragedy of patricide and fratricide back into the ordinary Russian himself – to be read by the literate.[6] Such literary pronouncement of individual responsibility parallels the growth of political responsibility. Russian literature and Russian history were late and explosive in reaching – in one terrifyingly condensed century – the preliminary stages of an effective literary consciousness and of a political conscience, while the backwardness of the vast peasant masses continued to reflect a primitive historical level which the West had left behind in Hellenic days.

Let us pause here also to remember that at the time of the Russian revolution four-fifths of the Russian population were peasants. The gigantic task of the outer transformation and inner conversion of these masses of peasants can hardly be over-estimated, not because they wanted another form of government, but because they had never thought of an organized interlocking of their daily lives with any form of government.

The moving-picture's characterization of the moody 'breed' points to at least one collective complex of a singularly archaic character which has kept the peasant masses of Russia (and, in fact, of much of the Eurasian continent) in inner serfdom as their

---

[6] Freud, in his paper 'Dostoevski and Patricide', likened *The Brothers Karamazov* to Shakespeare's *Hamlet* and to Sophocles' *King Oedipus*, and this because these three works measure up to a common artistic greatness, while they take father-murder as their central theme.

outer serfdom was assured by princes and priests. I refer to the psychological consequences of an ancient technological upheaval: the agricultural revolution. Here the mysteries of pre-history are as deep as those of early childhood. They both force us to mythologize in order to gain the beginning of an understanding.

In connection with the hunters and fishermen of prehistoric North America we employed one key which opened certain primitive rituals to interpretation. We pointed out that pre-literate human beings try to understand and to master the great Unknown in its expansion in space and time by projecting the attributes of human structure and growth on it: thus geographic environment is personified, and historical past is endowed with the imagery of human childhood. In this sense, then, the earth becomes a mother who, once upon a time, gave of her own free will. The transition from nomadic to agricultural life implied the usurpation of segments of land, and their partition; the violation of the soil with coercive tools; the subjugation of the earth as an enforced provider. Whatever inner evolution accompanied this technological step, it was (as myths and rituals attest) associated with that primal sin which, in individual life, consists of the first awareness of the violent wish to control the mother with the maturing organs of bite and grasp.

The 'cursed breed' then represents the children who in their rapacity would jealously usurp and destroy the mother; and the men, whom the task of collectively tilling the soil made ambitious, jealous, and exploitive. Thus the sense of a primal guilt, which we discussed earlier, chains the peasant to the cycle of sorrowful atonement and manic feasting as it makes him dependent on the productive year. Christianity, of course, took hold of this self-perpetuating cycle and superimposed on it its own yearly calendar of sin and expiation, of death and redemption.

I can conclude this dark subject only by referring to a memoir of Gorky's which betrays the identification of cultivated earth and conquered woman and the manic challenge of her master.[7]

He [Chekhov] used to say:
'If every man did all he could on the piece of earth belonging to him, how beautiful would this world be!'
I had started to write a play called Vasska Busslaev and one day I read to him Vasska's boastful monologue:

[7] Maxim Gorky, op. cit.

'Ha, were I only endowed with more strength and power
I'd breathe a hot breath – and make the snows melt!
I'd go round the earth and plough it through and through!
I'd walk for years and years and build town after town,
Put up churches without number, and grow gardens without end;
I'd adorn the earth – as though it were a maiden fair;
Clasp it in my arms – as though it were my bride;
Lift it to my heart, and carry it to God: . . .

'I'd have given it to you, Lord, as a fine gift –
Only – no – it would not do – I am too fond of it myself!'

Chekhov liked this monologue very much, and coughing excitedly said:
'That's very fine indeed! Very true, and very human! In this lies the essence of all philosophy. Man has made the earth habitable – therefore he must also make it comfortable for himself.'
He shook his head in obstinate affirmation and repeated:
'He will!'
He asked me to read Vasska's boastful speech over again. I did so and he listened attentively to the end, then he remarked:
'The last two lines are unnecessary – they are impertinent. There is no necessity for that . . .'

THE EXPLOITED

Saint and Beggar

Gypsy, the foundling, was not born in sin like the rest of the breed, the uncles, the 'wild animals'. Not having been born in sin, he has, as the grandmother puts it, a 'simple soul'. He has a graceful body, as he well demonstrated in his squatting dance, while the other men seem wooden and unfree in their motions and when drunk or enraged are like trucks without brakes. Not being anybody's son, Gypsy expects no property and envies none. It is as if his orphanhood suggested immaculate conception. And, indeed, in a subtle way, Gypsy is pictured as a primal Christian, charitable and always in hope.

Gypsy speaks to Alyosha of his dead father. He was different: *he understood*. For this reason he was hated by the Kashirins. Here a theme is introduced which is later taken up at the appearance of the anarchist, the representative of those who understand and accept homelessness. They are hated by the fathers and their rapacious sons as bearers of an entirely new principle which cannot be fought with old weapons: they read, think, plan. Thus it is Gypsy who provides Alyosha's eager soul with the imagery of his future identity.

Gypsy recognizes those who understand but he himself does not 'understand'. He has another fault and is dangerously different in another way: he is '*good*'. After the flogging his arm shows bloody welts, and he confesses cheerfully that in holding the boy down on the bench he had let his arms absorb the heaviest blows. 'I took the blows for love,' he tells the spellbound boy, whose heart goes out to him. But then Gypsy expounds on methods of how to take blows. Don't shrink back, he tells him, but try to relax. And shout as much as you wish. He confesses that he has taken so many blows that his hide would make good book-covers.

Again, the implication of this scene is not formulated. But it seems to concern the temptation of naïve non-violence, of Christian goodness and of learning to endure the pains of the world by adjusting to its beatings. Alyosha is touched and fascinated, but remains reserved. And indeed, soon after, Gypsy dies in a picturesque and symbolic way and he must bear the loss.

One of the uncles wants to erect a huge cross for his dead wife (whom, as Gypsy knows, he has murdered). He asks Gypsy to help him carry it up the designated hill. As everybody can see, the enormous cross is too heavy for one man. But Gypsy in childlike pride boasts that he can carry it on his back – all alone. Alyosha for a moment feels an urge to help him; the audience trembles with fear that the little boy may try to help support that big cross, but then – as at several highly critical moments – Alyosha simply lets himself be deflected, and leaves his friend to his fate.

In a scene obviously intended to suggest Calvary, Gypsy is seen in silhouette stumbling up a far-away hill with the huge cross on his bent back. It apparently crushes him, for soon he is carried back to the house, where he dies on the floor. A little white mouse, with which he has endlessly entertained himself and the children, escapes from his clothing and runs over to Alyosha, who catches it. It is as if Gypsy's 'white soul' had found a new home, in Alyosha.

If the grandmother represents the primitive folkways, and the grandfather and the uncles the greedy era of the ownership of lands and goods and wives and titles, then Gypsy is the simple saint of a primitive Christian era. He is cheerfully good, and charitable to the end.

This boy Alyosha, then, watches the pre-ordained destruction around him and yet maintains a sleepwalker's surefootedness in the avoidance of fatal involvements and of traditional pitfalls. Does Alyosha have no sympathy, no morality?

Take his encounter with old Gregory, the very individual who drags him away as Gypsy's Calvary approaches (for Gregory, nearly blind, can see what lies ahead). He is an impressive, a prophetic figure. But he has worked in the grandfather's dye factory for nearly four decades, and faces unemployment when his waning eyesight is gone. Because the grandfather refuses to take care of him, Gregory will have to go begging. Alyosha is horrified. 'I will go with you,' he cries compassionately. 'I will lead you by the hand!'

But after the fire, as blinded Gregory stumbles around with outstretched arms, miserably calling Alyosha, the boy hides from him and lets him stumble on alone in his eternal night. Two or three times he is later shown following Gregory, then a beggar on the street and on the fairground. In fact, Alyosha stalks Gregory as if fascinated by the sight.

The Western movie-goer cannot help thinking what a touching picture they would make together, the tall blinded patriarchal figure and the boy who leads him by the hand. He envisages an ending where the tormented grandfather reforms and sends out a state-wide alarm for the two, when it may be almost too late. The sheriff's posse or the state motor-cycle patrol reaches the old man and the small boy just as they are about to reach a bridge weakened by a flooded river . . .

But it is clear that what we are watching in this picture is the emergence of a new frame of mind, which to us is primarily characterized by its omissions. What is omitted, again and again, is action based on a sense of guilt. Thus neither remorse nor reform seem to count in this new frame of mind. What counts is critical caution, incorruptible patience, absolute avoidance of wrong action, the ripening of clear inner direction, and then – action.[8]

[8] See the following exchange at the Moscow trials:
VISHINSKY: 'Did you endorse these negotiations [with the Germans]?'

The Western observer at this point decides that the picture has less than a moral, that it is amoral. It may be, however, that the picture merely poses moral alternatives quite different from those to which our Judaeo-Christian world is committed. When Alyosha avoids being drawn into the temptation of sacrificing his young life to the blind old man he breaks, it is true, a promise to an individual – a promise possibly made on the basis of a sense of shared guilt, a sense that he should make up for his grandfather's economic sins. Opposed to this 'temptation', however, there is an inner vow, a vow to follow a direction, an as yet indistinct plan which, instead of the self-perpetuation of inner guilt, will lead to cooperative action beyond good and evil. Such a vow is personified by another member of the cast: the anarchist.

But a final scene should be noted which in its crude imagery shows the utter contempt of the new generation for the moral collapse of the old. As the by now thoroughly senile grandfather begs his way through the crowd at the fair, old Gregory, his erstwhile foreman, responds to his wail and hands him a piece of bread. The grandfather, now recognizing the blind man, throws the bread away, crying: 'You have eaten me out of my house!' It is a cruel scene, from our point of view; but little Alyosha turns away from it, not even with visible disgust. To leave the ruins of men and systems behind seems to be a job which does not call for any expenditure of emotion.

The Stranger

All this time there is a man in the village, in fact in a room of grandfather's house, who belongs nowhere and speaks with no one. He is not a serf, and yet he owns nothing; he has nothing to sell, and yet he seems to eat. He calls himself a chemist, yet he does not seem to hold a job. With his black hair, his high forehead, and his sharp, bespectacled eyes, he looks like a youngish, somewhat starved Trotsky.

As Alyosha one day trustingly slides through this man's window into his underground room, the man quickly hides a book. Then he calmly gasses the boy out of his room by opening

---

BUKHARIN: 'Or disavow? I did not disavow, consequently I endorsed.'
VISHINSKY: 'But you say that you learned of this post factum.'
BUKHARIN: 'Yes, the one does not contradict the other.'

a bottle with some malodorous vapours. The boy is offended, but even more fascinated.

He sees the man again at a meeting at which the grandmother sings ancient legends and ballads. In simple and strong words we hear her recite a long legend which contains the sentence: '*Behind the conscience of others he did not hide.*' At this the man gets strangely excited as if hearing an oracle. He mumbles something concerning 'the people, our people' (which apparently refers to the quality of old folk-wisdom) and leaves the room hurriedly. It may be symbolical that, thus swayed with emotions he leaves his glasses behind. At any rate, Alyosha picks them up.

In the next scene Alyosha sees the strange man lying in the grass on top of the cliff overlooking the river. The man hardly thanks him for the glasses. In fact, he somewhat rudely indicates that the boy may sit beside him if he can manage to be quiet and to join his contemplative mood. Thus this man, the river, the vast horizon, and a new frame of mind become and remain associated. The man's commanding presence seems to proclaim that you must be able to be silent; you must be able to meditate; you must be willing to envisage the distant horizon. Explicitly he says: 'You must remember all the legends the grandmother knows. You must learn to read and to write.' Alyosha is astonished, but apparently takes a deep liking to the man's fervour and sincerity.

Their friendship does not last long; or rather, their friendship must outlast a very short acquaintance, for the greedy grandfather forces the stranger to vacate his room and the man decides to leave town.

A gang of homeless boys accompany him to the river. But he puts his arm on Alyosha's shoulder. According to the English caption, he passionately tells the boy: 'One must learn how to take life.' He says this with such missionary fervour that one senses a significance in it which surpasses the words used. Here we must turn linguist.

The man's gestures indicate that he means 'take' in the sense of grasping or holding on, and not in the sense of enduring or holding out. Yet when I saw the picture the first time, my Russian interpreter insisted that the man had said '*brat*'' – take = endure. For reasons to be discussed presently, this difference seemed so basic that I persisted in inquiring into the origin of the discrepancy between the word and the gesture. And indeed, in the book on which this movie is based, the revolutionary says: 'One must know how to take (Russian *wyzat*') each single thing. Do you understand? It is very difficult to learn how to take (*wyzat*').' *Wyzat*' means 'to take' in the sense of 'grasp'. It is apparent, then, that the word but not the meaning was lost somewhere between the book and the picture.

The meaning is: one must learn not to wait until one is given, one must grasp what one wants and hold on to it. We have discussed this alternative in connection with the social modalities of the oral stages. Obviously this man does not only mean to say that one must grasp, but also that one must do so with a good conscience, with a new conscience; that one must grasp and not regress from sheer sense of sin over having grasped.

As we shall see, this determined 'grasping', paired with a resistance against sinking back into dependence, is of outstanding importance in the Bolshevik psychology. We have already reported on Alyosha's piercing, cutting way of reacting to the grandfather's hateful glance; we have pointed to the importance of focusing, comprehending, grasping in vision and foresight; and we have shown his incorruptibility of purpose, irrespective of personal feelings.

It later becomes apparent that the stranger was a revolutionary. The police were looking for him. They caught up with him somewhere beyond the horizon; for one day when a miserable group of shabby, shackled prisoners pass through Alyosha's street on their way to the boat and to Siberia, the stranger is among them, pale and ghostlike but almost gay.

The caption says, 'Thus ended my friendship with the first of a series of strangers in their own country – the best people.'

Alyosha, then, has come face to face with a member of the underground of professional revolutionaries, called for a time intelligentsia because of their religious belief in the necessity not only of reading and writing but also of mental discipline as the salvation from apathy, lethargy, and serfdom.

Fatherless Gang and Legless Child

As the anarchist disappears, Alyosha seems to grow in stature. He now has a goal, a fellowship. We must remember that his father, too, 'understood' – and disappeared. Yet we are horrified to watch this mere boy identify with the martyred ghost of a man whose ethos was contained in a few obscure remarks. Alyosha is a mere child; where is his childhood, who are his age mates? Does he ever play? [9]

We saw the abortive participation in the practical jokes of his cousins and their malicious and devious ways of getting even with the old man. The flogging scene – or, shall we say, the greater maturity following the grandfather's moral defeat after the flogging scene – put an end to that. In a later scene, as Alyosha looks around the neighbourhood, he comes across a group of well-fed children who with stones and yells have fallen upon an idiot boy. Alyosha immediately stands up for the idiot, whereupon they turn on him by calling him a 'Kashirin'. He protests, 'I am a Pyeshkov.' Like boys all the world over, they end up by throwing words at one another: Kashirin! Pyeshkov! Kashirin! Pyeshkov! But as the boys begin to beat and kick him, a gang of starved and ragged young creatures appears suddenly, frees him, and immediately befriends him.

This gang consists of homeless boys – 'proletarians' in the original sense. Alyosha becomes one of them, economically, in that he joins their occupation of searching garbage pits for items that can be sold to junk dealers; spiritually, in that he shares their feeling that they cannot rely on their parents – if, indeed, they have any. Thus in a few scenes Alyosha's proletarization is dramatically demonstrated. He, a fatherless Pyeshkov, takes the side of the idiot boy who is born with inferior endowment; he associates with those who have sunk below all caste and class. In one impressive scene he stumbles upon the fact that one of the gang, a boy with Asiatic features, does not even know where he came from. Alyosha laughs; it is the last display of thoughtless gaiety. Seeing the Asiatic's despair and rage, he becomes immune to one more temptation: to be proud of the name Pyeshkov. (As we know, he later chose his father's first name, Maxim, and the last name Gorky, which means bitter.)

Now he is a proletarian too. After 'work' he and his gang lie up on the cliff – that mild elevation from which the dispossessed look towards the horizon and the future. There they dream –

[9] Tolstoy once said to Gorky: 'It is not easy to believe that you were once a child' (Gorky, op. cit.).

of what? Of keeping pigeons so that they can set them free: 'I love to see pigeons circling in the bright summer sky.'

This suggestion of freedom is counterpointed by one more encounter. One day Alyosha hears a gay young voice from a cellar window. He follows the voice and finds Lyenka, a crippled boy, in bed. His legs are paralysed, they 'don't live, they are just there', as he explains. He is thus imprisoned in his cellar. But he proves to be living in a world of his own, a world of play and daydreams. He keeps little animals in boxes and cages. They must share his captivity. But he lives for the day when he will see the meadows and the prairie, and then he will open all the little boxes and set the animals free. In the meantime they are his microcosm: they reflect the world outside. One little roach is 'the landlord', another the 'official's wife'. The very oppressors of the real world are the captives of his play world. It is as if his crippled state permitted him to be the only child with a playful mind in the picture. His laugh is the gayest and freest; his eyes are full of a delighted sparkle. His sense of power seems to know no bounds; he is sure, he tells Alyosha excitedly, that 'a mouse could grow to be a horse'.

Seeing the boy's love for the animal companions of his imprisonment and his necessity and ability to invest a small thing like a mouse with mythical possibilities, Alyosha after a faint trace of hesitation gives him Gypsy's white mouse. This little mouse, we remember, had been Gypsy's dying gift to him. It was his last link to gaiety; it was his last toy. Why does he give it away? Is it pity, charity? Again Alyosha seems to grow in moral stature by sacrificing a comfort, and by resisting a temptation: the temptation to play, to dream, to hang on to fetishistic substitutes which make prisons more bearable, and thus add to their shackles. He knows that he will have to go without a toy. Thus, each of Alyosha's acts (or refusals to act) is like a vow. One after another, the bridges of regression are cut and the infantile comforts of the soul forever denied.

Lyenka, however, can get free only if somebody will make him free, will give him legs. And this is what Alyosha puts the 'gang' to work on. From among the treasures which they salvage from the garbage heaps, they save items of machinery out of which they build him a carriage, a mechanical prosthesis of locomotor freedom.

The Swaddled Baby

The figure of Lyenka does not seem to be taken from Gorky's book. I do not know who invented it. But it seems significant that this most emotive and gay of all the children is, as it were, the least motional. His delight reaches to the horizons, but his legs are tied, 'are not alive, just there'. This suggests a discussion of an outstanding Russian problem of child training which has assumed an almost ludicrous prominence in recent discussions of the Russian character: swaddling.

Is the Russian soul a swaddled soul? Some of the leading students of Russian character, to which I owe my first acquaintance with this moving-picture, definitely think so.[10]

In the great Russian peasant population, and to a varying degree in all the regions and classes which shared and continue to share the common cultural heritage of the great central plains of Russia, the item of child care called swaddling was developed to an extreme. While the custom of bandaging newborn infants is widespread, the ancient Russian extreme insists that the baby be swaddled up to the neck, tightly enough to make a handy 'log of wood' out of the whole bundle, and that swaddling be continued for nine months, for the greater part of the day and throughout the night. Such procedure does not result in any lasting locomotor deficiency, although the unswaddled infant apparently has to be taught to crawl.

When asked why babies must be swaddled, simple Russians have answered with astonishment: what other way was there to carry a baby and to keep him warm through a Russian winter? And besides, how could one otherwise keep him from scratching and harming himself, and of scaring himself with the sight of his own hands? Now it is probably true that a swaddled baby, especially when just unswaddled, has not sufficient mastery over his own movements to keep from scratching and hitting himself. The further assumption that *therefore* he has to be swaddled again is a favourite trick of cultural rationalization. It makes a particular pattern of infant-restraint culturally self-

[10] Geoffrey Gorer, 'Some Aspects of the Psychology of the People of Great Russia', *The American Slavic and Eastern European Review*, 1949. See also Geoffrey Gorer and John Rickman, *The People of Great Russia*, W. W. Norton & Co., 1962.

supporting. You must swaddle the infant to protect him against himself; this causes violent vasomotor needs in him; he must remain emotionally swaddled in order not to fall victim to wild emotion. This, in turn, helps to establish a basic, a pre-verbal, indoctrination, according to which people, for their own good, must be rigidly restrained, while being offered, now and then, ways of discharging compressed emotion. Thus, swaddling falls under the heading of those items of child training which must have a significant relation to the world image of the whole culture.

And indeed, there is no literature which, like the Russian, abounds in vasomotor excess. People in Russian fiction seem both isolated and effusive. It is as if each individual were strangely imprisoned in himself as in a restraining box of strangled emotions. Yet he is forever seeking other souls by sighing, paling, and blushing, by weeping and fainting. Many of the characters populating this literature seem to live for the moment when some intoxication – glandular, alcoholic, or spiritual – will permit a temporary fusion of emotion, often only an illusory mutuality which must end in exhaustion. But we need not look beyond the motion picture under discussion: if daily Russian reality of young Gorky's time manifested a fraction of the loudness, intensity, and variety of emotional expression which we see in this picture, the small child's awareness of emotion must be vivid and kaleidoscopic.

It is interesting to reflect, then, that the swaddled baby, when he becomes aware of such emotionality, is himself hindered from responding to it in a 'motional' way, such as kicking with arms and legs or moving his fingers. He is hindered from lifting his head, from grasping support, and from extending his visual field over the auditory sources of the perceived commotion. Such an arrangement can, indeed, be thought of as burdening the vasomotor system with the task of buffeting and balancing all these vivid impressions. Only during the periodical experience of being unswaddled would the baby partake of his elder's effusiveness.

However, in order to evaluate the significance of an item of child training such as swaddling in the totality of a culture's configuration, it would be necessary to assume not a single one-way chain of causality in the sense that Russians are the way they are – or like to appear or to picture themselves – because they have been swaddled. As in our discussion of other cultures we must rather assume a reciprocal amplification of a number of themes. Thus the almost universal – and incidentally, quite practical – custom of swaddling would have received amplification as a result of that synthesizing trend which put geography, history, and human childhood over a few common denominators. We observe a configurational affinity between these facts of Russian tradition.

1. The compact social life in a lonely stockade isolated in the rigours of the central plains and its periodic liberation after the spring thaws;
2. The long periods of tight swaddling alternating with moments of rich interchange of joyous affection at the time of unswaddling; and
3. The sanctioned behaviour of wooden endurance and apathetic serfdom on the one hand, and on the other, periodic emotional catharsis achieved by effusive soul-baring.

Historically and politically seen, swaddling, then, would appear to be part of a system of stubborn institutions which have helped to support and prolong the Russian combination of serfdom and 'soul'. And, indeed, Gorky said in his play *Philistines*: 'When a man is tired of lying on one side, he turns over on the other, but when he is tired of the conditions in which he lives he only grumbles. Then make an effort – and *turn over*!' A man, properly motivated, can make an effort to turn over or indeed, as we would say, to get up; but in the face of the adversity of being chained to certain conditions his mind may act according to its earliest experience of being tied down. And what the swaddled baby can do least of all is turn over. He can only sink back, give in, be patient, and hallucinate, dwelling on his vasomotor sensations and on the adventures of his bowels, till the moment of locomotor liberation comes again upon him.

Something of this kind may well be symbolized by Lyenka, the child with the greatest emotion and with the most impaired motion; the child with the most vivid imagination and the greatest dependence on others. When Alyosha gives him the little white mouse it is as if he were growing beyond the necessity of holding on to a play fetish and to dreams of omnipotence such as swaddled and imprisoned souls may be in need of. He does not pity Lyenka. Rather, he recognizes his state, compares it with his own, and acts accordingly. He sees to it that Lyenka gets mechanized legs – but he does not identify with him.

While the motion picture does not show Alyosha and his gang at play, Gorky's *Reminiscences* gives an account of a fantastic game indulged in by these young 'outlaws'. As we shall see, Gorky's interpretation of this game is entirely in tune with the theories advanced in our chapter on play.

As a lad of about ten I used to *lie down under a ballast train*, competing in audacity with my chums, one of whom, the postman's son, played the game with particular cool-headedness. It is an almost safe amusement, provided the furnace of the locomotive is raised high enough and the train is moving up-hill, not down-hill – for then the brake-chains of the cars are tightly stretched, and can't strike you or, having caught you, fling you on to the sleepers. For a few seconds you experience an eerie sensation, you *try to press as flat and close to the ground* as possible, and with the exertion of your whole will to *overcome the passionate desire to stir, to raise your head*. You feel that the stream of iron and timber, rushing over you, tears you off the ground and *wants to drag you off* somewhere, and the rumble and grinding of the iron rings as it were in your bones. Then, when the train has passed, you lie motionless for a minute or more, *powerless to rise*, seeming to swim along after the train; and it is as if your body stretches out endlessly, grows, *becomes light, melts into air*, and – the next moment you will be flying above the earth. It is very pleasant to feel all this.

'What fascinated you in such an absurd game?' asked Andreyev.

I said that perhaps we were testing the power of our wills, by opposing to the mechanical motion of huge masses the conscious immobility of our puny little bodies.

'No,' he replied, 'that is too good; no child could think of that.'

Reminding him of how children love to 'tread the cradle' – to swing on the supple ice of a new frozen pond or of a shallow riverbank, I said that they generally liked dangerous games.[11]

I have italicized those passages which suggest (in accordance with our theories of trauma and play) a further meaning in this game. An audacious gang could be said here to challenge a ballast train to provide them with an experience in which the

[11] Gorky, op. cit.

essential elements of a childhood trauma common to all are eerily repeated: immobility and violent motion, utter powerlessness and the lightest of emotion.

Whatever the 'swaddling hypothesis' proves or fails to prove in regard to the transformation of infantile experience into juvenile and adult patterns, it does seem to point to configurations of experience singularly alive in Russian behaviour and imagination.

In the moving-picture, Alyosha does not participate in any games. He keeps his eyes open, if often narrow with inquisitiveness: he 'lifts his head', focuses his vision, tries to apprehend and to perceive with clarity and to concentrate with discipline – all of this in order eventually to grasp life. The picture says more about the things he frees himself *from* than about the things he wants to be free *for*.

THE PROTESTANT

Alyosha is leaving. The gang accompanies him to the fields. On the little wagon, now completed, they take Lyenka along. Lyenka is beside himself with joy and anticipation: he is in motion and he is going to set his animals free. In a scene which would well have marked the happy ending of the movie in any other culture, Lyenka throws his precious birds up in the air and lets them take to their wings and to the endless spaces. But as the gang waves and shouts good-bye, Alyosha simply and unemotionally set his face towards the horizon.

Where is he going, the youth with steel in his eyes? The picture does not say. Obviously he is leaving to become Gorky, and beyond that, to become a new kind of Russian. What became of young Gorky, and what marked the new Russian?

Gorky went to study in the University of Kazan. 'If anybody had proposed to me "Go and study, but on condition that you'll be publicly birched every Sunday on Nikolayewsky Square" I most likely would have agreed.' [12] But he soon felt the discrimination against him as a penniless peasant. He therefore became a student in what he called the 'free' university of the revolutionary youth.

[12] Roskin, op. cit.

354

But Gorky had always been sensitive and impressionable, and his basic, sentimental sadness was counteracted only by his determination to 'grasp' life, almost to force it to respond to his faith. His discipline as a writer consisted of a struggle to say the essential by using fewer words. Against a deeply nostalgic trend young Gorky determined to develop a heart that could grasp, yet love a soul with teeth in it. As with so many of his like-minded contemporaries, the struggle nearly killed him.

At the age of twenty he attempted suicide by shooting himself in the side. 'I lay the blame of my death,' he wrote in a remarkable suicide-note, 'on the German poet Heine who invented a *toothache of the heart* . . . It will be seen from my passport that I am A. Pyeshkov, but from this note, I hope, nothing will be seen.'[13] He will now forgive us if we do see a meaningful relationship between this toothache of the heart and his, and his nation's struggle to overcome regressive nostalgia and 'to learn to grasp life'. The term used had, indeed, been invented by the bitterly (or may we say bitingly) nostalgic Heine, who recommended as a remedy for the heart's tooth-aches a certain toothpowder invented by Bertold Schwarz – the inventor of gunpowder. Gorky later formulated to Chekhov his depressive period as a time of 'stony darkness', of '*immobility forever poised*'. Having broken the deadlock by risking self-destruction, he recovered and set out to wander and to work.

'I have come into the world not to compromise', he said in his first epic poem. Alyosha had followed Gregory and all the others, watching in order to find out where he should and should not be involved in living the life of the people; Gorky literally stalked people and situations to see where he could wrest from life, as a homeless wanderer, those 'rare and positive' phenomena which would keep his faith alive.

His analytic incorruptibility 'lifted to the point of inspiration' is never more epically expressed than in the famous letter which he wrote upon the receipt of the gripping news that old Tolstoy had wandered off from home, wife, and estate.[14]

. . . There is a dog howling in my soul and I have a foreboding of some misfortune. Yes, newspapers have just arrived and it is already

[13] Roskin, op. cit.
[14] Gorky, op. cit.

355

clear: you at home are beginning to 'create a legend'; idlers and good-for-nothings have gone on living and have now produced a saint. Only think how pernicious it is for the country just at this moment, when the heads of disillusioned men are bowed down, the souls of the majority empty, and the souls of the best full of sorrow. Lacerated and starving they long for a legend. They long so much for alleviation of pain, for the soothing of torment. And they will create just what he desires, but what is not wanted – the life of a holy man and saint.

... Well, now he is probably making his last assault in order to give his ideas the highest possible significance, so that he might assert his holiness and obtain a halo. That is dictatorial, although his teaching is justified by the ancient history of Russia and by his own sufferings of genius. Holiness is attained by flirting with sin, by subduing the will to live. People do desire to live, but he tries to persuade them: 'That's all nonsense, our earthly life.' It is very easy to persuade a Russian of this: he is a lazy creature who loves beyond anything else to find an excuse for his own inactivity.

... A strange impression used to be produced by his words: 'I am happy, I am very happy, I am too happy.' And then immediately afterwards: 'To suffer.' To suffer – that too was true in him. I don't doubt it for a second, that he, only half convalescent, would have been really glad to be put into prison, to be banished, in a word to embrace a martyr's crown.

In the last analysis, he saw in Tolstoy's conversion the ancient curse of Russia:[15]

... He always greatly exalted immortality on the other side of this life, but he preferred it on this side. A writer, national in the truest and most complete sense, he embodied in his great soul all the defects of his nation, all the mutilations we have suffered by the ordeals of our history; his misty preaching of 'non-activity', of 'non-resistance to evil', the doctrine of passivism, all this is the unhealthy ferment of the old Russian blood, envenomed by Mongolian fatalism and almost chemically hostile to the West, with its untiring creative labor, with its active and indomitable resistance to the evils of life. What is called Tolstoy's 'anarchism' essentially and fundamentally expresses our Slav anti-Statism, which, again, is really a national characteristic, ingrained in our flesh from old times, our desire to scatter nomadically. Up to now we have indulged that desire passionately, as you and everyone else know. We Russians know it too, but we always break away along the lines of least resistance; we see that this is pernicious, but still we crawl further and further away from one another; and these mournful cockroach journeyings are called 'the history of

[15] Gorky, op. cit.

Russia', the history of a State which has been established almost incidentally, mechanically – to the surprise of the majority of its honest-minded citizens – by the forces of the Variags, Tartars, Baltic Germans, and petty officials . . .

In viewing this motion picture and in trying to determine what Alyosha became free *for*, it is hard to avoid two pitfalls, a biographical and a historical one. It seems clear that Alyosha, as the collective myth of the film, has great affinity to Gorky's image of himself, to his ideals, and to the legend which he, as any great writer, worked so hard to become. Yet the real Gorky's ways of solving, by creativity and by neurosis, the problem which he shouldered as a youth, is tangential to our discussion.

The historical pitfall would lie in a hostile comparison of this picture's simple humanity and earthiness, its implicit revolutionary spirit, with the stilted and stagnant revolutionary 'line' which we have become used to in what reaches us now of Soviet writings and movies. Beyond the cruel abuse of revolutions by the super-managers whom they bring to power, we must look for the root of revolution in the needs of the led – and the misled.

The importance of the picture for this book lies in its simple relevance for a few psychological trends which are basic to revolutions in general; and specifically to those in areas which face industrialization while still immersed in the imagery of an ancient agricultural revolution. True, our motion picture offers for discussion only some of the imagery of one of these areas: the great Russian plains. While other ethnic areas would call for the consideration of different or related imageries, yet Russia has so far been as decisive and pervading an influence in the Communist revolution as, say, the Anglo-Saxons were in the history of America.

To summarize: in the imagery suggested by this movie, the grandmother has a dominant place. She seems to represent the people in their mystical unity with flesh and earth: good in itself but cursed by the greediness of the 'breed': Paradise lost. To become or remain a party to the grandmother's strength would mean surrender to timelessness, and eternal bondage to the faith of primitive economy. It is that faith which makes the primitive hang on to the methods of ancient tools and of magical influence over the forces of nature; it is that faith which, in turn,

357

provides him with a simple remedy for any sense of sin; projection. Badness all lies in evil forces, in spirits, in curses: you must regulate them with magic – or be possessed by them. To the Bolshevik revolutionary the grandmother's goodness reaches back into times before good and evil entered the world; and, one assumes, it reaches into the far future when classless society will overcome the morality of greed and exploitation. In the meantime grandmother is a danger. She is the political apathy of the Russian's very timelessness and childish trust. Maybe she is the virtue, as it has been put recently, which permits the Kremlin to wait, and the Russian people to wait longer.

A second set of images seems to concern the wood-fire dichotomy. The uncles, and the other men, are stout, square, heavy, awkward, and dull, like logs of wood; but they are highly combustible. They are wood – and they are fire. The swaddled 'log of wood' with its smouldering vasomotor madness, the wooden Russian people with their explosive souls: are such images left-overs of a very recent or, in Russia, even contemporary *wooden age*? Wood provided the material for the stockades as well as for the overheated ovens through the long winters. It was the basic material for tools. But it also incorporated the danger of being consumed by its own combustibility. Houses and villages and wood supplies burned beyond recovery – a fatal tendency in view of the fact that the forests themselves perished in fires and receded from prairies and marshes. What tragic means were invoked to save them?

A third set of images centres in *iron* and *steel*. In the picture it is present only in the appearance of the little wheel for Lyenka's cart. The scavenger boys find it, but instead of turning it into money they use it to complete the prosthesis for Lyenka's locomotor liberation. But then, the wheel takes a special place among the basic human inventions. It goes beyond the tools which represent mere extensions of and prostheses for the limbs; moving within itself, it is basic for the idea of the machine, which, man-made and man-driven, yet develops a certain autonomy as a mechanical organism.

Beyond this, however, steel is, in many ways, suggested as a symbol of the new frame of mind. While the wood and fire imagery suggests a cyclic personality structure characterized by apathetic drudgery, childlike trust, sudden outbreaks of consuming passion, and a sense of depressing doom, the imagery of steel suggests incorruptible realism and enduring, disciplined struggle. For steel is forged in fire, but it is not combustible or subject to destruction by fire. To master it means to triumph over the weakness of the flesh-soul and the deadness and combustibility of the wood-mind. As it is forged, steel forges a new generation and a new élite. Such, at least, must be the connotation of names like Stalin (steel) and Molotov (hammer), and of official behaviour which underscores without cessation the incorruptibility of Bolshevik perception, the long range of its vision, its steel-like clarity of decision, and the machine-like firmness of action. On the defensive, such composure again becomes woodenness – or combustible oratory.

We see now where Gorky meant to stand and where this motion picture of the early days of the Russian revolution puts him: into that vanguard of revolutionaries called the 'intelligentsia', which – with all its morbid ruminations – prepared the new morality by learning to grasp and hold, first facts and ideas, and then political and military control itself. It is hard for us to realize what superhuman inspiration seemed involved at the time in Lenin's decision to ask the workers and peasants on the collapsing fronts to hold on to their guns; and what a miracle it must have seemed that the worn-out masses complied. It was Gorky who called writers 'the engineers of society', and, in turn, spoke of an inventor as 'a poet in the domain of scientific technique, who arouses that sensible energy which creates goodness and beauty'. As the revolution established itself, the highly educated and in many ways Westernized intellectual élite gave place to a planned, meticulously trained élite of political, industrial, and military engineers who believed themselves to be the aristocracy of the historical process itself. They are our cold, our dangerous adversaries today.

But there was a time when the intelligentsia wanted passionately to be of the people and for the people; and, no doubt, they once amplified and were amplified by a dark and illiterate tendency in the Russian masses (or, at any rate, in a decisive segment of these masses) to find its national identity in a mystical international cause. In Alyosha we see the son of a mystic and earthy past as well as a potential founding father of an industrial world future.

359

The American farmer's boy is the descendant of Founding Fathers who themselves were rebel sons. They had refused to hide behind any crown or cross. They were heirs of a reformation, a renaissance, the emergence of nationalism and of revolutionary individualism. They had before them a new continent which had not been their motherland and which had never been governed by crowned or ordained fathers. This fact permitted an exploitation of the continent which was crudely masculine, rudely exuberant, and, but for its women, anarchic. The Americans have, if any people has, fulfilled Chekhov's dream. They have made conquered earth comfortable and machinery almost pleasant, to the ambivalent envy of the rest of the world. Protestantism, individualism, and the frontier together created an identity of individual initiative which in industrialization found its natural medium. In an earlier chapter we pointed to the problems which this identity faced as the continent was gradually exploited in its width and depth, and as voracious initiative began to eat into the human resources of the nation; and we have pointed to some of the derivatives of the protestant revolution.

I shall now try to make more explicit what I meant earlier when referring to Alyosha's new frame of mind as a form of delayed Eastern protestantism.

The temptations Alyosha turns away from – and a protestant turns away from and against – are not dissimilar to those which the early Protestants felt emanated from Rome: the enchantment of God as a spirit that enters through the senses as the light of the stained windows, the fume of the incense and the lullaby of the chant; the mystic immersion in the mass; the 'clinical' view of life as a childhood disease of the soul; and most of all, the permission 'to hide behind another's conscience'.

If we turn to the community of men which Alyosha seems to be turning towards, the parallelism with protestant patterns becomes even clearer. For from a centralized organization for mediated salvation (and thus the exploitation of infantile and primitive fears) Alyosha and his comrades turn to the establishment of a responsible *élite*. Their means of selection is not faith in the Invisible, but conduct within a community which examines, selects, and judges. Their conscience is not based on the paroxysms of the sin-and-expiation cycle, but on a discipline of mind. This discipline determines their form of sacrifice, which is the emphasis on a systematic discipline of the senses rather than on spectacular atonement. Their state of salvation is not determined by the inner glow of faith and of love for the believers, but in disciplined success in this world, in a determined alignment with contemporary economic and technical forces. Their damnation and their death is not the consciousness of sin and the certainty of hell, but the exclusion from the revolutionary community, and even the self-exclusion from the historical process, a moral annihilation compared with which death from whatever hand is a mere biological trifle.

The framework of this Eastern protestant reorientation is of course radically different from the Western one; it is proletarian and industrial, and it is Russian and Orthodox. The latter two elements have determined the pitfalls of this orientation and the enormity of its tragedy.

We can continue and conclude our analogy here. The Communist Party, in absorbing an emerging protestantism, could not tolerate an important protestant ingredient: *sectarianism*. To maintain absolute power it felt the need for absolute unity. The Party's desperate and finally cruel attempts at warding off sectarian splits are well documented in the minutes of its early conventions, which were characterized by a hair-splitting most reminiscent of ecclesiastic history: the issues were the *truth* of dialectic history, the *infallibility* of the Politburo, and the mystic *wisdom* of the masses. We know how this hair-splitting ended.

Max Weber's prediction that an attempt at dictatorship for the proletariat could only lead to a dictatorship of the middleman, of bureaucracy, now proves to have been prophetic. Again, the Russian people believe in one man in the Kremlin, whom they do not blame for the cruelties of his middlemen and whom they believe to be their defender against usurpers and exploiters, foreign and domestic.

As of today, they believe this honestly, because there is nothing else that they could believe on the basis of what they know. Therefore, their best is invested in this belief. Our devoted studies should concern the fact that the original emergence of a revolutionary frame of mind in Russia and Asia, volcanic as it was, may have been an attempt, and in view of the historical process an unavoidable one, to approach the stage of human conscience which characterized our protestant revolution. Whether or not a few men on the Eurasian continent or some nervous council of ministers will plunge us into war, we do not know. But it may well be that the future – with or without war – will belong to those who will harness the psychological energies freed from the wasteful superstitions of ancient agricultural moralities on the European, Asiatic, and African continents. Physics, in learning to split the atom, has released new energy, for peace and for war. With the help of psychoanalysis we can study another kind of energy which is released when the most archaic part of our conscience is 'split'. As civilization enters into an industrialized era, such a split is inevitable. The enormous energy thus released can be benevolent, and it can be malevolent. In the end, it may be more decisive than material weapons.

As we Americans, with the friendly coerciveness of a Paul Bunyan (the Russians would say, a Vassily Buslaiev), throw gadgets and robots into the world market, we must learn to understand that we help to create revolutionized economic conditions. We must be able to demonstrate to grim Alyoshas everywhere that our new and shiny goods (so enticingly wrapped in promises of freedom) do not come to them as so many more sedatives to make them subservient to their worn-out upper classes, as so many more opiates to lull them into the new serfdom of hypnotized consumership. They do not want to be granted freedom; what they want is to be given the opportunity to grasp it, as equals. They do not want progress where it undermines their sense of initiative. They demand autonomy, together with unity; and identity together with the fruits of industry. We must succeed in convincing the Alyoshas that – from a very long-range point of view – their protestantism is ours, and ours theirs.

11 Conclusion: Beyond Anxiety

Feeling under his right thumb the thin sheaf of pages left of this book, the reader may wonder what kind of short conclusion could do justice to the matters of immediate concern illustrated in the last chapter. Here I must concede that whatever message has not been conveyed by my description and discourse has but a slim chance of being furthered by a formal conclusion. I have nothing to offer except a way of looking at things. From the periphery of our illustrations, I must now re-trace this viewpoint to its centre in psychoanalytic work.

This return to our point of departure is not an evasion. It must be remembered that until quite recently our clinical insights into the relationship of childhood and society have found little or no corollary in the sciences of sociology and history. As we clarify these matters as far as our methods will permit, we must be cautious in suggesting practical application. There is no time left in which to be as naïve historically as, in all past history, the historians have been psychologically.

To reconcile historical and psychological methodologies, we must first learn to deal jointly with the fact that psychologies and psychologists are subject to historical laws and that historians and historical records are subject to those of psychology. Having learned in clinical work that the individual is apt to develop an amnesia concerning his most formative experiences in childhood, we are also forced to recognize a universal blind spot in the makers and interpreters of history: they ignore the fateful function of childhood in the fabric of society. Historians and philosophers recognize a 'female principle' in the world, but not the fact that man is born and reared by women. They debate principles of formal education, but neglect the fateful dawn of individual consciousness. They forever insist on a mirage of progress which promises that man's (the male's) logic will lead to reason, order, and peace, while each step towards this mirage brings new hostile alignments which lead to war, and worse. Moralistic man and rationalizing man continues to identify himself with abstractions of himself, but refuses to see how he became what he really is and how, as an emotional and political being, he undoes with infantile compulsions and impulsions what his thought has invented and what his hands have built. All of this has its psychological basis – namely, the individual's unconscious determination never to meet his childhood anxiety face to face again, and his superstitious apprehension lest a glance at the infantile origins of his thoughts and schemes may destroy his single-minded stamina. He therefore prefers enlightenment away from himself; which is why the best minds have often been least aware of themselves.

But may it not be mainly superstition that makes man turn away from his latent anxiety as if from the head of a Medusa? May it not be that man, at this stage of the game, must and can expand his tolerant awareness to his latent anxieties and to the infantile origins of his preconceptions and apprehensions?

Every adult, whether he is a follower or a leader, a member of a mass or of an *élite*, was once a child. He was once small. A sense of smallness forms a substratum in his mind, ineradicably. His triumphs will be measured against this smallness, his defeats will substantiate it. The questions as to who is bigger and who can do or not do this or that, and to whom – these questions fill the adult's inner life far beyond the necessities and the desirabilities which he understands and for which he plans.

Every society consists of men in the process of developing from children into parents. To assure continuity of tradition, society must early prepare for parenthood in its children; and it must take care of the unavoidable remnants of infantility in its adults. This is a large order, especially since a society needs many beings who can follow, a few who can lead, and some who can do both, alternately or in different areas of life.

Man's childhood learning, which develops his highly specialized brain–eye–hand co-ordination and all the intrinsic mechanisms of reflection and planning, is contingent on prolonged dependence. Only thus does man develop conscience, that dependence on himself which will make him, in turn, dependable; and only when thoroughly dependable in a number of fundamental values (truth, justice, etc.) can he become independent and teach and develop tradition. But this dependability offers a problem because of its very origin in childhood, and because of the forces employed in its development. We have discussed the retardation of sexual development and its concentration on and deflection from the family; and we have discussed the importance of early patterns of aggressive approach (organ modes) for the development of social modalities. Both of these developments force the very origins of his ideals into an association with images denoting infantile tension and rage.

Thus the immature origin of his conscience endangers man's maturity and his works: infantile fear accompanies him through life. This we, the psychoanalysts, are attempting to correct in individual cases; this we try to explain and to conceptualize, because there is no universal cure – only, maybe, an alleviation by gradual insight – for the fact that each generation must develop out of its childhood and, overcoming its particular brand of childhood, must develop a new brand, potentially promising, potentially dangerous.

Mark Twain, probably in one of his depressed moods, called man 'the immodest animal', the only creature who knows that he is naked, or, as we would put it, the creature with a self-conscious sexuality. Here Mark Twain failed to mention the redeeming human speciality in which he himself specialized: humour, the ability at rare moments to play with and to reflect fearlessly on the strange customs and institutions by which man must find self-realization. But the fact remains that the human being in early childhood learns to consider one or the other aspect of bodily function as evil, shameful, or unsafe. There is no culture which does not use a combination of these devils to develop, by way of counterpoint, its own style of faith, pride, certainty, and initiative. Thus there remains in man's sense of achievement the suspicion of its infantile roots; and since his earliest sense of reality was learned by the painful testing of inner and outer goodnesses and badnesses, man remains ready to expect from some enemy, force, or event in the outer world that which, in fact, endangers him from within: from his own angry drives, from his own sense of smallness, and from his own split inner world. Thus he is always irrationally ready to fear invasion by vast and vague forces which are other than himself;

strangling encirclement by everything that is not safely clarified as allied; and devastating loss of face before all-surrounding, mocking audiences. These, not the animal's fears, characterize human anxiety, and this in world affairs as well as in personal affairs.

In conclusion I shall summarize at least some of the basic fears. But first let me hope that I have succeeded in indicating my recognition of the obvious – namely, that the existence of power spheres, of spheres of influence, jurisdiction, and possession, and, above all, of spheres of exploitation, are matters pertaining to the social process and are not in themselves to be explained as originating in infantile anxiety: they are the expression of the geographic–historical actuality in which we exist. The problem to be elucidated is that of the extent to which man is apt to project on political and economic necessity those fears, apprehensions, and urges which are derived from the arsenal of infantile anxiety.

And another reservation: we must learn to differentiate between fears and anxieties. Fears are states of apprehension which focus on isolated and recognizable dangers so that they may be judiciously appraised and realistically countered. Anxieties are diffuse states of tension (caused by a loss of mutual regulation and a consequent upset in libidinal and aggressive controls) which magnify and even cause the illusion of an outer danger, without pointing to appropriate avenues of defence or mastery. These two forms of apprehension obviously often occur together, and we can insist on a strict separation only for the sake of the present argument. If, in an economic depression, a man is afraid that he may lose his money, his fear may be justified. But if the idea of having to live on an income only ten times, instead of twenty-five times, as large as that of his average fellow-citizen causes him to lose his nerve and to commit suicide, then we must consult our clinical formulas. They may help us find out, for example, why wealth was the cornerstone of the man's identity and that the economic depression coincided with his climacteric. The fear of losing his money, then, became associated with the anxiety aroused by the idea of having to live a role not characterized by unlimited resources, and this at a time when the fear of losing his sexual potency had mobilized an infantile anxiety once connected with ideas of being inactivated and castrated. In the adult, then, impairment of judgement by infantile rage is the result of a state of irrational tension brought about by a short circuit between rational adult fears and associated infantile anxieties. This is the truth behind Franklin D. Roosevelt's simple yet magic statement that we have nothing to fear but fear itself, a statement which for the sake of our argument must be paraphrased to read: we have nothing to fear but anxiety. For it is not the fear of a danger (which we might be well able to meet with judicious action), but the fear of the associated state of aimless anxiety which drives us into irrational *action*, irrational *flight* – or, indeed, irrational *denial* of danger. When threatened with such anxiety, we either magnify a danger which we have no reason to fear excessively – or we ignore a danger which we have every reason to fear. To be able to be aware of fear, then, without giving in to anxiety; to train our fear in the face of anxiety to remain an accurate measure and warning of that which man must fear – this is a necessary condition for a judicious frame of mind. This is the more important since political and religious institutions, in vying for the allegiance of men, have learned to exploit infantile panics common to all mankind or to particular sections of it. To their own eventual disadvantage 'shrewd' leaders, cliques, and pressure groups can make people see exaggerated dangers – or make them ignore existing danger until it is too late. Thus it comes about that even enlightened and democratic men are blunted in their capacity to fear accurately and to cooperate judiciously.

We can only summarize some of the anxieties involved and let each (author and reader alike) ask himself in what way his own walk of life may help to combat the panic which shadows man as he progresses.

In childhood, of course, fear and anxiety are so close to one another that they are indistinguishable, and this for the reason that the child, because of his immature equipment, has no way of differentiating between inner and outer, real and imagined, dangers: he has yet to learn this, and while he learns, he needs the adult's reassuring instruction. In so far as the child fails to be convinced by the adult's reasoning and especially where he perceives instead the adult's latent horror and bewilderment, a panicky sense of vague catastrophe remains as an ever ready potentiality. A child has a right, then, to develop anxiety when he is afraid, even as he has a right to have 'childish' fears until guidance has helped him, step for step, to develop judgement and mastery. For this reason, we will call a number of the child's apprehensions fears, although we will call the same apprehensions anxieties in the adult in whom they persist in sharp contrast to his ability to judge danger and to plan against it.

In the following, we will recount primarily infantile fears which are tied to the experience of the growing organisms. These fears, it will be noted, are the precursors of many irrational anxieties entertained by adults in their spheres of concern, such as the preservation of individual identities and the protection of collective territories.

Babies are startled by a number of things, such as a sudden loss of support or a sudden intense noise or beam of light. Such events are accidental and rare, and are quickly adjusted to, unless a baby has learned to *fear suddenness* in the changes around him. From here on it is difficult to say when he fears the recurrence of a particular event, or suddenness as such, and when he reacts with anxiety to the adult ineptness or tension which is expressed in recurring suddenness. 'Instinctive' fear of such objective things as loss of support or noise thus easily becomes social anxiety connected with the sudden loss of attentive care.

The unavoidable imposition on the child of outer controls which are not in sufficient accord with his inner control at the time, is apt to produce in him a cycle of anger and anxiety. This leaves a residue of an *intolerance of being manipulated* and coerced beyond the point at which outer control can be experienced as self-control. Connected with this is an *intolerance of being interrupted* in a vital act, or of not being permitted to conclude an act in an idiosyncratically important way. All of these anxieties lead to impulsive self-will – or, by contrast, to exaggerated self-coercion by stereotypy and lonely repetition. Here we find the origins of compulsion and obsession and the concomitant need for the vengeful manipulation and coercion of others.

The intolerance of not being permitted to bring experiences to completion has its counterpart in the *fear of being impoverished* in a particular organ-mode. On the oral level, there is something of a fear of being left empty (nutritional) and of being starved of stimulation (sensory and sensual). These fears later become interchangeable, so that thrill-seeking and fear of starvation may characterize people who have more than enough to eat but less than enough sensual intimacy.

The anxiety caused by the *fear of losing autonomy*, in its intestinal form, concerns the possible emptying and robbing of one's inside by inimical people and inner saboteurs who can make the bowels let go against one's own sovereign wish. Corresponding to the ambivalent aspect of this stage, an alternate fear would concern the *danger of being closed up*, of being forced to contain the bulging bowel, of having no 'outlet'.

In the muscular area there is also a double intolerance: the anxiety caused by the *sense of being restrained* and held to the point of muscular impotence has its counterpart in that of not being held at all, of *losing outer bounds* and boundaries, and with them the necessary orientation for the definition of one's autonomy. The alliance of muscular and anal sadism, then, seems to foster the fear of *being attacked from the rear*, of being either overwhelmed and bound, or raped rectally, in the apparent way of animals.

Standing alone has many connotations of pride and isolation, of wishing to be admired, and of the *fear of being exposed* to devastating inspection and, of course, of *falling*.

In the centre of the boy's locomotor–phallic fears lurks that of 'castration', of being *deprived of an intrusive weapon*. The clinical evidence for the strategic existence of a fear for that sensitive organ, the penis, which so defiantly 'sticks its neck out' is overwhelming. More generally, there is a *fear of remaining small* either in one's total size or in one's genital stature, of not having been provided with 'the right stuff'.

On the ambulatory side, there is the *fear of being immobilized* and imprisoned, and yet, again, also a fear *of not being guided*, of not finding borderlines defined so that one may fight and assert one's initiative. Here is the infantile origin of (the man's) need for an enemy so that he may arm himself against and fight a concrete adversary and thus be freed of the constant anxiety of unknown enemies who, at unpredictable times, may find him unarmed and uncovered.

The fear of remaining empty (oral) or being emptied (anal) has a special quality in girls, since the body image of the girl (even before she 'knows' her inner anatomic arrangements) includes a valuable inside, an inside on which depends her fulfilment as an organism, a person, and as a role-bearer. This *fear of being left empty*, and, more simply, that of *being left*, seems to be the most basic feminine fear, extending over the whole of a woman's existence. It is normally intensified with every menstruation and takes its final toll during the menopause. No wonder, then, that the anxiety aroused by these fears can express itself either in complete subjection to male thought, in desperate competition with it, or in efforts to catch the male and make him a possession.

Here I must take special note of one of the most paradoxical and far-reaching consequences of the feminine fear of being left. Lest their men discard and abandon them in the periodical pursuits of competition, conquest, and war, women are apt to refrain from questioning these pursuits, which, again and again, lead to the disruption of the home and to the slaughter of sons. They pretend that they really believe in war and in man's magnificent equipment, where actually they have merely learned to accept as inevitable a martial excitement which is essentially outside their comprehension. It may well be that war cannot be banned until women, for the sake of a worthwhile survival, dare to recognize and to support the as yet undeveloped power of unarmed resistance. But here women must first learn to understand their fear of being abandoned, and their unwillingness to question judiciously man's cultivation of war for war's sake.

Somewhere, of course, the little girl learns to hate him who so smugly has what it takes – and can take it with him. By way of a 'projection' too complicated for a brief account, the little girl's hate intensifies her *fear of being raped*, leading to an anxiety easily fused with the various pregenital fears of being eaten into, being robbed, and being emptied. Men, in turn, make ample use of this anxiety when they need women's consent to their martial fantasies and aggressive provocations: there is always a woman, a country, or a principle, symbolized as a superhuman woman, who must be protected against capture and rape.

These, then, are some of the basic intolerances, fears, and resulting anxieties which arise from the mere fact that human life begins with a long, slow childhood and sexuality with an attachment to parental figures. Fears based on the structure and growth of the organism are emphasized here because they are the earliest, the most pervasive, and the least conscious themes of fear. A complete summary would give equal weight to the little being's bewilderment in the face of those unpredictable tensions and rages which periodically overwhelm the adults around him. In later childhood and in early adolescence, of course, all these fears become part and parcel of interpersonal involvements ('oedipus complex', 'sibling rivalry') which concern bigger and smaller rivals and their conflicting demands. For the former claims a right of ownership based on having been there first and being stronger, the latter an equal right on the basis of having come last and being weaker – contradictions not easily reconciled either in systems of child training or in political systems.

We concluded that only a gradually accruing sense of identity, based on the experience of social health and cultural solidarity at the end of each major childhood crisis, promises that periodical balance in human life which – in integration of the ego stages – makes for a sense of humanity. But wherever this sense is lost, wherever integrity yields to despair and disgust, wherever generativity yields to stagnation, intimacy to isolation, and identity to confusion, an array of associated infantile fears are apt to become mobilized: for only an identity safely anchored in the 'patrimony' of a cultural identity can produce a workable psychosocial equilibrium.[1]

[1] The concept of ego identity may be misunderstood in two ways. One may suspect that all identity is conformist, that a sense of identity is achieved primarily through the individual's complete surrender to given social roles and through his unconditional adaptation to the demands of social change. No ego, it is true, can develop outside of social processes which offer workable prototypes and roles. The healthy and strong individual, however, adapts these roles to the further processes of his ego, thus doing his share in keeping the social process alive.

The second misconception concerns those individuals who devote themselves to the study and the lonely pursuit of human integrity and who in doing so seem to live beside and above the group from which they have emerged. Are they above all identity? Such individuals were, in their development, by no means independent of their group's identity, which, in

In the last section of this book I illustrated some of the problems which face the youth of the world of today. Industrial revolution, world-wide communication, standardization, central-ization, and mechanization threaten the identities which man has inherited from primitive, agrarian, feudal, and patrician cultures. What inner equilibrium these cultures had to offer is now endangered on a gigantic scale. As the fear of loss of identity dominates much of our irrational motivation, it calls upon the whole arsenal of anxiety which is left in each individual from the mere fact of his childhood. In this emergency masses of people become ready to seek salvation in pseudo-identities.

I have indicated only by a few suggestions that the anxieties outlined reach into adult life, and this not only in the form of neurotic anxiety, which, after all, is recognizable as such, kept in bounds by most, and can be cured in some. More terrifyingly, they reappear in the form of collective panics and in afflictions of the collective mind. The anxieties named in the preceding pages could be taken out of their context of childhood and serve as headings for a treatise on group panics and their propagand-istic exploitation.

This then is one of our jobs: to perfect methods which, in given situations, facilitate the elucidation of such prejudices, apprehensions, and lapses of judgement as emanate from infantile rage and from the adult's defences against his latent infantile anxiety.

Assuming that our clinical experience has led us to detect meaningful connections in the relationship between the anxieties of infancy and the upheavals of society, what order of insight is this and what kind of power does it offer us? Will the utilization of this knowledge help us create synthetic child-training systems which will manufacture the desired kind of personality in our children? Can it help us to look through the infantile weaknesses of our enemies so that we may outsmart them? And – should we harbour such hopes – would insight thus applied remain insightful?

---

fact, they may have absorbed to the point of outgrowing it. Nor are they free from a new common identity, though they may share it only with a very few who may not even be living in the same era (I am thinking here of Gandhi, and his relationship both to India and to Jesus of Nazareth).

Our knowledge of these matters is based on the study of anxiety and therefore highlights primarily the ways in which anxiety is produced and exploited. We can (as I pointed out in the first chapter) make the origin of individual anxiety retroactively plausible by analysis: but we have only begun to study the combination of elements which, in a given case, would have resulted in an interesting variation of, rather than a neurotic deviation from, human functioning. We have studied variations less than we have studied deviations, and this for the reason that variations get along so well without us.

In psychoanalytic circles, we have witnessed a little private history of tentative child-training systems dedicated to instinctual indulgence or to the avoidance of anxiety in our children. We know that not infrequently only a new system of 'scientific' superstitions has resulted. Obsessively comparing variations of childhoods to deviations encountered in the childhood memories of adult patients, some of us have inadvertently driven our children into an identification with our patients. At least, one little son of a psychiatrist recently expressed it in so many words: when this carefully and considerately brought up child was asked what he wanted to be when big and strong he said, 'A patient.' He meant, of course, that he wanted to be the kind of being who seemed so absorbingly interesting to his parents. Since he has said it, he may not need to do it, and his parents may learn from him in time. But such experiences should show us that it is not easy to construct by mere scientific synthesis a foolproof system which will lead our children in a desired direction and avoid an undesirable one. Obviously, good can come only from a continuing interplay between that which we, as students, are gradually learning and that which we believe in, as people.

This is not easy. When men concentrate on an uncharted area of human existence, they aggrandize this area to become the universe, and they reify its centre as the prime reality. Thus, as I pointed out when discussing the theory of infantile sexuality, the 'id' was reified in psychoanalysis, and the instincts became the universe, in spite of the fact that Freud sovereignly referred to them as his 'mythology'. He knew that man, in building theories, patches up his world-image in order to integrate what he knows with what he needs, and that he makes of it all (for he must live as he studies) a design for living. Will we escape doing the same with the ego? It is a central principle of organization[2] in man's experience and action, to be understood as such, and not to be reified. For man's understanding must always step back from what he has discerned. A strong identity as well as a healthy and sensual body and a discerning and curious mind are what man lives by, but he has not understood either the strength or the illusions which come from them as long as he permits any of them to dominate his life or thought.

In the matter of societal processes, too, we begin to know something about the place of anxiety, superstition, and unscrupulous propaganda in collective grumblings, upheavals, and transformations. But we do not know half so well in what way a new idea suddenly does the seemingly impossible and creates or maintains a variation of civilization in the midst of an apparent chaos of deviant contradictions.

The situation here is rather similar to that in the field of atomic research. There, physicists have, under the pressure of a danger to our civilization, striven in shortest order to perfect work of the highest theoretical and most far-reaching practical significance. The public, on the whole, is inclined to accept as given an inconceivable weapon, leaving it to the scientists to find defence weapons equal to the offensive danger which they have created, and relying, for the rest, on the good old ways of professional diplomacy. The scientists have organized to enlighten the public, but they themselves cannot create and govern a new international organization which alone would meet the danger which they know so well. To build a super-cyclotron is one thing; to build a super-national organization another. The scientists have at their disposal only the voice of enlightenment, hope in mankind, and their own scientific ethics. They do not have an easy time of it, because (whatever their declared loyalties and unalterable commitments) there is a point where scientific ethos and armament races do not live well together in one identity, and on being forced to merge endanger the very spirit of inquiry.

In our field, too, we know some of the story, but not the whole story. We have seen spectacular evidences of the fact that psychoanalytic constructs serve to clarify unconscious dynamics.

[2] And only in this sense 'the individual's core', as I called it on the first page of the First Edition.   E.H.E.

We have studied convincing cures and shocking reverses. We have offered surprising clarifications in the field of motivational forces, and we are firmly approaching the study of society. Yet emergencies prevail upon us to offer our judgement regarding societal and international events. Some of us respond by analysing the problems of social organization as clinical situations. Others put their faith in what is called interdisciplinary teamwork, a kind of halt-and-blind cooperation, in which a social scientist with little psychological vision carries in piggy-back fashion a psychologist who has not learned to move with ease in the public events of this world, so that together they may grope their way through contemporary history. But I think that our work must contribute more significantly to a new manner of man, one whose vision keeps up with his power of locomotion, and his action with his boundless thinking. Only in so far as our clinical way of work becomes part of a judicious way of life can we help to counteract and reintegrate the destructive forces which are being let loose by the split in modern man's archaic conscience.

Judiciousness in its widest sense is a frame of mind which is tolerant of differences, cautious and methodical in evaluation, just in judgement, circumspect in action, and – in spite of all this apparent relativism – capable of faith and indignation. Its opposite is prejudice, an outlook characterized by prejudged values and dogmatic divisions; here everything seems to be clearly delineated and compartmentalized, and this by 'nature', wherefore it must stay forever the way it always has been. By thus relying on preconceived notions the prejudiced frame of mind creates a rigidity which can become uncomfortable; but it has the advantage of permitting the projection of everything that feels alien within one's own heart unto some vague enemy outside – a mechanism which makes for a certain limited stability and standardization, until a catastrophe endangers the whole brittle structure of preconceptions.[3] The judicious outlook, in turn, permits a greater flexibility and variability, but it admittedly endangers the unbalanced and neurotic individual who may choose to pursue it. As he abandons all prejudice, he forfeits the mechanism of projection: his danger becomes introspection and

[3] See the work of T. W. Adorno, Else Frenkel-Brunswik, Daniel J. Levinson, and R. Nevitt Sanford, *The Authoritarian Personality*, Harper & Brothers, New York, 1950.

'introjection', an over-concern with the evil in himself. One may say that he becomes prejudiced against himself. Some measure of this must be tolerated by men of good will. Men of good will must learn to fear accurately and to cope judiciously with the anxiety aroused by a renunciation of prejudice. Enlightenment has done the groundwork; new forms of communication must cement the foundation; society must provide the structure.

Clinical knowledge, then, like any knowledge, is but a tool in the hands of a faith or a weapon in the service of a superstition. Instead of coming to the conclusion that particular items of child training and their minute timing and dosage make and unmake men, and that we must, therefore, proceed with self-conscious circumspection and minute planning, we may allow for an alternative. We may consider that the relationships between infantile anxiety and adult destructiveness exist in the forms demonstrated in this book primarily because they serve systems of superstition and exploitation. It may well be that (within certain limitations designating what an organism can integrate and an ego synthesize) details become decisive only if and when preconceptions and apprehensions are attached to them by superstitious adults: in which case the decisive question is whether these adults and their children are living in a system which balances its superstitions, or whether their superstitions are fragmentary and individualized retardations and regressions, contrasting sharply with known facts, conscious methods and formulated aspirations.

Our concerted efforts, therefore, should focus on a relaxation of unconscious superstition in the handling of infants and on the reduction of political and economic prejudice which denies a sense of identity to youth. To this end, however, it is necessary to understand the basic fact that human childhood provides a most fundamental basis for human exploitation. The polarity Big–Small is the first in the inventory of existential oppositions such as Male and Female,[4] Ruler and Ruled, Owner and Owned, Light Skin and Dark, over all of which emancipatory struggles are now raging both politically and psychologically. The aim of these struggles is the recognition of the divided function of partners who are equal not because they are essentially alike, but

[4] This is comprehensively discussed by Margaret Mead in *Male and Female*, William Morrow & Co., New York, 1949.

because in their very uniqueness they are both essential to a common function.

Here we must qualify, at least in its simplified interpretation, the statement which summarized the first impact of psycho-analytic enlightenment on this country – namely, that frustration leads to aggression. Man, in the service of a faith, can stand meaningful frustration. Rather, we should say that exploitation leads to fruitless rage: exploitation being the total social context which gives a specific frustration its devastating power. Exploitation exists where a divided function is misused by one of the partners involved in such a way that for the sake of his pseudo-aggrandizement he deprives the other partner of whatever sense of identity he had achieved, of whatever integrity he had approached. The loss of mutuality which characterizes such exploitation eventually destroys the common function and the exploiter himself.

In our country, probably more than in any other large country, the child is the adult's partner. We treasure as a promise of things to come the simple daily observation that wherever the spirit of partnership pervades a home and wherever childhood provides a status of its own, a sense of identity, fraternal conscience, and tolerance results. We are also aware of the fact that the inhumanity of colossal machine organization endangers these very gains of what is so specifically American. Responsible Americans know the danger emanating from a 'total war' machine and from its facsimile in peace-time. But it is not super-organization alone which today makes cultural values relative. The rapid spread of communication and the increasing knowledge of cultural relativity endanger people who are in a marginal position, people who are traumatically exposed to a numerical increase or the closer proximity or the greater power of others-than-themselves. Among such people the drive for tolerance has its point of diminishing returns: it causes anxiety. Similarly, the drive for judiciousness is by no means as immediately conducive to civic peace or, for that matter, to mental health as the new American peace ship 'Mental Hygiene' would have us believe: for the tolerant appraisal of other identities endangers one's own. The super-ego, so long the mainstay of morals, will make real tolerance dangerous until the identity of judiciousness becomes relevant and inescapable. Such judiciousness is essentially a matter of personal and civic morality; all that psychology can contribute is instruction in the tolerance of anxiety, and the concomitant recognition of hidden coerciveness and exploitiveness.

Here psychology faces its humanistic crisis. For psychology, in many respects, plays the role of the manipulator of man's will. We have quoted William Blake as nominating, for the 'fruits of the two seasons', the child's toys and the old man's reasons. We presumed that he thus intended to acknowledge the dignity of the child's play; but maybe he meant to point also to a latent infantility in mature reason. For in the use of reason lies the eternal temptation to do with human data in experiment and argument what the child does with them in play: namely, to reduce them to a size and an order in which they seem manageable. Thus human data are treated as if the human being were an animal, or a machine, or a statistical item. Much naïve sense of power can be derived from the fact that, properly approached, the human being up to a point is all of these things, and under certain conditions can be reduced to being nothing but their facsimiles. But the attempt to make man more exploitable by reducing him to a simpler model of himself cannot lead to an essentially human psychology.

The alternative to an exploitation of the lowest common denominator of men is the deliberate appeal to their latent intelligence, and the systematic cultivation of new forms of group discussion. On this, however, the psychoanalyst can only advise to the extent to which he has grasped, in addition to the infantile origins of adult anxieties, the social and political safeguards of the individual's strength and freedom.

I suggested that in reading this conclusion, the reader think of his own area of competences. I will conclude with two examples out of mine.

An opportunity, some years ago, to hear from a small group of pioneering doctors about the development of the technique of 'natural' childbirth (reintroduced into our mechanized Western culture by Dr Grantly D. Read) has been one of the most encouraging experiences of my professional life. The facts are by now well known. In the terms used here, we would say that the objective is childbirth without anxiety. The expectant mother will feel some fear because she knows that pain is inevitable. But the fact that the mother has learned, by exercise and instruction, to be aware of the location and the function of the contractions which cause the pain; and the fact that she expects, at the height of the curve of pain, to have the privilege of choosing consciously whether or not she wishes to receive relief by drugs: this entirely judicious situation keeps her from developing the state of anxiety which in the recent past was caused by ignorance and superstition and which, more often than not, was the real cause of excessive pain. Thus, the mother is able, if she so wishes, to watch in an overhead mirror her child's arrival into this world: nobody sees it before she does and nobody has to tell her what sex it is. She has known the attending nurse for months. She and the nurse are partners in a job; there is no condescending nurses' chat. There are a number of surprising physiological advantages for both mother and child, in the absence of an artificial amnesia during this most natural process. But more: the emotional impact of this unique experience and of the full reactivity to the clarion call of the baby's first cry, so the mothers agree, arouses in them a permeating sense of mutuality. With the additional innovation of rooming-in, the baby remains close enough to be heard, touched, watched, held, and fed, and the mother thus has the opportunity to observe and to learn to know her baby's idiosyncrasies.

In the early days of this new development it was somewhat astounding to hear the doctors refer to their work of preparing the mothers by instruction as the 'indoctrination' period; and to hear the final success of the procedure explained as a result of the mother's 'father-transference' on the obstetrician. To such an extent had we, in this age of woman's emancipation, forgotten that childbirth is woman's 'labour' and accomplishment. To such an extent has the expert developed the illusion that he must teach and inspire life, when all that is needed is the dispelling of superstitions which he and his teachers have helped to create, and a restriction of his technical interference to the task of protecting mother and child against hazards and accidents. But these men, whatever they called it, engaged in the experiment,

379

and women in all walks of life knew with a somewhat surprised 'naturalness' what it was all about. Their daughters will know it even more naturally.

Such examples could mark the beginning of a new era. Natural childbirth is, of course, no true innovation. But its reintroduction represents a judicious mixture of eternally natural and progressively technical methods. In this way, the whole formidable array of worries and superstitions discussed in this book could, step by step, become subject to a more judicious approach; and this especially if group instruction by experts and the mutual enlightenment of parents in group discussion is carried over into all phases of parenthood: for I fully believe that the new techniques of discussion which are now being developed – and this in industry as well as in education – have a good chance of replacing the reassurance which once emanated from a continuity of tradition.

'Natural' childbirth is not a return to primitivity. For some time to come it is going to be the most expensive form of childbirth, if we consider the investment of time and attention which must be added to the technical appointments of modern delivery. Let us hope, then, that our society will not begrudge its new citizens this investment in time and money; and that it will make it well worth their while to have entered this world less drugged and more ready to open their eyes.

In this book I have attempted to demonstrate the origin in psychoanalytic practice and theory of insights concerning the prolonged inequality of child and adult as one of the facts of existence which make for exploitability, as well as for technical and cultural virtuosity, in human life. I am painfully aware of the fact that for the purpose of this demonstration I have exploited my clinical experience without conveying the nature of the psychoanalytic process itself as a new form of judicious partnership in another basic inequality – that of healer and sick. Here one remembers with gratitude the moral step which Freud took when he repudiated hypnosis and suggestion: a matter much too easily rationalized on the grounds of therapeutic expediency. When Freud decided that he must make the patient's conscious ego face his anxieties and his resistances, and that the only way to cure anxiety is to invite it to be transferred into the doctor–patient relationship, he demanded both from his patients and from his doctors that they realize a step in the evolution of conscience. True, Freud substituted the psycho-analytic couch for the hypnotic one, thus exposing the patient's inhibited will and unavoidable infantile regression to some sadistic and faddish exploitation. But the moral idea was clearly stated for all to behold: the 'classical arrangement' was only a means to an end – namely, a human relationship in which the observer who has learned to observe himself teaches the observed to become self-observant. In his last days, Freud must have been grimly aware of the frailties which emerged in many of us who tried to live up to this revolutionary idea: it is an idea not easily lived with and not easily sustained in a time of upset identities; an idea difficult to organize according to professional custom and difficult to fit into a framework of remuneration. It is, therefore, only with humility that we may specify what manner of human relationship was suggested in Freud's technical innovations. What are the dimensions of the psychoanalyst's job?

The first dimension extends along the axis of *cure–research*. The psychotherapist in the very act of curing has at his disposal a model 'experiment' which permits an approach to human problems while the human being is alive and fully motivated to participation. True, a human being can lend parts of himself (vision, audition, memory, etc.), as if they were isolated functions, to experiments; and an experimenter can put a human being in an experimental situation as if the subject were a conflict-ridden animal or a rattling robot and the experimenter an objective observer. But only in the clinical situation does the full motivational struggle of a human being become part of an interpersonal situation in which observation and self-observation become contemporaneous expressions of a mutuality of motiva-tion, of a division of labour, of a common research. The observer's frank and self-observing participation in this job marks the second dimension: *objectivity–participation*. To be objective, the clinician must know. But he must know how to keep knowledge in abeyance: for each case, each problem is new, not only because each event is individual, and each individual is a distinct cluster of events, but also because both he and his patient are subject to historical change. Neuroses change, as do the wider implications of therapy. The clinician's knowledge, therefore, must ever again yield to interpersonal experiment; fresh impressions must ever again be re-grouped into their common denominators in configurations; and the configurations, finally, must be abstracted into suggestive conceptual models. The third dimension of clinical work, therefore, is ordered along the axis of *knowledge-imagination*. By using a combination of both, the clinician applies selected insights to more strictly experimental approaches.

Finally, I would consider *tolerance-indignation* a dimension of the psychotherapist's work. Much has been said and is being said about the therapist's moral detachment from the multitude of patients who bring to him varieties of conflicts and solutions: naturally, he must let them find their own style of integrity. But the analyst has gone further. In analogy to a certain bird, he has tried to pretend that his values remained hidden because his classical position at the head of the 'analytic couch' removed him from the patient's visual field. We know today that communication is by no means primarily a verbal matter: words are only the tools of meanings. In a more enlightened world and under much more complicated historical conditions the analyst must face once more the whole problem of judicious partnership which expresses the spirit of analytic work more creatively than does apathetic tolerance or autocratic guidance. The various identities which at first lent themselves to a fusion with the new identity of the analyst – identities based on Talmudic argument, on Messianic zeal, on punitive orthodoxy, on faddist sensationalism, on professional and social ambition – all these identities and their cultural origins must now become part of the analyst's analysis, so that he may be able to discard archaic rituals of control and learn to identify with the lasting value of his job of enlightenment. Only thus can he set free in himself and in his patient that remnant of judicious indignation without which a cure is but a straw in the changeable wind of history.

The 'psychoanalytic situation' is a Western and modern contribution to man's age-old attempts at systematic introspection. It began as a psycho-therapeutic method and has led to an encompassing psychological theory. I have emphasized in conclusion the possible implications of both theory and practice for a more judicious orientation in the unlimited prospects and dangers of our technological future.

The Published Writings of
Erik H. Erikson Since the First Edition
of *Childhood and Society*

'Growth and Crises of the "Healthy Personality"'. In *Symposium on the Healthy Personality*, M. J. E. Senn, ed. New York: Josiah Macy, Jr, Foundation, 1950.

'Sex Differences in the Play Configurations of Pre-adolescents'. *Amer. J. Orthopsychiat.*, 21:667–692, 1951.

'On the Sense of Inner Identity'. In *Health and Human Relations*: Report of a Conference held at Hiddesen near Detmold, Germany. New York: Blakiston, 1953.

'The Power of the Newborn' (with Joan Erikson). *Mademoiselle*, June, 1953.

'Wholeness and Totality'. In *Totalitarianism*, Proceedings of a Conference held at the American Academy of Arts and Sciences, C. J. Friedrich, ed. Cambridge: Harvard University Press, 1954.

'The Dream Specimen of Psychoanalysis'. *J. Amer. Psa. Assoc.*, 2:5–56, 1954.

'Freud's "The Origins of Psychoanalysis"'. *International Journal of Psychoanalysis*, Vol. 36, Part 1, 1955.

'The Problem of Ego Identity'. *J. Amer. Psa. Assoc.*, 4:56–121.

'The First Psychoanalyst'. *Yale Review*, 46:40–62.

'Ego Identity and the Psychosocial Moratorium'. In *New Perspectives for Research in Juvenile Delinquency*, H. L. Witmer and R. Kosinsky, eds. U.S. Children's Bureau: Publication No. 356, 1956.

'The Confirmation of the Delinquent' (with Kai T. Erikson). *Chicago Review*, Winter, 1957.

'Trieb und Umwelt in der Kindheit'. In *Freud in der Gegenwart*, T. W. Adorno and W. Dirks, eds. Europäische Verlagsanstalt, 1957.

'Sex Differences in the Play Constructions of Pre-Adolescents', 'The Psychosocial Development of Children', and 'The Syndrome of Identity Diffusion in Adolescents and Young Adults'. In *Discussions in Child Development*, World Health Organization, Vol. III. New York: International Universities Press, 1958.

'The Nature of Clinical Evidence'. *Daedalus*, 87:65–87.

'Identity and Uprootedness in Our Time'. Address at the 11th Annual Meeting of the World Federation for Mental Health, Vienna. In *Uprooting and Resettlement*: Bulletin of the Federation, 1959.

Young Man Luther. New York: W. W. Norton, 1958.

'Late Adolescence'. In *The Student and Mental Health*: An International View, Daniel H. Funkenstein, ed. World Federation of Mental Health and International Association of Universities, 1959.

'Identity and the Lifecycle'. Monograph, *Psychological Issues*, Vol. I, No. 1. New York: International Universities Press, 1959. With an introduction by D. Rapaport, 'A Historical Survey of Psychoanalytic Ego Psychology'.

'Psychosexual Development'. In *Discussions in Child Development*, World Health Organization, Vol. IV. New York: International Universities Press, 1960.

Introduction to *Emotional Problems of the Student*, Graham B. Blaine, Jr and Charles C. McArthur. New York: Appleton-Century-Crofts, Inc., 1961.

'The Roots of Virtue'. In *The Humanist Frame*, Sir Julian Huxley, ed. New York: Harper, 1961.

'Youth: Fidelity and Diversity'. *Daedalus*, 91:5–27, 1962.

'Reality and Actuality'. *J. Amer. Psa. Assoc.*, 10:451–73, 1962.

Editor, *Youth: Change and Challenge*. New York: Basic Books, 1963.

'The Golden Rule and the Cycle of Life'. *Harvard Medical Alumni Bulletin*, Winter, 1963.

Insight and Responsibility. New York: W. W. Norton, 1964.

Revised in: *Psychoanalysis – A General Psychology*. Essays in honour of Heinz Hartmann, ed. Rudolph M. Lowenstein *et al.* New York: International Universities Press, 1966.

In German: 'Ontogenese der Ritualisievung'. *Psyche*, XXII, 7, 1968.

'Concluding Remarks on Ritualization of Behaviour in Animals and Man'. In *Philosophical Transactions of the Royal Society of London*, Series B., No. 772, Vol. 251: 513–24, 1966.

'Words for Paul Tillich'. *Harvard Divinity Bulletin*, 30, No. 2, 1966.

'Gandhi's Autobiography: The Leader as a Child'. *The American Scholar*, Autumn, 1966.

Book Review: 'Thomas Woodrow Wilson, by Sigmund Freud and William C. Bullitt'. *The New York Review of Books*, Vol. VIII, No. 2, 1967.

'Memorandum on Youth for the Committee on the Year 2000', *Daedalus*, Summer, 1967.

'Memorandum on the Military Draft'. In *The Draft: Facts and Alternatives*, Sol Tax, ed. Chicago: University of Chicago Press, 1968.

'The Human Life Cycle'. In *International Encyclopedia of the Social Sciences*. New York: Crowell-Collier, 1968.

Identiy: Youth and Crisis. New York: W. W. Norton, 1968.

'Psychosocial Identity'. In *International Encyclopedia of the Social Sciences*. New York: Crowell-Collier, 1968.

'The Nature of Psycho-Historical Evidence: In Search of Gandhi'. *Daedalus*, Summer, 1968.

'Insight and Freedom'. The T. B. Davie Memorial Lecture on Academic Freedom. South Africa: University of Capetown, 1968.

'On Student Unrest, and Remarks on Receiving the Foneme Prize'. Second International Convention. Milano: Foneme Institute, 1969.

Gandhi's Truth. New York: W. W. Norton, 1969.

'Reflections on the Dissent of Contemporary Youth'. *Daedalus*, Winter, 1970; also in *Int. J. Psa.*, Vol. 51, 1970, No. 1.

'Autobiographic Notes on the Identity Crisis'. *Daedalus*, Fall, 1970; also in *The Twentieth Century Sciences*, Gerald Holton, ed. New York: W. W. Norton, 1972.

'Notes on the Life Cycle'. In *Ekistics*, 32, 191, Athens, October 1971.

On 'Play'. In *Play and Development*, Maria Piers, ed. New York: W. W. Norton, 1972.

'Words at Delos'. In *Ekistics*, 32, 191, Athens, October 1971.

'Environment and Virtues'. In *Arts of the Environment*, G. Kepes, ed. New York: Braziller, 1972.

'On Protest and Affirmation'. Address, Class Day, Harvard Medical School, *Harvard Medical Alumni Bulletin*, July–August 1972.

'By Way of a Memoir'. In *Clinician and Therapist, Selected Papers of Robert P. Knight*, Stuart C. Miller, ed. New York: Basic Books, 1972.

'Thoughts on the City for Human Development'. In *Ekistics*, 35, 209, Athens, April 1973.

'Conversations with Huey P. Newton'. In *In Search of Common Ground*, Kai T. Erikson, ed. New York: W. W. Norton, 1973.

Dimensions of a New Identity. 1973 Jefferson Lectures. New York: W. W. Norton, 1974.

'Reminiscences, First Peter Blos Biennial Lecture', *Psychosocial Process*, Vol. III, No. 2, Fall, 1974.

Life History and the Historical Moment. New York: W. W. Norton, 1975.

Index

instinct of, 59
Defence mechanism, 29–30, 136, 175, 226 ff.
Delinquency, and role diffusion, 234 ff., 277–8
Democracy, 260, 285–6
Depression, infantile, 69–70
Despair *vs.* ego integrity, 241–2
Development, epigenetic, 29 ff., 56
  organic, 57–8
  processes, 28 ff.
Deviations, pregenital, 81–2
  Sioux, 137–8
  Yurok, 162
Diderot, Denis, 76
Dirt, attitude towards, *see* Cleanliness
Distantiation and prejudice, 237
Donskoi, Mark, 324
Dostoevsky, Fyodor, 325
Doubt
  origin of, 74, 228
  vs. initiative, 74, 226
Dreams, 135, 171–2; *see also* Fantasy
  Sioux, 135–6
Drives, human, 83, 192; *see also* Instincts; Body zones

Education, *see also* Culture patterns
  Sioux, 105, 129–30, 139, 141–2
Ego, *see also* Autonomy; Identity
  defences, 136, 174–5
  defined, 174–5, 374
  development of, 167–8, 171 ff., 251 ff.
  equilibrium, 171–2
  integrity *vs.* despair, 235 ff., 241–2
  qualities, 222 ff.
  restriction, 235, 280 ff.
  self-made, 266
  synthesis, 213 ff., 255
  and trust, 242
  weakness, 186
Einstein, Albert, 322
Epigenetic charts, 62 ff., 243 ff.
  definition of, 56
  development, 29 ff., 56
Erikson, Erik H., 165, 278
Erikson, K. T., 278
Ethos, 237
  economic, 232

technological, 234
Evil, sense of, 69, 70, 218

Fables, Yurok, 160
Fanny, the Shaman, 155
Fantasy, and ego, 171
  and guilt, 79
  obsessional, 72
  oedipal, 79
  and play, 195–6
  pregnancy, 47–51
Father
  American, 267 ff.
  German, 298 ff.
  identification, 214 ff., 301
  Russian, 337 ff.
Fear
  and anxiety, 367
  of autonomy loss, 71–2, 369
  of castration, 369
  of death, 21, 25, 146, 242
  of encirclement, 365–6
  feminine, 370
  of identity loss, 371
  and inactivity, 34
  infantile, 364
  interpretation of, 47, 50
  of invasion, 365
  of organ mode impoverishment, 368–9
  paranoiac, 72–3, 228
  of rape, 130, 369 ff.
  of violence, 25–6, 28
Federal Writers' Project, 219
Feeding, demand, *see* Breast feeding
Femininity, 77 ff.; *see also* Sex differences
Festivals, *see* Rituals
  Sioux, *see* Sun Dance
  Yurok, *see* Fish dam building
Fetish, 178, 183
Finger play, 183 ff.
Fire setting as symptom, 215
Fischer, John, 285
Fish dam building, Yurok, 152, 164
Fixation, *see* Regression; Anal Fixation
Flanner, Janet, 316
Folk songs and tales, American, 271 ff.
Frenkel-Brunswick, Else, 375
Freud, Anna, 175, 209, 277

Freud, Sigmund, 40, 50 ff., 52 ff.,
    54 ff., 60–1, 70, 75, 99, 135, 161,
    167, 168, 172, 174 ff., 188, 193 ff.,
    200, 238, 253 ff., 322, 340, 373,
    380–1
Frigidity, 81, 265

Generativity vs. stagnation, 240–1
Genital attitudes, 114
    Sioux, 139, 162
    Yurok, 162, 163–4
Genitality, ideal, 237 ff.
    infantile, 72, 74 ff.
    in boys, 76, 77
    in girls, 77
    and pregenitality, 81 ff.
    neurotic, 81 ff.
Genital love, 237–8
    maturity, 238 ff.
German, see under subject
Gesell, Arnold, 61
Gorer, Geoffrey, 324, 350
Gorky, Maxim, 324 ff.
Grandfathers
    American, 282
    Russian, 328 ff.
Grandmothers
    American, 262 ff.
    Russian, 327 ff.
Guilt, sense of, 79, 134–5
    vs. initiative, 79

Hartmann, H., 84
Hendrick, Ives, 233
History, interpretation of
    American, 265 ff.
    German, 311 ff.
    Russian, 336 ff.
Hitler, Adolf, 294 ff.
Homosexuality, 73
    Sioux, 137
Honzik, M. P., 89
Humour, 365
Huxley, Julian, 247

Id, 173–4
    daemonic, 254
Identification
    with conqueror, Sioux, 102
    with dominant race, Negro, 217–
        18

with father, 214 ff.
with giver, 66
with machines, 213–14, 271
with nature, 213, 271
and play, 215
as result of loss, 50
with tormentor, Russian, 335
Identity, 234 ff.
    American, 37, 258 ff.
    beginnings of, 211 ff.
    collective, Sioux, 138
    cultural, 252–6 ff.
    deprivation, 214 ff.
    evil, 218 ff.
    German, 294 ff., 322–3
    ideal, Sioux, 115, 119, 148
    infantile, 211
    Jewish, 23, 26, 31, 254–5, 309, 319
    loss of, 36, 38, 138, 181, 217–18,
        256
    in modern world, 251, 255–6, 293,
        361–2, 371
    national, 257, 323 ff.
    Negro, 217 ff.
    and play, 211 ff.
    psychosocial, 217, 255, 320
    vs. role confusion, 234 ff.
    sexual, 235
Incest taboos, 54, 79, 127
India, pre-adolescents in, 95
Indian, see Sioux, Yurok; see also
    under subject
Indian childhood, 99 ff.
    life, recent changes in, 141 ff.
Industry vs. inferiority, 232 ff.
Indian Service, 102, 104 ff., 112
Infantile
    anger, see Infantile rage
    anxiety, 175, 364, 367
    compulsions, 226–7, 364
    conscience, 226
    depression, 69–70
    fantasy, 47, 79
    fears, 364, 367 ff.
    genitality, 74 ff.
    paradise, 224, 271
    play, 199–200
    rage, 59, 68–9, 365, 372
        Sioux, 123 ff., 129
    schizophrenia, 176, 187, 223, 227–
        8, 268

392

sexuality, 40, 62 ff., 74–5, 238–9
    Freud's theory of, 52–6
Inferiority
    sense of, 230, 233–4
    vs. industry, 232 ff.
Initiative, lack of, Sioux, see Apathy,
    Sioux
Initiative vs. Guilt, 79, 229 ff.
Instincts
    animal, 82 ff.
    human, 83
Integration, of personality, 235 ff.
Intellect, Freud's theory of the pri-
    macy of, 254–5
Intimacy vs. isolation, 237 ff.
Intolerances
    constitutional, 24 ff.
    convergence of, 31–2
Introjection, 223
Isolation, 237 ff.
    à deux, 239

Jesus, 134
Jewish identity, 23, 26, 31, 254–5,
    308 ff., 309, 319
Jim the Sioux, 107 ff.
John Henry, 268 ff.
Johnson, M. and T., 274

Kinsey, Alfred Charles, 238
Kris, Ernst, 84
Kroeber, Alfred, 100, 150, 152, 153,
    155, 165

Latency Period, 53–4, 232
    definition of, 75
Law and order, principle of, 229
Leites, Nathan, 324
Lenin, 325, 336
Levinson, Daniel J., 375
Levy, David, 70
Lewis, Alfred H., 271
Libido, 40, 58, 82
    and aggression, 50 ff.
    Freud's theory of, 52 ff.
Lincoln, Abraham, 61
Lincoln, T. S., 137
Lomax, J. A. and Alan, 270
Love, 59
    adolescent, 235–6
    genital, 237 ff.

between sexes, Sioux, 130–1
Lowenstein, R., 84

Macfarlane, J. W., 85
MacGregor, Gordon, 105, 142
    study of Sioux, 141 ff.
Machines, see also Cultural pattern,
    American
    identification with, 213–14, 271
Macrosphere, 199
Magic, and play, 213 ff.
    among Sioux, 156, 173
    among Yurok, 156, 157, 165, 167,
    173
'Make', being on the, 79, 229
Mann, Thomas, 316 ff.
Marx, Karl, 241, 321–2
Masturbation, see Autoeroticism
Maternal relationship, 62 ff., 76,
    222 ff., 260 ff.; see also Mothers;
    'Mom'; Parent–child interac-
    tion
    attachment, Hitler's, 305 ff.
    estrangement, 178
    favour, contest for, 230
    rejection, 187, 270
    separation and teething, 67–8
Maturity, 232 ff., 237 ff., 242
Mead, Margaret, 95, 289, 324, 376
Mekeel, H. Scudder, 100, 102, 107,
    109, 112, 115, 117, 120
'Melting pot', 266
Menstruation
    Sioux attitude towards, 120
    Yurok attitude towards, 152
Mistrust, 70; see also Trust
Modalities, 62 ff., 66, 67, 69, 70 ff.,
    79; see also Cultural patterns
    and pregenitality, 82
    spacial, 85
Modes, organ, 45 ff., 50, 51, 62 ff.,
    71–2, 79–80, 84–5; see also
    Psychosexual stages; Psycho-
    social stages
Molotov, Vyacheslav, 325
'Mom', 260 ff., 267
Montessori touch method, 184
Moscow trials, 344
Mother, see also Maternal relation-
    ship; Mothers; 'Mom'; Parent–
    child interaction

393

Teething, 68 ff., 223
Tension
  neurotic, 53
  somatic, 30
Thumb sucking, 41, 199
  Sioux, 124-5
Trauma, oral, and schizophrenia,
    178-9
Tolstoy, Leo, 325
Toys, 188 ff.
  macrosphere, 199
Trotsky, Leon, 336
Tom Sawyer, 188 ff.
Trust, 62 ff.
  basic, *vs.* mistrust, 222 ff., 226
  loss of, 69-70, 222 ff., 226
  and orality, 66 ff.
Twain, Mark, 188 ff., 365

Underhill, Ruth, 212
United States Indian Service, *see*
    Indian Service
Unity, need for, Russian, 362

Violence, fear of, 25-6, 28
Visions, Sioux, 135 ff.

Waelder, Robert, 168
War neurosis
  case of, 32 ff.
  loss of identity in, 35, 32

Waterman, T. T., 150
Weaning, 69-70
  Sioux, 122
  Yurok, 159
Weber, Max, 300, 312 ff., 361
Wellman, P. I., 103
'Will', Schopenhauer's, and Id, 174
Will, affirmation by law, 228-9
Wissler, C., 103-4, 136
Wolfenstein, Martha, 95
Woman, *see also* Maternal relation-
    ship; Mothers
  and war, 370
  emancipated American, 266 ff.
Work, 232 ff.

Youth, 236, 251 ff.
  American, 277 ff.
  German, 294 ff.
  Russian, 350 ff.
Yurok
  ambivalence, 171
  anality, 166
  breast feeding, 159
  child psychiatry, 155
  cultural pattern, 149 ff.
  magic, 166
  summary, comparative, 163

Ziemer, G., 309, 310
Zones, *see* Body zones

397